The Java Work

A New, Interactive Approach to Learning Java

David Cuartielles

Andreas Göransson

Eric Foster-Johnson

The Java Workshop

Authors: David Cuartielles, Andreas Göransson, and Eric Foster-Johnson

Technical Reviewers: Scott Cosentino, Ashley Frieze, Corey Hendrey, David Parker, Darryl Pierce, and Shubham Shrivastava

Managing Editor: Manasa Kumar

Acquisitions Editor: Sarah Lawton

Production Editor: Shantanu Zagade

Editorial Board: Shubhopriya Banerjee, Bharat Botle, Ewan Buckingham, Megan Carlisle, Mahesh Dhyani, Manasa Kumar, Alex Mazonowicz, Bridget Neale, Dominic Pereira, Shiny Poojary, Abhishek Rane, Erol Staveley, Ankita Thakur, Nitesh Thakur, and Jonathan Wray

First Published: October 2019

Production Reference: 3171219

ISBN: 978-1-83898-669-8

Published by Packt Publishing Ltd.

Livery Place, 35 Livery Street

Birmingham B3 2PB, UK

Experience the Workshop Online

Thank you for purchasing the print edition of *The Java Workshop*. Every physical print copy includes free online access to the premium interactive edition. There are no extra costs or hidden charges.

With the interactive edition you'll unlock:

- **Screencasts and Quizzes.** Supercharge your progress with screencasts of all exercises and activities. Take optional quizzes to help embed your new understanding.

- **Built-In Discussions.** Engage in discussions where you can ask questions, share notes and interact. Tap straight into insight from expert instructors and editorial teams.

- **Skill Verification.** Complete the course online to earn a Packt credential that is easy to share and unique to you. All authenticated on the public Bitcoin blockchain.

- **Download PDF and EPUB.** Download a digital version of the course to read offline. Available as PDF or EPUB, and always DRM-free.

To redeem your free digital copy of *The Java Workshop* you'll need to follow these simple steps:

1. Visit us at https://courses.packtpub.com/pages/redeem.

2. Login with your Packt account, or register as a new Packt user.

3. Select your course from the list, making a note of the three page numbers for your product. Your unique redemption code needs to match the order of the pages specified.

4. Open up your print copy and find the codes at the bottom of the pages specified. They'll always be in the same place:

Sorting Collections

As we have seen, there are some classes in the collections framework that force the items within them to be sorted. Examples of that are TreeSet and TreeMap. The aspect to explore in this section is how to use existing sorting mechanisms for lists, but also for cases that have datasets with more than one value per data point.

The exercise we are doing throughout this chapter is a good example of a case where there are data points with more than one value. For each data point, we need to store the word for which we are calculating the frequency and the frequency itself. You might think that a good technique to sort that out is by storing the information in the form of maps. The unique words could be the keys, while the frequencies could be the values. This could be achieved by modifying the final part of the previous program to look like this:

```
Map map = new HashMap();
while (iterator.hasNext()) {
    //  point to next element
    String s = (String) iterator.next();
    // get the amount of times this word shows up in the text
```

AB 2 1 C

---

5. Merge the codes together (without any spaces), ensuring they are in the correct order.

6. At checkout, click **Have a redemption code?** and enter your unique product string. Click **Apply**, and the price should be free!

Finally, we'd like to thank you for purchasing the print edition of *The Java Workshop*! We hope that you finish the course feeling capable of tackling challenges in the real world. Remember that we're here to help if you ever feel like you're not making progress.

If you run into issues during redemption (or have any other feedback) you can reach us at workshops@packt.com.

Table of Contents

Chapter 3: Object-Oriented Programming   67

Chapter 6: Libraries, Packages, and Modules   169

Chapter 7: Databases and JDBC   219

Chapter 8: Sockets, Files, and Streams 249

Chapter 10: Encryption   311

Chapter 11: Processes 329

Chapter 12: Regular Expressions 339

Chapter 13: Functional Programming with Lambda Expressions

Chapter 14: Recursion

Chapter 15: Processing Data with Streams   401

Chapter 16: Predicates and Other Functional Interfaces   441

Preface

About

This section briefly introduces the coverage of this book, the technical skills you'll need to get started, and the software requirements required to complete all of the included activities and exercises.

About the Book

You already know you want to learn Java, and a smarter way to learn Java 12 is to learn by doing. *The Java Workshop* focuses on building up your practical skills so that you can develop high-performance Java applications that work flawlessly within the JVM across web, mobile and desktop. You'll learn from real examples that lead to real results.

Throughout The Java Workshop, you'll take an engaging step-by-step approach to understanding Java. You won't have to sit through any unnecessary theory. If you're short on time you can jump into a single exercise each day or spend an entire weekend learning about Reactive programming and Unit testing. It's your choice. Learning on your terms, you'll build up and reinforce key skills in a way that feels rewarding.

Every physical print copy of *The Java Workshop* unlocks access to the interactive edition. With videos detailing all exercises and activities, you'll always have a guided solution. You can also benchmark yourself against assessments, track progress, and receive free content updates. You'll even earn a secure credential that you can share and verify online upon completion. It's a premium learning experience that's included with your printed copy. To redeem, follow the instructions located at the start of your Java book.

Fast-paced and direct, *The Java Workshop* is the ideal companion for Java beginners. You'll build and iterate on your code like a software developer, learning along the way. This process means that you'll find that your new skills stick, embedded as best practice. A solid foundation for the years ahead.

About the Chapters

Chapter 1, Getting Started, covers the basics of writing and testing programs, a first step towards building all the code that you will find in this book.

Chapter 2, Learning the Basics, covers the basic syntax of the Java language, especially ways to control the flow of your applications.

Chapter 3, Object-Oriented Programming, provides an overview of OOP and details the aspects that make Java a popular language.

Chapter 4, Collections, Lists, and Java's Built-In APIs, covers the popular Java collections framework, which is used to store, sort, and filter data.

Chapter 5, Exceptions, provides recommendations on how to deal with exceptions on a more conceptual level, providing a list of best practices that any professional programmer will follow.

Chapter 6, Libraries, Packages, and Modules, introduces you to various ways to package and bundle Java code, along with tools to help you build Java projects.

Chapter 7, Databases and JDBC, shows how to use JDBC to access relational databases from your Java applications.

Chapter 8, Sockets, Files, and Streams, aids you in working with external data storage systems.

Chapter 9, Working with HTTP, explains how to create programs that connect to a specific web server and downloads data.

Chapter 10, Encryption, explores how applying encryption to your software is vital to safeguard yours, or your customers, integrity, data, and business.

Chapter 11, Processes, briefly discusses how processes function and are dealt with in Java.

Chapter 12, Regular Expressions, decrypts what regular expressions mean and looks at how this comes in handy in Java.

Chapter 13, Functional Programming with Lambda Expressions, discusses how Java doubles up as a functional programming language, and how lambda expressions are used to perform pattern matching in Java.

Chapter 14, Recursion, looks at a couple of problems that are solved using the recursion technique.

Chapter 15, Processing Data with Streams, explains how you can use streams to write more expressive programs with fewer lines of code, and also how you can easily chain multiple operations on large lists.

Chapter 16, Predicates and Other Functional Interfaces, explores some of the valid use cases of functional interfaces.

Chapter 17, Reactive Programming with Java Flow, talks about the Java Flow API and the advantages of the Reactive Streams specification.

Chapter 18, Unit Testing, delves into testing with JUnit, one of the primary testing frameworks for Java.

Conventions

Code words in text, database table names, folder names, filenames, file extensions, pathnames, dummy URLs, user input, and Twitter handles are shown as follows: "You can nest **if** statements within any block of code, including the block of code that follows an if statement.".

Words that you see on the screen, for example, in menus or dialog boxes, also appear in the text like this: "**Click** on **Create New Project**."

A block of code is set as follows:

```
if (i == 5) {
System.out.println("i is 5");
}
i = 0;
```

New terms and important words are shown like this: "This kind of data is what we call a **variable type**."

Large code snippets are truncated and the corresponding names of the code files on GitHub are placed at the top of the truncated code. The permalinks to the entire code are placed below the code snippet. It should look as follows:

Exercise02.java

```
6   if (distanceToHome > maxDistance) {
7   System.out.println("Distance from the store to your home is");
8   System.out.println(" more than " + maxDistance + "km away.");
9   System.out.println("That is too far for free delivery.");
```

https://packt.live/32Ca9YS

Before You Begin

Each great journey begins with a humble step. Our upcoming adventure with Java is no exception. Before we can do awesome things using Java, we must be prepared with a productive environment. In this small note, we shall see how to do that.

Installation of JRE

To install JRE on your systems, refer to: https://www.java.com/en/download/manual.jsp.

Installation of JDK

To install JDK on your systems, refer to: https://www.oracle.com/technetwork/java/javase/downloads/index.html.

Installation of IntelliJ IDEA

While all the code present in the course runs on all Java compilers, we have used IntelliJ IDEA on our systems. All the instructions in the exercises and the activities are tailored to work on IntelliJ. To install IntelliJ on your system, visit jetbrains.com/idea/.

If you have any issues or questions about installation please email us at workshops@packt.com.

Installing the Code Bundle

Download the code files from GitHub at https://packt.live/2Jgzz6D and place them in a new folder called C:\Code. Refer to these code files for the complete code bundle.

Getting Started

Overview

In this chapter, we will be covering the fundamentals of Java. You will first learn to write and compile your first "Hello World!" program—traditionally the first step to practicing any new language. We will then discuss the differences between the **command-line interface (CLI)** and **Graphical User Interface (GUI)**, and the relative benefits of both. By the end of this chapter, you will understand the basic concepts behind variables, know how to hold data within them, and, even, how to comment on your own code.

Introduction

When learning how to program in almost any programming language, the first example you will typically test is called "hello world." It is the simplest application possible; the aim is to write the expression "hello world" to whatever user interface the programming environment offers. Executing this program will introduce you to the basics of writing code using the IntelliJ editor, utilizing different types of data to be printed to the user interface and adding comments to your code.

When writing your first program, you will also discover how Java's syntax is constructed and how it relates to other languages such as C or C++. Understanding the syntax is key to starting to read code. You will learn how to distinguish where commands and functions begin and end, how parameters are passed over between blocks of code, and how to leave comments that will help you when revisiting your software in the future.

This chapter covers the basics of writing and testing programs as a first step toward building all the code that you will find in this book.

Writing, Compiling, and Executing Your Hello World Program

In the preface, you saw how to install the IntelliJ development environment. While it is possible to write Java code with literally any text editor, we believe it is good to see how to create applications using state-of-the-art tools such as the aforementioned software package.

However, prior to guiding you step by step through getting your first program to run, we should take a look at the code that will become your first executable running on Java. The following code listing shows the program. Read through it, and we will later revise what each one of the parts is doing:

```
public class Main {
    public static void main (String[] args) {
        System.out.println("Hello World!");
    }
}
```

The first line is what we call a class definition. All programs in Java are called **classes**. A program might consist of several classes. Classes carry inside them everything they need to perform the task they were designed for. For a class to be executable in Java, it must contain a method called `main`. In this program, you can see how the `Main` class contains a method called `main` that will be printing the sentence "Hello World!" to the system's default output.

The code included in the class definition (**public class Main**) indicates that the class itself is public, which means that it will be accessible from other programs running on your computer. The same happens for the method definition (**public static void main(String[] args)**). There is, however, a series of other things that require our attention:

- **static** signifies that there is nothing in the system instantiating the **main** method. Because of the way the Java Virtual Machine works, the **main** method needs to be static, or it will not be possible to execute it.

- **void** indicates that the **main** method will not be returning anything to any code calling it. Methods could, in fact, send an answer to a piece of code executing it, as we will see later in the book.

- **main** is the name of the method. You cannot assign this a different name, since it is the method that makes the program executable and needs to be named this way.

- **String[] args** are the parameters of the **main** method. Parameters are passed as a list of strings. In other words, the program could take arguments from other parts within your computer and use them as data. In the particular case of the **main** method, these are strings that could be entered on the **command-line interface** (**CLI**) when calling the program.

Exercise 1: Creating Your Hello World Program in Java

IntelliJ provides you with a pre-made "hello world" template. Templates help you to get started faster with your code, as they provide the components you may need to speed up development. Templates can also be used for educational purposes; this is the case when it comes to testing "hello world."

For this first exercise, start with the editor. We will leave some options as they are by default. We will later see how to personalize some of the options to better suit our needs:

1. Open IntelliJ and you will see a window giving you several options. Click on **Create New Project**. It should be the first option in the list:

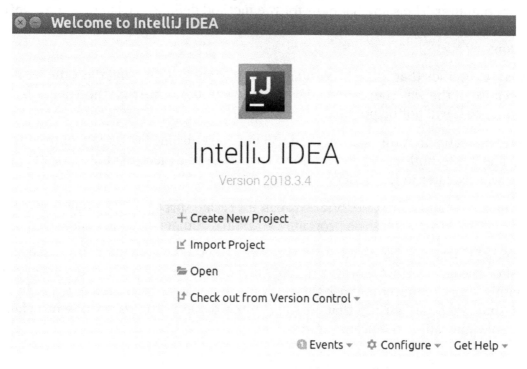

Figure 1.1: Creating a new project on IntelliJ IDE

2. A new interface should appear. The default options here are meant for creating a Java program, so you just need to click **Next**:

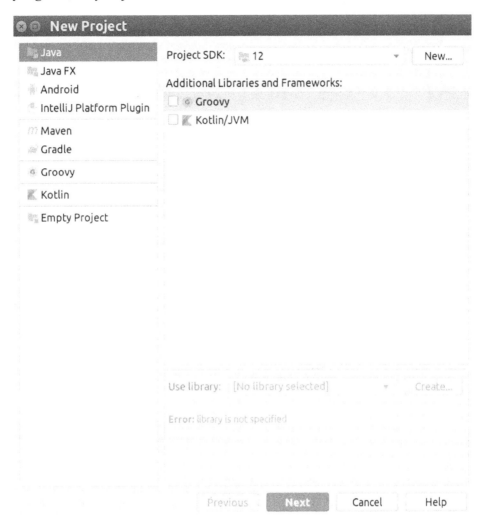

Figure 1.2: Creating a new Java project

3. Check the box to create the project from a template. Click on **Java Hello World** and then click **Next**:

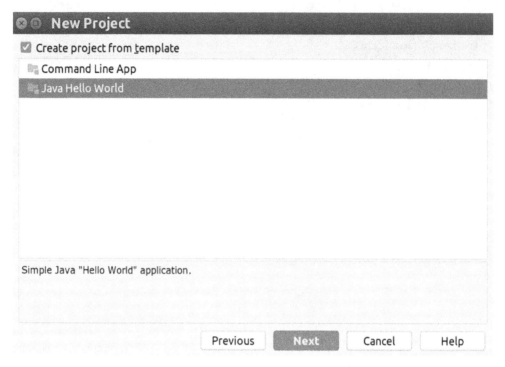

Figure 1.3: Create a Java Hello World project from template

4. Name the project **chapter01**. Then, click **Finish**:

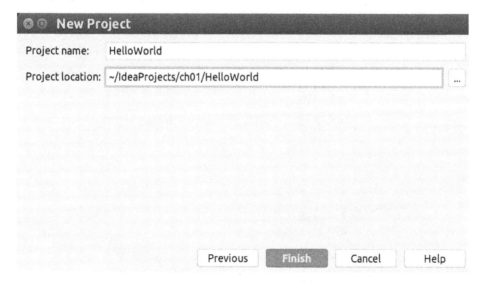

Figure 1.4: Create a Hello World Project

5. As we haven't chosen a folder to store the projects (intentionally), IntelliJ will offer you the possibility to create a default project folder inside your user space. Click **OK**:

Figure 1.5: Default project folder option on IntelliJ IDE

6. You will see a popup with tips on how to use the software. If you have never used a development environment of this type before, then this is a good way to get information about how it functions every time IntelliJ boots up. Choose your preferences and then click **Close**:

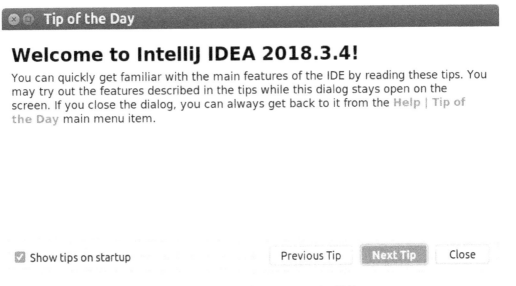

Figure 1.6: Tip on how to use the IDE

7. IntelliJ reminds you regarding the possibility of using a special tab dedicated to learning more about the environment in relation to programming. Click **Got It**.

8. The editor presents a menu bar, a code navigation bar, a project navigation area, and the actual editor where you can see the code we explained earlier. Now it is time to test it. Click on the **Run** button (this is the triangle on the right-hand side of the code navigation bar).

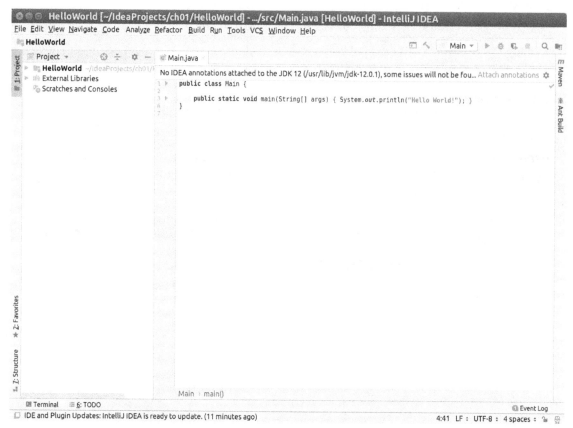

Figure 1.7: Execute the program by clicking on the Run button

9. When the program runs, a terminal window unfolds at the bottom of IntelliJ. Here, you can see how the software called your JVM, the program's outcome, and a line from the editor reading **Process finished with exit code 0**, which means that no errors occurred.

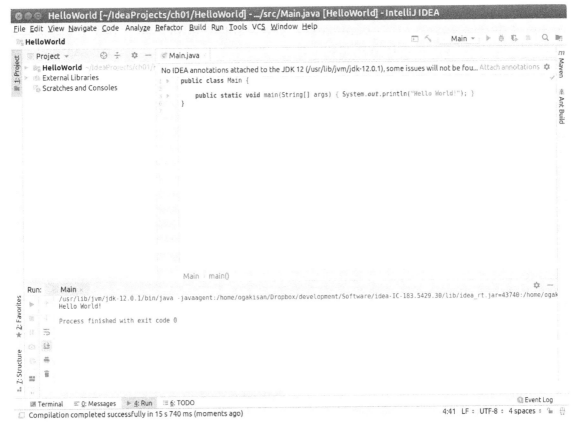

Figure 1.8: JVM showing the output

> **Note**
>
> Since we took all the options by default for this example, you will see that our program is called **Main.java**. In the following chapter, we will see how to create programs that we then name ourselves.

Basic Syntax and Naming Conventions

The first thing you will have noticed in the **hello world** program, when it comes to syntax, is how we group the code into blocks marked within sets of curly braces—**{** and **}**. The **Main** class contains the **main** method. In other words, **main** is nested inside **Main**. This is how classes are defined in Java – in principle, they contain all of the methods they are going to use.

Another aspect of the Java syntax is that capitalization matters. If a command is defined as **Print**, it differs from another command called **print**, and the compiler will identify them as different. Capitalization falls under a convention, an unwritten rule among programmers on how names should be formatted in Java. You will have noticed that the class is called **HelloWorld**. In Java, the convention establishes that methods, classes, variables, and so on should be named by joining words together using capitals as a way to mark the separation between words. In addition, the names of classes should start with capitals.

> **Note**
>
> When you are starting off, it is easy to get confused between syntax, which is rigid and must be respected for the compiler to function, and conventions, which are intended for developers to better understand how code is supposed to function.

To some extent, the Java compiler doesn't care about whitespace characters, but there is a convention about using them to make code more readable. The first code listing you saw (**Example01.java**) can be rewritten as follows, and will have the exact same result once compiled and executed:

```java
public class Main {
    public static void main(String[] args) {
        System.out.println("Hello World!");
    }
}
```

The **System.out.println("Hello World!")** function call will print out the expected message on the CLI. The command is nested inside the **main(String[] args)** method definition, which is nested inside the **class** definition. You could add more blank spaces, but it will not affect the functionality of the program. This is part of the syntax of Java, but also of other programming languages such as C, C++, and Scala.

Also, note that "**Hello World!**" is a **String**, a type of data. The following section will explore what types of data can be sent as parameters to the **System.out.println()** method call.

Printing Out Different Data Types

In Java, it is common to define methods that have the capability to use different sets of parameters. For example, the **System.out.println()** method can print other types of data that are not just pieces of text. You could, as an example, try to print out a simple number and see the result. **Example03.java** adds a couple of lines to the code to showcase different types of data:

```
public class Main {
    public static void main(String[] args) {
        System.out.println("This is text");
        System.out.println('A');
        System.out.println(53);
        System.out.println(23.08f);
        System.out.println(1.97);
        System.out.println(true);

    }
}
```

The previous example will print out four lines to the CLI, representing the different arguments given to the **System.out.println()** method. The outcome will look as follows:

```
This is text
A
53
23.08
1.97
true
Process finished with exit code 0
```

You see six different types of data in this result: some text, a character, an integer number, two different kinds of decimal numbers, and a truth statement. In the Java programming language, we define those types of data as **String**, **char**, **int**, **float**, **double**, and **boolean**, respectively. There is a lot more to learn about data types, but let's first introduce a new topic: **variables**. This will help to understand why data types are important.

Variables and Variable Types

Variables are human-readable names given to slots of your computer memory. Each one of those slots can store some data, such as a number, a piece of text, a password, or the value of the temperature outside. This kind of data is what we call a **variable type**. There are as many variable types as there are data types in our programming language. The type of data we are using defines the amount of memory allocated to store the data. A byte (which is made up of 8 bits) is smaller than an integer (which is made up of 32 bits). A **string** comprises several characters, hence making it bigger than an integer.

byte, **int** (short for integer), **String**, and **char** (short for character) are variable types. To make use of a variable, you need to define it for the compiler to understand that it needs it in order to allocate some space for storing data. The variable definition is done by first determining its type, followed by the variable's name, and then you can optionally initialize it with a certain value.

The following code listing shows how to define a couple of variables of different types:

```
// a counter
int counter = 0;
// a String
String errMsg = "You should press 'NEXT' to continue";
// a boolean
boolean isConnected = false;
```

This next exercise will take you through how to modify the code listing from **Example03. java** in order to print out the values coming from the variables.

Exercise 2: Printing Different Types of Data

In this exercise, we shall declare variables of different data types and print it as an output. To do so, perform the following steps:

1. Open IntelliJ. If you didn't get to try the code listing from **Example03.java**, let's start by creating a new project using the **HelloWorld** template:

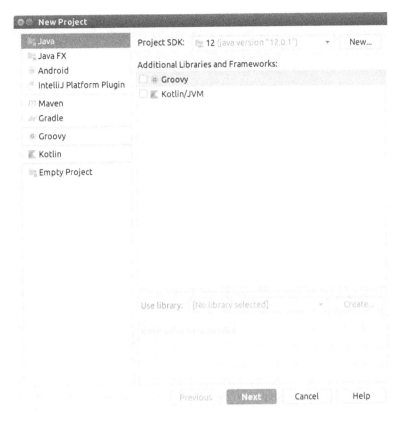

Figure 1.9: Create a new Java project

2. Once you have reached the step where you have the code generated by the development environment, copy all of the code, erase it, and paste in the code from the **Example03.java** listing instead:

3. Try out the code, and check that the outcome is what it should be, as explained in *Printing Out Different Data Types*.

4. Start by declaring a new variable of the **String** type and initialize it:

```
public class Main {
    public static void main(String[] args) {
        String t = "This is text";
        System.out.println("This is text");
        System.out.println('A');
        System.out.println(53);
        System.out.println(23.08f);
        System.out.println(1.97);
        System.out.println(true);
    }
}
```

5. Next, substitute the text in the first **System.out.println()** command with the variable. As the variable is linked to the piece of memory containing the string, executing the program will give the same result:

```java
public class Main {
    public static void main(String[] args) {
        String t = "This is a text";
        System.out.println(t);
        System.out.println('A');
        System.out.println(53);
        System.out.println(23.08f);
        System.out.println(1.97);
        System.out.println(true);
    }
}
```

6. Continue by declaring a variable of the **char** type, another of the **int** type, one of the **double** type, and finally, one of the **boolean** type. Proceed to use the variable names instead of the values when printing out to the CLI:

```java
public class Main {
    public static void main(String[] args) {
        String t = "This is a text";
        char c = 'A';
        int i = 53;
        float f = 23.08f;
        double d = 1.97;
        boolean b = true;
        System.out.println(t);
        System.out.println(c);
        System.out.println(i);
        System.out.println(f);
        System.out.println(d);
        System.out.println(b);
    }
}
```

With this example, not only have you learned about different types of data and the variables that store this data, but also about how methods can handle more than one data type.

> **Note**
>
> Notice how the float type, when defined, requires the letter f to be appended after the number. This way, Java will be able to distinguish between these two types of decimal variables.

Primitive versus Reference Data Types

Some data types are built on top of others. For example, strings are made of sequences of characters, so, in a sense, without characters, there would be no strings. You could say that characters are more core to the language than strings are. Like characters, there are other data types that are used to define the properties of a programming language. These data types, fundamental for the construction of the language itself, are what we call primitive data types.

The following table describes some of the basic types of variables you will find in Java, along with their characteristics:

Type name	Range of values	Default value	Size
boolean	true or false	false	1 bit
byte	-128 .. 127	0	8 bit
short	-32,768 .. 32,767	0	16 bit
int	-2,147,483,648 .. 2,147,483,647	0	32 bit
long	-9,223,372,036,854,775,808 .. 9,223,372,036,854,775,807	0	64 bit
float	$3.40282347 \times 10^{38}$, $1.40239846 \times 10^{45}$	0.0	32 bit
double	$1.7976931348623157 \times 10^{308}$, $4.9406564584124654 \times 10^{-324}$	0.0	64 bit
char	Unicode character	\u0000	16 bit

Figure 1.10: Basic types in Java

The eight primitive data types represent **truth levels** (boolean), **integral numbers** (byte, short, int, and long), **floating point numbers** (float and double), and **characters** (char). *Exercise 2, Printing Different Types of Data* showcased how to use variables from some of these types within our programs.

> **Note**
>
> String is not a primitive data type. It is what we call a reference data type. A mnemotechnic that could help you remember why it is called "reference" is that it is not linking to the actual data, but to the position in memory where the data is stored; hence, it is "a reference." There are other reference data types that you will be introduced to later in the book. Note that **float** and **double** are not precise enough to deal with some uses of decimal numbers, such as currencies. Java has a high-precision decimal data type called **BigDecimal**, but it is not a primitive type.

Null

In the same way that primitive data types have a default value, reference data types, which could be made of any kind of data, have a common way to express that they contain no data. As an example of a reference typed variable, the default value for a string that is defined as **empty** is **null**.

Null is a lot more complex than that, though—it can also be used to determine termination. Continuing with the example of the string, when stored in memory, it will be made of an array of characters ending with **null**. In this way, it will be possible to iterate within a string, since there is a common way to signify that you have reached its end.

It is possible to modify the content of the computer memory during the execution of a program. We do this using variables in code. The next code listing will show you how to create an empty variable of the **String** type and modify its value while the program is running:

```
public class Main {
    public static void main(String[] args) {
        String t = null;
        System.out.println(t);
        t = "Joe ...";
        System.out.println(t);
```

```
        t = "went fishing";
        System.out.println(t);
    }
}
```

The previous example shows how to declare an empty string, how its value can be modified throughout the program, and how the program will cope with displaying the content of an empty string. It literally prints out the word **null** on the CLI. See the full outcome of the program:

```
null
Joe ...
went fishing
Process finished with exit code 0
```

The program declares an empty variable, and by assigning new values to it, overwrites the variable's contents with new content.

Chars and Strings

As explained in *Primitive versus Reference Data Types*, strings are made of sequences of characters. A character is a symbol representing a letter in the alphabet, a digit, a human-readable symbol such as the exclamation mark, or even symbols invisible to the eye, such as the blank space, end-of-line, or tabulation characters. Strings are variables that refer to a part of the memory containing a one-dimensional array of characters.

Java allows the use of the mathematical composition of characters into strings. Let's take the previous example that printed the message "**Joe . . . went fishing**." Let's modify this so that it will add the different parts of the string together instead of overwriting the variable at each step:

```
public class Main {
    public static void main(String[] args) {
        String t = null;
        System.out.println(t);
        t = t + "Joe . . . ";
        System.out.println(t);
        t = t + "Joe . . . went fishing";
        System.out.println(t);
    }
}
```

The outcome for this program will be the following:

```
null
nullJoe ...
nullJoe ... went fishing
Process finished with exit code 0
```

What happens here is that the program prints the string as we make it grow longer by appending new parts to it. However, the result is a non-desired one (unless you really want the program to print **null** in front of the string).

Now it is time to see what happens when you do not declare a variable properly. Modify the previous code listing, and observe the outcome from the development environment.

Exercise 3: Declaring Strings

Modify the code example from **Example05.java** to see how the development environment will respond to the non-valid declaration of a variable. To do so, perform the following steps:

1. Start by creating a program using the **HelloWorld** template and overwrite all of the code with the listing from the **Example05.java** file.

2. Try the program. You should get the outcome presented earlier in this section.

3. Modify the line where the string is declared to be as follows:

   ```
   String t;
   ```

4. When executing the program, you will get an error as the result:

   ```
   Error:(4, 28) java: variable t might not have been initialized
   ```

5. Declare the string to be empty, as in, containing no characters. You can do this by using the following line of code to declare the string:

   ```
   String t = "";
   ```

   After making this modification, the program's result will be as follows:

   ```
   Joe ...
   Joe … went fishing
   Process finished with exit code 0
   ```

Doing Some Math

You could say that the code presented in the **Example05.java** file's listing represents a way to *add* strings. This operation of adding strings is called *concatenation*. At the same time, it is possible to run all kinds of simple and complex mathematical operations using variables as part of the equation.

The basic mathematical operators in Java are addition (+), subtraction (-), multiplication (*), and division (/). An example of some operations being performed is presented here:

```
t = a + 5;
b = t * 6.23;
n = g / s - 45;
```

The order in which operations will be performed is that of normal math: multiplication and division first, followed by addition and subtraction. If nesting is needed, you could use braces:

```
h = (4 + t) / 2;
f = j * (e - 5 / 2);
```

There are other mathematical operators, such as square root (**sqrt()**), minimum (**min()**), and round up a number (**round()**). Calling to some of these more advanced operations will require calling the methods from the **Math** library within Java. Let's see some example code that will execute some mathematical operations to see how this works, later using this to try and solve a simple equation from trigonometry:

```
public class Main {
    public static void main(String[] args) {
        float f = 51.49f;
        System.out.println(f);
        int i = Math.round(f);
        System.out.println(i);
    }
}
```

In the preceding example, you declare a variable of the **float** type and print it. Next, you declare a variable of the **int** type and initialize it with the result of rounding the previous variable, which eliminates the fractional part of the number. You can see that **round()** is part of Java's **Math** library and therefore has to be called this way.

`Math.round()` and `System.out.println()` are examples of calls to methods that belong to the standard Java libraries `Math` and `System`, respectively. Java comes with a plethora of useful methods that will make your interaction with the software quick and easy. We will look at them later in the book.

Exercise 4: Solving a Simple Trigonometry Problem

The goal of this exercise is to solve the hypotenuse of a right triangle, given the lengths of the other two sides. Note that the formula for calculating the hypotenuse of a right-angled triangle is as follows: $h^2 = a^2 + b^2$

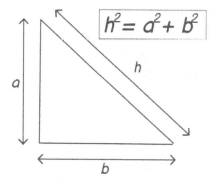

Figure 1.11: A right angled triangle with sides as a and b and h as the hypotenuse

To do this, perform the following steps:

1. Take, once more, the `HelloWorld` template as a point of departure for the exercise, create the program, and then let's build a new program by modifying its contents.

2. Declare the values to each one of the problem's variables. Initialize the one corresponding to the hypotenuse with `0`. Make all the variables of the **double** type:

```
double a = 3;
double b = 4;
double h = 0;
```

3. Given that the addition of the squares of **a** and **b** equals the square of **h**, rewrite the equation as follows:

```
h = Math.sqrt(a*a + b*b);
```

The **sqrt()** method is used to obtain the square root of a number.

4. Add the necessary code to print out the result:

```
System.out.println(h);
```

The expected outcome of this program should be the following:

```
5.0
Process finished with exit code 0
```

5. Programming languages typically offer more than one way to solve a problem. In this particular case, you could solve the calculation of the square of the **a** and **b** variables by using the **Math.pow()** method. This will calculate the power of a base by an exponent that is given as a parameter:

```
h = Math.sqrt(Math.pow(a,2) + Math.pow(b,2));
```

The form of the final program, given all the modifications, is as follows:

```
public class Main {
    public static void main(String[] args) {
        double a = 3;
        double b = 4;
        double h = 0;
        h = Math.sqrt(Math.pow(a,2) + Math.pow(b,2));
        System.out.println(h);
    }
}
```

Comments Help You to Share Code

Until now, you have just been writing programs and testing them. But if you intend to be part of a large software project where you will collaborate with others in the making of an application, you will have to share your code with others. Sharing code is an important part of the work of the contemporary developer, and, in order to share code, you will have to annotate it so that others can understand why you decided to solve certain challenges the way you did in your code.

There are two ways to comment code in Java: inline comments, which are marked using a double-slash, //; and more extensive comments, typically used at the beginning of large blocks of code, which are marked with an opening tag comprising a slash and an asterisk, /*, and a closing tag comprising an asterisk and a slash, */.

The following example showcases how to add comments to the resulting program from the previous exercise:

```java
public class Main {
    public static void main(String[] args) {
        double a = 3; // first side of the triangle
        double b = 4; // second side of the triangle
        double h = 0; // hypotenuse, init with value 0
        // equation to solve the hypotenuse
        h = Math.sqrt(Math.pow(a,2) + Math.pow(b,2));
        System.out.println(h); // print out the results
    }
}
```

In the previous example, we commented both the opening of the program and each one of the lines. The idea is to highlight different ways to comment code—inline, before a line, at the beginning of the code. You will notice some special things in the comments; for instance, the opening comment includes the author of the code (eventually, you will also include your contact information) as well as a copyright notice, letting people know to what extent they are allowed to reuse your code.

> **Note**
>
> Copyright notices for code depend on a specific company's policies most of the time, and vary for almost every project. Be careful when adding these to your code.

CLI versus GUI

In this book, we are going to be using the CLI as a way to test and deploy code. On the other hand, we will be writing the code using the IntelliJ development environment, which has a **Graphical User Interface** (GUI). We are intentionally avoiding making programs that will be using a GUI to interact with users. Java, in its current form, is mostly used as a service running on a server, and therefore the generation of GUIs is not the main goal behind the use of Java.

Up to this point, this book has invited you to run the code from the IntelliJ environment. The following exercise will help you to create a fully compiled application and run it from the CLI.

Exercise 5: Running the Code from the CLI

We will start from the creation of the **HelloWorld** example. We will compile it and then look for it from a terminal window. You have to remember which folder you created your program in, as we will be executing it from there. In this example, we called the folder **chapter01**. If you named it differently, you will have to remember to use the correct folder name when necessary in the code for this exercise:

1. Click on the **Build Project** button (this is the hammer on the toolbar), and check that the system is not throwing any errors. If there are any, the console at the bottom of the window will open up, indicating the possible errors.

2. Next, open the terminal within the editor, and you will see a button at the bottom of the environment's window. This will show a CLI starting at the location where the program was created. You can see the contents of the folder by typing the **ls** command:

```
usr@localhost:~/IdeaProjects/chapter01$ ls
chapter01.iml   out   src
```

3. There will be two different folders and one file. We are interested in checking the folder named **out**. It is the one containing the compiled version of our program.

4. Navigate to that folder by issuing the **cd out** command. This folder contains a single subfolder called **production** – enter it, as well as the subsequent **chapter01** subfolder:

```
usr@localhost:~/IdeaProjects/chapter01$ cd out
usr@localhost:~/IdeaProjects/chapter01/out$ cd production
usr@localhost:~/IdeaProjects/chapter01/out/production$ cd chapter01
usr@localhost:~/IdeaProjects/chapter01/out/production/chapter01$ ls
Main.class
```

5. Once at the right folder, you will find a file called **Main.class**. This is the compiled version of your program. To execute it, you need to call the **java Main** command. You will see the program's outcome directly at the CLI:

```
usr@localhost:~/IdeaProjects/chapter01/out/production/chapter01$ java Main
Hello World!
```

Activity 1: Obtaining the Minimum of Two Numbers

Write a program that will check two numbers entered as variables and print out the message "`The minimum of numbers: XX and YY is ZZ`", where **XX**, **YY**, and **ZZ** represent the values of the two variables and the result of the operation, respectively. To do this, perform the following steps:

1. Declare 3 double variables: **a**, **b**, and **m**. Initialize them with the values **3**, **4** and **0** respectively.

2. Create a **String** variable **r**, it should contain the output message to be printed.

3. Use the **min()** method to obtain the minimum of the two numbers and store the value in m.

4. Print the results.

> **Note**
>
> The solution for the activity can be found on page 532.

Summary

This chapter introduced you to the use of the IntelliJ development environment, which is the basic tool that will be used throughout the book. Many of IntelliJ's features are common in other tools, along with the language used in menus and the overall programming interface.

You have seen some basic aspects of Java's syntax: how classes are defined, how code is nested inside curly braces, and how semicolons end each one of the commands. Comments help make the code more readable, both for others with whom you may collaborate and for yourself when reviewing your code in the future.

The primitive types offer a collection of possible variable types to be used in your programs to carry data, store the results of operations, and transfer information between different blocks of code.

All examples in this chapter are built from modifying an initial example that we used as a point of departure: "hello world"–that is, printing a string on the CLI. In later chapters, you will learn how to create your own classes from scratch, name them according to your needs, and store them in different folders. The next chapter will specifically cover statements in Java that control the flow of the programs.

Learning the Basics

Overview

In this chapter, we will be executing programs that do not have the typical linear flow that we have seen so far. You will first learn to use if, else, else if, and switch-case statements to control the flow of your programs. You will practice running for, while, and do-while loops in order to perform repetitive tasks in Java, and how to pass command-line arguments to modify how programs run. By the end of this chapter, you will be able to implement immutable, static (global) variables, alongside Java's variable type inference mechanism.

Introduction

Business applications have lots of special-case conditions. Such conditions may include finding changes in allocation rules starting at a particular year, or handling different types of employees differently based on their designation. To code for such special cases, you will require conditional logic. You basically tell the computer to perform a set of actions when a particular condition is met.

Before we delve into advanced Java topics, you need to know the basics of Java syntax. While some of this material might seem simple, you'll find you need to use the techniques and syntax shown in this chapter repeatedly in your applications.

As you've seen in *Chapter 1, Getting Started*, Java's syntax borrows heavily from C and C++. That's true for conditional statements that control the flow of your programs as well. Java, like most computer languages, allows you to do this. This chapter covers the basic syntax of the Java language, especially ways in which you can control the flow of your applications.

This chapter, and the next one on object-oriented programming, will give you a good working knowledge of how Java programs work. You'll be able to take on more advanced APIs and topics. Work your way through this basic material, and you will be ready to move on to the more complex code to come.

Controlling the Flow of Your Programs

Imagine paying a bill from your e-wallet. You will only be able to make the payment if the credit balance in your e-wallet is greater than or equal to the bill amount. The following flowchart shows a simple logic that can be implemented:

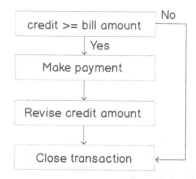

Figure 2.1: A representative flow chart for an if-else statement

Here, the credit amount dictates the course of action of the program. To facilitate such scenarios, Java uses the **if** statement.

With the **if** statement, your application will execute a block of code *if* (and only if) a particular condition is true. In the following code, if the **happy** variable is **true**, then the block of code immediately following the **if** statement will execute. If the **happy** variable is not **true**, then the block of code immediately following the **if** statement will not execute.

```
boolean happy = true;// initialize a Boolean variable as true
if (happy) //Checks if happy is true
    System.out.println("I am happy.");
```

Exercise 1: Creating a Basic if Statement

In most software industries, you are only working on a module of the code, and you might already know the value stored in a variable. You can use **if** statements and **print** statements in such cases. In this exercise, use an **if** statement to check if the values of variables assigned are **true** or **false**:

1. Create a directory for examples from this chapter and others. Name the folder **sources**.

2. In IntelliJ, select **File** -> **New** -> **Project** from the **File** menu.

3. In the **New Project** dialog box, select a **Java** project. Click **Next**.

4. Check the box to create the project from a template. Click on **Command Line App**. Click on **Next**.

5. Name the project **chapter02**.

6. For the project location, click the button with three dots (...) and then select the **sources** folder you created previously.

7. Delete the base package name so that this entry is left blank. You will use Java packages in the *Chapter 6, Libraries, Packages, and Modules*.

8. Click **Finish**.

IntelliJ will create a project named **chapter02**, as well as a **src** folder inside **chapter02**. This is where your Java code will reside. IntelliJ also creates a class named **Main**:

```
public class Main {
    public static void main(String[] args) {
    // write your code here
    }
}
```

Rename the class named **Main** to **Exercise01**. (We're going to create a lot of small examples in this chapter.)

9. Double-click in the text editor window on the word **Main** and then right-click it.

10. From the contextual menu, select **Refactor | Rename...**, enter **Exercise01**, and then press **Enter**.

You will now see the following code:

```
public class Exercise01 {
    public static void main(String[] args) {
    // write your code here
    }
}
```

11. Within the **main()** method, define two Boolean variables, **happy** and **sad**:

```
        boolean happy = true;
        boolean sad = false;
```

12. Now, create two **if** statements, as follows:

```
if (happy)
    System.out.println("I am happy.");
// Usually put the conditional code into a block.
if (sad) {
    // You will not see this.
    System.out.println("The variable sad is true.");
}
```

The final code should look similar to this:

```java
public class Exercise01 {
    public static void main(String[] args) {
        boolean happy = true;
        boolean sad = false;
        if (happy)
            System.out.println("I am happy.");
        // Usually put the conditional code into a block.
        if (sad) {
        // You will not see this.
            System.out.println("The variable sad is true.");
        }
    }
}
```

13. Click the green arrow that is just to the left of the text editor window that points at the class name **Exercise01**. Select the first menu choice, **Run Exercise01.main()**.

14. In the **Run** window, you'll see the path to your Java program, and then the following output:

```
I am happy.
```

The line **I am happy.** comes from the first **if** statement, since the **happy** Boolean variable is true.

Note that the second **if** statement does not execute, because the **sad** Boolean variable is false.

You almost always want to use curly braces to define the code block following an **if** condition. If you don't, you may find odd errors in your programs. For example, in the following code, the second statement, which sets the **i** variable to zero, will always get executed:

```java
if (i == 5)
    System.out.println("i is 5");
    i = 0;
```

Unlike languages such as Python, indentation doesn't count in Java. The following shows what will actually execute with greater clarity:

```
if (i == 5) {
    System.out.println("i is 5");
}
i = 0;
```

The last line is always executed because it is outside the **if** statement after the curly braces closes.

Comparison Operators

In addition to Java's Booleans, you can use comparisons in conditional statements. These comparisons must form a Boolean expression that resolves to **true** or **false**. Comparison operators allow you to build Boolean expressions by comparing values. Java's main comparison operators include the following:

Operator	Name	Explanation
==	is equal to	a==b indicates that the value stored in variable a is equal to the value stored in b
!=	is not equal to	a!=b indicates that the value stored in variable a is not equal to the value stored in b
<	is less than	a<b indicates that the value stored in variable a is lesser than value stored in b
<=	is less than or equal to	a<=b indicates that the value stored in variable a is lesser than or equal to the value stored in b
>	is greater than	a>b indicates that the value stored in variable a is greater than the value stored in b
>=	is greater than or equal to	a>=b indicates that the value stored in variable a is greater than or equal to the value stored in b

Figure 2.2: The comparison operators in Java

The comparison operators such as == do not work the way you would expect for textual values. See the *Comparing Strings* section later in this chapter to see how to compare text values.

Exercise 2: Using Java Comparison Operators

An online retail store provides free delivery only if the destination is within a 10-kilometer (km) radius of the store. Given the distance between the nearest store location and home, we can code this business logic with comparison operators:

1. In the **Project** pane in IntelliJ, right-click on the folder named **src**.

2. Choose **New** -> **Java Class** from the menu.

3. Enter **Exercise02** for the name of the new class.

4. Define the method named **main()**:

```
public static void main(String[] args) {
}
```

5. Inside the **main()** method, define the variables we'll use for comparisons:

```
int maxDistance = 10;       // km
int distanceToHome = 11;
```

6. Enter the following **if** statements after the variable declarations:

```
if (distanceToHome > maxDistance) {
    System.out.println("Distance from the store to your home is");
    System.out.println("  more than " + maxDistance + "km away.");
    System.out.println("That is too far for free delivery.");
}
if (distanceToHome <= maxDistance) {
    System.out.println("Distance from the store to your home is");
    System.out.println("  within " + maxDistance + "km away.");
    System.out.println("You get free delivery!");
}
```

The final code should look similar to the following: https://packt.live/32Ca9YS

7. Run the **Exercise02** program using the green arrow to the left.

In the **Run** window, you'll see the path to your Java program, and then the following output:

```
Distance from the store to your home is
  more than 10km away.
That is too far for free delivery.
```

Nested if Statements

Nesting implies embedding a construct within another code construct. You can nest **if** statements within any block of code, including the block of code that follows an **if** statement. Here is an example of how the logic in a nested **if** statement is evaluated:

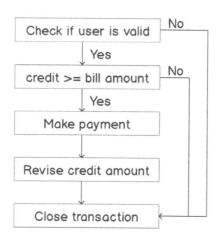

Figure 2.3: A representative flow chart for a nested if-else statement

Exercise 3: Implementing a Nested if Statement

In the following exercise, we will nest an **if** statement within another **if** statement to check if the speed of the vehicle is above the speed limit, and if so, whether it is above the finable speed:

1. Using the techniques from the previous exercise, create a new class named **Exercise03**.

2. Declare the **speed**, **speedForFine**, and **maxSpeed** variables with the values of **75**, **70**, and **60** respectively:

```java
public class Exercise03 {
    public static void main(String[] args) {
        int speed = 75;
        int maxSpeed = 60;
        int speedForFine = 70;

    }
}
```

3. Create a nested **if** statement, where the outer **if** statement checks if the speed is greater than or equal to the maximum speed limit, and the inner loop checks if the speed is greater than or equal to the speed limit for a fine:

```java
// Nested if statements.
if (speed >= maxSpeed) {
    System.out.println("You're over the speed limit!");
if (speed >= speedForFine) {
    System.out.println("You are eligible for a fine!");
}
```

4. Run the **Exercise03** program using the green arrow to the left.

In the **Run** window, you'll see the path to your Java program, and then the following output:

```
You're over the speed limit!
You are eligible for a fine!
```

> **Note**
>
> Try changing the value of speed in the code and then running the program again. You will see how different speed values produce different outputs.

Branching Two Ways with if and else

An **else** statement following the code block for an **if** statement gets executed if the **if** statement condition is not true. You can also use **else if** statements to provide for an additional test.

The basic syntax is as follows:

```
if (speed > maxSpeed) {
    System.out.println("Your speed is greater than the max. speed limit");
} else if (speed < maxSpeed) {
    System.out.println("Your speed is less than the max. speed limit");
} else {
    System.out.println("Your speed is equal to the max. speed limit");
}
```

The third line (in the **else** block) will only print if neither of the first two lines (the **if** or **else if** code blocks) was true. Whatever the value of speed, only one of the lines will print.

Exercise 4: Using if and else Statements

A fair-trade coffee roaster offers a discount of 10% if you order more than 5 kg of whole coffee beans, and a discount of 15% if you order more than 50 kg. We'll code these business rules using **if**, **else if**, and **else** statements:

1. Using the techniques from the previous exercise, create a new class named **Exercise04**.

2. Enter the **main** method and declare the variables as follows:

```
public static void main(String[] args) {
    int noDiscount = 0;
    int mediumDiscount = 10;    // Percent
    int largeDiscount = 15;
    int mediumThreshold = 5;    // Kg
    int largeThreshold = 50;
    int purchaseAmount = 40;
}
```

3. Enter the following **if**, **else if**, and **else** statements:

```
if (purchaseAmount >= largeThreshold) {
    System.out.println("You get a discount of " + largeDiscount + "%");
} else if (purchaseAmount >= mediumThreshold) {
    System.out.println("You get a discount of " + mediumDiscount + "%");
} else {
    // Sorry
    System.out.println("You get a discount of " + noDiscount + "%");
}
```

Notice that we check against the largest threshold first. The reason for this is that a value greater than or equal to **largeThreshold** will also be greater than or equal to **mediumThreshold**.

> **Note**
>
> The full source code for this exercise can be found at: https://packt.live/33UTu35.

4. Run the **Exercise04** program using the green arrow to the left.

   In the **Run** window, you'll see the path to your Java program, and then the following output:

```
You get a discount of 10%
```

Using Complex Conditionals

Java allows you to create complex conditional statements with logical operators. Logical operators are generally used on only Boolean values. Here are some of the logical operators available in Java:

- **AND (&&): a && b** will be evaluated to **true** if both a and b are **true**
- **OR (||): a || b** will be evaluated to **true** if either a or b, or both are **true**
- **NOT (!): !a** be evaluated to true if **a** is **false**

Use the conditional operators to check more than one condition in an **if** statement. For example, the following shows an **if** statement where both conditions must be true for the overall **if** statement to execute:

```
boolean red = true;
boolean blue = false;
if ((red) && (blue)) {
    System.out.println("Both red AND blue are true.");
}
```

In this case, the overall expression resolves to **false**, since the **blue** variable is false, and the **print** statement will not execute.

> **Note**
>
> Always use parentheses to make your conditionals clear by grouping the conditions together.

You can also check if either, or both, of the expressions are true with the **||** operator:

```
boolean red = true;
boolean blue = false;
if ((red) || (blue)) {
    System.out.println("Either red OR blue OR both are true.");
}
```

In this case, the overall expression resolves to true, since at least one part is true. Therefore, the **print** statement will execute:

```
boolean blue = false;
if (!blue) {
    System.out.println("The variable blue is false");
}
```

The value of **blue** is initialized to **false**. Since we are checking the NOT of the blue variable in the **if** statement, the **print** statement will execute. The following exercise shows how we can use logical operators.

Exercise 5: Using Logical Operators to Create Complex Conditionals

This exercise shows an example of each of the conditional operators previously described. You are writing an application that works with data from a fitness tracker. To accomplish this, you need to code a check against normal heart rates during exercise.

If a person is 30 years old, a normal heart rate should be between 95 beats per minute (bpm) and 162 bpm. If the person is 60 years old, a normal heart rate should be between 80 and 136 bpm.

Use the following steps for completion:

1. Using the techniques from the previous exercise, create a new class named **Exercise05** in the **main** method and declare variables.

```java
public static void main(String[] args) {
    int age = 30;
    int bpm = 150;
}
```

2. Create an **if** statement to check the heart rate of a 30-year old person:

```java
if (age == 30) {
    if ((bpm >= 95) && (bpm <= 162)) {
        System.out.println("Heart rate is normal.");
    } else if (bpm < 95) {
        System.out.println("Heart rate is very low.");
    } else {
        System.out.println("Heart rate is very high.");
    }
```

We have nested conditionals to check the allowable range for 30-year-olds.

3. Create an **else if** statement to check the heart rate of a 60-year old person:

```java
} else if (age == 60) {
    if ((bpm >= 80) && (bpm <= 136)) {
        System.out.println("Heart rate is normal.");
    } else if (bpm < 80) {
        System.out.println("Heart rate is very low.");
    } else {
        System.out.println("Heart rate is very high.");
    }
}
```

We have nested conditionals to check the allowable range for 60-year-olds.

4. Run the **Exercise05** program using the green arrow to the left.

   In the **Run** window, you'll see the path to your Java program, and then the following output:

   ```
   Heart rate is normal.
   ```

5. Change **age** to **60** and re-run the program; your output should be as follows:

   ```
   Heart rate is very high.
   ```

   > **Note**
   >
   > The full source code for this exercise can be found at: https://packt.live/2W3YAHs.

Using Arithmetic Operators in an if Condition

You can use arithmetic operators as well in Boolean expressions, as shown in **Example01.java**:

```java
public class Example01 {
    public static void main(String[] args) {
        int x = 2;
        int y = 1;
        if ((x + y) < 5) {
            System.out.println("X added to Y is less than 5.");
        }
    }
}
```

The output in this case would be as follows:

```
X added to Y is less than 5
```

Here, the value of (**x** + **y**) is calculated, and then the result is compared to **5**. So, since the result of **x** added to **y** is **3**, which is less than **5**, the condition holds true. Therefore, the **print** statement is executed. Now that we have seen the variations of the **if else** statement, we will now see how we can use the ternary operator to express the **if else** statements.

The Ternary Operator

Java allows a short-hand version of an **if else** statement, using the ternary (or three-part) operator, ?:. This is often used when checking variables against an allowed maximum (or minimum) value.

The basic format is: *Boolean expression* ? *true block* : *false block*, as follows:

```
x = (x > max) ? max : x;
```

The JVM resolves the **(x > max)** Boolean expression. If true, then the expression returns the value immediately after the question mark. In this case, that value will be set into the **x** variable since the line of code starts with an assignment, **x =**. If the expression resolves to false, then the value after the colon, :, is returned.

Exercise 6: Using the Ternary Operator

Consider the minimum height requirement for a roller coaster to be 121 centimeters (cm). In this exercise, we will check for this condition using the ternary operator. Perform the following steps:

1. Using the techniques from the previous exercise, create a new class named **Exercise06**.

2. Declare and assign values to the **height** and **minHeight** variables. Also, declare a string variable to print the output message:

```
public static void main(String[] args) {
    int height = 200;
    int minHeight = 121;
    String result;
```

3. Use the ternary operator to check the minimum height requirement and set the value of **result**:

```
result = (height > minHeight) ? "You are allowed on the ride" : "Sorry you do not
meet the height requirements";
System.out.println(result);
}
```

So, if height is greater than **minHeight**, the first statement will be returned (**You are allowed on the ride**). Otherwise, the second statement will be returned (**Sorry you do not meet the height requirements**).

Your code should look similar to this:

```java
public class Exercise06 {
    public static void main(String[] args) {
        int height = 200;
        int minHeight = 121;
        String result;
        result = (height > minHeight) ? "You are allowed on the ride" :
            "Sorry you do not meet the height requirements";
        System.out.println(result);
    }
}
```

4. Run the **Exercise06** program.

    In the **Run** window, you'll see the path to your Java program, and then the following output:

    ```
    You are allowed on the ride
    ```

Equality Can Be Tricky

Java decimal types such as **float** and **double** (and the object versions, **Float** and **Double**) are not stored in memory in a way that works with regular equality checks.

When comparing decimal values, you normally need to define a value that represents what you think is close enough. For example, if two values are within .001 of each other, then you may feel that is close enough to consider the values as equal.

Exercise 7: Comparing Decimal Values

In this exercise, you'll run a program that checks if two double values are close enough to be considered equal:

1. Using the techniques from the previous exercise, create a new class named **Exercise07**.

2. Enter the following code:

```java
public class Exercise07 {
    public static void main(String[] args) {
        double a = .6 + .6 + .6 + .6 + .6 + .6;
        double b = .6 * 6;
        System.out.println("A is " + a);
        System.out.println("B is " + b);
        if (a != b) {
            System.out.println("A is not equal to B.");
        }
        // Check if close enough.
        if (Math.abs(a - b) < .001) {
            System.out.println("A is close enough to B.");
        }
    }
}
```

The **Math.abs()** method returns the absolute value of the input, making sure the input is positive.

We will learn more about the **Math** package in *Chapter 6, Libraries, Packages, and Modules*.

3. Run the **Exercise07** program using the green arrow to the left.

In the run window, you'll see the path to your Java program, and then the following output:

```
A is 3.6
B is 3.5999999999999996
A is not equal to B.
A is close enough to B.
```

Note how **a** and **b** differ due to the internal storage for the double type.

> **Note**
>
> For more on how Java represents floating-point numbers, see https://packt.
> live/2VZdaQy.

Comparing Strings

You cannot use == to compare two strings in Java. Instead, you need to use the **String** class' **equals** method. This is because == with **String** objects just checks whether they are the exact same object. What you'll normally want is to check if the string values are equal:

```java
String cat = new String("cat");
String dog = new String("dog");
if (cat.equals(dog)) {
    System.out.println("Cats and dogs are the same.");
}
```

The **equals** method on a **String** object called **cat** returns true if the passed-in **String**, **dog**, has the same value as the first **String**. In this case, these two strings differ. So, the Boolean expression will resolve to false.

You can also use literal strings in Java, delineating these strings with double quotes. Here's an example:

```java
if (dog.equals("dog")) {
    System.out.println("Dogs are dogs.");
}
```

This case compares a **String** variable named **dog** with the literal string **"dog"**.

Example09 shows how to call the equals method:

Example09.java

```java
15            if (dog.equals(dog)) {
16                System.out.println("Dogs are dogs.");
17            }
18
19            // Using literal strings
20            if (dog.equals("dog")) {
21                System.out.println("Dogs are dogs.");
22            }
23
24            // Can compare using a literal string, too.
25            if ("dog".equals(dog)) {
26                System.out.println("Dogs are dogs.");
```

https://packt.live/2BtrKGz

You should get the following output:

```
Cats and dogs are not the same.
Dogs are dogs.
Dogs are dogs.
Dogs are dogs.
```

Using switch Statements

The **switch** statement is similar to a group of nested **if-else-if** statements. With **switch**, you can choose from a group of values.

The basic syntax follows:

```
switch(season) {
    case 1: message = "Spring";
        break;
    case 2: message = "Summer";
        break;
    case 3: message = "Fall";
        break;
    case 4: message = "Winter";
        break;
    default: message = "That's not a season";
        break;
}
```

With the **switch** keyword, you place the variable to be checked. In this case, we're checking a variable called **season**. Each case statement represents one possible value for the **switch** variable (season). If the value of season is **3**, then the **case** statement that matches will be executed, setting the **message** variable to the String **Fall**. The **break** statement ends the execution for that case.

The **default** statement is used as a catch-all for any unexpected value that doesn't match the defined cases. The best practice is to always include a **default** statement. Let's see how to implement this logic in a program.

Exercise 8: Using switch

In this exercise, you'll run a program that maps a number to a season:

1. Using the techniques from the previous exercise, create a new class named **Exercise08**.

2. Enter in the **main()** method and set up these variables:

```
public static void main(String[] args) {
    int season = 3;
    String message;
}
```

3. Enter the following **switch** statement.

```
switch(season) {
    case 1: message = "Spring";
        break;
    case 2: message = "Summer";
        break;
    case 3: message = "Fall";
        break;
    case 4: message = "Winter";
        break;
    default: message = "That's not a season";
        break;
}
```

4. And enter a **println** statement to show us the results:

```
System.out.println(message);
```

> **Note**
>
> You can find the code for this exercise here: https://packt.live/35WXm58.

5. Run the **Exercise08** program using the green arrow to the left.

In the **Run** window, you'll see the path to your Java program, and then the following output:

```
Fall
```

Because the **season** variable is set to **3**, Java executes the **case** with **3** as the value, so in this case, setting the **message** variable to **Fall**.

> **Note**
>
> There is no one rule for when to use a **switch** statement as opposed to a series of **if-else** statements. In many cases, your choice will be based on the clarity of the code. In addition, **switch** statements are limited in only having cases that hold a single value, while **if** statements can test much more complicated conditions.

Normally, you'll put a **break** statement after the code for a particular case. You don't have to. The code will keep executing from the start of the **case** until the next **break** statement. This allows you to treat multiple conditions similarly.

Exercise 9: Allowing Cases to Fall Through

In this exercise, you will determine a temperature adjustment for the porridge in *Goldilocks and the Three Bears*. If the porridge is too hot, for example, you'll need to reduce the temperature. If it's too cold, raise the temperature:

1. Using the techniques from the previous exercise, create a new class named **Exercise09**.

2. Enter in the **main()** method and set up these variables:

```
public static void main(String[] args) {
    int tempAdjustment = 0;
    String taste = "way too hot";
}
```

3. Next, enter the following **switch** statement:

```
switch(taste) {
    case "too cold":     tempAdjustment += 1;
        break;
    case "way too hot": tempAdjustment -= 1;
    case "too hot":      tempAdjustment -= 1;
        break;
    case "just right":  // No adjustment
    default:
        break;
}
```

4. Print out the results:

```
System.out.println("Adjust temperature: " + tempAdjustment);
```

5. Run the **Exercise09** program using the green arrow to the left.

   In the run window, you'll see the path to your Java program, and then the following output:

```
Adjust temperature: -2
```

Look carefully at the **switch** statement. If the value of the taste variable is too cold, then increment the temperature by 1. If the value is too hot, decrement the temperature by 1. But notice there is no break statement, so the code keeps executing and adjusts the temperature down by another 1. This implies that if the porridge is too hot, the temperature is decremented by 1. If it's way too hot, it's decremented by 2. If the porridge is just right, there is no adjustment.

> **Note**
>
> Starting with Java 7, you can use Strings in switch statements. Prior to Java 7, you could not.

Using Java 12 Enhanced switch Statements

Java 12 offers a new form of the **switch** statement. Aimed at **switch** statements that are essentially used to determine the value of a variable, the new **switch** syntax allows you to assign a variable containing the result of the **switch**.

The new syntax looks like this:

```
int tempAdjustment = switch(taste) {
    case "too cold" ->     1;
    case "way too hot" -> -2;
    case "too hot" ->    -1;
    case "just right" -> 0;
    default -> 0;
};
```

This **switch** syntax does not use break statements. Instead, for a given case, only the code block after -> gets executed. The value from that code block is then returned as the value from the switch statement.

We can rewrite the **Exercise09** example using the new syntax, as shown in the following exercise.

> **Note**
>
> IntelliJ needs a configuration to support Java 12 **switch** statements.

Exercise 10: Using Java 12 switch Statements

In this exercise, we will work on the same example as in the previous exercise. This time, though, we will implement the new switch case syntax that is made available by Java 12. Before we start with the program there, you'll have to make changes to the IntelliJ configuration. We will set that up in the initial few steps of the exercise:

1. From the **Run** menu, select **Edit** Configurations.

2. Click on **Edit** Templates.

3. Click on **Application**.

4. Add the following to the **VM** options:

    ```
    --enable-preview
    ```

5. Click **OK**.

    This turns on the IntelliJ support for Java 12 enhanced switch statements.

6. Using the techniques from the previous exercise, create a new class named **Exercise10**.

7. Enter in the **main()** method and set up this variable:

    ```
    public static void main(String[] args) {
        String taste = "way too hot";
    }
    ```

8. Define a **switch** statement as follows:

    ```
    int tempAdjustment = switch(taste) {
        case "too cold" ->    1;
        case "way too hot" -> -2;
        case "too hot" ->    -1;
        case "just right" -> 0;
        default -> 0;
    };
    ```

    Note the semi-colon after **switch**. Remember, we are assigning a variable to a value with the whole statement.

9. Then print out the value chosen:

    ```
    System.out.println("Adjust temperature: " + tempAdjustment);
    ```

10. When you run this example, you should see the same output as in the previous example:

```
Adjust temperature: -2
```

The full code is as follows:

```java
public class Exercise10 {
    public static void main(String[] args) {
        String taste = "way too hot";
        int tempAdjustment = switch(taste) {
            case "too cold" ->     1;
            case "way too hot" -> -2;
            case "too hot" ->    -1;
            case "just right" -> 0;
            default -> 0;
        };
        System.out.println("Adjust temperature: " + tempAdjustment);
    }
}
```

Looping and Performing Repetitive Tasks

In this chapter, we cover using loops to perform repetitive tasks. The main types of loop are as follows:

- **for** loops
- **while** loops
- **do-while** loops

for loops repeat a block a set number of times. Use a **for** loop when you are sure how many iterations you want. A newer form of the **for** loop iterates over each item in a collection.

while loops execute a block while a given condition is true. When the condition becomes false, the **while** loop stops. Similarly, **do-while** loops execute a block and then check a condition. If true, the **do-while** loop runs the next iteration.

Use **while** loops if you are unsure how many iterations are required. For example, when searching through data to find a particular element, you normally want to stop when you find it.

Use a **do-while** loop if you always want to execute the block and only then check if another iteration is needed.

Looping with the for Loop

A **for** loop executes the same block of code for a given number of times. The syntax comes from the C language:

```
for(set up; boolean expression; how to increment) {
    // Execute these statements...
}
```

In the preceding code, we can see that:

- Each part is separated by a semicolon, (;).

- The **set up** part gets executed at the beginning of the entire for loop. It runs once.

- The **boolean expression** is examined at each iteration, including the first. So long as this resolves to true, the loop will execute another iteration.

- The **how to increment** part defines how you want a loop variable to increment. Typically, you'll add one for each increment.

The following exercise will implement a classic for loop in Java.

Exercise 11: Using a Classic for Loop

This exercise will run a **for** loop for four iterations, using the classic for loop syntax:

1. Using the techniques from the previous exercise, create a new class named **Exercise11**.

2. Enter a **main()** method and the following code:

    ```
    public static void main(String[] args) {
        for (int i = 1; i < 5; i++) {
            System.out.println("Iteration: " + i);
        }
    }
    ```

3. Run the **Exercise11** program using the green arrow to the left.

    In the **Run** window, you'll see the path to your Java program, and then the following output:

    ```
    Iteration: 1
    Iteration: 2
    Iteration: 3
    Iteration: 4
    ```

Here is how the program executes:

- `int i = 1` is the **for** loop set up part.

- The Boolean expression checked each iteration is `i < 5`.

- The how to increment part tells the **for** loop to add one to each iteration using the **++** operator.

- For each iteration, the code inside the parentheses executes. It continues like this until the Boolean expression stops being **true**.

In addition to the old classic **for** loop, Java also offers an enhanced for loop designed to iterate over collections and arrays.

We will cover arrays and collections in greater detail later in the book; for now, think of arrays as groups of values of the same data type stored in a single variable, whereas collections are groups of values of different data types stored in a single variable.

Exercise 12: Using an Enhanced for Loop

Iterating over the elements of arrays means that the increment value is always 1 and the start value is always 0. This allows Java to reduce the syntax of a form to iterate over arrays. In this exercise you will loop over all items in a **letters** array:

1. Using the techniques from the previous exercise, create a new class named **Exercise12**.

2. Enter a **main()** method:

```
public static void main(String[] args) {

}
```

3. Enter the following array:

```
String[] letters = { "A", "B", "C" };
```

Chapter 4, Collections, Lists, and Java's Built-In APIs, will cover the array syntax in greater depth. For now, we have an array of three **String** values, **A**, **B**, and **C**.

4. Enter an enhanced **for** loop:

```
for (String letter : letters) {
    System.out.println(letter);
}
```

Notice the reduced syntax of the **for** loop. Here, the variable letter iterates over every element in the letters array.

5. Run the **Exercise12** program using the green arrow to the left.

In the **Run** window, you'll see the path to your Java program, and then the following output:

```
A
B
C
```

Jumping Out of Loops with Break and Continue

A **break** statement, as we saw in the **switch** examples, jumps entirely out of a loop. No more iterations will occur.

A **continue** statement jumps out of the current iteration of the loop. Java will then evaluate the loop expression for the next iteration.

Exercise 13: Using break and continue

This exercise shows how to jump out of a loop using **break**, or jump to the next iteration using continue:

1. Using the techniques from the previous exercise, create a new class named **Exercise13**.

2. Enter a **main()** method:

```
public static void main(String[] args) {
}
```

3. Define a slightly longer array of **String** values:

```
String[] letters = { "A", "B", "C", "D" };
```

4. Enter the following for loop:

```
for (String letter : letters) {
}
```

This loop will normally iterate four times, once for each letter in the **letters** array. We'll change that though, with the next code.

5. Add a conditional to the loop:

```
if (letter.equals("A")) {
    continue;    // Jump to next iteration
}
```

Using **continue** here means that if the current letter equals A, then jump to the next iteration. None of the remaining loop code will get executed.

6. Next, we'll print out the current letter:

```
System.out.println(letter);
```

For all iterations that get here, you'll see the current letter printed.

7. Finish the **for** loop with a conditional using **break**:

```
if (letter.equals("C")) {
    break;     // Leave the for loop
}
```

If the value of **letter** is **C**, then the code will jump entirely out of the loop. And since our array of letters has another value, **D**, we'll never see that value at all. The loop is done when the value of letter is **C**.

8. Run the **Exercise13** program using the green arrow to the left.

In the **Run** window, you'll see the path to your Java program, and then the following output:

```
B
C
```

Exercise13.java holds the full example:

> **Note**
>
> Source code for Exercise 13 can be found at the following link: https://packt.live/2MDczAV.

Using the while Loop

In many cases, you won't know in advance how many iterations you need. In that case, use a **while** loop instead of a **for** loop.

A **while** loop repeats so long as (or *while*) a Boolean expression resolves to true:

```
while (boolean expression) {
    // Execute these statements...
}
```

Similar to a **for** loop, you'll often use a variable to count iterations. You don't have to do that, though. You can use any Boolean expression to control a **while** loop.

Exercise 14: Using a while Loop

This exercise implements a similar loop to *Exercise10*, which shows a **for** loop:

1. Using the techniques from the previous exercise, create a new class named **Exercise14**.

2. Enter a **main()** method:

```
public static void main(String[] args) {
}
```

3. Enter the following variable setting and **while** loop:

```
int i = 1;
while (i < 10) {
    System.out.println("Odd: " + i);
    i += 2;
}
```

Note how this loop increments the **i** variable by two each time. This results in printing odd numbers.

4. Run the **Exercise14** program using the green arrow to the left.

In the **Run** window, you'll see the path to your Java program, and then the following output:

```
Odd: 1
Odd: 3
Odd: 5
Odd: 7
Odd: 9
```

> **Note**
>
> A common mistake is to forget to increment the variable used in your Boolean expression.

Using the do-while Loop

The **do-while** loop provides a variant on the **while** loop. Instead of checking the condition first, the **do-while** loop checks the condition after each iteration. This means with a **do-while** loop, you will always have at least one iteration. Normally, you will only use a **do-while** loop if you are sure you want the iteration block to execute the first time, even if the condition is false.

One example use case for the **do-while** loop is if you are asking the user a set of questions and then reading the user's response. You always want to ask the first question.

The basic format is as follows:

```
do {
    // Execute these statements...
} while (boolean expression);
```

Note the semicolon after the Boolean expression.

A **do-while** loop runs the iteration block once, and then checks the Boolean expression to see if the loop should run another iteration.

Example17.java shows a **do-while** loop:

```
public class Example17 {
    public static void main(String[] args) {
        int i = 2;
        do {
            System.out.println("Even: " + i);
            i += 2;
        } while (i < 10);
    }
}
```

This example prints out even numbers.

> **Note**
>
> You can use **break** and **continue** with **while** and **do-while** loops too.

Handling Command-Line Arguments

Command-line arguments are parameters passed to the **main()** method of your Java program. In each example so far, you've seen that the **main()** method takes in an array of **String** values. These are the command-line arguments to the program.

Command-line arguments prove their usefulness by giving you one way of providing inputs to your program. These inputs are part of the command line launching the program, when run from a Terminal shell window.

Exercise 15: Testing Command-Line Arguments

This exercise shows how to pass command-line arguments to a Java program, and also shows how to access those arguments from within your programs:

1. Using the techniques from the previous exercises, create a new class named **Exercise15**.

2. Enter the following code:

```
public class Exercise15 {
    public static void main(String[] args) {
        for (int i = 0; i < args.length; i++) {
            System.out.println(i + " " + args[i]);
        }
    }
}
```

This code uses a **for** loop to iterate over all the command-line arguments, which the **java** command places into the **String** array named **args**.

Each iteration prints out the position (**i**) of the argument and the value (**args[i]**). Note that Java arrays start counting positions from 0 and **args.length** holds the number of values in the **args** array.

To run this program, we're going to take a different approach than before.

3. In the bottom of the IntelliJ application, click on **Terminal**. This will show a command-line shell window.

When using IntelliJ for these examples, the code is stored in a folder named **src**.

4. Enter the following command in the **Terminal** window:

```
cd src
```

This changes to the folder with the example source code.

5. Enter the **javac** command to compile the Java program:

```
javac Exercise15.java
```

This command creates a file named **Exercise15.class** in the current directory. IntelliJ normally puts these .*class* files into a different folder.

6. Now, run the program with the **java** command with the parameters you want to pass:

```
java Exercise15 cat dog wombat
```

In this command, **Exercise15** is the name of the Java class with the **main()** method, **Exercise15**. The values following **Exercise15** on the command line are passed to the **Exercise15** application as command-line arguments. Each argument is separated by a space character, so we have three arguments: *cat, dog,* and *wombat.*

7. You will see the following output:

```
0 cat
1 dog
2 wombat
```

The first argument, at position **0** in the **args** array, is **cat**. The argument at position **1** is **dog**, and the argument at position **2** is **wombat**.

> **Note**
>
> The **java** command, which runs compiled Java programs, supports a set of command-line arguments such as defining the available memory heap space. See the Oracle Java documentation at https://packt.live/2BwqwdJ for details on the command-line arguments that control the execution of your Java programs.

Converting Command-Line Arguments

Command-line arguments appear in your Java programs as String values. In many cases, though, you'll want to convert these *String values* into numbers.

If you are expecting an integer value, you can use **Integer.parseInt()** to convert a **String** to an **int**.

If you are expecting a double value, you can use **Double.parseDouble()** to convert a **String** to a **double**.

Exercise 16: Converting String to Integers and Doubles

This exercise extracts command-line arguments and turns them into numbers:

1. Using the techniques from the previous exercises, create a new class named **Exercise16**.

2. Enter the **main()** method:

```java
public class Exercise16 {
    public static void main(String[] args) {
    }
}
```

3. Enter the following code to convert the first argument into an **int** value:

```java
if (args.length > 0) {
    int intValue = Integer.parseInt(args[0]);
    System.out.println(intValue);
}
```

This code first checks if there is a command-line argument, and then if so, converts the **String** value to an **int**.

4. Enter the following code to convert the second argument into a **double** value:

```java
if (args.length > 1) {
    double doubleValue = Double.parseDouble(args[1]);
    System.out.println(doubleValue);
}
```

This code checks if there is a second command-line argument (start counting with 0) and if so, converts the **String** to a **double** value.

5. Enter the **javac** command introduced in *Chapter 1, Getting Started*, to compile the Java program:

```
javac Exercise16.java
```

This command creates a file named **Exercise16.class** in the current directory.

6. Now, run the program with the **java** command:

    ```
    java Exercise16 42 65.8
    ```

    You will see the following output:

    ```
    42
    65.8
    ```

    The values printed out have been converted from String values into numbers inside the program. This example does not try to catch errors, so you have to enter the inputs properly.

> **Note**
>
> Both **Integer.parseInt()** and **Double.parseDouble()** will throw **NumberFormatException** if the passed-in String does not hold a number. See *Chapter 5, Exceptions*, for more on exceptions.

Diving Deeper into Variables — Immutability

Immutable objects cannot have their values modified. In Java terms, once an immutable object is constructed, you cannot modify the object.

Immutability can provide a lot of advantages for the JVM, since it knows an immutable object cannot be modified. This can really help with garbage collection. When writing programs that use multiple threads, knowing an object cannot be modified by another thread can make your code safer.

In Java, **String** objects are immutable. While it may seem like you can assign a **String** to a different value, Java actually creates a new object when you try to change a **String**.

Comparing Final and Immutable

In addition to immutable objects, Java provides a **final** keyword. With **final**, you cannot change the object reference itself. You can change the data within a **final** object, but you cannot change which object is referenced.

Contrast **final** with immutable. An immutable object does not allow the data inside the object to change. A **final** object does not allow the object to point to another object.

Using Static Values

A *static* variable is common to all instances of a class. This differs from instance variables that apply to only one instance, or object, of a class. For example, each instance of the **Integer** class can hold a different **int** value. But, in the **Integer** class, **MAX_VALUE** and **MIN_VALUE** are static variables. These variables are defined once for all instances of integers, making them essentially global variables.

> **Note**
>
> *Chapter 3, Object-Oriented Programming,* delves into classes and objects.

Static variables are often used as constants. To keep them constant, you normally want to define them as **final** as well:

```
public static final String MULTIPLY = "multiply";
```

> **Note**
>
> By convention, the names of Java constants are all uppercase.

Example20.java defines a constant, **MULTIPLY**:

```
public class Example20 {
    public static final String MULTIPLY = "multiply";
    public static void main(String[] args) {
        System.out.println("The operation is " + MULTIPLY);
    }
}
```

Because the **MULTIPLY** constant is a final value, you will get a compilation error if your code attempts to change the value once set.

Using Local Variable Type Inference

Java is a statically typed language, which means each variable and each parameter has a defined type. As Java has provided the ability to create more complex types, especially related to collections, the Java syntax for variable types has gotten more and more complex. To help with this, Java version 10 introduced the concept of local variable type inference.

With this, you can declare a variable of the **var** type. So long as it is fully clear what type the variable really should be, the Java compiler will take care of the details for you. Here's an example:

```
var s = new String("Hello");
```

This example creates a new **String** for the **s** variable. Even though s is declared with the **var** keyword, **s** really is of the **String** type. That is, this code is equivalent to the following:

```
String s = new String("Hello");
```

With just a **String** type, this doesn't save you that much typing. When you get to more complex types, though, you will really appreciate the use of the **var** keyword.

> **Note**
>
> *Chapter 4, Collections, Lists, and Java's Built-In APIs,* covers collections, where you will see really complex types.

Example21.java shows local variable type inference in action:

```
public class Example21 {
    public static void main(String[] args) {
        var s = new String("Hello");
        System.out.println("The value is " + s);
        var i = Integer.valueOf("42");
```

```
        System.out.println("The value is " + i);
    }
}
```

When you run this example, you will see the following output:

```
The value is Hello
The value is 42
```

Activity 1: Taking Input and Comparing Ranges

You are tasked with writing a program that takes a patient's blood pressure as input and then determines if that blood pressure is within the ideal range.

Blood pressure has two components, the systolic blood pressure and the diastolic blood pressure.

According to https://packt.live/2oaVsgs, the ideal systolic number is more than 90 and less than 120. 90 and below is low blood pressure. Above 120 and below 140 is called pre-high blood pressure, and 140 and over is high blood pressure.

The ideal diastolic blood pressure is between 60 and 80. 60 and below is low. Above 80 and under 90 is pre-high blood pressure, and over 90 is high blood pressure.

Component	Ideal Range
Systolic blood pressure	90-120
Diastolic blood pressure	60-80

Figure 2.4: Ideal ranges for systolic and diastolic blood pressures

For the purpose of this activity, if either number is out of the ideal range, report that as non-ideal blood pressure:

1. Write an application that takes two numbers, the systolic blood pressure and the diastolic blood pressure. Convert both inputs into **int** values.

2. Check if there is the right number of inputs at the beginning of the program. Print an error message if any inputs are missing. Exit the application in this case.

3. Compare against the ideal rates mentioned previously. Output a message describing the inputs as low, ideal, pre-high, or high blood pressure.

    To print an error message, use `System.err.println` instead of `System.out.println`.

4. Try out your program with a variety of inputs to ensure it works properly.

    You'll need to use the Terminal pane in IntelliJ to compile and run the program with command-line input. Look back at Exercises 15 and 16 for details on how to do this.

5. The blood pressure is typically reported as systolic blood pressure/diastolic blood pressure.

    > **Note**
    >
    > The solution for this activity can be found on page 533.

Summary

This chapter covered a lot of Java syntax—things you need to learn to be able to tackle the more advanced topics. You'll find yourself using these techniques in just about every Java application you write.

We started out by controlling the flow of the program using conditional statements such as `if`, `else if`, `else`, and `switch` statements. We then moved on to the different loops that can be used to perform repetitive tasks. After this, we looked at how to provide values during runtime using command-line arguments. This is one way to pass inputs to your Java applications. Every example in this chapter created a class, but we have not yet done much with these classes.

In the next chapter, you'll learn about classes, methods, and object-oriented programming, and how you can do a lot more with classes.

3

Object-Oriented Programming

Overview

In this chapter, we will consider the way in which Java implements **object-oriented programming (OOP)** concepts. For these purposes, you will first practice creating and instantiating your own classes so that you can later create methods that can handle data within them. We will then take you through how to code recursive methods, and even how to override existing methods in favor of your own. By the end of the chapter, you will be fully equipped to overload the definition of methods in order to accommodate different scenarios with different parameters to the same method or constructor, and annotate code to inform the compiler about specific actions that must be taken.

Introduction

A Java class is a template that is used to define data types. Classes are composed of objects carrying data and methods that are used to perform operations on that data. Classes can be self-contained, extend other classes with new functionalities, or implement features from other classes. In a way, classes are categories that allow us to define what kind of data can be stored within them, as well as the ways in which that data can be handled.

Classes tell the compiler how to build a certain object during runtime. Refer to the explanation of what objects are in the *Working with Objects in Java* topic.

The basic structure of a class definition looks like this:

```
class <name> {
    fields;
    methods;
}
```

> **Note**
>
> Class names should start with a capital letter, as in **TheClass**, **Animal**, **WordCount**, or any other string that somehow expresses the main purpose of the class. If contained in a separate file, the filename containing the source should be named like the class: **TheClass.java**, **Animal.java**, and so on.

The Anatomy of a Class

There are different software components in classes. The following example shows a class that includes some of the main ones.

Example01.java

```
1   class Computer {
2       // variables
3       double cpuSpeed;   // in GHz
4
5       // constructor
6       Computer() {
7           cpuSpeed = 0;
8       }
9
10      //methods
11      void setCpuSpeed ( double _cpuSpeed ) {
12          cpuSpeed = _cpuSpeed;
13      }
```

https://packt.live/32w1ffg

The outcome of this example is:

```
2.5
Process finished with exit code 0
```

The previous code listing shows the definition of a basic class called **Computer**, which includes variables and methods to deal with one of the properties of the class computer – in this case, **cpuSpeed**. The code shows two different classes. The first one is the blueprint for how to define objects of the **Computer** type in your programs. The second one, **Example01**, is the one that will be executed after compilation and will make an instance of the **Computer** class in the form of an object called **myPC**.

There is one more component inside the class, the constructor, which is optional, as Java includes a default constructor for all your classes. **Constructors** are used to initializing the basic properties of classes, and so are used when assigning values to variables, for instance. In our case, the operation performed by the constructor is initializing the **cpuSpeed** variable with a value of **0**:

```
// constructor
Computer() {
    cpuSpeed = 0;
}
```

It is also possible for constructors to have parameters. You could have the constructor of the class be this:

```
// constructor
Computer( double _c ) {
    cpuSpeed = _c;
}
```

In this way, you could call the constructor with:

```
Computer myPC = new Computer( 2.5 );
```

That would also require a parameter. In addition, classes can have more than one constructor. This will be explained later in the chapter.

Working with Objects in Java

Objects are to classes what variables are to data types. While classes define the structure and possible actions of a certain data type, objects are actual usable parts of the computer memory containing that data. The action of creating an object is known as making an instance of a class. In a sense, it is like making a copy of the template and then modifying it by accessing its variables or methods. Let's see this in action:

```
Computer myPC = new Computer( 2.5 );
```

myPC is the actual object. We would say that myPC is an object of the **class Computer** in colloquial terms.

The different fields and methods inside the class can be accessed by typing the name of the object followed by a period and the name of the variable or method you want to address. Making any changes to the variables or calling the methods will take effect only within the scope of that object. If you had more objects of the same class in your program, each one of them would have a piece of memory of its own. An example of how to address a method is as follows:

```
myPC.setCpuSpeed( 2.5 );
```

An example of how to address a variable, on the other hand, would be the following assignment:

```
myPC.cpuSpeed = 2.5;
```

Because of the way the **Computer** class has been defined, the last two code listings have the exact same effect. The whole class has been defined—by default—as **public**, which means that all the methods, variables, and objects from the class are available to be called with the mechanism described previously. It could be necessary to prevent users from directly interacting with the variables within the class and only allow their modification through certain methods.

The different components within a class can be defined as **public** or **private**. The former will make the component available to be used as shown so far, while the latter will hinder the ability of other developers to access that part. The following example shows how to make the **cpuSpeed** variable **private**:

Example02.java

```
1   class Computer {
2       // variables
3       private double cpuSpeed;   // in GHz
4
5       // constructor
6       Computer() {
7           cpuSpeed = 0;
8       }
9
10      // methods
11      void setCpuSpeed ( double _cpuSpeed ) {
12          cpuSpeed = _cpuSpeed;
13      }
14
15      double getCpuSpeed () {
16          return cpuSpeed;
17      }
18 }
```

https://packt.live/2pBgWTS

The result of this code listing is the same as before:

```
2.5
Process finished with exit code 0
```

If you tried to access the **cpuSpeed** variable directly from the **Example02** class, the program would throw an exception. The following example shows such a case. Try it out to see how the debugger informs you when you try to access a **private** variable:

Example03.java

```
20 public class Example03 {
21      public static void main(String[] args) {
22          Computer myPC = new Computer();
23          myPC.setCpuSpeed( 2.5 );
24          System.out.println( myPC.cpuSpeed );
25      }
26 }
```

https://packt.live/2pvLu9Q

The result of this program is:

```
Example03.java:23: error: cpuSpeed has private access in Computer
        System.out.println( myPC.cpuSpeed );
1 error
Process finished with exit code 1.
```

What the compiler shows is an error in the **Computer** class, which has been derived from **java.lang**.

Checking the Precedence of a Class with instanceof

You can check whether an object is an instance of a specific class. This can be convenient for things such as error checking, handling data in different ways depending on its precedence, and more. The following example shows the **checkNumber** method, which can discriminate between different types of variables and will print different messages based on that:

```java
public class Example04 {
    public static void checkNumber(Number val) {
        if( val instanceof Integer )
            System.out.println("it is an Integer");
        if( val instanceof Double )
            System.out.println("it is a Double");
    }
    public static void main(String[] args) {
        int val1 = 3;
        double val2 = 2.7;
        checkNumber( val1 );
        checkNumber( val2 );
    }
}
```

The outcome of the previous example is:

```
it is an Integer
it is a Double
Process finished with exit code 0
```

Exercise 1: Creating the WordTool Class

WordTool is a class that will help you to perform a series of operations on a piece of text, including counting the number of words, looking at the frequency of letters, and searching for the occurrence of a specific string:

1.   Open IntelliJ and click on the **File** | **New** | **Project** menu options:

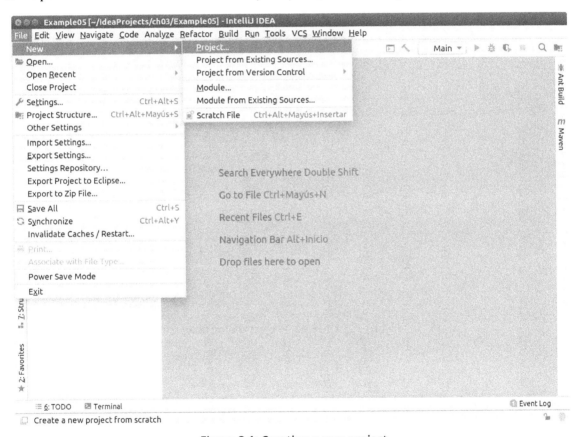

Figure 3.1: Creating a new project

2. A new interface unfolds. The default options are meant for creating a Java program. You just need to click **Next**:

Figure 3.2: The New Project dialog box

3. Check the box to create the project from a template. Select the template for the **Command Line App.** Click **Next**:

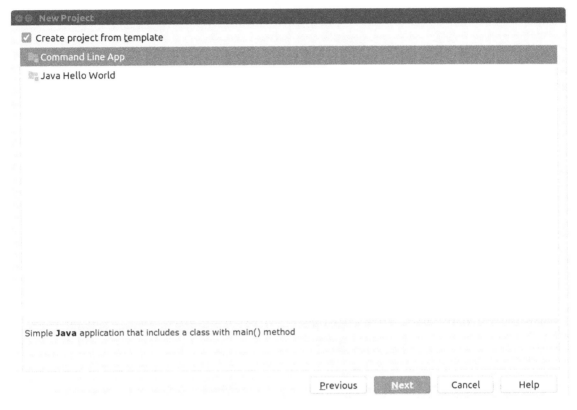

Figure 3.3: Creating a project from template

Name the project **WordTool**. Click **Finish**:

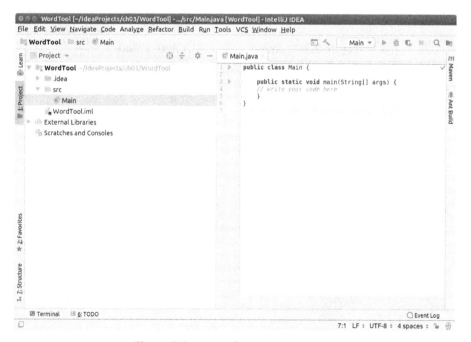

Figure 3.4: Adding the Project name

1. By default, the template calls your basic class **Main**. Let's change that to **WordTool**.
   First, navigate within the new project to the **Main.java** file; it is displayed as the
   main entry in the list:

Figure 3.5: A template Java program

2. Right-click on the **Main** entry and, in the drop-down list, select the **Refactor** option. Within that, select **Rename…**:

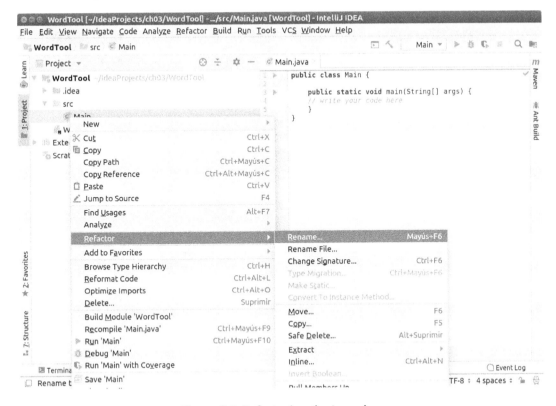

Figure 3.6: Refactoring the Java class

3. A dialog window pops up. Write in it the name of the class, **WordTool**. The checkboxes allow you to choose which parts of the code will be refactored to fit the new name of the class:

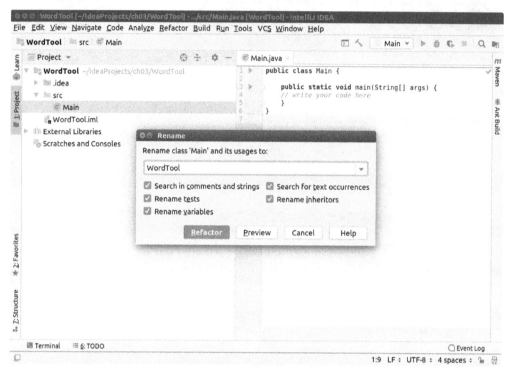

Figure 3.7: Renaming the class in IntelliJ

4. You will see that the class is now called **WordTool** and the file is **WordTool.java**:

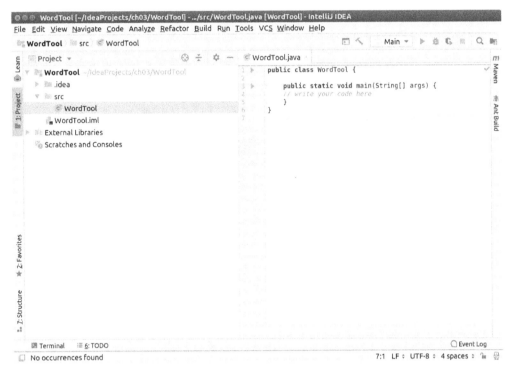

Figure 3.8: WordTool

5. Create the constructor for the class; it will be empty, in this case:

```
WordTool() {};
```

6. Add a method to count the number of words in a string:

```
public int wordCount ( String s ) {
    int count = 0;    // variable to count words
    // if the entry is empty or is null, count is zero
    // therefore we evaluate it only otherwise
    if ( !(s == null || s.isEmpty()) ) {
        // use the split method from the String class to
        // separate the words having the whitespace as separator
        String[] w = s.split("\\s+");
        count = w.length;
    }
    return count;
}
```

7. Add a method to count the number of letters in a string, and add the ability to count both with and without whitespace characters:

```java
public int symbolCount ( String s, boolean withSpaces ) {
    int count = 0;  // variable to count symbols
    // if the entry is empty or is null, count is zero
    // therefore we evaluate it only otherwise
    if ( !(s == null || s.isEmpty()) ) {
        if (withSpaces) {
            // with whitespaces return the full length
            count = s.length();
        } else {
            // without whitespaces, eliminate whitespaces
            // and get the length on the fly
            count = s.replace(" ", "").length();
        }
    }
    return count;
}
```

8. In the **main** class, create an object of the **WordTool** class and add a **String** variable containing some text of your choice:

```java
WordTool wt = new WordTool();
String text = "The river carried the memories from her childhood.";
```

9. Add code inside the main method to print out the calculations made by **WordTool**:

```java
System.out.println( "Analyzing the text: \n" + text );
System.out.println( "Total words: " + wt.wordCount(text) );
System.out.println( "Total symbols (w. spaces): " + wt.symbolCount(text, true) );
System.out.println( "Total symbols (wo. spaces): " + wt.symbolCount(text, false) );
```

10. Run the program; the outcome should be as follows:

```
Analyzing the text:
The river carried the memories from her childhood.
Total words: 8
Total symbols (w. spaces): 50
Total symbols (wo. spaces): 43
Process finished with exit code 0
```

> **Note**
>
> You can use the trick presented in this exercise to create classes for all the examples in this book, just by using the template and refactoring them to have the example name. After that, you will just need to copy the code in a fresh project.

Activity 1: Adding the Frequency-of-Symbol Calculation to WordTool

Add a method to the previously created **WordTool** class to calculate the frequency of a certain symbol. To do so, perform the following steps:

1. Add a method to count the number of words in a string.

2. Add a method to count the number of letters in a string, and add the possibility of separating the case of having whitespaces or not.

3. In the **main** class, create an object of the **WordTool** class and add a string variable containing a line of text of your choice.

4. Add code inside the main method to print out the calculations made by WordTool.

    The expected outcome of this activity is as follows:

```
Analyzing the text:
The river carried the memories from her childhood.
Total words: 8
Total symbols (w. spaces): 50
Total symbols (wo. spaces): 43
Total amount of e: 7
Process finished with exit code 0
```

> **Note**
>
> The solution for this activity can be found on page 534.

Inheritance in Java

Inheritance is a key principle of object-oriented programming. It entails the transfer of the existing structure of one class, including its constructor, variables, and methods, to a different class. The new class is called the child class (or subclass), while the one it's inheriting from is called the parent class (or superclass). We say that the child class extends the parent one. The child class is said to extend the parent class in the sense that it not only inherits whatever structures are defined by the parent, but it also creates new structures. The following example shows a parent class and how the child class extends it by adding a new method to it. We will take the **Computer** class we defined earlier as a parent and create a new class called **Tablet**, which is a type of computer.

Example05.java

```
20 class Tablet extends Computer {
21     // variables
22     private double screenSize;  // in inches
23
24     // methods
25     void setScreenSize ( double _screenSize ) {
26         screenSize = _screenSize;
27     }
28
29     double getScreenSize () {
30         return screenSize;
31     }
32 }
33
34 public class Example05 {
35     public static void main(String[] args) {
36         Tablet myTab = new Tablet();
37         myTab.setCpuSpeed( 2.5 );
38         myTab.setScreenSize( 10 );
39         System.out.println( myTab.getCpuSpeed() );
40         System.out.println( myTab.getScreenSize() );
41     }
42 }
```

https://packt.live/2o3NaqE

Notice how the definition of the **Tablet** class does not include any methods called **setCpuSpeed()** or **getCpuSpeed()**; however, when calling them, not only does the program not give any errors, but the commands are also successfully launched.

This is because the definition of the **Tablet** class extends the **Computer** class, thus inheriting all its internal objects, variables, and methods. When creating an object of the **Tablet** class, such as **myTab**, the JVM reserves space in memory for a **cpuSpeed** variable and the setter and getter methods that go with it.

Overriding and Hiding Methods

When extending a class, it is possible to redefine some of the methods that are part of it. Overriding means to rewrite something's functionality. This is done by making a new declaration of the method with the same name and properties of the method from the original class. This is demonstrated in the following example. Note that we're continuing, for the sake of clarity, with **Computer** and **Tablet**, but they have been cleaned up so as not to make the example programs too long.

```
class Computer {
    public void whatIsIt() {
        System.out.println( "it is a PC");
    }
}
class Tablet extends Computer {
    public void whatIsIt() {
```

```
            System.out.println( "it is a tablet");
        }
    }
    class Example06 {
        public static void main(String[] args) {
            Tablet myTab = new Tablet();
            myTab.whatIsIt();
        }
    }
```

Since **Tablet** extends **Computer**, you could modify the main class in the program to be as follows:

```
    class Example06 {
        public static void main(String[] args) {
            Computer myTab = new Tablet();
            myTab.whatIsIt();
        }
    }
```

Technically, tablets are computers, which means that you can create an object of the **Tablet** class by defining it as **Computer** in the first place. The result for both cases will be the same:

```
    it is a tablet
    Process finished with exit code 0
```

The result is the same for both classes because both the child and parent classes include a non-static method called **whatIsIt()**. When calling the method, the overriding one will have priority. This is done by the JVM at runtime. This principle is what we call runtime polymorphism. There can be multiple definitions of the same method, and which definition will be executed is decided during the execution of the program.

But what would happen if the method you called was static? This could be a design decision taken by the developer who is creating the class you are extending and therefore is a situation out of your control. In this case, it is not possible to override the method. The child class can, however, hide the method defined by the parent using the same mechanism. The next code listing demonstrates this.

```
    class Computer {
        public static void whatIsIt() {
            System.out.println( "it is a PC");
        }
    }
    class Tablet extends Computer {
```

```
    public static void whatIsIt() {
        System.out.println( "it is a tablet");
    }
}
class Example07 {
    public static void main(String[] args) {
        Computer myTab = new Tablet();
        myTab.whatIsIt();
    }
}
```

The outcome of this example is:

```
it is a PC


Process finished with exit code 0
```

The decision of what method should be used with static methods is not taken at runtime but during compilation, and this ensures that the method from the parent class is the one being called. This action is called **hiding instead of overriding**. It is still possible to call the method in the **Tablet** class. To do so, you should modify the code in the **main** class to the following:

```
class Example07 {
    public static void main(String[] args) {
        Computer myTab = new Tablet();
        Tablet.whatIsIt();
    }
}
```

Note how we clearly specify the actual class you call for this. The result of the modified example is:

```
it is a tablet
Process finished with exit code 0
```

Avoiding Overriding: Final Classes and Methods

If you want to stop other developers from overriding parts of your class, you can declare the methods you want to protect as **final**. An example of this could be a class that deals with temperature. The method that converts from Celsius into Fahrenheit is final, as it makes no sense to override such a method.

```java
class Temperature {
    public double t = 25;
    public double getCelsius() {
        return t;
    }
    final public double getFahrenheit() {
        return t * 9/5 + 32;
    }
}
class Example08 {
    public static void main(String[] args) {
        Temperature temp = new Temperature();
        System.out.println( temp.getCelsius() );
        System.out.println( temp.getFahrenheit() );
    }
}
```

This program will give this result:

```
25.0
77.0
Process finished with exit code 0
```

> **Note**
>
> Alternatively, you can declare a whole class **final**. A **final** class cannot be extended. An example of such a class is **String**. You could ask whether it defeats the purpose of object-oriented programming to have a class that cannot be extended. But there are some classes that are so fundamental to the programming language, such as **String**, that they are better kept as they are.

Overloading Methods and Constructors

One very interesting property of Java is how it allows you to define methods that have the same conceptual functionality as each other by using the same name but changing either the type or number of parameters. Let's see how this could work.

```java
class Age {
    public double a = 0;
    public void setAge ( double _a ) {
        a = _a;
    }
    public void setAge ( int year, int month ) {
        a = year + (double) month / 12;
    }
    public double getAge () {
        return a;
    }
}
class Example09 {
    public static void main(String[] args) {
        Age age = new Age();
        age.setAge(12.5);
        System.out.println(age.getAge());
        age.setAge(9, 3);
        System.out.println(age.getAge());
    }
}
```

> **Note**
>
> Look at the highlighted portion in the preceding code. As we are taking the integer parameter **month** and dividing it by a number, the result of the operation will be a double. To avoid possible errors, you need to convert the integer into a floating comma number. This process, called casting, is done by adding the new type between brackets in front of the object, variable, or operation we want to convert.

The result of this example is:

```
12.5
9.25
Process finished with exit code 0
```

This shows that both methods modify the **a** variable in the **Age** class by taking different sets of parameters. This same mechanism for having conceptually equivalent results from different blocks of code can be used for the constructors of a class, as shown in the following example.

```
class Age {
    public double a = 0;
    Age ( double _a ) {
        a = _a;
    }
    Age ( int year, int month ) {
        a = year + (double) month / 12;
    }
    public double getAge () {
        return a;
    }
}
class Example10 {
    public static void main(String[] args) {
        Age age1 = new Age(12.5);
        Age age2 = new Age(9, 3);
        System.out.println(age1.getAge());
        System.out.println(age2.getAge());
    }
}
```

In this case, as a way to show the functionality, instead of instantiating a single object and calling the different methods to modify its variables, we had to create two different objects, **age1** and **age2**, with one or two parameters, as those are the possible options offered by the constructors available in the **Age** class.

Recursion

Programming languages allow the usage of certain mechanisms to simplify solving a problem. Recursion is one of those mechanisms. It is the ability of a method to call itself. When properly designed, a recursive method can simplify the way a solution to a certain problem is expressed using code.

Classic examples in recursion include the computation of the factorial of a number or the sorting of an array of numbers. For the sake of simplicity, we are going to look at the first case: finding the factorial of a number.

```
class Example11 {
    public static long fact ( int n ) {
        if ( n == 1 ) return 1;
        return n * fact ( n - 1 );
    }
    public static void main(String[] args) {
        int input = Integer.parseInt(args[0]);
        long factorial = fact ( input );
        System.out.println(factorial);
    }
}
```

To run this code, you will need to go to the terminal and call the example from there with **java Example11 m**, where **m** is the integer whose factorial will be calculated. Depending on where you created the project on your computer, it could look like this (note that we have shortened the path to the example to keep it clean):

```
usr@localhost:~/IdeaProjects/chapter03/[...]production/Example11$ java Example11 5
120
```

Or, it could look like this:

```
usr@localhost:~/IdeaProjects/chapter03/[...]production/Example11$ java Example11 3
6
```

The result of the call is the factorial: **120** is the factorial of **5**, and **6** is the factorial of **3**.

While it might not seem so intuitive at first sight, the **fact** method calls itself in the return line. Let's take a closer look at this:

```
public static long fact ( int n ) {
    if ( n == 1 ) return 1;
    return n * fact ( n - 1 );
}
```

There are a couple of conditions that you need to meet when designing a functional recursive method. Otherwise, the recursive method will not converge to anything:

1. There needs to be a base condition. This means you need something that will stop the recursion from happening. In the case of the **fact** method, the base condition is **n** being equal to 1:

```
if ( n == 1 ) return 1;
```

2. There needs to be a way to computationally reach the base condition after a certain number of steps. In our case, every time we call fact, we do it with a parameter that is one unit smaller than the parameter of the current call to the method:

```
return n * fact ( n - 1 );
```

Annotations

Annotations are a special type of metadata that can be added to your code to inform the compiler about relevant aspects of it. Annotations can be used during the declaration of classes, fields, methods, variables, and parameters. One interesting aspect of annotations is that they remain visible inside classes, indicating whether a method is an override to a different one from a parent class, for example.

Annotations are declared using the @ symbol followed by the annotation's name. There are some built-in annotations, but it is also possible to declare your own. At this point, it is important to focus on some of the built-in ones, as it will help you to understand some of the concepts presented so far in this chapter

The most relevant built-in annotations are **@Override**, **@Deprecated**, and **@SuppressWarnings**. These three commands inform the compiler about different aspects of the code or the process of producing it.

@Override is used to indicate that a method defined in a child class is an override of another one in a parent class. It will check whether the parent class has a method named the same as the one in the child class and will provoke a compilation error if it doesn't exist. The use of this annotation is displayed in the following example, which builds on the code we showcased earlier in the chapter about the **Tablet** class extending the **Computer** class.

```
class Computer {
    public void whatIsIt() {
        System.out.println( "it is a PC");
    }
}
class Tablet extends Computer {
    @Override
```

```
      public void whatIsIt() {
          System.out.println( "it is a tablet");
      }
}
class Example12 {
    public static void main(String[] args) {
        Tablet myTab = new Tablet();
        myTab.whatIsIt();
    }
}
```

@Deprecated indicates that the method is about to become obsolete. This typically means that it will be removed in a future version of the class. As Java is a living language, it is common for core classes to be revised and new methods to be produced, and for the functionality of others to cease being relevant and get deprecated. The following example revisits the previous code listing, if the maintainer of the **Computer** class has decided to rename the **whatIsIt()** method **getDeviceType()**.

Example13.java

```
1  class Computer {
2      @Deprecated
3      public void whatIsIt() {
4          System.out.println( "it is a PC");
5      }
6
7      public void getDeviceType() {
8          System.out.println( "it is a PC");
9      }
10 }
11
12 class Tablet extends Computer {
13     @Override
14     public void whatIsIt() {
15         System.out.println( "it is a tablet");
16     }
17 }
```

https://packt.live/35NGCgG

Calling the compilation of the previous example will issue a warning about the fact that the **whatIsIt()** method will soon be no longer used. This should help developers plan their programs, as they'll know that some methods may disappear in the future:

```
Warning:(13, 17) java: whatIsIt() in Computer has been deprecated
```

@SuppressWarnings makes the compiler hide the possible warnings that will be defined in the annotation's parameters. It should be mentioned that annotations can have parameters such as **overrides**, **deprecation**, **divzero**, and **all**. There are more types of warnings that can be hidden, but it is too early to introduce them. While we are not going to go deeper into this concept at this point, you can see an example of this in the following code listing.

Example14.java

```
1   class Computer {
2       @Deprecated
3       public void whatIsIt() {
4           System.out.println( "it is a PC");
5       }
6
7       public void getDeviceType() {
8           System.out.println( "it is a PC");
9       }
10 }
11
12 @SuppressWarnings("deprecation")
13 class Tablet extends Computer {
14     @Override
15     public void whatIsIt() {
16         System.out.println( "it is a tablet");
17     }
18 }
```

https://packt.live/33GKnTt

When calling the compilation of the latest example, you will see a difference in comparison to the previous one, as the compilation of this one will not produce any warnings regarding the deprecation of the **whatIsIt()** method.

> **Note**
>
> You should be careful when using **@SuppressWarnings** as it can hide risks derived from potential malfunctions of your code. Especially avoid using **@SuppressWarnings("all")**, as it could mask warnings that could be producing runtime errors in other parts of your code.

Interfaces

Interfaces are reference types in Java. As such, they define the skeleton of classes and objects but without including the actual functionality of methods. Classes implement interfaces but do not extend them. Let's look at an example of a simple interface, further developing the idea of building classes to represent different types of computers.

```java
interface Computer {
    public String getDeviceType();
    public String getSpeed();
}
class Tablet implements Computer {
    public String getDeviceType() {
        return "it is a tablet";
    }
    public String getSpeed() {
        return "1GHz";
    }
}
class Example15 {
    public static void main(String[] args) {
        Tablet myTab = new Tablet();
        System.out.println( myTab.getDeviceType() );
        System.out.println( myTab.getSpeed() );
    }
}
```

As you might have guessed, the output for this example is:

```
it is a tablet
1GHz
Process finished with exit code 0
```

Some relevant notes on interfaces follow:

- Interfaces can extend other interfaces.

- Unlike classes, which can only extend one class at a time, interfaces can extend multiple interfaces at once. You do so by adding the different interfaces separated by commas.

- Interfaces have no constructors.

Inner Classes

Classes, as we have seen so far, cannot be hidden to other parts of the program. In code terms, they cannot be made private. To offer this kind of security mechanism, Java developed so-called **inner classes**. This type of class is declared nested within other classes. A quick example of this follows:

Example16.java

```java
1  class Container {
2      // inner class
3      private class Continent {
4      public void print() {
5          System.out.println("This is an inner class");
6          }
7      }
8
9      // method to give access to the private inner class' method
10     void printContinent() {
11         Continent continent = new Continent();
12         continent.print();
13     }
14 }
```

https://packt.live/2P2vc30

The result of the previous example is:

```
This is an inner class
Process finished with exit code 0
```

The previous example is a case of a non-static inner class. There are two more: method-local inner classes (these are defined inside a method) and anonymous classes. There is no big difference in how method-local classes are declared in comparison to what you've seen so far. A method-local inner class's main characteristic is that it is defined only for the scope of that method; it cannot be called by other parts of the program.

When it comes to anonymous inner classes, they make for an interesting case that deserves to be studied. The reason for their existence is to make code more concise. With anonymous classes, you declare and instantiate the class at the same time. This means that for such a class, only one object is created. Anonymous classes are typically created by extending existing classes or interfaces. Let's look at an example defining one of these specific types of anonymous classes:

```java
class Container {
    int c = 17;
    public void print() {
        System.out.println("This is an outer class");
    }
}
class Example17 {
    public static void main(String[] args) {
        // inner class
        Container container = new Container() {
            @Override
            public void print() {
                System.out.println("This is an inner class");
            }
        };
        container.print();
        System.out.println( container.c );
    }
}
```

This example shows how an anonymous class can be created in an ad hoc way to override a single method from the original class. This is one of the many possible applications of this type of inner class. The output of this program is:

```
This is an inner class
17
Process finished with exit code 0
```

Documenting with JavaDoc

Javadoc is a tool that comes with the JDK that can be used to generate documentation of classes directly from properly commented code. It requires the use of a specific type of commenting that is different from the ones seen in *Chapter 1, Getting Started*. There, we saw that comments can be added to code using either // or /* or */. JavaDoc uses a specific type of marking to detect what comments were intentionally made for documentation purposes. Javadoc comments are contained within /** and */. A simple example follows.

Example18.java

```
1  /**
2   * Anonymous class example
3   * This example shows the declaration of an inner class extending
4   * an existing class and overriding a method. It can be used as a
5   * technique to modify an existing method for something more suitable
6   * to our purpose.
7   *
8   * @author Joe Smith
9   * @version 0.1
10  * @since 20190305
11  */
```

https://packt.live/2J5u4aT

> **Note**
>
> If you are going to generate documentation from a class, you need to make sure the class is public, otherwise, the JavaDoc generator will complain about the fact that it makes no sense to document classes that aren't public.

The new comments include information about the program itself. It is good practice to explain, in some detail, what the program does. Sometimes, it may be convenient to even add blocks of code. In order to support that extra information, there are tags that allow the addition of specific features or metadata to the documentation. **@author**, **@version**, and **@since** are examples of such metadata – they determine who made the code, the version of the code, and when it was first created, respectively. There is a long list of possible tags that you can use; visit https://packt.live/2J2Px4n for more information.

JavaDoc renders the documentation as one or more HTML files. Therefore, it is possible to also add HTML markup to help messages. You could change the documentation part of the previous example as follows:

```
/**
 * <H1>Anonymous class example</H1>
 * This example shows the declaration of an <b>inner class</b> extending
 * an existing class and overriding a method. It can be used as a
 * technique to modify an existing method for something more suitable
 * to our purpose.
 *
 * @author Joe Smith
 * @version 0.1
 * @since 20190305
 */
```

Finally, you can create the documentation file by selecting **Tools** | **Generate JavaDoc** from the menu:

Figure 3.9: Generating JavaDoc

The JavaDoc generation dialog box will pop up and give you some options. Make sure that you insert the folder where you want the documentation file to be stored (/tmp in the example) and tick the checkboxes for the **@author** and the **@version**:

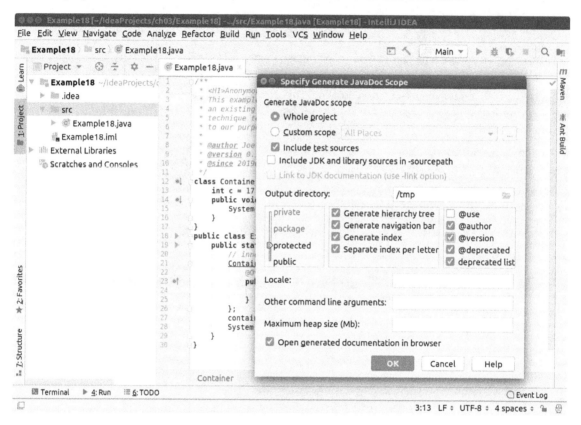

Figure 3.10: Specifying the scope for the JavaDoc

This will generate an HTML file that is formatted in the same way that official Java documentation is:

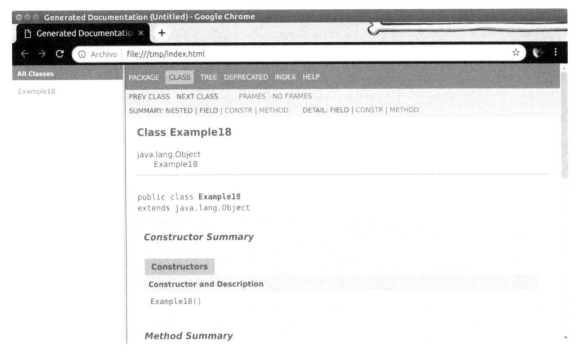

Figure 3.11: The generated JavaDoc

Activity 2: Adding Documentation to WordTool

Create documentation for the class created in *Exercise 1, Creating the WordTool Class*.

1. Make sure you document each one of the examples and add enough metadata for people to know how to handle the different methods.

2. Export the resulting documentation file.

> ### Note
> The solution for this activity can be found on page 536.

Summary

This chapter introduced you to the core of object-oriented programming–the creation of classes and those operations which can be performed with them, such as extending them, using them to override parts of the code, or creating local instances.

The examples provided here showed you the importance of creating classes to better structure your code and improve it economically. If there are several classes within a specific context, it is very likely that they will have common characteristics that could be described in a parent class or even an interface.

A part of the chapter was dedicated to operations done with the compiler. As a developer, you may want to inform others when certain parts of your code will be deprecated, or whether a method from a specific class has been overridden. Annotating code is a good technique for maintaining communication with others. You also saw how to turn off possible warnings coming from annotations that occurred during development.

Finally, we discussed the process of documentation. This is relevant when sharing code or passing it over to other people. In the next chapter, we will take a look at Java collections framework which will simplify your dealings with complex data structures.

Collections, Lists and Java's Built-In APIs

Overview

This chapter introduces you to the powerful Java collections framework, which is used to store, sort, and filter data. It will first take you through the structure of the built-in Collections **Application Programming Interface** (**API**), the Java collections framework, which will simplify your dealings with complex data structures and allow you to use and create APIs with minimal effort. Through this framework, you will examine the relationship between lists and arrays, and learn to populate lists from arrays. Finally, in this chapter's final activity, you will create and complete a program in which you will be asked to perform standard operations on data stored in sets, lists, and maps in preparation for future chapters.

Introduction

Java comes with a built-in Collections API, allowing you to manipulate data structures with very little effort. A collection is an object that contains multiple elements. Collections are used to store, share, process, and communicate aggregated data. We call this system the **Java collections framework**.

As part of this framework, there are different components that are used to optimize our interaction with the actual data:

- **Interfaces**: Abstract data types that represent collections
- **Implementations**: Specific implementations of the collection interfaces
- **Algorithms**: Polymorphic methods used to process the data within a collection for operations such as sorting and searching

> **Note**
>
> Other programming languages have their own collection frameworks. For example, C++ has the **Standard Template Library** (**STL**). Java boasts simplicity when it comes to its collection framework.

Using the collections framework has many benefits, including a reduction in the complexity of creating programs that deal with data structures, an increase in the performance of programs, a simplification of API creation and use, and an increase in the reuse of functioning software.

The collections framework is relevant even when handling data that can be accessed by several processes simultaneously, as this would be the case in multithreaded programming scenarios. However, it is not the intention of this chapter to deal with concurrent programming.

The Collections API comes with five main interfaces:

- **Set**: A collection that contains no duplicates
- **List**: An ordered collection or sequence, allowing for duplicates
- **Queue**: A collection that sorts data in the order of its arrival, typically handled as a **First In First Out** (**FIFO**) process
- **Deque**: Essentially a queue that allows for data insertion at both ends, meaning that it can be handled both as FIFO and **Last In First Out** (**LIFO**)
- **Map**: Relates keys—which must be unique—to values

In this chapter, we will define the main interfaces (lists, sets, and maps), and explore examples of their respective uses. The framework has even more interfaces than the ones listed previously, but the others are either just variations of those listed or are outside the scope of this chapter. Furthermore, we will look at how arrays work in much more depth than we have previously.

The definition of a simple collection—in this case, a specific type of set would be as follows:

```
Set mySet = new HashSet();
```

> **Note**
>
> The different available classes for sets, lists, queues, deques, and maps are named after the interfaces. The different classes present different properties, as we will see later in the chapter.

Arrays

Arrays are part of the collections framework. There are some static methods that can be used to manipulate arrays. The operations you can perform are creating, sorting, searching, comparing, streaming, and transforming arrays. You were introduced to arrays in *Chapter 2, Learning the Basics*, where you saw how they can be used to store data of the same type. The declaration of an array is quite straightforward. Let's see what an array of strings would look like:

```
String[] text = new String[] { "spam", "more", "buy" };
```

Running operations on an array is as easy as calling some of the methods contained in the **java.util.Arrays** package. For example, sorting the previous array would require calling the following:

```
java.util.Arrays.sort( text );
```

The methods dedicated to handling arrays include one method that could be used to print out full arrays as if they were strings. This can be very handy when debugging a program:

```
System.out.println( java.util.Arrays.toString( text ) );
```

This will print the arrays and display each element separated by commas and within square brackets, **[]**. If you executed the previous command after sorting the declared array of strings, the outcome would be:

```
[buy, more, spam]
```

As you can see, the array has been sorted in ascending alphabetical order. There is a difference between that way of printing out an array and using a **for** loop to iterate throughout an array:

```
for (int i = 0; i < text.length; i++)
    System.out.print(text[i] + " ");
```

This would give the following as the result:

```
buy more spam
```

If you want to write your code in a slightly cleaner way, you could import the whole **java.util.Arrays** API at the beginning of your program, which would allow you to call the methods by omitting the **java.util** part of the command. See the following example highlighting this technique:

```
import java.util.Arrays;
public class Example01 {
    public static void main(String[] args) {
        String[] text = new String[] { "spam", "more", "buy" };
        Arrays.sort(text);
        System.out.println(Arrays.toString(text));
        for (int i = 0; i < text.length; i++)
            System.out.print(text[i] + " ");
    }
}
```

The outcome will be:

```
[buy, more, spam]
buy more spam
Process finished with exit code 0
```

If you were to make a new array that you wanted to be filled up with the same data for all cells, there is the possibility of calling the **java.util.Arrays.fill()** method, as shown here:

```
int[] numbers = new int[5];
Arrays.fill(numbers, 0);
```

Such a command would create an array filled with zeros:

```
[0, 0, 0, 0, 0]
```

Creating arrays with prefilled data can also be done with a copy of a preexisting array. It is possible to create an array by copying part of one array, or by instantiating a larger one where the old one would just be part of it. Both methods are shown in the following example, which you can test in your editor:

```
import java.util.Arrays;
public class Example02 {
    public static void main(String[] args) {
        int[] numbers = new int[5];
        Arrays.fill(numbers, 1);
        System.out.println(Arrays.toString(numbers));
        int [] shortNumbers = Arrays.copyOfRange(numbers, 0, 2);
        System.out.println(Arrays.toString(shortNumbers));
        int [] longNumbers = Arrays.copyOf(numbers, 10);
        System.out.println(Arrays.toString(longNumbers));
    }
}
```

This example will print the **numbers**, **shortNumbers** (which is shorter), and **longNumbers** (which is longer) arrays. The newly added positions in the array will be filled with zeros. If it was an array of strings, they would be filled up with **null**. The outcome of this example is:

```
[1, 1, 1, 1, 1]
[1, 1]
[1, 1, 1, 1, 1, 0, 0, 0, 0, 0]
Process finished with exit code 0
```

You can compare arrays by calling the **java.utils.Arrays.equals()** or **java.util.Arrays.deepEquals()** methods. The difference between them is that the latter can look through nested arrays. A simple comparison example of the former method in use follows:

```
import java.util.Arrays;
public class Example03 {
    public static void main(String[] args) {
        int[] numbers1 = new int[3];
        Arrays.fill(numbers1, 1);
        int[] numbers2 = {0, 0, 0};
        boolean comparison = Arrays.equals(numbers1, numbers2);
        System.out.println(comparison);
        int[] numbers3 = {1, 1, 1};
        comparison = Arrays.equals(numbers1, numbers3);
        System.out.println(comparison);
        int[] numbers4 = {1, 1};
```

```
        comparison = Arrays.equals(numbers1, numbers4);
        System.out.println(comparison);
    }
}
```

In this example, we create four arrays: **numbers1**, **numbers2**, **numbers3**, and **numbers4**. Only two of them are the same, containing three instances of **1**. In the example, you can see how the last three arrays are compared to the first one. You can also see how the last array differs not in content, but in size. The outcome of this code is:

```
false
true
false
Process finished with exit code 0
```

> **Note**
>
> Since this chapter is not looking into such a complex data structure as nested arrays, we will not show an example of **java.util.Arrays.deepEquals()**. If you're interested, you should consider checking the Java reference at https://packt. live/2MuRrNa.

Searching within arrays is done through different algorithms behind the scenes. It is obviously a lot faster to perform searches on sorted arrays than on unsorted ones. The method to be invoked to run such a search on a sorted array is **Arrays.binarySearch()**. As it has many possible parameter combinations, it is recommended to visit the official documentation for the method. The following example illustrates how it works:

```java
import java.util.Arrays;
public class Example04 {
    public static void main(String[] args) {
        String[] text = {"love","is", "in", "the", "air"};
        int search = Arrays.binarySearch(text, "is");
        System.out.println(search);
    }
}
```

This code is going to search for the word **the** inside the array text. The result is:

```
-4
Process finished with exit code 0
```

This is wrong! **binarySearch** is an optimized search algorithm within the collections framework, but it is not optimal when used with unsorted arrays. This means that **binarySearch** is mainly very useful for determining whether an object can be found within an array (by sorting it first). At the same time, we will need a different algorithm when we must search through unsorted arrays and when there are multiple occurrences of a value.

Try the following modification of the previous example:

```
String[] text = {"love","is", "in", "the", "air"};
Arrays.sort(text);
int search = Arrays.binarySearch(text, "is");
System.out.println(search);
```

The outcome, since the array is sorted, will be:

```
2
Process finished with exit code 0
```

It is only a coincidence in this case that "**is**" happens to be in the same place in the unsorted and the sorted versions of the array. Making use of the tools you've been learning about, it should be possible for you to create an algorithm that can iterate throughout an array and count all the existing items, even if they are repeated, as well as locating their positions within the array. See *Activity 1, Searching for Multiple Occurrences in an Array* in this chapter, where we challenge you to write such a program.

You can also transform objects of the **java.util.Arrays** class into strings with the **Arrays.toString()** method, as we saw at the beginning of this section, into a list with **Arrays.asList()** (we will see this in a later section, as well as in **Example05**) or into a set with **Arrays.setAll()**.

Arrays and collections play important roles in software development. This section of the chapter dives into the differences between them as well as how they can be used together. If you search the internet for the relationship between these two constructs, most references you find will be focused on the differences, such as:

- Arrays have fixed sizes, while collections have variable sizes.

- Arrays can hold objects of any kind, but also primitives; collections cannot contain primitives.

- Arrays will hold homogeneous elements (elements that are all the same nature), while collections can hold heterogeneous elements.

- Arrays have no underlying data structure, while collections are implemented using standard structures.

If you know the amount of data you are going to be dealing with, arrays are the preferred tool, mainly because arrays perform better than lists or sets in such cases. However, there will be countless occasions when you don't know the amount of data you will be dealing with, which is where lists will be handy.

Also, arrays can be used to programmatically populate collections. We will be doing this throughout this chapter as a way of saving you the time of having to manually type all the data that will end up inside a collection, for example. The following example shows how to populate a set using an array:

```java
import java.util.*;
public class Example05 {
    public static void main(String[] args) {
        Integer[] myArray = new Integer[] {3, 25, 2, 79, 2};
        Set mySet = new HashSet(Arrays.asList(myArray));
        System.out.println(mySet);
    }
}
```

In this program, there is an array of **Integer** used to initialize an object of the **HashSet** class, which is later printed out.

The outcome of this example is:

```
[2, 3, 25, 79]
Process finished with exit code 0
```

The previous code listing shows a couple of interesting things. First of all, you will notice that the output to the program is sorted; that is because the conversion of the array to a list using **Arrays.asList()** will make the dataset inherit the properties of a list, which means that it will be sorted. Also, since the data has been added to a set and sets do not include duplicates, duplicate number two is left out.

It is important to note that with collections, you can specify the type to be stored. As such, there would be a difference between the declaration in the previous example, where we displayed a generic declaration, and what follows. The type is declared here using the name given within angle brackets, **<>**. In this case, it is **<Integer>**. You could rewrite the instantiation of the object as follows:

```
Set<Integer> mySet = new HashSet<Integer>(Arrays.asList(myArray));
```

You will see that the result of executing the program will be the same.

Activity 1: Searching for Multiple Occurrences in an Array

Write a program that will search for multiple occurrences of a certain word in an array of strings, where each one of the objects is a single word. Use the following array, a famous quote by Frank Zappa, as a point of departure:

```
String[] text = {"So", "many", "books", "so", "little", "time"};
```

The word to search for is **so**. but you will have to consider that it shows up twice and that one instance is not in lowercase. As a hint, the method to compare two strings without looking at the specific casing of any of the letters in them is **text1.compareToIgnoreCase(text2)**. To do so, perform the following steps:

1. Create the **text** array.

2. Create the variable that contains the word to be searched for: **so**

3. Initialize the variable **occurrence** to -1.

4. Create a for loop to iterate through the array to check for the occurrence.

That will give the following result:

```
Found query at: 0
Found query at: 3
Process finished with exit code 0
```

> **Note**
>
> The solution for this activity can be found on page 538.

Sets

Sets within the collections framework are the programmatic equivalent of mathematical sets. This means that they can store objects of a specific type while avoiding duplicates. In the same way, sets offer methods that will let you handle data as you would in mathematics. You can add objects to a set, check whether a set is empty, combine the elements of two sets to add all their elements into a single set, see what objects coincide with each other between two sets, and calculate the difference between two sets.

In the **java.util.Sets** class, we find three interfaces used to represent sets: **HashSet**, **TreeSet**, and **LinkedHashSet**. The differences between them are straightforward:

- **HashSet** will store data without guaranteeing the order of iteration.

- **TreeSet** orders a set by value.

- **LinkedHashSet** orders a set by arrival time.

Each of these interfaces is meant to be used under specific circumstances. Let's look at a couple of examples of sets, departing from the one in **Example05**, and look at how we can add other methods to check how to operate sets. The first step is populating a set from an array. There are several methods for doing so; let's use the one that is probably the quickest to implement:

```java
import java.util.*;
public class Example06 {
    public static void main(String[] args) {
        String[] myArray = new String[] {"3", "25", "2", "79", "2"};
        Set mySet = new HashSet();
        Collections.addAll(mySet, myArray);
        System.out.println(mySet);
    }
}
```

The above line of code shows how to add all the elements of the array to the set; when printing the results, we get:

```
[2, 79, 3, 25]
Process finished with exit code 0
```

Please note that the order of the resulting print may vary for you. As explained earlier, **HashSet**, because of the way it is implemented, cannot guarantee any sorting of the content. If you performed the following example using **Integer** instead of **String** for the data, it would end up being sorted:

```java
import java.util.*;
public class Example07 {
    public static void main(String[] args) {
        Integer[] myArray = new Integer[] {3, 25, 2, 79, 2};
        Set mySet = new HashSet();
        Collections.addAll(mySet, myArray);
        System.out.println(mySet);
    }
}
```

The result of this program is:

```
[2, 3, 25, 79]
Process finished with exit code 0
```

This means that the results end up being sorted, even if we don't request it.

> **Note**
>
> The fact that the set in this example is sorted is a mere coincidence. Please be aware that this may not be the case in other situations. **Example08** will show the union operation between two sets, and there the data will not be sorted.

Working with sets involves working with packages of data and performing operations with them. The union operation for two sets is displayed in the following example:

```java
import java.util.*;
public class Example08 {
    public static void main(String[] args) {
        Integer[] numbers1 = new Integer[] {3, 25, 2, 79, 2};
        Integer[] numbers2 = new Integer[] {7, 12, 14, 79};
        Set set1 = new HashSet();
        Collections.addAll(set1, numbers1);
        Set set2 = new HashSet();
        Collections.addAll(set2, numbers2);
        set1.addAll(set2);
        System.out.println(set1);
```

```
        }
}
```

This program will print, as its output, the resulting set from the union of the two sets described by the two arrays at the beginning of the main method of the example:

```
[2, 3, 7, 25, 12, 14, 79]
Process finished with exit code 0
```

Besides **HashSet**, we also find **TreeSet**, and here is where data will be sorted by value. Let's simply change the types of the sets in the previous example and see the result:

```
Set set1 = new TreeSet();
Collections.addAll(set1, numbers1);
Set set2 = new TreeSet();
Collections.addAll(set2, numbers2);
```

This, when changed in the previous example, will give the following sorted set as a result:

```
[2, 3, 7, 12, 14, 25, 79]
```

You might be wondering about the pros and cons of using each type of set. When sorting, you are trading speed for tidiness. Therefore, if you are working with large sets of data and speed is a concern, you will have to decide whether it is more convenient to have the system operate faster, or have the results sorted, which would allow faster binary searches through the dataset.

Given this last modification, we could perform other operations with the data, such as the intersection operation, which is invoked with the **set1.retainAll(set2)** method. Let's see it in action:

```
import java.util.*;
public class Example09 {
    public static void main(String[] args) {
        Integer[] numbers1 = new Integer[] {3, 25, 2, 79, 2};
        Integer[] numbers2 = new Integer[] {7, 12, 14, 79};
        Set set1 = new TreeSet();
        Collections.addAll(set1, numbers1);
        Set set2 = new TreeSet();
        Collections.addAll(set2, numbers2);
        set1.retainAll(set2);
        System.out.println(set1);
    }
}
```

For the output, given that the arrays are used to populate the arrays, we will get only those numbers that exist in both arrays; in this case, it is just the number **79**:

```
[79]
Process finished with exit code 0
```

The third type of set, **LinkedHashSet**, will sort the objects in order of their arrival. To demonstrate this behavior, let's make a program that will add elements to the set one by one using the **set.add(element)** command.

```
import java.util.*;
public class Example10 {
    public static void main(String[] args) {
        Set set1 = new LinkedHashSet();
        set1.add(35);
        set1.add(19);
        set1.add(11);
        set1.add(83);
        set1.add(7);
        System.out.println(set1);

    }

}
```

When running this example, the result will be sorted by the way the data arrived in the set:

```
[35, 19, 11, 83, 7]
Process finished with exit code 0
```

For the sake of experimentation, use the next 2 minutes to chalk out the set construction into **HashSet** once more:

```
Set set1 = new LinkedHashSet();
```

The result of this modified program is uncertain. For example, we get:

```
[35, 19, 83, 7, 11]
Process finished with exit code 0
```

This is, again, an unsorted version of the same set of data.

To close our explanation of the possible methods that you can use with sets, let's use **LinkedHashSet** to run an experiment where we will find the difference between two sets.

```
import java.util.*;
public class Example11 {
    public static void main(String[] args) {
        Set set1 = new LinkedHashSet();
        set1.add(35);
        set1.add(19);
        set1.add(11);
        set1.add(83);
        set1.add(7);
        Set set2 = new LinkedHashSet();
        set2.add(3);
        set2.add(19);
        set2.add(11);
        set2.add(0);
        set2.add(7);
        set1.removeAll(set2);
        System.out.println(set1);
    }
}
```

In this case, both sets are slightly different, and by determining the difference, the algorithm behind **set1.removeAll(set2)** will look for the occurrences of each item in **set2** within **set1** and eliminate them. The result of this program is:

```
[35, 83]
Process finished with exit code 0
```

Finally, if you just want to check whether the whole of a set is contained within another set, you can call the **set1.containsAll(set2)** method. We'll leave that for you to explore – just be aware that the method simply responds with a Boolean stating whether the statement is true or false.

Lists

Lists are ordered collections of data. Unlike sets, lists can have repeated data. Having data contained within lists allows you to perform searches that will give the locations of certain objects within a given list. Given a position, it is possible to directly access an item in a list, add new items, remove items, and even add full lists. Lists are sequential, which makes them easy to navigate using iterators, a feature that will be explored in full in a later section in the chapter. There are also some methods for performing range-based operations on sublists.

There are two different list implementations: **ArrayList** and **LinkedList**. Each of them is ideal depending on the circumstances. Here, we will work with **ArrayList** mainly. Let's start by creating and populating an instance, then search for a certain value, and given its location within the list, we'll print out the value.

```java
import java.util.*;
public class Example12 {
    public static void main(String[] args) {
        List list = new ArrayList();
        list.add(35);
        list.add(19);
        list.add(11);
        list.add(83);
        list.add(7);
        System.out.println(list);
        int index = list.indexOf(19);
        System.out.println("Find 19 at: " + index);
        System.out.println("Component: " + list.get(index));
    }
}
```

The output of this example is:

```
[35, 19, 11, 83, 7]
Find 19 at: 1
Component: 19
Process finished with exit code 0
```

The **indexOf** method informs you about the location of an object passed to the method as a parameter. It's sibling method, **lastIndexOf**, reports the location of the last occurrence of an object in the list.

You should look at a list as a series of nodes connected by links. If one of the nodes is eliminated, the link that used to point to it will be redirected to the following item in the list. When adding nodes, they will be attached by default at the end of the list (if they are not duplicated). As all the nodes in the collection are of the same type, it should be possible to exchange the locations of two nodes in a list.

Let's experiment with removing an item from a list and ascertaining the locations for objects located immediately before and after the removed item:

```java
import java.util.*;
public class Example13 {
    public static void main(String[] args) {
        List list = new ArrayList();
        list.add(35);
        list.add(19);
        list.add(11);
        list.add(83);
        list.add(7);
        System.out.println(list);
        int index = list.lastIndexOf(83);
        System.out.println("Before: find 83 at: " + index);
        list.remove(index - 1);
        System.out.println(list);
        index = list.lastIndexOf(83);
        System.out.println("After: find 83 at: " + index);
    }
}
```

This program creates a list, prints it out, looks for a node in the list, and prints its location. Then, it removes an item in the list and repeats the previous process to show that the node has been removed from the list. This is a clear difference from the case with arrays, where it is not possible to remove items from them, and thus it is not possible to change their size. Observe the output of the previous example:

```
[35, 19, 11, 83, 7]
Before: find 83 at: 3
[35, 19, 83, 7]
After: find 83 at: 2
Process finished with exit code 0
```

It is also possible to change the content of a node. In the previous example, instead of removing a node, change **list.remove(index-1);** to the following and check the outcome:

```
list.set(index - 1, 99);
```

The final array will have substituted **11** for **99**.

If instead of deleting one node, you wanted to empty the whole list, the command to the issue would be:

```
list.clear();
```

Using **subList()**, an operator that generates lists from lists, it is possible to, for example, delete a range of cells within a list. See the following example, which deletes part of a string array, changing its meaning when printing it:

```
import java.util.*;
public class Example14 {
    public static void main(String[] args) {
        List list = new ArrayList();
        list.add("No");
        list.add("matter");
        list.add("what");
        list.add("you");
        list.add("do");
        System.out.println(list);
        list.subList(2,4).clear();
        System.out.println(list);
    }
}
```

Look at the following result:

```
[No, matter, what, you, do]
[No, matter, do]
Process finished with exit code 0
```

The **list** object has been modified by running the example code so that it becomes shorter. The two index numbers used in the **subList()** method is the places in the list where the method starts and stops. The result of **subList()** can also be assigned to a different variable of the same **List** type, resulting in a reduced copy of the list in the code, after performing the **subList()** operation.

Look at the following modification in the latest code listing:

```
List list1 = list.subList(2,4);
System.out.println(list1);
```

This will print out the list that was made of the nodes that were deleted in the previous example.

There are a lot of interesting algorithms within the collections framework that offers relevant functionality for operating with lists:

- **sort**: Put the elements of a list in a certain order.

- **shuffle**: Randomize the locations of all objects in a list.

- **reverse**: Invert the order of a list.

- **rotate**: Move objects to the end of a list, and when they reach the end, have them show up at the other end.

- **swap**: Swap two elements with one another.

- **replaceAll**: Replace all occurrences of an element in a list using a parameter.

- **fill**: Fill the content of a list with one value.

- **copy**: Make more instances of a list.

- **binarySearch**: Perform optimized searches within a list.

- **indexOfSubList**: Search for the occurrence of a piece (a set of consecutive nodes) of a list.

- **lastIndexOfSubList**: Search for the last occurrence of a piece of a list.

> **Note**
>
> Lists generated from arrays using **Arrays.asList()** do not behave in the same way as the objects of the **List** class described in this section. The lists coming from arrays have a fixed length, which means that elements cannot be removed from the array. The reason for this is that **java.util.Arrays** implement its own **ArrayList** class inside the package, one that is different from the one in the collections framework. Confusing, isn't it?

Exercise 1: Creating the AnalyzeInput Application

In this exercise, we will create a new application that will respond to the CLI by storing whatever strings are provided to it, then run some statistical operations on the data, such as word counting (determining the most frequent word or the most frequent letter, and so on). The intent is to give you an idea of how to use the collections framework instead of other tools to do such operations. This time, we will do something special; instead of getting the data from the CLI as arguments to the script, we will use the **java.io.Console** API, which allows the reading of different types of strings from the terminal, such as usernames (plain strings) and passwords. The goal of this application is to read the input until a line with only the "*" symbol (asterisk) is captured. Once the termination symbol is entered, the text will be processed, and the statistics will be delivered to the terminal:

1. Open IntelliJ and create a new Java program using the CLI template. Name the project **AnalyzeInput**.

2. Start by creating a simple program that can read a line from the terminal and printing it out:

```
import java.io.Console;
public class AnalyzeInput {
  public static void main(String[] args) {
    Console cons;
    String line = "";
      if ((cons = System.console()) != null && (line = cons.readLine()) !=
        null) {
        System.out.println("You typed: " + line);
    }
  }
}
```

3. Execute the program from the CLI by calling **java AnalyzeInput** from the right folder and interact with it:

```
usr@localhost:~/IdeaProjects/ch04/out/production/ch04$ java AnalyzeInput
hej this is an example
You typed: hej this is an example
```

4. You must import **java.io.Console**, which allows you to instantiate objects of the **Console** class. You can also see the call to **cons = System.console()**, which will make sure that the terminal is ready for you to read the data, and **line = cons. readLine()**, which will ensure that when hitting the *Enter* key on the keyboard, the resulting data is not empty.

5. The next step is storing the data we are capturing in a collection. Since we don't know the size this could be, we should be using **ArrayList <String>** to store the data. Also, to store data for as long as we want, we can modify the **if** statement and make it into a **while** loop. Finally, use the **add** method to add the lines into a list (note that the following code listing will never exit, so bear with us and do not execute it yet):

```java
import java.util.*;
import java.io.Console;
public class Exercise01 {
  public static void main(String[] args) {
    ArrayList <String> text = new ArrayList<String>();
    Console cons;
    String line = "";
    while ((cons = System.console()) != null && (line = cons.readLine())
       != null) {
    text.add(line);
    }
    System.out.println("You typed: " + text);
  }
}
```

6. Modify the **while** loop to include the condition we established for finishing the data capture process – the arrival of a line with only an asterisk symbol:

```java
while (!line.equals("*")
       && (cons = System.console()) != null
       && (line = cons.readLine()) != null) {
```

7. The outcome will happen only when you type the asterisk symbol alone in a line, as seen in this log while interacting with the program:

```
usr@localhost:~/IdeaProjects/ch04/out/production/ch04$ java AnalyzeInput
this is the array example
until you type *
alone in a line
*
You typed: [this is the array example, until you type *, alone in a line, *]
```

8. Since we used **ArrayList** to store the different strings, you could be typing until you exhaust the computer's memory. Now it is possible to execute some commands to work with the strings. The first step will be turning the whole of the text into a list. This will require going through the different strings and splitting them into parts that will be added to a larger list. The easiest trick is to use the **split()** method using a whitespace character as a separator. Modify the **main** method to look like the following, and you will see that the result is now a list with all the words separated as single nodes in the list:

```
public static void main(String[] args) {
    ArrayList <String> text = new ArrayList<String>();
    Console cons;
    String line = "";
    while (!line.equals("*")
        && (cons = System.console()) != null
        && (line = cons.readLine()) != null) {
            List<String> lineList = new
                ArrayList<String>(Arrays.asList(line.split(" ")));
        text.addAll(lineList);
    }
    System.out.println("You typed: " + text);
}
```

9. Having all the data stored in this way allows for the use of a lot of the methods available in the collections framework that will let you do operations with data. Let's start by counting all the words in the text (including the closing symbol, "*"). Just add the following at the end of the **main** method:

```
System.out.println("Word count: " + text.size());
```

The result of this exercise is a program that is ready to be used for further analysis of the data. But in order to continue doing so, we need to make use of a tool that has not yet been introduced—the iterator. We will come back to this example later in the chapter and finish off the application by adding some extra functionality to it.

Maps

The collections framework offers one more interface, **java.util.Map**, which can be used when dealing with data that is stored as key-value pairs. This type of data storage is becoming more and more relevant as data formats such as JSON are slowly taking over the internet. JSON is a data format that is based on having data stored in the form of nested arrays that always respond to the key-value structure.

Having data organized in this way offers the possibility of having a very simple way to look for data – by means of the keys instead of using, for example, an index, as we would do in an array. Keys are the way we can identify the block of data we are looking for within a map. Let's look at a simple example of a map before looking at alternatives to maps:

The following example shows how to create a simple map and how to print some messages based on the information available within it. The first thing that you will notice in comparison to other interfaces in the collections framework is that we do not *add* elements to the map – we *put* elements in the map. Also, elements have two parts: the **key** (in our case, we are using strings) and the **value** (which can be heterogeneous in nature):

```java
import java.util.*;
public class Example15 {
    public static void main(String[] args) {
        Map map = new HashMap();
        map.put("number", new Integer(1));
        map.put("text", new String("hola"));
        map.put("decimal", new Double(5.7));
        System.out.println(map.get("text"));
        if (!map.containsKey("byte")) {
            System.out.println("There are no bytes here!");
        }
    }
}
```

This program will give the following result:

```
hola
There are no bytes here!
Process finished with exit code 0
```

Since there is no key named "**bytes**" in the code, the `maps.containsKey()` method will answer accordingly, and the program will inform the user about it. The main methods available in this interface are:

- **put** (Object key, Object value)
- **putAll** (Map map)
- **remove** (Object key)
- **get** (Object key)

- **containsKey** (Object key)

- **keySet()**

- **entrySet()**

All but the last two are self-explanatory. Let's focus on augmenting our previous example to see what those two methods do. Make the following addition to the code to see what **keySet()** and **entrySet()** have to offer:

```
System.out.println(map.entrySet());
System.out.println(map.keySet());
```

The outcome of the modified code listing will be:

```
hola
There are no bytes here!
[number=1, text=hola, decimal=5.7]
[number, text, decimal]
Process finished with exit code 0
```

In other words, **entrySet()** will print the whole map using the key = value formula, while **keySet()** will respond with the set of keys within the map.

> **Note**
>
> You might have realized this by now: keys must be unique – there cannot be two of the same keys in a map.

We will not go deeper into maps at this point because they are, to an extent, a repetition of what we saw with sets. There are three different classes for maps: **HashMap**, **TreeMap**, and **LinkedHashMap**. The last two are put in order, while the first one is neither sorted nor arranged in order of arrival. You should use these classes according to your needs.

Iterating through Collections

Earlier in this chapter, when working with *Exercise 01, Creating the AnalyzeInput Application* we stopped when we were about to make searches through the data. We made it to the point where we had to iterate through the data and look for characteristics such as word frequency.

Iterators are used in Java to browse through collections. Let's look at a simple example that involves extracting the elements from a simple list one by one and printing them out.

```java
import java.util.*;
public class Example16 {
    public static void main(String[] args) {
        List array = new ArrayList();
        array.add(5);
        array.add(2);
        array.add(37);
        Iterator iterator = array.iterator();
        while (iterator.hasNext()) {
            //   point to next element
            int i = (Integer) iterator.next();
            // print elements
            System.out.print(i + " ");
        }
    }
}
```

The output of this program is:

```
5 2 37
Process finished with exit code 0
```

Iterators such as this one are the most generic ones in the collections framework and can be used with lists, sets, queues, and even maps. There are other less-broad implementations of the iterators that allow for different ways to browse through data, for example, in lists. As you saw in the latest code listing, the `iterator.hasNext()` method checks whether there is a node after the one we are at in the list. When starting the iterator, the object points to the first element in the list. Then, `hasNext()` responds with a Boolean stating whether there are more nodes hanging from it. The `iterator.next()` method will move the iterator to the following node in the collection. This kind of iterator does not have the possibility of going back in the collection; it can only move forward. There is one final method in the iterator, called `remove()`, which will eliminate the current element that the iterator is pointing to from the collection.

If we used **listIterator()** instead, we would have had a lot more options for navigating collections, such as adding new elements and changing elements. The following code listing demonstrates how to go through a list, add elements, and modify them. **listIterator** works only with lists:

```java
import java.util.*;
public class Example17 {
    public static void main(String[] args) {
        List <Double> array = new ArrayList();
        array.add(5.0);
        array.add(2.2);
        array.add(37.5);
        array.add(3.1);
        array.add(1.3);
        System.out.println("Original list: " + array);
        ListIterator listIterator = array.listIterator();
        while (listIterator.hasNext()) {
            //  point to next element
            double d = (Double) listIterator.next();
            // round up the decimal number
            listIterator.set(Math.round(d));
        }
        System.out.println("Modified list: " + array);
    }
}
```

In this example, we create a list of **Double**, iterate through the list, and round up each of the numbers. The outcome of this program is:

```
Original list: [5.0, 2.2, 37.5, 3.1, 1.3]
Modified list: [5, 2, 38, 3, 1]
Process finished with exit code 0
```

By calling **listIterator.set()**, we modify each of the items in the list and the second **System.out.println()** command shows where the numbers have been rounded up or down.

The final iterator example we are going to see in this section is a trick to iterate through a map. This could come in handy in scenarios where you want to perform some operations on data within a map. By using the **entrySet()** method – which returns a list – it is possible to have an iterator over a map. See the following example to understand how this works:

```java
import java.util.*;
public class AnalyzeInput {
    public static void main(String[] args) {
        Map map = new HashMap ();
        map.put("name", "Kristian");
        map.put("family name", "Larssen");
        map.put("address", "Jumping Rd");
        map.put("mobile", "555-12345");
        map.put("pet", "cat");
        Iterator <Map.Entry> iterator = map.entrySet().iterator();
        while (iterator.hasNext()) {
            Map.Entry entry = iterator.next();
            System.out.print("Key = " + entry.getKey());
            System.out.println( ", Value = " + entry.getValue());
        }
    }
}
```

This program will iterate through a map and print the contents as they were stored in **HashMap**. Remember that these types of objects are not sorted in any specific way. You can expect an output like the following:

```
Key = address, Value = Jumping Rd
Key = family name, Value = Larssen
Key = name, Value = Kristian
Key = mobile, Value = 555-12345
Key = pet, Value = cat
Process finished with exit code 0
```

Given that we now have ways to iterate through collections, we can move on to an exercise that picks up where we left off: iterating through a list for data analysis.

Exercise 2: Bringing Analytics into the AnalyzeInput Application

We are going to start from where we left off at the end of *Exercise 1, Creating the AnalyzeInput Application*. We managed to capture the text typed in the terminal and store it as a list of strings. This time, we are going to use a method from the collections framework called **frequency**, which will respond with the number of times a certain object can be found inside a list. As words could be repeated in a sentence, we first need to figure out a way to extract the unique elements in a list:

1. Sets are objects in the collections framework that keep only one copy of each element. We saw an example of this earlier in the chapter. We will create a **HashSet** instance and copy all the elements from the list into it. This will automatically eliminate duplicates:

    ```
    Set <String> textSet = new HashSet <String> ();
    textSet.addAll(text);
    ```

2. The next step, now that we have the set, is to create an iterator that will check how many copies of each element from the set can be found in the list:

    ```
    Iterator iterator = textSet.iterator();
    ```

3. Using the same technique that we saw in previous examples for how to iterate through a set, we will find the next node in the set and check in the list for the frequency of the string stored in the node:

    ```
    while (iterator.hasNext()) {
        //point to next element
        String s = (String) iterator.next();
        // get the amount of times this word shows up in the text
        int freq = Collections.frequency(text, s);
        // print out the result
        System.out.println(s + " appears " + freq + " times");
    }
    ```

    > **Note**
    >
    > The final code can be referred at: https://packt.live/2BrplvS.

4. The outcome will depend on the kind of text you type. For the sake of testing, try the following (we will stick to this data entry for the rest of the chapter – you can copy and paste it to the terminal each time you call the application):

```
this is a test
is a test
test is this
*
```

5. The full outcome of this input will be:

```
You typed: [this, is, a, test, is, a, test, test, is, this, *]
Word count: 11
a appears 2 times
test appears 3 times
this appears 2 times
is appears 3 times
* appears 1 times
```

While the result is correct, it is not easy to read through. Ideally, results should be sorted. For example, by descending values of frequency, so that it is easy to see at a glance the most and least frequent words. This is the time to make yet another stop in the exercise as we need to introduce the idea of sorting before we move on with it.

Sorting Collections

As we have seen, there are some classes in the collections framework that force the items within them to be sorted. Examples of that are **TreeSet** and **TreeMap**. The aspect to explore in this section is how to use existing sorting mechanisms for lists, but also for cases that have datasets with more than one value per data point.

The exercise we are doing throughout this chapter is a good example of a case where there are data points with more than one value. For each data point, we need to store the word for which we are calculating the frequency and the frequency itself. You might think that a good technique to sort that out is by storing the information in the form of maps. The unique words could be the keys, while the frequencies could be the values. This could be achieved by modifying the final part of the previous program to look like this:

```
Map map = new HashMap();
while (iterator.hasNext()) {
    //  point to next element
    String s = (String) iterator.next();
    // get the amount of times this word shows up in the text
```

```
        int freq = Collections.frequency(text, s);
        // print out the result
        System.out.println(s + " appears " + freq + " times");
        // add items to the map
        map.put(s, freq);
    }
    TreeMap mapTree = new TreeMap();
    mapTree.putAll(map);
    System.out.println(mapTree);
```

While this is an interesting and simple approach to sorting (copying the data into a structure that is sorted by nature), it presents the problem that data is sorted by key and not by value, as the following result of the previous code highlights:

```
Word count: 11
a appears 2 times
test appears 3 times
this appears 2 times
is appears 3 times
* appears 1 times
{*=1, a=2, is=3, test=3, this=2}
```

So, if we want to sort these results by value, we need to figure out a different strategy.

But let's step back for a second and analyze what tools are offered in the collections framework for sorting. There is a method called **sort()** that can be used to sort lists. An example of this is as follows:

```
import java.util.*;
public class Example19 {
    public static void main(String[] args) {
        List <Double> array = new ArrayList();
        array.add(5.0);
        array.add(2.2);
        array.add(37.5);
        array.add(3.1);
        array.add(1.3);
        System.out.println("Original list: " + array);
        Collections.sort(array);
        System.out.println("Modified list: " + array);

    }
}
```

The result of this program is:

```
Original list: [5.0, 2.2, 37.5, 3.1, 1.3]
Modified list: [1.3, 2.2, 3.1, 5.0, 37.5]
Process finished with exit code 0
```

Given a list, we could sort it this way just fine; it would even be possible to navigate through it backward using **listIterator** to sort a list in descending order. However, these methods do not solve the issue of sorting data points with multiple values. In such a case, we would need to create a class to store our own key-value pair. Let's see how to implement this by continuing with the exercise we have been dealing with throughout the chapter.

Exercise 3: Sort the Results from the AnalyzeInput Application

We now have a program that, given some input text, identifies some basic characteristics of the text, such as the number of words in the text or the frequency of each of the words. Our goal is to be able to sort the results in descending order to make them easier to read. The solution will require the implementation of a class that will store our key-value pairs and make a list of objects from that class:

1. Create a class containing the two data points: the word and its frequency. Implement a constructor that will take values and pass them to class variables. This will simplify the code later:

```
class DataPoint {
    String key = "";
    Integer value = 0;
    // constructor
    DataPoint(String s, Integer i) {
        key = s;
        value = i;
    }
}
```

2. When calculating the frequency for each word, store the results in a newly created list of objects of the new class:

```
List <DataPoint> frequencies = new ArrayList <DataPoint> ();
while (iterator.hasNext()) {
//point to next element
String s = (String) iterator.next();
// get the amount of times this word shows up in the text
```

```
        int freq = Collections.frequency(text, s);
        // print out the result
        System.out.println(s + " appears " + freq + " times");
        // create the object to be stored
        DataPoint datapoint = new DataPoint (s, freq);
        // add datapoints to the list
        frequencies.add(datapoint);
    }
```

3. Sorting is going to require the creation of a new class using the **Comparator** interface, which we are just introducing now. This interface should implement a method that will be used to run comparisons within the objects in the array. This new class must implement **Comparator <DataPoint>** and include a single method called **compare()**. It should have two objects of the class being sorted as parameters:

```
class SortByValue implements Comparator<DataPoint>
{
    // Used for sorting in ascending order
    public int compare(DataPoint a, DataPoint b)
    {
        return a.value - b.value;
    }
}
```

4. The way we call the **Collections.sort()** algorithm using this new comparator is by adding an object of that class as a parameter to the **sort** method. We instantiate it directly in the call:

```
Collections.sort(frequencies,new SortByValue());
```

5. This will sort the frequencies list in ascending order. To print the results, it is no longer valid to make a direct call to **System.out.println(frequencies)** because it is now an array of objects and it will not print the contents of the data points to the terminal. Iterate through the list in the following way instead:

```
System.out.println("Results sorted");
for (int i = 0; i < frequencies.size(); i++)
    System.out.println(frequencies.get(i).value
                    + " times for word "
                    + frequencies.get(i).key);
```

6. If you run the program using the same input that we have been using for the last couple of examples, the outcome will be:

```
Results sorted
1 times for word *
2 times for word a
2 times for word this
3 times for word test
3 times for word is
```

7. Our goal is to sort the results in descending order and, to do that, we will need to add one more thing to the call to the **sort** algorithm. When instantiating the **SortByValue()** class, we need to tell the compiler that we want the list to be sorted in reverse order. The collections framework already has a method for this:

```
Collections.sort(frequencies, Collections.reverseOrder(new SortByValue()));
```

> **Note**
>
> For the sake of clarity, the final code can be referred at: https://packt.live/2W5qhzP.

8. A full interaction path with this program, from the moment we call it to include the data entry, would be as follows:

```
user@localhost:~/IdeaProjects/ch04/out/production/ch04$ java AnalyzeInput
this is a test
is a test
test is this
*
You typed: [this, is, a, test, is, a, test, test, is, this, *]
Word count: 11
a appears 2 times
test appears 3 times
this appears 2 times
is appears 3 times
```

```
* appears 1 times
Results sorted
3 times for word test
3 times for word is
2 times for word a
2 times for word this
1 times for word *
```

Properties

Properties in the collections framework are used to maintain lists of key-value pairs where both are of the **String** class. Properties are relevant when obtaining environmental values from the operating system, for example, and are the grounding class for many other classes. One of the main characteristics of the **Properties** class is that it allows the definition of a default response in the case of a search for a certain key not being satisfactory. The following example highlights the basics of this case:

Example20.java

```
1   import java.util.*;
2
3   public class Example20 {
4
5       public static void main(String[] args) {
6           Properties properties = new Properties();
7           Set setOfKeys;
8           String key;
9
10          properties.put("OS", "Ubuntu Linux");
11          properties.put("version", "18.04");
12          properties.put("language", "English (UK)");
13
14          // iterate through the map
15          setOfKeys = properties.keySet();
```

https://packt.live/2N0CzoS

Before diving into the results, you will notice that in properties, we put rather than add new elements/nodes. This is the same as we saw with maps. Also, you will have noticed that to iterate, we used the **keySet()** technique that we saw when iterating through maps earlier. Finally, the particularity of **Properties** is that you can set a default response in the case of the searched-for property not being found. This is what happens in the example when searching for **keyboard layout**—it was never defined, so the **getProperty()** method will answer with its default message without crashing the program.

The result of this program is:

```
version = 18.04
OS = Ubuntu Linux
language = English (UK)
keyboard layout = not found
Process finished with exit code 0
```

Another interesting method to be found in the **Properties** class is the **list()**; it comes with two different implementations that allow you to send the contents of a list to different data handlers. We can stream the whole properties list to a **PrintStreamer** object, such as **System.out**. This offers a simple way of displaying what is in a list without having to iterate through it. An example of this follows:

```java
import java.util.*;
public class Example21 {
    public static void main(String[] args) {
        Properties properties = new Properties();
        properties.put("OS", "Ubuntu Linux");
        properties.put("version", "18.04");
        properties.put("language", "English (UK)");
        properties.list(System.out);
    }
}
```

That will result in:

```
version=18.04
OS=Ubuntu Linux
language=English (UK)
Process finished with exit code 0
```

The **propertyNames()** method returns an **Enumeration** list, and by iterating through it, we will obtain the keys to the whole list. This is an alternative to creating a set and running the **keySet()** method.

```java
import java.util.*;
public class Example22 {
    public static void main(String[] args) {
        Properties properties = new Properties();
        properties.put("OS", "Ubuntu Linux");
```

```
        properties.put("version", "18.04");
        properties.put("language", "English (UK)");
        Enumeration enumeration = properties.propertyNames();
        while (enumeration.hasMoreElements()) {
            System.out.println(enumeration.nextElement());
        }
    }
}
```

That will result in:

```
version
OS
language
Process finished with exit code 0
```

The final method we will introduce you to from **Properties** at this point is
setProperty(). It will modify the value of an existing key, or will eventually create a new
key-value pair if the key is not found. The method will answer with the old value if the
key exists, and answer with **null** otherwise. The next example shows how it works:

```
import java.util.*;
public class Example23 {
    public static void main(String[] args) {
        Properties properties = new Properties();
        properties.put("OS", "Ubuntu Linux");
        properties.put("version", "18.04");
        properties.put("language", "English (UK)");
        String oldValue = (String) properties.setProperty("language", "German");
        if (oldValue != null) {
            System.out.println("modified the language property");
        }
        properties.list(System.out);
    }
}
```

Here is the outcome:

```
modified the language property
-- listing properties --
version=18.04
OS=Ubuntu Linux
language=German
Process finished with exit code 0
```

> **Note**
>
> There are more methods in the **Properties** class that deals with storing and retrieving lists of properties to/from files. While this is a very powerful feature from the Java APIs, as we haven't yet introduced the use of files in this book, we will not discuss those methods here. For more information at this point, please refer to Java's official documentation.

Activity 2: Iterating through Large Lists

In contemporary computing, we deal with large sets of data. The purpose of this activity is to create a random-sized list of random numbers to perform some basic operations on data, such as obtaining the average.

1. To start, you should create a random list of numbers.

2. To compute the average, you could create an iterator that will go through the list of values and add the weighted value corresponding to each element.

3. The value coming from the `iterator.next()` method must be cast into a **Double** before it can be weighed against the total number of elements.

If you've implemented everything properly, the results of the averaging should similar to:

```
Total amount of numbers: 3246
Average: 49.785278826074396
```

Or, it could be:

```
Total amount of numbers: 6475
Average: 50.3373892275651
```

> **Note**
>
> The solution for this activity can be found on page 539.

If you managed to make this program work, you should think about how to take advantage of being able to simulate large sets of data like this one. This data could represent the amount of time between different arrivals of data in your application, temperature data from the nodes in an Internet of Things network being captured every second. The possibilities are endless. By using lists, you can make the size of the dataset as endless as their working possibilities.

Summary

This chapter introduced you to the Java collections framework, which is a very powerful tool within the Java language that can be used to store, sort, and filter data. The framework is massive and offers tools in the form of interfaces, classes, and methods, some of which are beyond the scope of this chapter. We have focused on **Arrays**, **Lists**, **Sets**, **Maps**, and **Properties**. But there are others, such as queues and dequeues, that are worth exploring on your own.

Sets, like their mathematical equivalents, store unique copies of items. Lists are like arrays that can be extended endlessly and support duplicates. Maps are used when dealing with key-value pairs, something very common in contemporary computing, and do not support the use of two of the same keys. Properties work very much like **HashMap** (a specific type of **Map**) but offer some extra features, such as the listing of all their contents to streams, which simplifies the printing out of the contents of a list.

Some of the classes offered in the framework are sorted by design, such as **TreeHash** and **TreeMap**, while others are not. Depending on how you want to handle data, you will have to decide which is the best collection.

There are standard techniques for looking through data with iterators. These iterators, upon creation, will point to the first element in a list. Iterators offer some basic methods, such as **hasNext()** and **next()**, that state whether there is more data in the list and extract data from the list, respectively. While those two are common to all iterators, there are others, such as **listIterator**, that are much more powerful and allow, for example, the addition of new elements to a list while browsing through it.

We have looked at a chapter-long example that used many of these techniques, and we have introduced the use of the console to read data through the terminal. In the next chapter, we will cover exceptions and how to handle them.

5

Exceptions

Overview

This chapter discusses how exceptions are dealt with in Java. You will first learn how to identify the situations that produce exceptions in your code. This knowledge will simplify the process of handling these exceptions by alerting you to those circumstances in which they are most likely to arise. In this endeavor, this chapter also provides a list of best practices guiding you through common scenarios and the best methods of either catching exceptions or throwing them to the calling class, logging their details as you go. You will further learn to differentiate between different types of exceptions, and practice the techniques for handling each. By the end of the chapter, you will even be able to create your own exception class, capable of logging each type of exception in order of severity.

Introduction

Exceptions are not errors, or, more accurately, exceptions are not bugs, even if you might perceive them to be when they crash your programs. Exceptions are situations that occur in your code when there is a mismatch between the data you are handling and the method or command you are using to process it.

In Java, there is a class that is dedicated to errors. Errors are unexpected situations that affect programs on the **Java Virtual Machine** (**JVM**) level. For example, if you fill-up the program stack through an unconventional use of memory, then your whole JVM will crash. Unlike errors, exceptions are situations that your code, when properly designed, can catch on the fly.

Exceptions are not as drastic as errors, even if the result for you, the developer, will be the same—that is, a non-working program. In this chapter, we are inviting you to make your programs crash by intentionally provoking exceptions that you will later learn how to catch (that is, handle) and avoid. Depending on how you develop the catch mechanism, you can decide whether to get your program to recover and continue operating or to gracefully end its execution with a human-readable error message.

A Simple Exception Example

Start by provoking a simple exception in your code. First, type in the following program in the **Integrated Development Environment** (**IDE**) and execute it:

```java
public class Example01 {
    public static void main(String[] args) {
        // declare a string with nothing inside
        String text = null;
        // you will see this at the console
        System.out.println("Go Java Go!");
        // null'ed strings should crash your program
        System.out.println(text.length());
        // you will never see this print
        System.out.println("done");
    }
}
```

Here is the output:

```
Go Java Go!
Exception in thread "main" java.lang.NullPointerException
    at Example01.main(Example01.java:11)
Process finished with exit code 1
```

The previous code listing shows how the program starts executing a command that works fine. The sentence **Go Java Go!** is printed on the console, but then a **NullPointerException** shows up, highlighting that something exceptional happened. In this case, we tried to print the length of a string initiated to null by calling **text. length()**. Since there is no length to be calculated (that is, we don't even have an empty string), either **System.out.println()** or **text.length()** provoked the exception. Additionally, there was an error at that point, so the program exited and the final call to **System.out.println("done")** was not executed. You could try to separate both commands to see what the outcome will be:

```
// null'ed strings should crash your program
int number = text.length();
System.out.println(number);
```

Here is the output:

```
Go Java Go!
Exception in thread "main" java.lang.NullPointerException
      at Example01.main(Example01.java:11)
Process finished with exit code 1
```

If you check the line numbers in the IDE, you will see that the exception takes place on the line where we are trying to get the length of the string. Now that we know the cause of the problem, there are two ways around this issue: either we fix the data (note that there will be situations where this will be impossible), or we include a countermeasure in our code to detect the exceptions and then handle or ignore them. The action of handling an unexpected event is what we call catching the exception. On the other hand, bypassing the event is called throwing the exception. Later in the chapter, we will explore different ways of doing both of these actions, as well as good practices for when writing code-handling exceptions.

However, before learning about how to avoid or handle exceptions, let's provoke some more. Almost every Java API includes the definition of an exception that can help to propagate errors towards the main class, and thus the developer. In that way, it will be possible to avoid situations where the code will break in front of the user's eyes.

The exceptions covered by the Java APIs are what we call built-in exceptions. It is also possible to create your own when you define a class. Talking about classes, let's try to get a character from a non-existing location within an object instantiated from **String** and see what happens:

```java
public class Example02 {
    public static void main(String[] args) {
        // declare a string of a fixed length
        String text = "I <3 bananas"; // 12 characters long
        // provoke an exception
        char character = text.charAt(15); // get the 15th element
        // you will never see this print
        System.out.println("done");
    }
}
```

The IDE will respond with the following:

```
Exception in thread "main" java.lang.StringIndexOutOfBoundsException: String index out of
range: 15
        at java.lang.String.charAt(String.java:658)
        at Example02.main(Example02.java:8)
Process finished with exit code 1
```

Note that the text variable is only 12 characters long. When trying to extract the 15th character, the IDE will issue an exception and terminate the program. In this case, we got one called **StringOutOfBoundsException**. There are many different types of built-in exceptions.

Here's a list of the various types of exceptions:

- **NullPointerException**
- **StringOutOfBoundsException**
- **ArithmeticException**
- **ClassCastException**
- **IllegalArgumentException**
- **IndexOutOfBoundsException**
- **NumberFormatException**

- `IllegalAccessException`

- `InstantiationException`

- `NoSuchMethodException`

As you can see, the names of the different exceptions are quite descriptive. When you get one, it should be quite easy to figure out where to find more information about it within the Java documentation in order to mitigate the problem. We classify exceptions as checked or unchecked:

- **Checked exceptions**: These are highlighted during compilation. In other words, your program will not make it to the end of the compilation process, and therefore you will not be able to run it.

- **Unchecked exceptions**: These show up during program execution; therefore, we also call them runtime exceptions. The examples that have been shown in this chapter so far (**NullPointerException** and **StringOutOfBoundsException**) are both unchecked.

> ### Why Two Types of Exception?
>
> There are two possibilities for exceptions: either we, as developers, make a mistake and don't realize that our way of handling data is going to produce an error (such as when we are trying to get the length of an empty string or when we are dividing a number by zero), or the error happens because we are uncertain about the nature of the data we will be gathering during an exchange with something external to our program (such as when getting parameters from the CLI and they are of the wrong type). In cases like the first one, checked exceptions make more sense. The second scenario is the reason why we need unchecked exceptions. In this second case, we should develop strategies to handle potential threats to the proper execution of the program.

Making an example of a checked exception is slightly more complicated because we have to anticipate things that will not be introduced in depth until a later chapter. However, we consider that the following example, which displays an example of **IOException**, is simple enough even if it includes a couple of classes that haven't been touched on in the book yet:

```java
import java.nio.file.*;
import java.util.*;
public class Example03 {
    public static void main(String[] args) {
```

```
        // declare a list that will contain all of the files
        // inside of the readme.txt file
        List<String> lines = Collections.emptyList();
        // provoke an exception
        lines = Files.readAllLines(Paths.get("readme.txt"));
        // you will never see this print
        Iterator<String> iterator = lines.iterator();
        while (iterator.hasNext())
            System.out.println(iterator.next());
    }
}
```

The newest thing in this code listing is the use of **java.nio.file.***. This is an API that includes classes and methods to manage files, among other things. The goal of this program is to read a whole text file called readme.txt into a list that will then be printed using an iterator, as we saw in *Chapter 4, Collections, Lists, and Java's Built-In APIs*.

This is a case where a checked exception could occur when calling **Files. readAllLines()** if there is no file to be read because of, for example, having a wrongly declared filename. The IDE knows this and, therefore, it flags that there is a potential risk.

Note how the IDE displays a warning from the moment we write the code. Furthermore, when trying to compile the program, the IDE will respond with the following:

```
Error:(11, 35) java: unreported exception java.io.IOException; must be caught or declared
to be thrown
```

Catching and **throwing** are the two strategies that you can use to avoid exceptions. We will talk about them in more detail later in the chapter.

NullPointerException – Have No Fear

We presented the concept of **null** within Java in a previous chapter. As you may recall, **null** is the value that is implicitly assigned to an object upon creation, that is, unless you assign a different value to it. Related to **null** is the **NullPointerException** value. This is a very common event that can and will happen to you for a variety of reasons. In this section, we will highlight some of the most common scenarios of this in an effort to introduce you to a different way of thinking when dealing with any type of exception in your code.

In *Example01*, we examined the process of trying to perform operations on an object that was pointing to **null**. Let's look at some other possible cases:

```java
public class Example04 {
    public static void main(String[] args) {
        String vehicleType = null;
        String vehicle = "car";
        if (vehicleType.equals(vehicle)) {
            System.out.println("it's a car");
        } else {
            System.out.println("it's not a car");
        }
    }
}
```

The outcome of this example would be the following:

```
Exception in thread "main" java.lang.NullPointerException
        at Example04.main(Example04.java:5)
Process finished with exit code 1
```

You could have prevented this exception if you had written your code to compare the existing variable with the potentially **null** one instead.

```java
public class Example05 {
    public static void main(String[] args) {
        String vehicleType = null;
        String vehicle = "car";
        if (vehicle.equals(vehicleType)) {
            System.out.println("it's a car");
        } else {
            System.out.println("it's not a car");
        }
    }
}
```

The preceding code will produce the following result:

```
it's not a car
Process finished with exit code 0
```

As you can see, there is no conceptual difference between the examples; however, there is a difference at the code level. This difference is enough for your code to issue an exception upon compilation. This is because the **equals()** method for the **String** class is prepared to handle the situation of its parameter being **null**. On the other hand, a **String** variable that is initialized to **null** cannot have access to the **equals()** method.

A very common situation for provoking a **NullPointerException** occurs when trying to call non-static methods from an object initialized to **null**. The following example shows a class with two methods that you can call to see whether they produce the exception. You can do this by simply commenting or uncommenting each of the lines calling the methods from **main()**. Copy the code in the IDE and try the two cases:

```
public class Example06 {
    private static void staticMethod() {
        System.out.println("static method, accessible from null reference");
    }
    private void nonStaticMethod() {
        System.out.print("non-static method, inaccessible from null reference");
    }
    public static void main(String args[]) {
        Example06 object = null;
        object.staticMethod();
        //object.nonStaticMethod();
    }
}
```

There are other cases when this exception can appear, but let's focus on how to deal with exceptions. The following sections will describe different mechanisms you can use to enable your programs to recover from unexpected situations.

Catching Exceptions

As mentioned earlier, there are two ways to handle exceptions: catching and throwing. In this section, we will deal with the first of these methods. Catching an exception requires encapsulating the code that might generate an unwanted result into a specific statement, as shown in the following code snippet:

```
try {
    // code that could generate an exception of the type ExceptionM
} catch (ExceptionM e) {
    // code to be executed in case of exception happening
}
```

We can put this code to test with any of the previous examples. Let's demonstrate how we could stop the exception we found in the first example of the chapter, where we tried to check the length of a string that was initialized to null:

```java
public class Example07 {
    public static void main(String[] args) {
        // declare a string with nothing inside
        String text = null;
        // you will see this at the console
        System.out.println("Go Java Go!");
        try {
            // null'ed strings should crash your program
            System.out.println(text.length());
        } catch (NullPointerException ex) {
            System.out.println("Exception: cannot get the text's length");
        }
        // you will now see this print
        System.out.println("done");
    }
}
```

As you can see, we have wrapped the potentially broken code inside a **try-catch** statement. The result of this code listing is very different from the result that we saw previously:

```
Go Java Go!
Exception: cannot get the text's length
done
Process finished with exit code 0
```

Mainly, we find that the program is not interrupted until the end. The **try** section of the program detects the arrival of the exception, and the **catch** part will execute a specific code if the exception is of the **NullPointerException** type.

Several **catch** statements can be placed in sequence after the call to **try** as a way to detect different types of exceptions. To try this out, let's go back to the example where we were trying to open a non-existing file and try to catch the reason for **readAllLines()** stopping the program:

Example08.java

```
5   public class Example08 {
6       public static void main(String[] args) {
7           // declare a list that will contain all of the files
8           // inside of the readme.txt file
9           List<String> lines = Collections.emptyList();
10
11          try {
12              // provoke an exception
13              lines = Files.readAllLines(Paths.get("readme.txt"));
14          } catch (NoSuchFileException fe) {
15              System.out.println("Exception: File Not Found");
16          } catch (IOException ioe) {
17              System.out.println("Exception: IOException");
18          }
```

https://packt.live/2VU59wh

As we saw earlier in the chapter, we have made a program that tries to open a non-existing file. The exception that we got then was **IOException**. In reality, that exception is triggered by **NoSuchFileException**, which is escalated and triggers **IOException**. Therefore, we get that exception on the IDE. When implementing the multiple try-catch statements, as shown in the previous example, we get the following outcome:

```
Exception: File Not Found
Process finished with exit code 0
```

This means that the program detects the **NoSuchFileException** and, therefore, prints the message included in the corresponding catch statement. However, if you want to see the full sequence of exceptions triggered by the non-existing readme.txt file, you can use a method called **printStackTrace()**. This will send to the output everything that was on the way to the proper execution of the program. To see this, simply add the following highlighted changes to the previous example:

```
try {
    // provoke an exception
    lines = Files.readAllLines(Paths.get("readme.txt"));
} catch (NoSuchFileException fe) {
    System.out.println("Exception: File Not Found");
```

```
        fe.printStackTrace();
    } catch (IOException ioe) {
        System.out.println("Exception: IOException");
    }
}
```

The output of the program will now include a full printout of the different exceptions triggered during program execution. You will see the output of the stack is inverted: first, you will see the reason why the program stopped (**NoSuchFileException**), and it will end with the method that starts the process that provokes the exception (**readAllLines**). This is due to the way exceptions are built. As we will discuss later, there are many different types of exceptions. Each one of these types is defined as a class of exceptions, which may be extended by several other subclasses of exceptions. If an extension of a certain type occurs, then the class that it is extending will also appear when printing out the stack. In our case, **NoSuchFileException** is a subclass of **IOException**.

> **Note**
>
> Depending on your operating system, the different nested exceptions for dealing with opening a file will probably be called differently.

We have been catching two different exceptions – one nested inside the other. It should also be possible to handle exceptions coming from different classes, such as **IOException** and **NullPointerException**. The following example demonstrates how to do this. If you are dealing with exceptions that are not a subclass of one another, it is possible to catch both exceptions using a logical OR operator:

```
import java.io.*; ·
import java.nio.file.*;
import java.util.*;
public class Example09 {
    public static void main(String[] args) {
        List<String> lines = Collections.emptyList();
        try {
            lines = Files.readAllLines(Paths.get("readme.txt"));
        } catch (NullPointerException|IOException ex) {
            System.out.println("Exception: File Not Found or NullPointer");
            ex.printStackTrace();
```

```
        }
        // you will never see this print
        Iterator<String> iterator = lines.iterator();
        while (iterator.hasNext())
            System.out.println(iterator.next());
    }
}
```

As you can see, it is possible to handle both exceptions in a single **catch** statement. However, if you want to handle the exceptions differently, you will have to work with the object containing the information about the exception, which, in this case, is **ex**. The keyword you need to distinguish the between the exceptions that you may be handling simultaneously is **instanceof**, as shown in the following modification of the previous example:

```
try {
    // provoke an exception
    lines = Files.readAllLines(Paths.get("readme.txt"));
} catch (NullPointerException|IOException ex) {
    if (ex instanceof IOException) {
        System.out.println("Exception: File Not Found");
    }
    if (ex instanceof NullPointerException) {
        System.out.println("Exception: NullPointer");
    }
}
```

How Many Different Exceptions Can You Catch in a Single Try?

The fact is that you can daisy chain as many catch statements as you need to. If you use the second method that we discussed in this chapter (that is, using the OR statement), then you should remember that it is not possible to have a subclass together with its parent class. For example, it is not possible to have NoSuchFileException and IOException together in the same statement – they should be placed in two different catch statements.

Exercise 1: Logging Exceptions

There are two main actions that you can perform when catching exceptions aside from any type of creative coding you may want to do to respond to the situation; these actions are logging or throwing. In this exercise, you will learn how to log the exception. In a later exercise, you will learn how to throw it instead. As we will reiterate in the *Best Practices for Handling Exceptions* section of this chapter, you should never do both at once:

1. Create a new Java project in IntelliJ using the template for CLI. Name it LoggingExceptions. You will be creating classes inside it that you can then use later in other programs.

2. In the code, you need to import the logging API by issuing the following command:

    ```
    import java.util.logging.*;
    ```

3. Declare an object that you will be using to log the data into. This object will be printed to the terminal upon program termination; therefore, you don't need to worry about where it will end up at this point:

    ```
    Logger logger = Logger.getAnonymousLogger();
    ```

4. Provoke an exception, as follows:

    ```
    String s = null;
    try {
        System.out.println(s.length());
    } catch (NullPointerException ne) {
        // do something here
    }
    ```

5. At the time of catching the exception, send the data to the logger object using the **log()** method:

    ```
    logger.log(Level.SEVERE, "Exception happened", ne);
    ```

6. Your full program should read as follows:

    ```
    import java.util.logging.*;
    public class LoggingExceptions {
        public static void main(String[] args) {
            Logger logger = Logger.getAnonymousLogger();
            String s = null;
            try {
                System.out.println(s.length());
    ```

```
        } catch (NullPointerException ne) {
            logger.log(Level.SEVERE, "Exception happened", ne);
        }
    }
}
```

7. When you execute the code, the output should be as follows:

```
may 09, 2019 7:42:05 AM LoggingExceptions main
SEVERE: Exception happened
java.lang.NullPointerException
        at LoggingExceptions.main(LoggingExceptions .java:10)
Process finished with exit code 0
```

8. As you can see, the exception is logged at the determined **SEVERE** level, but the code ends without an error code because we were able to handle the exception. The log is useful because it tells us where the exception happened in the code and, additionally, helps us to find the place of where we can dig deeper into the code and fix any potential issues.

Throws and Throw

You can choose not to deal with some caught exceptions in your code at a low level, as described in the previous section. It could be interesting to filter out an exception's parent class and focus on detecting a subclass that might be of more importance to us. The **throws** keyword is used in the definition of the method you are creating and where the exception may occur. In the following case, which is a modification of *Example 09*, we should call throws in the definition of **main()**:

```
import java.io.*;
import java.nio.file.*;
import java.util.*;
public class Example10 {
    public static void main(String[] args) throws IOException {
        // declare a list that will contain all of the files
        // inside of the readme.txt file
        List<String> lines = Collections.emptyList();
        try {
            lines = Files.readAllLines(Paths.get("readme.txt"));
        } catch (NoSuchFileException fe) {
            System.out.println("Exception: File Not Found");
```

```
                //fe.printStackTrace();
        }
        // you will never see this print
        Iterator<String> iterator = lines.iterator();
        while (iterator.hasNext())
            System.out.println(iterator.next());
    }
}
```

As you can see, we are throwing any **IOException** that is occurring during runtime. In this way, we can focus on catching the one that actually happens: **NoSuchFileException**. It is possible to throw more than one exception type in this way by separating them using commas.

An example of such a method definition is as follows:

```
public static void main(String[] args) throws IOException, NullPointerException {
```

The one thing that is not possible is having an exception class and its subclass being thrown in the same method definition – just as we saw when trying to catch more than one exception in a single **catch** statement. It is also interesting to see that **throws** is operating at a certain scope; for example, we could disregard a certain exception within a method in a class but not a different one.

On the other hand, there is yet another keyword that you will find relevant for dealing with exceptions as you advance in your understanding of the term. The **throw** keyword (note that this is not **throws**) will explicitly invoke an exception. You can use this to create your own exceptions and try them out in your code. We will demonstrate in a later section how you can create your own exception, and then we will use **throw** as part of the example to also see how exceptions propagate. The main reason to use **throw** is if you want your code to hand over an exception occurring within your class to another one higher up in the hierarchy. For the sake of learning about how this works, let's look at the following example:

```
public class Example11 {
    public static void main(String args[]) {
        String text = null;
        try {
            System.out.println(text.length());
        } catch (Exception e) {
```

```
                System.out.println("Exception: this should be a NullPointerException");
                throw new RuntimeException();
            }
        }
}
```

In this case, we reproduce the **NullPointerException** example we saw earlier by trying to call the **length()** method on a string initialized as **null**. However, if you run this code, you will see that the exception that is being displayed is **RuntimeException**:

```
Exception: this should be a NullPointerException
Exception in thread "main" java.lang.RuntimeException
        at Example11.main(Example11.java:9)
Process finished with exit code 1
```

The reason for this is the call to **throw new RuntimeException()** that we issued in the **catch** block. As you can see, when dealing with the exception, we are provoking a different exception. This can be very useful for catching exceptions and piping them through your own exceptions, or simply catching the exception, giving a meaningful message to help the user understand what went down, and then letting the exception continue its own path, and eventually crashing the program if the exception is not handled at a higher level in the code.

Exercise 2: Breaking the Law (and Fixing It)

In this example, you will create your own checked exception class. You will define a class and then experiment by provoking that exception, logging its results, and then analyzing them:

1. Create a new Java project in IntelliJ using the template for CLI. Name it **BreakingTheLaw**. You will be creating classes inside it that you can use later in other programs.

2. In the code, create a new class to describe your exception. This class should extend the base **Exception** class. Call it **MyException** and include the empty constructor:

```
public class BreakingTheLaw {
    class MyException extends Exception {
        // Constructor
        MyException() {};
```

```
        }
        public static void main(String[] args) {
            // write your code here
        }
    }
```

3. Your constructor should include all the possibilities to be thrown. This implies that the constructor needs to contemplate several different cases:

```
// Constructor
public MyException() {
    super();
}
public MyException(String message) {
    super(message);
}
public MyException(String message, Throwable cause) {
    super(message, cause);
}
public MyException(Throwable cause) {
    super(cause);
}
```

4. This will allow us to now wrap any exception with our newly formed exception. However, there are a couple of modifications that we should apply to our program in order for it to compile. First, we need to make the exception class static for it to work in the context we are using it in:

```
public static class MyException extends Exception {
```

5. Next, you need to make sure that the main class is throwing your new exception since you are going to be issuing that exception in the code:

```
public static void main(String[] args) throws MyException {
```

6. Finally, you need to generate some code that will provoke an exception, such as **NullPointerException**, when trying to get the length of a **String** initialized to **null**, **catch** it, and then **throw** it away using our newly created class:

```java
public static void main(String[] args) throws MyException {
    String s = null;
    try {
        System.out.println(s.length());
    } catch (NullPointerException ne) {
        throw new MyException("Exception: my exception happened");
    }
}
```

7. The result of running this code is as follows:

```
Exception in thread "main" BreakingTheLaw$MyException: Exception: my exception
happened
        at BreakingTheLaw.main(BreakingTheLaw.java:26)
Process finished with exit code 1
```

8. You can now experiment with the call to **throw** by using any other of the constructors in the class. We just tried one that includes our own error message, so let's add the stack trace for the exception:

```java
throw new MyException("Exception: my exception happened", ne);
```

9. What will make the output slightly more informative is that it will now include information about the exception that generated our own **NullPointerException**:

```
Exception in thread "main" BreakingTheLaw$MyException: Exception: my exception
happened
        at BreakingTheLaw.main(BreakingTheLaw.java:26)
Caused by: java.lang.NullPointerException
        at BreakingTheLaw.main(BreakingTheLaw.java:24)
Process finished with exit code 1
```

You have now learned how to use throw to wrap an exception into your own exception class. This can be very handy when dealing with a large codebase and having to look for the exceptions generated by your code in a long log file, or similar.

> **Note**
>
> The final code can be referred at: https://packt.live/2VVdy2f.

The finally Block

The **finally** block can be used to execute some common code after any of the **catch** blocks used to handle a series of different exceptions in the code. Going back to our example where we tried to open a non-existing file, a modified version of it including a **finally** statement would look like the following:

Example12.java

```
11        try {
12            // provoke an exception
13            lines = Files.readAllLines(Paths.get("readme.txt"));
14        } catch (NoSuchFileException fe) {
15            System.out.println("Exception: File Not Found");
16        } catch (IOException ioe) {
17            System.out.println("Exception: IOException");
18        } finally {
19            System.out.println("Exception: Case Closed");
20        }
```

https://packt.live/2VTBFOS

The output of the preceding example is as follows:

```
Exception: File Not Found
Exception: Case Closed
Process finished with exit code 0
```

After the **catch** block detecting the **NoSuchFileException**, the handling mechanism jumps into the **finally** block and executes whatever is in it, which, in this case, implies printing yet another line of text to the output.

Activity 1: Designing an Exception Class Logging Data

We have seen examples of how to log exceptions and how to throw them. We have also learned how to create exception classes and throw them. With all that information, the goal of this activity is to create your own exception class that should log the different exceptions in terms of severity. You should make an application that is based on the arguments to the program, and the program will respond to the logging exceptions in different ways. Just to have a common ground, use the following standard:

1. If the input is number 1, issue the **NullPointerException** with a severity level of SEVERE.

2. If the input is number 2, issue the **NoSuchFileException** with a severity level of WARNING.

3. If the input is number 3, issue the **NoSuchFileException** with a severity level of INFO.

4. In order to make this program, you will need to consider making your own methods for issuing exceptions, such as the following:

```
public static void issuePointerException() throws NullPointerException {
    throw new NullPointerException("Exception: file not found");
}
public static void issueFileException() throws NoSuchFileException {
    throw new NoSuchFileException("Exception: file not found");
}
```

> **Note**
>
> The solution for this activity can be found on page 540.

Best Practices for Handling Exceptions

Dealing with exceptions in your code requires following a set of best practices in order to avoid deeper issues when writing your programs. This list of common practices is of relevance to your code in order to keep some degree of professional programming consistency:

The first piece of advice is to avoid throwing or catching the main **Exception** class. You need to be as specific as possible when dealing with an exception. Therefore, a case like the following is not recommended:

```
public class Example13 {
    public static void main(String args[]) {
        String text = null;
        try {
            System.out.println(text.length());
        } catch (Exception e) {
            System.out.println("Exception happened");
        }
    }
}
```

This code listing will catch any exception, with no granularity. So, how are you supposed to properly handle the exception this way?

In the following section, we will do a quick recap of where the Exception class is located within the Java API structure. We will examine how it hangs from the Throwable class at the same level as the Error class. Therefore, if you were to catch the Throwable class, you would mask possible errors occurring in your code and not only exceptions. Remember that errors are those situations when your code should be exited because they alert to a real malfunction that could lead to the misuse of JVM resources.

Masking such a scenario behind a catch could stall the whole JVM. Therefore, avoid code like the following:

```
try {
    System.out.println(text.length());
} catch (Throwable e) {
    System.out.println("Exception happened");
}
```

In *Exercise 2, Breaking the Law (and Fixing It)* you saw how to make your own exception class. As discussed, it is possible to redirect exceptions toward others by using **throw**. It is good practice to not disregard the stack trace of the original exception since it will help you to debug the source of the issue in a better way. Therefore, when catching the original exception, you should consider passing over the whole stack trace as a parameter to the exception constructor:

```
} catch (OriginalException e) {
    throw new MyVeryOwnException("Exception trace: ", e);
}
```

In the same exercise, when making your own exception, you learned how to use the system's log to store the information of the exception. You should avoid both logging the exception and throwing it once more. You should try to log at the highest level possible in your code. Otherwise, you will get duplicated information about the situation inside your log, making the debugging a lot more complicated. Therefore, we recommend that you use the following:

```
throw new NewException();
```

Alternatively, you can use the following inside the same **catch** block, but not for both:

```
log.error("Exception trace: ", e);
```

Additionally, when logging information, try to use a single call to the system's log. As your code grows bigger, there will be multiple processes working in parallel, thus a lot of different sources will be issuing log commands:

```
log.debug("Exception trace happened here");
log.debug("It was a bad thing");
```

This will most likely not show up as two consecutive lines in the log, but as two lines that are far apart. Instead, you should do something like this:

```
log.debug("Exception trace happened here. It was a bad thing");
```

When dealing with multiple exceptions, some being subclasses of others, you should catch them in order, starting from the most specific. We have seen this in some of the examples in this chapter when, for example, dealing with **NoSuchFileException** and **IOException**. Your code should look like this:

```
try {
    tryAnExceptionCode();
} catch (SpecificException se) {
    doTheCatch1();
} catch (ParentException pe) {
    doTheCatch2();
}
```

If you are not planning to catch the exception at all, but you are still forced to use the try block for the code to compile, use a finally block to close whatever actions were initiated prior to the exception. An example of this is opening a file that should be closed prior to leaving the method, which will happen because of the exception:

```
try {
    tryAnExceptionCode();
} finally {
    closeWhatever();
}
```

The **throw** keyword is a very powerful tool, as you have noticed. Being able to redirect exceptions allows you to create your own strategy for handling different situations and, additionally, it means that you don't have to rely on the strategy provided by default by the JVM. However, you should be careful with placing **throw** in some of the blocks when catching. You should avoid using **throw** inside a **finally** block as it will mask the original reason for the exception.

In a way, this is in line with the "throw early, catch late" principle when dealing with Java exceptions. Imagine that you are doing a low-level operation that is part of a larger method. For example, you are opening a file as part of a piece of code that will parse its contents and look for patterns. If the action of opening the file fails due to an exception, it is a better option to simply **throw** that exception to the following method for it to put in context and be able to decide at a higher level how to proceed with the whole task. You should handle the exceptions only when you can make final decisions at a higher level.

We saw the use of **printStackTrace()** throughout the previous examples as a way to see the full source of an exception. While it is very interesting to be able to see that when debugging some code, it is also almost irrelevant when not being in that mindset. Therefore, you should make sure to either delete or comment away all the **printStackTrace()** commands you might have been using. Other developers will have to determine where they want to put their probes when analyzing the code later if that is ever needed.

In a similar manner, when dealing with exceptions in whatever way inside your methods, you should remember to document things properly in your Javadoc. You should add an **@throws** declaration to clarify what kind of exception arrives and whether it is handled, passed over, or what:

```
/**
 * Method name and description
 *
 * @param input
 * @throws ThisStrangeException when ...
 */
public void myMethod(Integer input) throws ThisStrangeException {
    ...
}
```

Where Do Exceptions Come from?

Moving away from the more-pragmatic approach we have followed in this chapter, it is now time to put things into perspective and understand where things come from in the larger schema of the Java API. Exceptions, as mentioned in a previous section, hang from the **Throwable** class, which is part of the **java.lang** package. They are on the same level as errors (which we explained earlier). In other words, both **Exception** and **Error** are subclasses of **Throwable**.

Only object instances of the **Throwable** class can be thrown by the Java **throw** statement; therefore, the way we had to define our own exception implied using this class as a point of departure. As stated in the Java documentation for the **Throwable** class, this includes a snapshot of the execution stack at the time of creation. This allows you to look for the source of the exception (or the error) because it includes the state of computer memory at that time. A throwable object can contain the reason for which it was constructed. This is what is known as the chained exception facility because one exceptional event might be caused by a certain chain of exceptions. This is something we have seen when analyzing the stack traces in some of the programs in this chapter.

Summary

We have taken a very hands-on approach with this chapter. We started by making your code break in different ways, and then explained the differences between an error and an exception. We focused on ways to handle the latter because those are the only ones that should not make your program crash immediately.

Exceptions can be handled by catching or throwing. The former is done by observing the different exceptions and defining different strategies to respond to the situations by means of a try-catch statement. You have the option of either resending the exception to a different class with the **throw** or responding within the **catch** block. Independently of what strategy you follow, you can set the system to execute some final lines of code after handling the exception using the **finally** block.

This chapter also included a series of recommendations on how to deal with exceptions on a more conceptual level. You have a list of best practices that any professional programmer will follow.

Finally, at the practical level, you worked on a number of exercises that guided you through classic scenarios of dealing with exceptions, and you have seen different tools that you can use to debug your code, such as logs and **printStackTrace()**.

6

Libraries, Packages, and Modules

Overview

This chapter will introduce you to the various ways of packaging and bundling Java code, as well as the tools required to help build your own Java projects. The first step is learning how to organize your code into packages, so that you can build a **Java ARchive (JAR)** file from those packages. From there, you will practice creating an executable JAR file using Java build tools like Maven and Gradle, which will further help you to include third-party open source libraries in your projects. By the end of this chapter, you will be well equipped to create your own Java module to group your packages together.

Introduction

Any sophisticated Java application will require many separate Java classes. Java provides several ways to help you organize your classes; one of which is the concept of packages. You can collect multiple compiled packages together into a Java library, or a **Java ARchive (JAR)** file. Furthermore, you can use modules to provide a higher level of abstraction in your code, exposing only those elements that you consider appropriate.

When you start to create larger applications, you'll want to take advantage of Java's handy build tools—of which Maven and Gradle are the most popular. Build tools make it easier to build large projects that might depend on other projects and libraries. Build tools also provide standard ways to run tests, as well as packaging the project.

Both Maven and Gradle help significantly with the inclusion of third-party open-source libraries in your applications. There are thousands of such libraries available.

Organizing Code into Packages

Java packages together related classes, interfaces, enums (a data type that contains a data type that contains a fixed group of constants), and annotations (contain metadata). In other words, a package is a collection of Java types brought together under a common name. Using a common name makes it easier to find code in larger projects, and helps to keep your code separate from other, perhaps similar, code. For example, more than one package might contain a class named **Rectangle**, so referring to the appropriate package will allow you to specify which **Rectangle** class you're looking for. Packages allow you to organize your code, which becomes more and more important as you work on larger and larger applications.

Java's API includes hundreds of classes divided into packages, such as **java.math** and **java.net**. As you'd expect, **java.math** has mathematics-related classes, and **java.net** has networking-related classes.

Importing Classes

When you use Java classes from packages other than **java.lang**, you need to import them using an **import** statement. The Java compiler imports all classes in the **java.lang** package by default. Everything else is up to you.

Here's an example:

```
import java.time.DayOfWeek;
import java.time.LocalDateTime;
```

This code imports two types from the **java.time** package, **DayOfWeek** and **LocalDateTime**. Now, **DayOfWeek** is a Java **enum** representing days of the week. **LocalDateTime** is a class that holds a date and a time.

Once you import these types, you can use them in your code, as follows:

```
LocalDateTime localDateTime = LocalDateTime.now();
DayOfWeek day = localDateTime.getDayOfWeek();
System.out.println("The week day is: " + day);
```

Exercise 1: Importing Classes

In this exercise, we will display the current day of the week and use the **java.time** package to extract system date and time.

1. In IntelliJ, select **File**, **New**, and then **Project** from the **File** menu.

2. In the **New Project** Dialog, select a Java project. Click **Next**.

3. Check the box to create the project from a template. Click on **Command Line App**. Click **Next**.

4. Name the project **chapter06**.

5. For the project's location, click the button with three dots (...), and then select the source folder you created previously.

6. Enter **com.packtpub.chapter06** as the base package name. We'll do more with packages later in this chapter.

7. Click **Finish**.

   IntelliJ will create a project named **chapter06**, as well as an **src** folder inside **chapter06**. This is where your Java code will reside. Inside this folder, IntelliJ will create subfolders for **com**, **packtpub**, and **chapter06**.

   IntelliJ also creates a class named **Main**:

   ```
   public class Main {
       public static void main(String[] args) {
       // write your code here
       }
   }
   ```

   Rename the class named **Main** to **Example01**.

8. Double-click in the text editor window on the word **Main**.

9. Right-click and select **Refactor | Rename...** from the menu.

10. Enter **Example01** and press *Enter*.

    You will now see the following code:

    ```
    public class Example01 {
        public static void main(String[] args) {
        // write your code here
        }
    }
    ```

    Now enter the following code inside the **main()** method:

    ```
    LocalDateTime localDateTime = LocalDateTime.now();
    DayOfWeek day = localDateTime.getDayOfWeek();
    System.out.println("The weekday is: " + day);
    ```

    IntelliJ should offer the option to import the two types, **DayOfWeek** and **LocalDateTime**. If, for some reason, you click the wrong button, you can add the following lines after the package statement and prior to the definition of the class:

    ```
    package com.packtpub.chapter06;
    import java.time.DayOfWeek;
    import java.time.LocalDateTime;
    public class Example01 {
    ```

11. Now, click on the green arrow just to the left of the text editor window that points to the class name, **Example01**. Select the first menu choice, **Run Example01.main()**.

12. In the **Run** window, you'll see the path to your Java program, and then some output such as this:

    ```
    The weekday is: SATURDAY
    ```

    You should see the current day of the week.

The package statement identifies the package in which this code resides. See the *Creating a Package* section later in this chapter for more information on this topic.

Fully Qualified Class Names

You don't have to use **import** statements. Instead, you can use the fully qualified class name, as shown here:

```
java.time.LocalDateTime localDateTime = java.time.LocalDateTime.now();
```

The fully qualified name includes both the package and the type name. the following example would also give us the same result as the *Exercise 01, Importing Classes*.

```
package com.packtpub.chapter06;
public class Example02 {
    public static void main(String[] args) {
        java.time.LocalDateTime localDateTime = java.time.LocalDateTime.now();
        java.time.DayOfWeek day = localDateTime.getDayOfWeek();
        System.out.println("The weekday is: " + day);
    }
}
```

Usually, importing classes and types makes your code easier to read and requires less typing. In large projects, you will find very long package names. Placing these long names in front of every declaration will make your code much harder to read. Most Java developers will import classes, unless you have two classes with the same name but stored in separate packages.

> **Note**
>
> Most IDEs, such as IntelliJ, can find most classes for you, and will offer to import the class.

Importing All Classes in a Package

You can import all classes in a package using an asterisk, *, to represent all the classes in a package, as follows:

```
import java.time.*;
```

The asterisk is considered a wildcard character and imports all public types from the given package, in this case, **java.time**. The Java compiler will automatically import any types from this package that you use in your code.

> **Note**
>
> Using the wildcard imports may bring in different classes to the ones you intended. Some packages use common class names, such as **Event**, **Duration**, or **Distance**, that may conflict with type names you want to use. So, if you use the wildcard import, you may end up with the wrong class imported. Normally, it is best to import only the types that you require.

Example03.java shows how to use wildcard imports:

```
package com.packtpub.chapter06;
import java.time.*;
public class Example03 {
    public static void main(String[] args) {
        LocalDateTime localDateTime = LocalDateTime.now();
        DayOfWeek day = localDateTime.getDayOfWeek();
        System.out.println("The weekend is: " + day);
    }
}
```

When you run this program, you will see output like the following, depending on the day of the week:

```
The weekday is: MONDAY
```

Dealing with Duplicated Names

If, for some reason, you have to use two different classes with the same name, you'll need to use the fully qualified class names.

When you work with third-party libraries, you may find that there are multiple classes in your project with the same name. **StringUtils**, for example, is defined in multiple packages in multiple libraries. In this case, use the fully qualified class names to disambiguate. Here is an example:

```
boolean notEmpty = org.springframework.util.StringUtils.isNotEmpty(str);
boolean hasLength = org.apache.commons.lang3.StringUtils.hasLength(str);
```

These are two classes with the same basic name, **StringUtils**, that come from different third-party libraries. You will learn more about third-party libraries later on in this chapter.

Static Imports

Many classes define constants, usually defined as **static final** fields. You can use these constants by importing the enclosing class and then referencing them from the class name, as shown in *Chapter 3, Object-Oriented Programming*. For example, Java defines the end of time with the **MAX** constant in the **LocalDateTime** class.

Example04.java shows how to statically import **LocalDateTime.MAX** to see when the universe will end, at least according to the company behind Java:

```
package com.packtpub.chapter06;
import java.time.LocalDateTime;
public class Example04 {
    public static void main(String[] args) {
        System.out.println("The end of time is: " + LocalDateTime.MAX);
    }
}
```

When you run this program, you will see the following output:

```
The end of time is: +999999999-12-31T23:59:59.999999999
```

Creating a Package

As discussed earlier, once you start writing more complex Java programs, you will want to bundle your code together in a package. To create a package, you should observe the following steps:

1. Name your package.

2. Create the appropriate source directory for the package.

3. Create classes and other types, as needed, in the new package.

Naming Your Package

Technically, you can name your Java packages anything you want, so long as you stick to the rules for naming variables and types in Java. Don't use characters that Java will interpret as code. For example, you cannot use a hyphen, -, in a Java package name. The Java compiler will think you are performing subtraction. You cannot use Java's reserved words, such as **class**, either.

Typically, you'll use your organization's domain name in reverse for your package names. For example, if the domain name is **packtpub.com**, then your package names would start with **com.packtpub**. You will almost always want to add descriptive names after the domain part to allow you to organize your code. For example, if you were making a medical application that pulled data from a fitness tracking device, you might create packages such as the following:

- `com.packtpub.medical.heartrate`

- `com.packtpub.medical.tracker`

- `com.packtpub.medical.report`

- `com.packtpub.medical.ui`

Use names that make sense for your organization, as well as for the purpose of the classes in the package.

The reason for using your organization's domain name is, in part, to prevent your Java packages from having the same name as packages in third-party libraries. The domain names are already made unique by domain name registrars. Using the domain names in reverse makes for more understandable names for packages as you delve deeper and deeper into the package tree, such as `com.packtpub.medical.report.daily.exceptions`. Furthermore, this convention helps separate packages from multiple organizations.

> **Note**
>
> The classes provided with Java APIs reside in packages starting with **java** or **javax**. Don't use these names for your packages.

Generally, you'll want to group classes, interfaces, enums, and annotations that are related to the same package.

Directories and Packages

Java makes heavy use of directories to define packages. Every dot in a package name, such as **java.lang**, indicates a sub-folder.

In the IntelliJ project you created for this chapter, you also created a package named **com.packtpub.chapter06**. Using IntelliJ's **Project** pane, you can see the folders created for the package.

1. Click on the gear icon in the **Project** pane.

2. Uncheck the **Compact Middle Packages** option.

3. You will now see a folder for **com.packtpub.chapter06**, as shown in *Figure 6.1*:

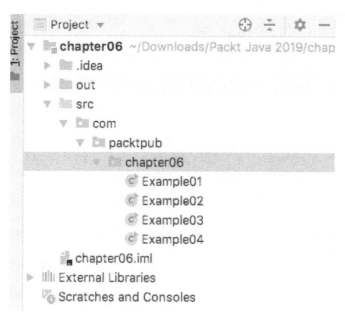

Figure 6.1: IntelliJ's Project pane can show the individual folders that make up a Java package

> **Note**
>
> The folder structure might vary based on the number of examples you have tried out in this chapter.

Normally, you'll want to leave IntelliJ's **Compact Middle Packages** setting on, as it makes the project organization easier to see at a glance.

Exercise 2: Creating a Package for a Fitness Tracking App

We've created a package, **com.packtpub.chapter06**, that acts as a catch-all for examples in this chapter. In this exercise, we'll create another package to gather together a related set of classes.

When creating an application that interacts with a fitness tracker, you want a package for classes that relate to tracking daily steps. Users will define a goal for the number of steps they want to take in a day, say 10,000. The tracker will record the number of steps taken so far, along with a collection of the daily totals:

1. In the IntelliJ Project pane for the **chapter06** project created previously, click the gear icon. Make sure **Flatten Packages** and **Hide Empty Middle Packages** are both selected.

2. Remain in the **Project** pane, and right-click on the **src** folder. Select **New**, and then **Package**. Enter the **com.packtpub.steps** package name, and then click **OK**. This is our new package.

3. Right-click on the **com.packtpub.steps** package, select **New**, and then select **Java Class**. Enter the **Steps** class name.

4. Enter the following field definitions:

```
private int steps;
private LocalDate date;
```

5. Allow IntelliJ to import **java.time.LocalDate**, or simply enter the following code after the package statement and before the definition of the class:

```
package com.packtpub.steps;
import java.time.LocalDate;
/**
 * Holds steps taken (so far) in a day.
 */
public class Steps {
    private int steps;
    private LocalDate date;
}
```

6. Right-click within the class definition. Choose **Generate…** from the menu. Then, select **Constructor**. Select both **steps** and the **date**, and then click **OK**.

   You'll see a brand-new constructor, as follows:

```
public Steps(int steps, LocalDate date) {
    this.steps = steps;
    this.date = date;
}
```

7. Right-click within the class definition again. Choose **Generate…**, and then select **Getter and Setter**. Select both **steps** and the **date**, and then click **OK**. You'll now see the getter and setter methods:

```
public int getSteps() {
    return steps;
}
public void setSteps(int steps) {
```

```
        this.steps = steps;
    }
    public LocalDate getDate() {
        return date;
    }
    public void setDate(LocalDate date) {
        this.date = date;
    }
```

We now have our first class in the new package. Next, we'll create another class.

8. Right-click on the `com.packtpub.steps` package in the **Project** pane, select **New**, and then select **Java Class**. Enter the `DailyGoal` class name.

9. Enter the following field definition:

    ```
    int dailyGoal = 10000;
    ```

    Note that we default the daily steps goal to 10,000 steps.

10. Right-click within the class definition. Choose **Generate…** from the menu. Then, select **Constructor**, followed by **dailyGoal**, and then click **OK**.

11. Define the following method, which is used to determine whether a **Steps** object has achieved the daily goal:

    ```
    public boolean hasMetGoal(Steps steps) {
        if (steps.getSteps() >= dailyGoal) {
            return true;
        }
        return false;
    }
    ```

12. Right-click on the `com.packtpub.steps` package in the **Project** pane, select **New**, and then select **Java Class**. Enter the `WeeklySteps` class name.

13. Enter the following fields:

    ```
    List<Steps> dailySteps = new ArrayList<>();
    DailyGoal dailyGoal;
    ```

    You will need to import `java.util.List` and `java.util.ArrayList`.

14. Right-click within the class definition again. Choose **Generate…**, and then select **Getter and Setter**. Select both **dailySteps** and **dailyGoal**, and then click **OK**. You'll now see the getter and setter methods.

To use this new class, we'll add some methods to determine the best day (the day with the greatest number of steps), total the steps, and format the output.

15. Enter the following method to determine the best day for steps:

```
public DayOfWeek bestDay() {
    DayOfWeek best = DayOfWeek.MONDAY;
    int max = 0;
    for (Steps steps : dailySteps) {
        if (steps.getSteps() > max) {
            max = steps.getSteps();
            best = steps.getDate().getDayOfWeek();
        }
    }
    return best;
}
```

16. Now, enter the following method to total the weekly number of steps:

```
public int getTotalSteps() {
    int total = 0;
    for (Steps steps : dailySteps) {
        total += steps.getSteps();
    }
    return total;
}
```

Note that both methods iterate over **dailySteps**. These two methods could be combined into one.

In a real fitness tracking application, you would probably have a smartphone or a web user interface. For this example, though, we'll simply generate a string of the results of the weekly steps.

17. Enter the following method:

WeeklySteps.java

```
36 public String format() {
37
38     StringBuilder builder = new StringBuilder();
39
40     builder.append("Total steps: " + getTotalSteps() + "\n");
41
42     for (Steps steps : dailySteps) {
43         if (dailyGoal.hasMetGoal(steps)) {
44             builder.append("YAY! ");
45         } else {
46             builder.append("      ");
47         }
```

https://packt.live/2quq4uh

This method uses **StringBuilder** and **DayOfWeek**, both part of the Java API. An encouraging message, **YAY!**, appears with each day the user met the step goal. The best day also gets an uplifting message.

18. To help initialize the weekly step data, we'll create a convenience method (a method that exists to simplify our code and reduce typing):

```
public void addDailySteps(int steps, LocalDate date) {
    dailySteps.add(new Steps(steps, date));
}
```

19. To test the entire step-tracking package, we'll create a **main()** method that shows how everything fits together:

WeeklySteps.java

```
84 public static void main(String[] args) {
85     // Initialize sample data.
86     DailyGoal dailyGoal = new DailyGoal(10000);
87
88     WeeklySteps weekly = new WeeklySteps();
89     weekly.setDailyGoal(dailyGoal);
90
91     int year = 2021;
92     int month = 1;
93     int day = 4;
```

https://packt.live/2pB8nIG

Normally, you would put this type of code into a unit test, which is a special code designed to make sure your classes and algorithms are correct. Refer to *Chapter 18, Unit Testing*, for more information on unit testing.

20. Click on the green arrow just to the left of the text editor window that points to the **WeeklySteps** class name. Select the first menu choice, **Run 'WeeklySteps.main()'**.

You'll see output along the lines of the following, for a week of fitness data (in the year 2021):

```
Total steps: 92772
YAY! MONDAY 11543
YAY! TUESDAY 12112
YAY! WEDNESDAY 10005
YAY! THURSDAY 10011
     FRIDAY 9000
YAY! SATURDAY 20053 ***** BEST DAY!
YAY! SUNDAY 20048
```

Now that you have an idea of the basics of Java code organization, we will look into a special kind of file known as the Java Archive.

Building JAR Files

A JAR file, short for Java Archive, holds multiple files and provides a platform-neutral way to distribute Java code. For a Java library, a JAR file will contain the compiled .class files, and perhaps additional files, such as the configuration data, certificates, and image files, called resources, that are required by the library. Specialized versions of JAR files are used to package and deploy server-side Java applications.

A **WAR** file, short for **web archive**, contains the compiled Java code and resources for a web application. An **EAR** file, short for **enterprise archive**, contains the compiled Java code and resources for a full server-side **Java Enterprise Edition (JavaEE)** application. Under the hood, a JAR file is a compressed ZIP file.

To build a JAR file, we can use the following command:

```
jar cvf jar_file_name files_to_put_in
```

The **c** option tells the **jar** command to create a new JAR file. The **f** option specifies the filename of the new JAR file. This filename should appear immediately after the options. Finally, you list all the files to place in the JAR file, typically, .**class** files.

> **Note**
>
> The **v** option (part of **cvf**) stands for verbose; that is, it is optional, and tells the JAR tool to output verbose output while it works.

Exercise 3: Building a JAR File

In this exercise, we'll compile the Java code for the **com.packtpub.steps** package and then build a JAR file:

1. In the Terminal pane in IntelliJ, run the following commands:

```
cd src
javac com/packtpub/steps/*.java
```

The **javac** command created **.class** files in the **com/packtpub/steps** folder.

2. Next, create a JAR file with the following command:

```
jar cvf chapter6.jar   com/packtpub/steps/*.class
```

This command will generate output because we are using the verbose option:

```
added manifest
adding: com/packtpub/steps/DailyGoal.class(in = 464) (out= 321)(deflated 30%)
adding: com/packtpub/steps/Steps.class(in = 622) (out= 355)(deflated 42%)
adding: com/packtpub/steps/WeeklySteps.class(in = 3465) (out= 1712)(deflated 50%)
```

You'll then see the new JAR file, **chapter6.jar**, in the current directory. By convention, use the **.jar** filename extension for JAR files.

> **Note**
>
> The name jar, and the command-line syntax, are based on a much earlier UNIX and Linux tool called **tar**.

Like with all compressed files, we will have to decompress the JAR files too, before we start using them. To extract all the files from a JAR file, use the **jar xvf** command:

```
jar xvf chapter6.jar
```

In this case, **chapter6.jar** is the name of the JAR file.

> **Note**
>
> The JAR command-line options are treated in order. In this case, the **f** option requires a filename parameter. If you add another option that also requires a parameter (such as **e**, mentioned later in *Exercise 04, Building an Executable JAR File*), then the filename needs to come before that additional parameter.

To see what is inside a JAR file, use the **jar tf** command. In this case, you can see inside your new JAR file by running the following command from the Terminal pane:

```
jar tf chapter6.jar
```

You will see a listing of the files in the JAR file as the output:

```
META-INF/
META-INF/MANIFEST.MF
com/packtpub/steps/DailyGoal.class
com/packtpub/steps/Steps.class
com/packtpub/steps/WeeklySteps.class
```

Notice how the **jar** command created a folder named **META-INF** and a file named **MANIFEST.MF** in that folder.

By default, the **jar** command will create a **MANIFEST.MF** file with the following content:

```
Manifest-Version: 1.0
Created-By: 11.0.2 (Oracle Corporation)
```

The file lists a version number, and the version of Java created that file—in this case, Java 11 from Oracle.

Defining the Manifest

The **MANIFEST.MF** file is used to provide information to Java tools regarding the content of the JAR file. You can add versioning information, electronically sign the JAR file, and so on. Probably the most useful thing to add to a JAR file's manifest is to identify the **main** class. This option names the class with a **main()** method that you would want to run from the JAR file. In essence, this creates an executable JAR file.

An executable JAR file allows you to run the Java application inside the JAR file with a command such as this:

```
java -jar chapter6.jar
```

To do this, you need to create an entry in the **MANIFEST.MF** file that defines the main class. For example, for the **WeeklySteps** Java class, you'd create an entry in the **MANIFEST. MF** file with the following:

```
Main-Class: com.packtpub.steps.WeeklySteps
```

Exercise 4: Building an Executable JAR File

In this exercise, we'll add a Main-Class entry to the **MANIFEST.MF** file inside a JAR file:

1. Recreate the JAR file with the following command (all on one line):

```
jar cvfe chapter6.jar com.packtpub.steps.WeeklySteps com/packtpub/steps/*.class
```

The **e** option defines an entry point, in other words, the Main-Class header. Since the JAR command-line options are dealt with in a sequential order, this means that you provide the JAR filename first, and then the name of the main class (the entry point). These options can easily be mixed up.

With this **jar** command, you'll see output like the following:

```
added manifest
adding: com/packtpub/steps/DailyGoal.class(in = 464) (out= 321)(deflated 30%)
adding: com/packtpub/steps/Steps.class(in = 622) (out= 355)(deflated 42%)
adding: com/packtpub/steps/WeeklySteps.class(in = 251) (out= 185)(deflated 26%)
```

2. Now we can run our Java application from the JAR file:

```
java -jar chapter6.jar
```

This command should generate the output shown in *Exercise 02, Creating a Package for a Fitness Tracking App*:

```
Total steps: 92772
YAY! MONDAY 11543
YAY! TUESDAY 12112
YAY! WEDNESDAY 10005
YAY! THURSDAY 10011
     FRIDAY 9000
YAY! SATURDAY 20053 ***** BEST DAY!
YAY! SUNDAY 20048
```

> **Note**
>
> You can find out more about the jar command, as well as the other Java tools, at https://packt.live/2MYsN6N.

Manually building a JAR file when you have a single package isn't that difficult. When you start to add more and more packages though, manually building JAR files and manipulating the contents becomes quite cumbersome. There are much easier ways to do this—most notably, by using a Java build tool that can aid in making JAR files.

Build Tools

As applications become more and more complex, you'll find it essential to use a Java build tool. Build tools allow you to do the following:

- Build Java applications that span multiple packages.

- Make your builds easier to run and maintain.

- Make your builds consistent.

- Create a library or multiple libraries from your code.

- Download and include third-party libraries in your applications.

These items just scratch the surface of what Java build tools can do for you.

The two main Java build tools are as follows:

- **Maven**, which issues XML configuration files

- **Gradle**, which uses a Groovy-based, domain-specific language for configuration

> **Note**
>
> Refer to https://packt.live/33Iqprj for more on Maven, and https://packt.live/35PNREO for more on Gradle.

Maven

Maven has very specific ideas about how your software projects should be structured. For example, Maven expects your source code to go into a folder named **src**. In general, it is best not to fight Maven's expectations.

> **Note**
>
> Refer to https://packt.live/2nVNI1A for more on Maven's expectations about the directory structure for your projects.

Exercise 5: Creating a Maven Project

IntelliJ provides some very handy features when working with Maven. We'll now use those features to create a Maven project:

1. In IntelliJ, go to the **File** menu, select **New**, and then **Project…**.

2. In the **New Project** dialog, select **Maven**. Then, click **Next**, as shown in *Figure 6.2*:

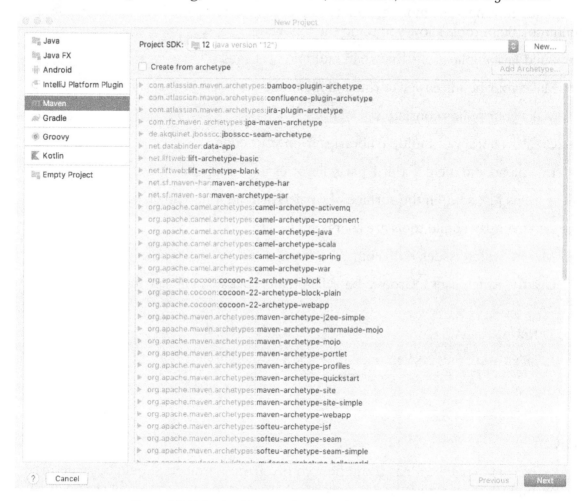

Figure 6.2: Selecting Maven when creating a Maven project

On the next screen, you'll need to enter three values, as shown in *Figure* 6.3:

Figure 6.3: Entering GroupId, ArtifactId, and Version

3. For **GroupId**, enter **com.packtpub.steps**.

   GroupId in Maven identifies the overall project. Normally, you'll use the main package name for your work as **GroupId**.

4. For **ArtifactId**, enter steps.

   ArtifactId is the name you want for any JAR file you create, without the version number. Maven will add the version information for you.

5. Leave the **Version** as **1.0-SNAPSHOT**.

   > **Note**
   >
   > In Maven, SNAPSHOT versions represent work in progress. When you come to make a release, you'll normally remove the SNAPSHOT portion of the version information.

6. Click **Next**.

7. On the next screen, it will default the IntelliJ project name to steps (from **ArtifactId**). Select a project location on disk and then click **Finish**.

You now have a Maven project.

In the **Project** pane, note the directory structure created. You will find an **src** folder. This holds the project source code. Under **src**, you'll see folders called **main** and **test**. The **main** folder is where your Java source code resides. The **test** folder is where your unit tests reside. Unit tests are Java classes that test the main code.

> **Note**
>
> Refer to *Chapter 18, Unit Testing*, for more information on unit tests.

In both the main and test folders, you'll see folders named **java**. This indicates Java source code (as opposed to Groovy or Kotlin code, for example).

Figure 6.4 shows the directory structure with the **src/main/java** and **src/test/java** folders:

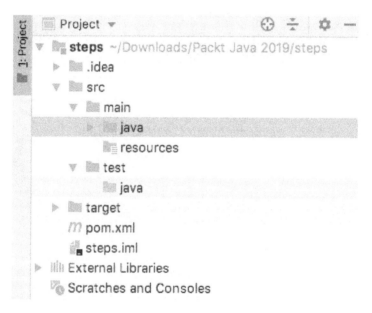

Figure 6.4: The src/main/java and src/test/java folders for a Maven project

When Maven builds your project, compiling the code and building JAR files, it incorporates the output of the build in a folder named target.

You'll also see a file named **pom.xml**. Short for **Project Object Model**, **POM** provides Maven's configuration, which tells Maven what you want to build and how to do it.

The default POM created by IntelliJ, **pom.xml**, has the following content:

```xml
<?xml version="1.0" encoding="UTF-8"?>
<project xmlns="http://maven.apache.org/POM/4.0.0"
    xmlns:xsi="http://www.w3.org/2001/XMLSchema-instance"
    xsi:schemaLocation="http://maven.apache.org/POM/4.0.0
      http://maven.apache.org/xsd/maven-4.0.0.xsd">
    <modelVersion>4.0.0</modelVersion>
    <groupId>com.packtpub.steps</groupId>
    <artifactId>steps</artifactId>
    <version>1.0-SNAPSHOT</version>
</project>
```

You should see **groupId**, **artifactId**, and the version information you entered when creating the project in IntelliJ.

Exercise 6: Adding Java Sources to the Maven Project

We'll now add the Java source to the Maven project as follows:

1. Start by going to the **src/main/java** folder.

2. Right-click, select **New**, and then select **Package**.

3. Enter **com.packtpub.steps** as the package name.

4. Next, bring in the three source files from **Exercise 02**. You can copy the files from before.

5. Copy **Steps.java**, **DailyGoal.java**, and **WeeklySteps.java** into this project.

   Now, let's have a look at the three files. First, here's **Steps.java**:

Steps.java

```
1   package com.packtpub.steps;
2
3   import java.time.LocalDate;
4
5   /**
6    * Holds steps taken (so far) in a day.
7    */
8   public class Steps {
9       private int steps;
10      private LocalDate date;
```

https://packt.live/2MVxFJO

Here is **DailyGoal.java**:

```
package com.packtpub.steps;
public class DailyGoal {
    int dailyGoal = 10000;
    public DailyGoal(int dailyGoal) {
        this.dailyGoal = dailyGoal;
    }
    public boolean hasMetGoal(Steps steps) {
        if (steps.getSteps() >= dailyGoal) {
            return true;
        }
        return false;
    }
}
```

And here is **WeeklySteps.java**:

WeeklySteps.java

```
1   package com.packtpub.steps;
2
3   import java.time.DayOfWeek;
4   import java.time.LocalDate;
5   import java.util.ArrayList;
6   import java.util.List;
7
8   public class WeeklySteps {
9       List<Steps> dailySteps = new ArrayList<>();
10      DailyGoal dailyGoal;
```

https://packt.live/32wiz3Q

6. Call up **Steps.java** in the IntelliJ editor window.

   You'll notice that a number of errors appear in the project. This is because Maven does not default to using Java 12. The next step fixes this.

7. Call up **pom.xml** in the IntelliJ editor window.

8. Enter the following after **groupId**, **artifactId**, and **version**:

```
<groupId>com.packtpub.steps</groupId>
<artifactId>steps</artifactId>
<version>1.0-SNAPSHOT</version>
<build>
    <plugins>
        <plugin>
            <groupId>org.apache.maven.plugins</groupId>
            <artifactId>maven-compiler-plugin</artifactId>
            <version>3.6.1</version>
            <configuration>
                <source>12</source>
                <target>12</target>
            </configuration>
        </plugin>
    </plugins>
</build>
```

As you enter this configuration, notice how IntelliJ offers to help you type in the XML elements.

9. When you finish, IntelliJ will display an alert that Maven projects need to be imported. Click on **Import Changes**.

The red error lines for **Steps** and **WeeklySteps** should disappear.

You should now be able to build your project. This is covered in *Exercise 07, Building the Maven Project.*

Exercise 7: Building the Maven Project

Now that we have added the Java sources, we will build the Maven project.

1. First, go to the **steps** project, and then click on the **Maven** tab near the top-right corner of the IntelliJ window.

2. Expand the **steps** project.

3. Expand **Lifecycle**.

You will now see a list of Maven goals, as shown in *Figure 6.5*:

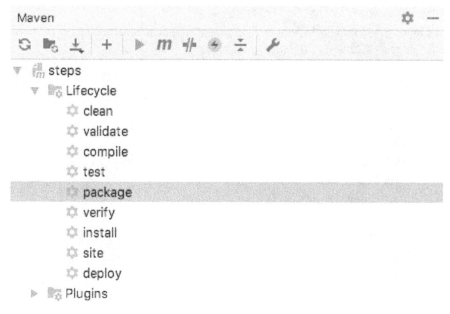

Figure 6.5: IntelliJ's Maven pane

4. Double-click on package. In the **Run** pane, you will see a lot of output. Maven is a very verbose tool by default. The project is now built.

5. Look in the target directory. You will see the output of the build.

Maven creates a JAR file named steps-`1.0-SNAPSHOT.jar`. This holds all the compiled `.class` files.

The Maven-created JAR file is not an executable JAR, though. *Exercise 08, Creating an Executable JAR with Maven* will show you how to configure Maven to create an executable JAR.

Exercise 8: Creating an Executable JAR with Maven

In this exercise, we will create an executable JAR with Maven.

1. In the **Steps** project, call up **pom.xml** in the IntelliJ editor window.

2. Enter the following after the **\<plugin\>** section for the Maven compiler plugin:

pom.xml

```
24 <plugin>
25     <groupId>org.apache.maven.plugins</groupId>
26     <artifactId>maven-shade-plugin</artifactId>
27     <executions>
28         <execution>
29             <goals>
30                 <goal>shade</goal>
31             </goals>
32             <configuration>
33                 <transformers>
34                     <transformer implementation=
35                         "org.apache.maven.plugins.shade.resource.ManifestResourceTransformer">
```

https://packt.live/33KFUPs

This configuration brings in the Maven shade plugin, which provides one of the main ways to create an executable JAR. The shade plugin will also create a JAR with all the necessary dependencies, such as third-party libraries, which makes this Maven plugin pretty handy.

3. Run the package goal in the **Maven** pane.

    You will see a lot more output.

4. Switch to the **Terminal** pane.

5. Change to the **target** directory:

    ```
    cd target
    ```

6. Run the executable JAR:

    ```
    java -jar steps-1.0-SNAPSHOT.jar
    ```

    You will see output such as the following:

    ```
    Total steps: 92772
    YAY! MONDAY 11543
    YAY! TUESDAY 12112
    YAY! WEDNESDAY 10005
    YAY! THURSDAY 10011
        FRIDAY 9000
    YAY! SATURDAY 20053 ***** BEST DAY!
    YAY! SUNDAY 20048
    ```

There is a lot more to Maven. This exercise has just touched the surface of this build tool.

> **Note**
>
> Refer to https://packt.live/33lqprj for a number of tutorials on Maven.

Using Gradle

While Maven can do a lot for you, it is often inflexible and confusing, especially for larger projects. Trying to solve those problems led to the creation of Gradle. For example, in Maven, each POM file builds one thing, such as a JAR file. With Gradle, you can perform additional tasks with the same build file (Gradle's equivalent of a POM file).

Gradle is a lot more flexible than Maven, and generally–but not always–easier to understand.

Exercise 9: Creating a Gradle Project

In this exercise, we will create a Gradle project.

1. First, go to IntelliJ, and, in the **File** menu, select **New** and then **Project**.

2. Select **Gradle** and, in the right-hand pane, leave Java checked, as shown in *Figure 6.6*:

Figure 6.6: Selecting Gradle when creating a new project

3. Click **Next**. Enter **GroupId**, **ArtifactId**, and **Version**, much like you did for the Maven project, as shown in *Figure 6.7*:

Figure 6.7: Entering GroupId, ArtifactId, and Version

4. Enter **com.packtpub.steps** for **GroupId**.

5. Enter **steps-gradle** for **ArtifactId**.

6. Leave the version information at **1.0-SNAPSHOT**.

    Note that Gradle uses the same mechanism as Maven for identifying dependencies.

7. Click **Next**.

8. Leave all the default options. Create a separate module for each source set, and use the default gradle wrapper.

9. Click **Next**.

10. On the next screen, it will default the IntelliJ project name to steps-gradle (from **ArtifactId**). Select a project location on disk and then click **Finish**.

    IntelliJ will build things for a bit, and then you can look at the new project directory.

IntelliJ creates Gradle projects along very similar lines to Maven projects. You will see the same **main** and **test** folders inside **src**, for example.

You'll also see two new files:

- **build.gradle** provides the main configuration file for Gradle.

- **settings.gradle** contains some additional settings.

The **build.gradle** file generated by IntelliJ holds the following configuration:

```
plugins {
    id 'java'
}
group 'com.packtpub.steps'
version '1.0-SNAPSHOT'
sourceCompatibility = 1.8
repositories {
    mavenCentral()
}
dependencies {
    testCompile group: 'junit', name: 'junit', version: '4.12'
}
```

Exercise 10: Building an Executable JAR with Gradle

In this exercise, we'll add the same three Java classes as used in the Maven example, and then configure the **build.gradle** file to create an executable JAR file. We'll work in the **steps-gradle** project created in the previous exercise.

1. In the **steps-gradle** project, go to the **src/main/java** folder.

2. Right-click, and select **New** and then **Package**.

3. Enter **com.packtpub.steps** as the package name.

4. Next, bring in the three source files from **Exercise 02**. You can copy the files from before.

5. Call up the **build.gradle** file in the IntelliJ text editor.

6. Set **sourceCompatibility** to 12:

```
sourceCompatibility = 12
```

7. Add the following section at the end of the **build.gradle** file:

```
jar {
    manifest {
        attributes 'Main-Class': 'com.packtpub.steps.WeeklySteps'
    }
}
```

8. Click on the **Gradle** tab near the top-right corner of the IntelliJ window.

9. Expand the **steps-gradle** project, then **Tasks**, and then **build**.

10. Double-click on **ASSEMBLE** to build the project.

You'll see that Gradle outputs much less text than Maven. When it's done, you'll see a build directory. This is similar to the target directory used by Maven. The Java **.class** files and JAR files are placed in the build directory.

11. Switch to the **Terminal** pane.

12. Change to the **build/libs** directory:

```
cd build
cd libs
```

13. Run the executable JAR:

```
java -jar steps-gradle-1.0-SNAPSHOT.jar
```

You should see the same output as before.

As with Maven, there are a lot more things you can do with Gradle.

> **Note**
>
> You can read more about Gradle at https://packt.live/2P3Hjg2. You can find more on how Gradle handles Java projects at https://packt.live/2Mv5CBZ.

Using Third-Party Libraries

One of the best things about developing with Java is the thousands of open source third-party libraries available. A third-party library is a group of ready-made packages that you can use in your own programs. This means you can implement specific functionality without having to code it from scratch.

Everything from the Spring Boot framework to logging libraries and simple utilities can be found online. And, to make things easier, both the Maven and Gradle build tools support the downloading of third-party libraries and the incorporation of these libraries into your project.

Finding the Libraries

There is a huge set of third-party libraries available for Java. To see a description of some, a good starting point is https://packt.live/2qnRAcx, which lists many Java libraries and frameworks.

The `Spring`, `Hibernate`, `Apache`, `Eclipse`, and `BouncyCastle` projects provide a huge number of libraries. They can all be found at the link mentioned previously, and are good places to search for whatever functionality you're looking for.

Before selecting an open source library, you will want to take a look at the following topics:

- **Documentation** – Good documentation not only helps you learn how to use the library, but acts as a good indicator for the maturity of the library. Can you understand how to use the library? If not, this library is probably not for you.

- **Community** – An active community shows that the library is being used. It also provides a glimpse into how the library's maintainers treat people who ask questions. Look for mailing lists and discussion groups about the library.

- **Momentum** – Check to see how often the library gets updates. You'll want to choose libraries that are under active development.

- **Does it work for you**? – Always try each library to see that it actually works for your project and that you can understand how to use the library.

- **License** – Can you legally use this library? Make sure first. Refer to https://packt.live/2MTZfqD for a listing of the most common open source licenses. Read the license and see whether this will work for your organization. If the license looks too weird or restrictive, avoid the library.

> **Note**
>
> Always look at the license for any open source library to make sure your organization can legally use the library in the manner you want to use it.

Once you find a library that looks promising, the next step is to import the library into your application.

Adding a Project Dependency

A third-party library that you include in your project is called a dependency. Think of this as meaning your project now depends on this library. Both Maven and Gradle identify dependencies similarly. You'll need the following:

- GroupId

- ArtifactId

- Version information

- A repository where the build tool can download the library

The most commonly used third-party open source libraries can be downloaded from a large repository called `Maven Central`, located at https://packt.live/2pvXmZs.

You can search for the group, artifact, and version information on a handy site located at https://packt.live/33UlfZF.

A good, useful open source library is `Apache Commons Lang`, which contains handy classes for working with strings and numbers.

Exercise 11: Adding a Third-Party Library Dependency

In this exercise, we'll add the Apache Commons Lang library to the Gradle project created in *Exercises 09 and 10* previously. In these exercises, we'll add just one to simplify the entire setup.

In large, complex projects, you will often see a lot of dependencies. The concepts used here apply when you start adding more dependencies:

1. Search on https://packt.live/33UlfZF for Apache Commons Lang. You should find the page on this library at https://packt.live/33JnQ8n.

2. Look for the latest released version. At the time of writing, the version is 3.8.1.

   Notice how many releases there are. This library seems to be under active development.

3. Click on the **3.8.1** link.

4. Look at the license information. The Apache license is compatible with most organizations.

   On this page, you will see a set of tabs for different Java build tools, with the Maven tab selected by default. Inside the tab, you'll see the group, artifact, and version information in the format used in a Maven POM file.

5. Click on the **Gradle** tab to see the same information formatted for Gradle, as shown in *Figure 6.8*:

Figure 6.8: Using the Gradle tab to see the Gradle dependency information

6. Copy this text and add it to the dependencies block in your **build.gradle** file.

7. Change the word *compile* to *implementation*:

```
implementation group: 'org.apache.commons', name: 'commons-lang3', version: '3.8.1'
```

The compile dependency in Gradle is replaced by the implementation dependency in more recent versions of Gradle.

8. In the IntelliJ alert that states that Gradle projects need to be imported, click **Import Changes.**

   We now have the library in the project. We next need to do two things. First, we need to configure Gradle to build an executable JAR with all the dependencies. Second, we need to use the new dependency—the new library—in our code.

   The next step is to add the Gradle shadow plugin to the project. This plugin combines your code in a project (along with any third-party libraries and other dependencies) into a single JAR file that holds everything needed.

   > **Note**
   >
   > You can find more information on the Gradle shadow plugin at https://packt. live/33Irb7H and https://packt.live/31qGIYs.

9. Call up **build.gradle** in the IntelliJ text editor.

10. Replace the **plugins** block with the following:

```
buildscript {
    repositories {
        jcenter()
    }
    dependencies {
        classpath 'com.github.jengelman.gradle.plugins:shadow:2.0.1'
    }
}
apply plugin: 'java'
apply plugin: 'com.github.johnrengelman.shadow'
```

   This tells Gradle to bring the shadow plugin into our project.

11. Go to the Gradle pane in IntelliJ. Click the **Refresh** icon (the two circular arrows).

12. Expand the new shadow tasks.

13. Double-click on **shadowJar**.

   This will build a new JAR file, **steps-gradle-1.0-SNAPSHOT-all.jar**, that contains the project code, along with all the dependencies. Notice that the format is artifact Id – version – **all.jar**.

14. Switch to the **Terminal** pane.

15. Enter the following commands:

```
cd build
cd libs
java -jar steps-gradle-1.0-SNAPSHOT-all.jar
```

You will then see the output of the **Steps** application.

In this exercise, we have added a third-party dependency library. Next, we'll use the new library in the application.

Using the Apache Commons Lang Library

When using a new library, it is usually good to start with a look at the documentation. For a Java utility library, Javadoc is a good first place to start.

For the Apache Commons Lang library, you can find the Javadoc at https://packt. live/32wkrJR. Open the first package, **org.apache.commons.lang3**.

In this package, you'll find a really handy set of utility classes, including the excellent **StringUtils** class. **StringUtils** provides a number of methods for working with strings. And, better yet, the methods are null safe, so if you pass in a null string, your code won't throw an exception.

Open the **StringUtils** Javadoc. You will see a lot of good documentation relating to this class.

Exercise 12: Using the Apache Commons Lang Library

In this exercise, we'll use two methods of the handy **StringUtils** class, **leftPad()** and **rightPad()**. These methods ensure that a string has a certain length by padding space characters on the left or right.

We'll use these methods to make the **Steps** application output look a bit better:

1. In IntelliJ, call up the **WeeklySteps** class into the text editor.

2. Scroll down to the **format()** method.

3. Replace that method with the following code:

```
public String format() {
    StringBuilder builder = new StringBuilder();
    builder.append("Total steps: " + getTotalSteps() + "\n");
    for (Steps steps : dailySteps) {
        if (dailyGoal.hasMetGoal(steps)) {
            builder.append("YAY! ");
```

```
        } else {
            builder.append("        ");
        }
        String day = steps.getDate().getDayOfWeek().toString();
        builder.append( StringUtils.rightPad(day, 11) );
        builder.append(" ");
        String stp = Integer.toString(steps.getSteps());
        builder.append( StringUtils.leftPad( stp, 6 ) );
        DayOfWeek best = bestDay();
        if (steps.getDate().getDayOfWeek() == best) {
            builder.append(" ***** BEST DAY!");
        }
        builder.append("\n");
    }
    return builder.toString();
}
```

This code pads out the days of the week to a consistent length. It does the same to the daily steps count.

4. Run the **shadowJar** build task again from the Gradle pane.

5. In the Terminal pane, in the **build/libs** directory, run the following command:

```
java -jar steps-gradle-1.0-SNAPSHOT-all.jar
```

You will see output that is now better aligned:

```
Total steps: 92772
YAY! MONDAY        11543
YAY! TUESDAY       12112
YAY! WEDNESDAY     10005
YAY! THURSDAY      10011
     FRIDAY         9000
YAY! SATURDAY      20053 ***** BEST DAY!
YAY! SUNDAY        20048
```

Just about every Java project you work on will require more than one dependency.

Using Modules

Java packages allow you to gather together related classes (and other types). You can then bundle a number of packages into a JAR file, creating a library you can use.

Modules go a step further and allow you encapsulate your libraries efficiently. This means you can declare which of a module's public classes (and other types) can be accessed outside the module.

> **Note**
>
> Java version 9 and higher supports modules called the **Java Platform Module System**, or **JPMS**.

In addition, modules can declare explicit dependencies on other modules. This helps clean up the mess of Java classpaths. Instead of searching the classpath for classes, a module will search directly for a named dependent module. This really helps when you bring in a lot of dependencies. With a large Java application, some libraries may depend on different versions of the same libraries, causing all sorts of problems. Instead, each module allows you to isolate its dependencies from the rest of the application.

Modules look in what is called a module path. The module path just lists modules, not classes.

Within a module, packages in a module can be exported. If a package in a module is not exported, then no other module can use that package.

A module that wants to use code from another module must indicate that it requires the other module. Inside a module, your code can only make use of packages that are exported in the dependent module.

> **Note**
>
> When you start using modules, you'll want to convert each Java library you create into one or more modules. You can only have one module per JAR file.

> **Note**
>
> The original project that created Java's module system was called PROJECT JIGSAW. Refer to https://packt.live/32yH1le for more on modules. A big part of the effort was to add modules to the **Java Development Kit**, or **JDK**. This allows you to create smaller JDKs aimed at mobile platforms, for example.

To see all the modules that make up the JDK, use the java command.

From the IntelliJ Terminal pane, run the following command:

```
java --list-modules
```

You will see a lot of modules in the output (shortened here):

```
java.base@11.0.2
java.compiler@11.0.2
java.datatransfer@11.0.2
java.desktop@11.0.2
java.instrument@11.0.2
java.logging@11.0.2
java.management@11.0.2
java.management.rmi@11.0.2
java.naming@11.0.2
java.net.http@11.0.2
...
jdk.hotspot.agent@11.0.2
jdk.httpserver@11.0.2
jdk.internal.ed@11.0.2
```

The modules with names starting with java are classes that we consider part of the JDK, that is, classes you can use in your Java code. Modules with names starting with jdk are modules that are required internally by the JDK. You should not use those classes.

Creating Modules

A module groups together a set of Java packages and additional resources (files). Each module requires a **module-info.java** file, which specifies what the module exports as well as what other modules are required.

Exercise 13: Creating a Project for a Module

In this exercise, we'll create an IntelliJ project that we can use to explore Java modules and then create a Java module inside the project:

1. From the **File** menu, select **New** and then **Project...**.

2. Select a **Java** project and click **Next**, as shown in *Figure 6.9*:

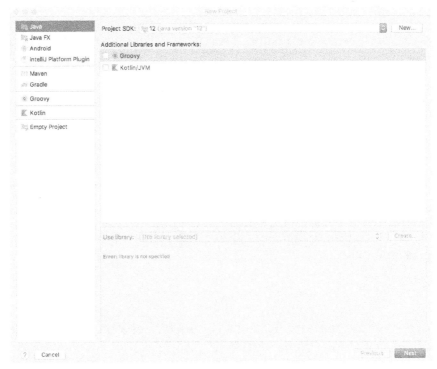

Figure 6.9: Selecting a Java project

3. Do not specify a project template. Click **Next**, as shown in *Figure 6.10*:

Figure 6.10: Do not select a project template

4. Name the project modules.

5. Click **Finish**. You now have an empty Java project. The next step will be to create a very simple module.

6. From the **File** menu, select **New** and then **Module…**.

7. Make sure Java is selected. Click **Next**.

8. Enter `com.packtpub.day.module` for the module name. Make sure that the content root and the file location both show `com.packtpub.day.module` under the modules folder.

9. Click **Finish**. You now have a module.

   It can be confusing at first that the module name, `com.packtpub.day.module`, gets created as a single directory.

   > **Note**
   >
   > Normally, with packages, each dot in the name indicates a separate subfolder. With modules, you get a folder name with dots.

   IntelliJ has created a folder named `com.packtpub.day`.module in the project, and also an **src** folder under `com.packtpub.day.module`.

10. Right-click on the **src** folder under `com.packtpub.day` module.

11. Select **New** and then **Package**.

12. Enter `com.packtpub.day` as the name of the package.

13. Right-click on the new package, `com.packtpub.day`, select **New**, and then **Java class**. Name the class **Today**.

14. In the text editor window, add a method to the new class:

```
public String getToday() {
    return LocalDate.now().getDayOfWeek().toString();
}
```

This method returns the day of the week for the current day as a string.

15. Right-click on the package `com.packtpub.day`, select **New**, and then select `module-info.java`.

16. In the text editor, add the following **exports** line inside the **module** block:

```
module com.packtpub.day.module {
    exports com.packtpub.day;
}
```

com.packtpub.day module exports one package, **com.packtpub.day**. Anything else added to this module will be hidden.

Now that we have a module, the next step is to use this module in another module. This will show how modules can control what classes get exported for use by other modules, and what classes remain private within the module. The modules exist side by side, but both need to be included in your project's module path–the module equivalent of Java's classpath.

Exercise 14: Creating a Second Module Using the First One

Next, we'll create a second very simple module that uses the **com.packtpub.day** module created previously.

1. From the **File** menu, select **New** and then **Module…**.

2. Make sure Java is selected, and then click **Next**.

3. Name this module **com.packtpub.message.module**.

4. Click **Finish**.

5. Right-click on the **src** folder under **com.packtpub.message** module.

6. Select **New** and then **Package**.

7. Name the **package com.packtpub.message** and click **OK**.

8. Right-click on the **com.packtpub.message** package. Select **New** and **module-info.java**.

9. Right-click on the **com.packtpub.message** package. Select **New** and **Java Class**.

10. Name the class **Message**.

11. In the text editor, edit the **Message** class and import the **Today** class:

```
import com.packtpub.day.Today;
```

12. Also in the text editor, create a **main()** method as follows:

```
public static void main(String[] args) {
    Today today = new Today();
    System.out.println("Today is " + today.getToday());
}
```

13. Edit the **module-info.java** file in the **com.packtpub.message.module** module. Add the following **requires** statement:

```
module com.packtpub.message.module {
    requires com.packtpub.day.module;
}
```

The **requires** statement will show an error. We need to add the **com.packtpub.day. module** module as a dependency within the IntelliJ project.

14. From the **File** menu, select **Project Structure**.

15. Click on **Modules**.

16. Select **message.module** under **com.packtpub**.

17. Click the **Dependencies** tab.

18. Click the + icon at the bottom of the dialog window and select **Module Dependency...**.

19. Select com.**packtpub.day.module** and click **OK**.

You should see the new module dependency added, as shown in Figure 6.11.

20. Click **OK** in the previous dialog. The error should no longer be present.

21. In the **Message** class, click the green arrow to the left of the class definition, and select **Run 'Message.main()'**.

You will see output like this:

```
Today is THURSDAY
```

Figure 6.11: The IntelliJ project structure dialog showing the new module dependency on the com. packtpub.day.module module

Activity 1: Tracking Summer High Temperatures

Studies on changing climate have determined what summer high temperatures will be like in the year 2100.

You can see this information for many world cities at https://packt.live/33IrCyR.

Create an application to display how high summer temperatures are projected to be in the year 2100 with no major emission cuts, or with moderate emission cuts.

To do this, follow these steps:

1. Create a new Gradle project in IntelliJ.

2. Bring in the Guava third-party library as a dependency. Refer to https://packt.live/2qkLutt for more on Guava.

3. Create a class named `City` that holds the name of a city, the name of the country where the city is located, and its summer high temperature. Remember that IntelliJ can generate getter and setter methods for you.

4. Create a class named `SummerHigh` that holds a base city, along with the city that most closely matches the 2100 summer projections if no emission cuts are made, and the city that matches the 2100 summer projections if moderate emission cuts are made (based on data from Climate Central).

5. Create a class named `SummerHighs` to hold the overall data store. This class should have methods to retrieve the data by city name (regardless of case) or country name (regardless of case).

6. Use a Guava Table to hold the underlying `SummerHigh` data, using a Table like this:

```
Table<String String, SummerHigh> data = HashBasedTable.create();
```

7. Create a `Main` class that takes in either a city or a country name, looks up the appropriate data, and then prints it out. Use a command-line parameter of `-city` for a city lookup and `-country` for a country lookup.

   The entire code base for the project should be incorporated in an executable JAR. Run this JAR from the IntelliJ Terminal pane.

   You should be able to run this JAR similarly to the following:

```
java -jar temps-1.0-all.jar  -city London
```

   You should generate output like the following:

```
In 2100, London, United Kingdom 20.4 C will be like
    Milan, Italy 25.2 C with no emissions cuts,
    Paris, France 22.7 C with moderate emissions cuts
```

8. Add a temperature converter class that can output the temperatures in degrees Fahrenheit instead of Celsius.

9. Add a `-f` command-line option that tells the application to return temperatures in degrees Fahrenheit.

10. Create a class called `TempConverter` to perform the conversion.

11. Use the following formula to convert the unit of temperature:

```
double degreesF = (degreesC * 9/5) + 32
```

   You should then be able to run the application:

```
java -jar temps-1.0-all.jar  -city London -f
```

You should then see the temperature output in degrees Fahrenheit. Here's an example:

```
In 2100, London, United Kingdom 68.72 F will be like
   Milan, Italy 77.36 F with no emissions cuts,
   Paris, France 72.86 F with moderate emissions cuts
```

> **Note**
>
> Refer to https://packt.live/2pvYxbk for more information on the **Table** class. **Hint:** look at the **row()** and **column()** methods. We use this class to allow lookups by city or country.

Summertime High Temperatures

Here are some selected cities from the Climate Central map. Each city is listed with its summertime high temperature. Feel free to include these cities in your program. You can add more cities from Climate Central if you like.

London, United Kingdom, 20.4 °C:

- Will be like Paris, France, 22.7 °C, with moderate emission cuts.

- Will be like Milan, Italy, 25.2 °C, with no emission cuts.

Stockholm, Sweden, 19.3 °C:

- Will be like Vilnius, Lithuania, 21.7 °C, with moderate emission cuts.

- Will be like Kiev, Ukraine, 24.2 °C, with no emission cuts.

Barcelona, Spain, 25.7 °C:

- Will be like Madrid, Spain, 28.9 °C, with moderate emission cuts.

- Will be like Izmir, Turkey, 32.2 °C, with no emission cuts.

New York, US, 27.7 °C:

- Will be like Belize City, Belize, 31.3 °C, with moderate emission cuts.

- Will be like Juarez, Mexico, 34.4 °C, with no emission cuts.

Tokyo, Japan, 26.2 °C:

- Will be like Beijing, China, 29.0 °C, with moderate emission cuts.

- Will be like Wuhan, China, 31.2 °C, with no emission cuts.

> **Note**
>
> The solution to this activity can be found on page 542.

Summary

In this chapter, we saw how packages allow you to better organize your code, which becomes essential when working on large projects. When you use classes from another package, you need to import these classes into your code.

When you create your own packages, place your code into packages based on the purpose of the code and name these packages based on your organization's internet domain name. For example, you might create packages called `com.packtpub.medical.report` and `com.packtpub.medical.heartrate`.

You will often incorporate your Java code into a JAR file. A JAR file is like a compiled library of Java code. Executable JAR files contain the name of a Java class with a `main()` method that you can run with the `java-jar` command.

Java build tools such as Maven or Gradle help a lot when working on large projects. These two build tools also support downloading and using third-party open source Java libraries—libraries that are used in just about every large Java project.

Modules form a newer way to separate code. In the next chapter, we shall cover relational databases and using Java with databases.

7

Databases and JDBC

Overview

In the following chapter, you will learn how to use **Java Database Connectivity (JDBC)** to access relational databases from your Java applications. This begins with creating tables in relational databases to store and sort data. Only then can you manipulate these tables by writing basic SQL queries to retrieve and modify that data. Once this baseline is established, you'll be able to apply these skills to Java applications, specifically, in order to access databases and run queries from JDBC. You will further practice using the JDBC PreparedStatement interface to allow for parameterized SQL statements, boosting your speed by cutting out time-consuming and repetitive keystrokes. By the end of this chapter, you will know how to insert and update data from the JDBC, and handle any exceptions it throws with confidence and skill.

Introduction

Databases—especially relational databases—are used in thousands of applications, from small home-based applications to huge enterprise systems. To help us write applications that access databases, Java provides a few very handy tools, starting with **Java Database Connectivity (JDBC)**.

JDBC allows Java applications to connect to a myriad of databases, provided you have the correct driver: a Java library designed to communicate with a given database. Once connected, JDBC provides an API for accessing databases in a manner that is mostly generic. You'll only encounter a few areas where you need to know the specifics of the underlying database implementation.

Relational Databases

Originally defined by E. F. Codd, relational databases store data in tables, made up of columns and rows. For example, the following table could be used to store customer information:

CUSTOMER_ID	USERNAME	FIRST_NAME	LAST_NAME
1	bobmarley	Bob	Marley
2	petertosh	Peter	Tosh
3	jimmy	Jimmy	Cliff

Figure 7.1: A database table of customers

In this customer table example, each row has four columns: an ID, a username, a first name, and a last name.

> **Note**
>
> In addition to celebrities such as Sting, Cher, and Bono, some ethnic groups use just one name. You will not always have first and last names.

Each row needs a unique way to distinguish that row from all others, called a **unique primary key**. In this case, the ID column acts as a unique key. In this table, you could also use the username as a unique key.

Some tables use a single column as a key, while others use the values in multiple columns to form the key, called a **composite key**.

Most databases use more than one table. You can relate tables to other tables based on information within a row.

For example, in an online system, each customer might have multiple email addresses. You can model this relationship using a separate table for email addresses, as shown in Table 2:

EMAIL_ID	CUSTOMER_ID	EMAIL_ADDRESS	EMAIL_TYPE
1	1	bob@example.com	HOME
2	1	bob.marley@big_company.com	WORK
3	2	petertosh888@example.com	HOME

Figure 7.2: A database table for email addresses

In table 2, each row has its own unique ID, with the `EMAIL_ID` column. Each row also links back to the customer table by holding an ID for the user table in the `CUSTOMER_ID` column. This allows the `EMAIL` table to link to the `CUSTOMER` table. User **bobmarley**, for example, has two email addresses in the system, one for home and one for work.

> **Note**
>
> These email addresses are not real.

In this hypothetical example, there may also be tables for postal addresses, customer preferences, billing, and other things. Each table would likely relate back to the customer table.

To use a relational database, you need a **Relational Database Management System (RDBMS)**, the software that manages the tables.

Relational Database Management Systems

Some of the most common RDBMSes include Oracle, MySQL, SQL Server, PostgreSQL, and DB2. In each case, you have software that runs on a server (or servers) to manage the data, along with separate client software to query and manipulate the data.

To use an RDMS, you first need to install the database software.

Installing a Database

In this chapter, we'll use an open-source database called H2. H2 is written entirely in Java, so you can run it wherever you run a JVM, such as in Windows, Linux, or macOS systems. On account of its portability and simplicity, H2 works well for the database tables we'll create in this chapter.

H2 has some nice features in that it comes with a browser-based database console that you can use to access the database.

> **Note**
>
> H2 can also be used inside your applications as an embedded in-memory database. In this case, the database server and client both exist within your Java application.

To install H2, go to https://packt.live/2MYw1XX and download the **All Platforms** zip file. Once downloaded, unzip the file. This will create a folder named **h2**.

Inside the **h2** folder, you will see sub-folders named **bin**, **docs**, **service**, and **src**. The documentation in the **docs** folder is also available online.

The bin folder contains the H2 database software bundled into a JAR file. It also contains a Windows batch file and a Unix/Linux shell script.

Exercise 1: Running the H2 Database

Now that you have installed the database, the next step is to get the database up and running. To do this, perform the following steps:

1. To run the H2 database, you can use one of the scripts in the **bin** folder, or simply run the **jar** file. For example:

   ```
   java -jar h2*.jar
   ```

   Regardless of how you launch the H2 database, you can access it from a browser. On some systems, such as macOS, H2 will open the database console in your default browser.

2. If it does not open automatically, you can simply point your browser to `http://10.0.1.7:8082/`.

3. You will see the login pane with the information filled in, as shown in *Figure 7.1*:

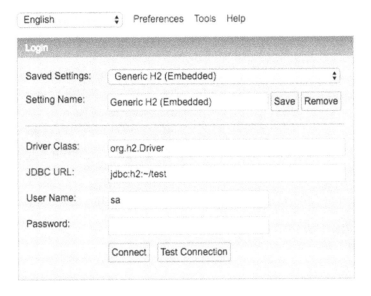

Figure 7.3: The login pane for the web database console

All the information should be filled in correctly when you start. The database driver (discussed later in this chapter) is **org.h2.Driver**, the JDBC URL is **jdbc:h2:~/test**, the username is **sa** (for system administrator), and the password is empty.

Obviously, on a real database, you'd use an actual password.

4. Click **Connect**.

In a few moments, you'll see the main console pane, and you're in.

> **Note**
>
> By default, H2 will store databases in your home directory. With this database named **test**, you should see two files in your home directory with names starting with **test** and ending with **db**.

Once you have the H2 database installed and running, the next step is to start creating tables. To do so, you need to write commands in a language called SQL.

Introducing SQL

Structured Query Language (**SQL** and often pronounced "sequ-el") provides a common language for querying and manipulating data in relational databases. While there are a few differences, SQL mostly works the same in relational database systems such as Oracle, SQL Server, MySQL, and H2.

The first thing you need to do is to create a table. To do so, use the **CREATE TABLE** SQL command. To create a table, you must provide the name of the table, the names and types of the columns, and any constraints.

Exercise 2: Creating the customer Table

Use the SQL **CREATE TABLE** command to create a **customer** table. It should contain the customer ID and the users' first and last names.

1. Enter the following SQL commands in the upper-right input pane:

```
CREATE TABLE IF NOT EXISTS customer
(
CUSTOMER_ID long,
USERNAME varchar(255),
FIRST_NAME varchar(255),
LAST_NAME varchar(255),
UNIQUE(USERNAME),
PRIMARY KEY (CUSTOMER_ID)
);
```

2. After entering the SQL command, click on the **Run** button.

    Figure 7.2 shows the main database console window:

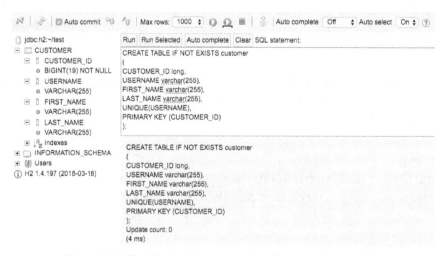

Figure 7.4: The H2 database console after creating a table

Notice in *Figure* 7.4 that once the table is created, you see the table name, **CUSTOMER**, in the left-hand pane. You can click on the **+** symbol to expand the table entry and see the columns, as shown in *Figure* 7.4.

The **CREATE TABLE** command can be broken down into its component parts. The command starts with **CREATE TABLE**. After that, **IF NOT EXISTS** means to not attempt to recreate the table if it already exists (the **ALTER TABLE** command is used to change the structure of an existing table):

```
CREATE TABLE IF NOT EXISTS customer
```

Next comes the table name, **customer**.

After a parenthesis, you will see the definition of the columns and then the constraints:

```
CUSTOMER_ID long,
USERNAME varchar(255),
FIRST_NAME varchar(255),
LAST_NAME varchar(255),
```

The **CUSTOMER_ID** column is of the **long** type, like the Java **long** type. This column will be the unique primary key.

The **USERNAME**, **FIRST_NAME**, and **LAST_NAME** columns are all of the **varchar** type. The **varchar** type holds variable-length character (text) data up to a maximum number of characters, specified here as **255** characters.

Next comes the constraints:

```
UNIQUE(USERNAME),
PRIMARY KEY (USER_ID)
```

The **USERNAME** column must be unique, and the **CUSTOMER_ID** column is the primary key. (The primary key must also be unique.) The database will enforce these constraints when you insert data. Note that you can list multiple columns names, separated by commas, to create a composite primary key. This means that the combination of values in those columns must be unique.

The entire command ends with a closing parenthesis and a semicolon. SQL uses a semicolon in the same way as Java to indicate the end of a statement.

Inserting Data into a Table

To insert data into a table, use the **INSERT INTO** command. The basic syntax is as follows:

```
INSERT INTO table_name
(column1, column2, column3, column4)
VALUES (value1, value2, value3, value4);
```

You first list the columns and then provide values for those columns. You must provide a value for all columns that do not allow nulls. In this case, the **CUSTOMER_ID** and the **USERNAME** are required. Each must also be unique.

> **Note**
>
> SQL uses a single quote character to delimit strings. If you need to enter a quote character, use two together, such as **Java''s**. Don't try smart quotes, as are used in some word processors.

Exercise 3: Inserting Data

This exercise again uses the H2 web console.

1. Enter the following SQL in the upper-right input pane:

```
INSERT INTO customer
(CUSTOMER_ID, USERNAME, FIRST_NAME, LAST_NAME)
VALUES (1, 'bobmarley', 'Bob', 'Marley');
```

2. After entering the SQL command, click on the **Run** button.

3. Repeat these two steps with the following two SQL statements:

```
INSERT INTO customer
(CUSTOMER_ID, USERNAME, FIRST_NAME, LAST_NAME)
VALUES (2, 'petertosh', 'Peter', 'Tosh');
INSERT INTO customer
(CUSTOMER_ID, USERNAME, FIRST_NAME, LAST_NAME)
VALUES (3, 'jimmy', 'Jimmy', 'Cliff');
```

> **Note**
>
> Most RDBMSs support types that will automatically manage ID numbers for a primary key. The syntax does differ in different database software, however. Refer to https://packt.live/2J6z5Qt for the **IDENTIIY** type for H2.

Retrieving Data

To retrieve data from a table (or tables), use the **SELECT** command. The SQL **SELECT** command lets you query for data. You must specify what you are looking for.

The basic syntax is as follows:

```
SELECT what_columns_you_want
FROM table_name
WHERE criteria_you_want;
```

You can provide a comma-delimited list of columns to return, or use an asterisk, *, to indicate you want all the columns returned. The simplest query follows:

```
SELECT * from customer;
```

You should now see all the rows returned, as displayed in *Figure* 7.3:

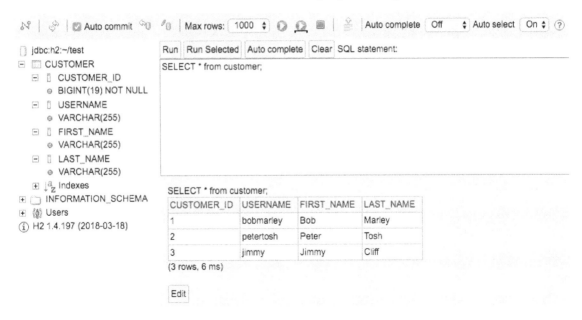

Figure 7.5: Querying all the rows from the customer table

You can refine your query with a **WHERE** clause. For example:

```
SELECT * from customer
WHERE first_name = 'Bob';
```

This will return all rows that have a **first_name** column value equal to **Bob**, which, so far, would be just one row.

You can use a wild card query with the **LIKE** modifier:

```
SELECT * from customer
WHERE username LIKE '%e%';
```

This query returns all rows where the username has an **e**.

In SQL, the percent sign acts as a wild card. This example has a wild card at the beginning of the value, and another at the end. You can use just one wild card, for example, to query for the end of a value:

```
SELECT * from customer
WHERE username LIKE '%ey';
```

This example queries for all records that have a username value that ends in **ey**.

You can make a more detailed query using **OR** or **AND** in the **WHERE** clause. For example:

```
SELECT * from customer
WHERE
    first_name = 'Peter'
OR
    last_name = 'Cliff';
```

This example returns all rows where the **first_name** is **Peter** or the **last_name** is **Cliff**, which is two rows in this example.

With an **OR** operator, the **SELECT** statement returns all rows that match either of the criteria. With an **AND** operator, both parts of the criteria must match:

```
SELECT * from customer
WHERE
    first_name = 'Peter'
AND
    last_name = 'Cliff';
```

This example will return zero rows since no row matches both criteria.

Thus far, we've used an asterisk to indicate that we want all columns returned. You can specify a comma-delimited list of column names instead. For example:

```
SELECT first_name, last_name from customer
order by
last_name, first_name;
```

This example also uses the **ORDER BY** clause to tell the database to return the records in a certain order, in this case, sorted by `last_name` and then `first_name`.

SQL uses two dashes, `--`, to indicate the start of a comment, as shown here:

```
-- This is a comment.
```

SQL queries can get quite complex. These examples just provide a small taste.

> **Note**
>
> For more information on SQL, you can refer to the following Packt video: https://packt.live/33Kli8S.

Relating Tables

Most databases include multiple tables, and many of these tables will be related. From the earlier example, we can relate the customer table to a separate table for email addresses. In the previous example, each row in the email table included the ID of the related row in the customer table.

Exercise 4: Creating the email Table

This exercise uses the H2 web console. In this exercise, we will create an email table and insert some values into it.

1. Enter the following SQL in the upper-right input pane:

```
CREATE TABLE IF NOT EXISTS email
(
EMAIL_ID long,
CUSTOMER_ID long,
EMAIL_ADDRESS varchar(255),
EMAIL_TYPE varchar(255),
PRIMARY KEY (EMAIL_ID)
);
```

2. After entering the SQL command, click the **Run** button.

3. Include the following **INSERT** statement, and then click the **Run** button:

```
INSERT INTO email
(EMAIL_ID, CUSTOMER_ID, EMAIL_ADDRESS, EMAIL_TYPE)
VALUES (1,1, 'bob@example.com', 'HOME');
```

4. Include the following **INSERT** statement, and then click on the **Run** button:

```
INSERT INTO email
(EMAIL_ID, CUSTOMER_ID, EMAIL_ADDRESS, EMAIL_TYPE)
VALUES (2,1, 'bob.marley@big_company.com', 'WORK');
```

5. Include the following **INSERT** statement, and then click on the **Run** button:

```
INSERT INTO email
(EMAIL_ID, CUSTOMER_ID, EMAIL_ADDRESS, EMAIL_TYPE)
VALUES (3,2, 'petertosh888@example.com', 'HOME');
```

Notice how we must manage the IDs, both **EMAIL_ID** and the related **CUSTOMER_ID**. This can become tedious. Java libraries, such as Hibernate, that map Java objects to relational tables can help with this.

> **Note**
>
> Hibernate is considered an ORM, or Object-Relational Mapper. For more information on Hibernate, refer to https://packt.live/2Bs5z3k.

Once you have data in multiple related tables, you can query from multiple tables at once, joining the results together.

Selecting Data from Multiple Tables

When you use the SQL select statement to query data from multiple tables, you need to list all the columns (from all the tables) that you wish to be returned, along with the criteria to search in the **WHERE** clause. In the **WHERE** clause, you will need to join the two tables on some common value.

For example, the **email** table has a **customer_id** column to join back to the **customer** table. To join that, write a query along the lines of the following:

```
SELECT username, email_address
FROM customer, email
WHERE email_type = 'HOME'
AND
email.customer_id = customer.customer_id;
```

In this query, we ask for the **username** from the customer table, along with the **email_address** from the email table. The **FROM** section lists both the customer and email tables.

The **WHERE** clause gets more interesting. This query looks for all email addresses where the type is **HOME**. To join this back to the customer table, and to ensure you are getting the right customer, the query adds a join where the **customer_id** email table column corresponds to the **customer_id** customer table column. This ensures that you get the correct customers aligned.

Modifying Existing Rows

The **UPDATE** command lets you modify existing rows. To update data, you need to specify which rows to change, along with the values to change. The basic syntax is as follows:

```
UPDATE table_name
SET column1 = value1, column2 = value2
WHERE where_clause_to_find_rows
```

Exercise 5: Modifying email Data

If a user, such as **bobmarley**, switches to a different work email, you would need to update the email table. To do so, perform the following steps:

1. Go to the H2 database console.

2. Include the following SQL query, and then click **Run**:

    ```
    SELECT * from email;
    ```

    This command lets you see what values are in the table now before we change anything.

3. Next, enter the following **UPDATE** statement, and then click **Run**:

    ```
    UPDATE email
    SET EMAIL_ADDRESS = 'bob.marley@another_company.com'
    WHERE customer_id = 1
    AND email_type = 'WORK';
    ```

    This query changes the **email_address** entry for the customer, **bobmarley**, but just the **WORK** email.

4. Now, run the select query again (and click **Run**) to see how the table has changed:

```
SELECT * from email;
```

You should now see the results as shown in the following table:

EMAIL_ID	CUSTOMER_ID	EMAIL_ADDRESS	EMAIL_TYPE
1	1	bob@example.com	HOME
2	1	bob.marley@another_company.com	WORK
3	2	petertosh888@example.com	HOME

Figure 7.6: Output of the query

Deleting Data

To remove data from a table, use the **DELETE** command:

```
DELETE FROM table_name
WHERE criteria_for_which_rows_to_delete;
```

For example, to remove the work email for the customer, **bobmarley**, you would use a command such as the following:

```
DELETE FROM email
WHERE customer_id = 1
AND email_type = 'WORK';
```

> **Note**
>
> When you have tables that are related, deleting data becomes trickier. If you delete a customer, for example, you need to delete all rows from the email table for this customer, too. In this example, the email table depends on the customer table, but the opposite is not true.

In all the examples so far in this chapter, we've used SQL in the H2 console to work with the data in a test database. In your Java applications, you will use JDBC to accomplish much the same goals.

JDBC—Accessing Databases from Java

JDBC provides a common API to work with databases. Mostly, JDBC works with relational databases, but you can work with any data source for which you have a **JDBC driver**, the Java library that communicates with the data source and implements the JDBC API.

> **Note**
>
> One of the best parts of JDBC is that most driver libraries are written in Java, so you can use these drivers from any platform that runs the JVM.

The first thing you need to do with JDBC is connect to a data source, typically a database.

Connecting to Databases

The simplest way to connect to a database using JDBC is to use the `getConnection()` method on the `java.sql.DriverManager` class:

```
Connection conn = DriverManager.getConnection("jdbc:h2:~/test", "sa", "");
```

This method takes three parameters:

- The JDBC URL, which starts with `jdbc:h2` tells `DriverManager` to look for an H2 JDBC driver. `~/test` tells H2 to look for a database named **test** in the current user's home directory. (This is the user—you—running the Java program.) **test** is the default database name created by H2.

- The username to connect under, in this case, **sa**, for the system administrator.

- The password, in this case, is empty.

> **Note**
>
> Other than H2, you will likely never have an empty password when connecting to a database. H2 sets up the **sa** account that you can use for testing by default.

The **getConnection()** method returns a **java.sql.Connection** object, which you can use as a starting point for working with a database.

> **Note**
>
> There are other ways to connect to a database, especially when using connection pools, described later in this chapter.

Almost every JDBC operation can throw a **java.sql.SQLException**, so you will usually wrap JDBC calls in a try-catch block.

When you are done with a JDBC connection, you should close the connection:

```
conn.close();
```

Querying Data with JDBC

To query from a database with JDBC, create **java.sql.Statement** and then execute a query:

```
String sql = "SELECT * from customer order by username";
statement = conn.createStatement();
ResultSet results = statement.executeQuery(sql);
```

Create a statement using the **Connection** object. You can then execute a SQL query using the **executeQuery()** method, which returns a **java.sql.ResultSet** object.

The **ResultSet** API can be confusing at first. It is based on the idea of a cursor, a record of the program's position within the data. By calling **next()** on a **ResultSet**, you move the cursor to the next row.

So, the normal flow for a query will look something like the following:

```
String sql = "SELECT * from customer order by username";
statement = conn.createStatement();
ResultSet results = statement.executeQuery(sql);
while (results.next()) {
    // Process the current row.
}
```

ResultSet starts with a position–the cursor–prior to the first row, so you need to call **next()** to get the very first row of data. The **next()** method returns false when it has reached the end of the data.

Part of the reason for iterating through a **ResultSet** like this is because some database tables hold so many records that you could not hold them all in memory at the same time. Hence, the general technique is to process one row at a time.

With each row of data, call **get** methods on the **ResultSet**. For example, to get a string value, call **getString()**:

```
String username = results.getString("USERNAME");
```

In this example, we pass the name of the column to **getString()**. It returns the value of the **USERNAME** column for the current row.

You can also pass the position of the column in the results. For example:

```
String username = results.getString(2);
```

The position number is the position of the column in the results, which is dependent on the query.

> **Note**
>
> Unlike almost everything else in Java, JDBC columns start counting at 1, not 0.

You have to know the type of data in the column to call the proper **get** method. For example, to get a **long** value, call **getLong()**:

```
Long id = results.getLong("CUSTOMER_ID");
```

> **Note**
>
> You can call **getObject()** if you are unsure of the type of data in the column.

When done with a **ResultSet**, call **close()**. Similarly, when you're done with a statement, call **close()**. Calling the **close()** method on these objects frees up resources.

Exercise 6: Querying Data with JDBC

This exercise will create an IntelliJ project, bring in a dependency for the H2 database JDBC driver, and then query the database:

1. Select **New** and then **Project...** from the **File** menu in IntelliJ.

2. Select **Gradle** for the type of project. Click **Next**.

3. For the **Group Id**, enter **com.packtpub.db**.

4. For the **Artifact Id**, enter **customers**.

5. For the **Version**, enter **1.0**.

6. Accept the default on the next pane. Click **Next**.

7. Leave the project name as **customers**.

8. Click **Finish**.

9. Call up **build.gradle** in the IntelliJ text editor.

10. Set **sourceCompatibility** to **12**:

    ```
    sourceCompatibility = 12
    ```

11. Replace the plugins block with the following, just as we did in *Chapter 6, Libraries, Packages, and Modules*:

    ```
    buildscript {
        repositories {
            jcenter()
        }
        dependencies {
            classpath 'com.github.jengelman.gradle.plugins:shadow:2.0.1'
        }
    }
    apply plugin: 'java'
    apply plugin: 'com.github.johnrengelman.shadow'
    ```

12. Add the following dependency to incorporate the H2 library in the project:

    ```
    // https://mvnrepository.com/artifact/com.h2database/h2
    implementation group: 'com.h2database', name: 'h2', version: '1.4.197'
    ```

    Note that the same jar file that provides the JDBC driver also includes the entire database software.

13. Add the following to the end of the project's **build.gradle** file to define the main class for the executable jar:

```
jar {
    manifest {
        attributes 'Main-Class': 'com.packtpub.db.Query
    }
}
```

14. In the **src/main/java** folder, create a new Java package.

15. Enter **com.packtpub.db** as the package name.

16. Right-click on this package in the **Project** pane and create a new Java class named **Query**.

17. Create a **main()** method for the **Query** class:

Query.java

```
6    public static void main(String[] args) {
7
8        String sql = "SELECT * from customer order by username";
9
10       Statement statement;
11
12       Connection conn;
13       try {
14           conn = DriverManager.getConnection("jdbc:h2:~/test", "sa", "");
15
16           statement = conn.createStatement();
17
18           ResultSet results = statement.executeQuery(sql);
```

https://packt.live/2PbKanp

This program establishes a connection to an H2 database. Notice how all the JDBC calls are wrapped in a try-catch block.

After establishing a **connection**, the program asks the **Connection** to create a **Statement**. Calling **executeQuery()** on the **Statement** runs the query, returning a **ResultSet**. With a **while** loop, the program iterates over each row in the **ResultSet**, extracting data, and printing.

In the end, the program closes the resources used.

This sets up an executable jar that will run the **Query** class. Remember to run the **shadowJar** Gradle task to build the executable jar with dependencies.

When you run this program, you should see output similar to the following:

```
1 bobmarley Bob Marley
3 jimmy Jimmy Cliff
2 petertosh Peter Tosh
```

Note that the query asked the database to order the results by username.

If you are connected to the database from the H2 web console, you will see an error like the following when you run this program:

```
org.h2.jdbc.JdbcSQLException: Database may be already in use: null. Possible solutions:
close all other connection(s); use the server mode [90020-197]
```

You should also see the full stack trace for the error. This error indicates that you are already logged into the database as user **sa**. Click on the disconnect icon in the upper-left corner of the H2 web console to close the web console's connection to the database.

In the **Query** class in *Exercise 6, Querying Data with JDBC*, we used a string for the SQL query. That works fine when your program generates the entire SQL statement itself. However, if you accept user input and then build a string for the SQL, your program may be vulnerable to SQL injection attacks, where a malicious user inputs SQL syntax designed to cause havoc to your database.

> **Note**
>
> For a more detailed look at SQL injection vulnerabilities, refer to https://packt.
> live/2OYGF3g.

Because of this risk, you should sanitize any user input prior to placing it in a SQL statement.

Sanitizing User Input

To sanitize user input:

- You can properly sanitize the data yourself. You could disallow characters that could form SQL syntax, for example.

- You can use the **PreparedStatement** interface and set the values on the prepared statement. JDBC will then sanitize the input for you.

Using Prepared Statements

A JDBC prepared statement takes in a SQL statement with placeholders for the data values. With most databases, JDBC sends the SQL to the database to be compiled. When you send a SQL statement to a database, the database needs to compile the SQL into an internal format that is native to the database, from which the database can execute the statement.

With a regular statement, you can provide a SQL statement to methods such as **executeQuery()** and **executeUpdate()**. You can reuse the **Statement** and provide a completely different SQL statement.

With a **PreparedStatement**, on the other hand, you prepare the statement with a SQL string, and that is all you get. Luckily, though, you provide placeholders for the data values. This means that you can reuse a **PreparedStatement** to insert multiple records into a table, for example.

From *Exercise 5*, *Modifying email Data*, we use an **UPDATE** statement:

```
UPDATE email
SET EMAIL_ADDRESS = 'bob.marley@another_company.com'
WHERE customer_id = 1
AND email_type = 'WORK';
```

With a **PreparedStatement**, you would use a question mark, ? as a placeholder for the input values:

```
String sql = "UPDATE email " +
    "SET EMAIL_ADDRESS = ? " +
    "WHERE customer_id = ? " +
    "AND email_type = ? ";
```

> **Note**
>
> In a prepared statement, you do not need to place single quotes around string placeholders. JDBC will take care of that for you.

These placeholders need to be filled in prior to using **PreparedStatement**. For example:

```
statement = conn.prepareStatement(sql);
statement.setString(1, "bob.marley@another_company.com");
statement.setLong(2, 1L);
statement.setString(3, "WORK");
int rowsChanged = statement.executeUpdate();
```

Pass your SQL string, with placeholders, to the **prepareStatement()** method on a connection. Then, call **setString()**, **setLong()**, and so on, to fill in the placeholder values. With each set method call, you pass the index of the placeholder to fill, starting with **1** for the first placeholder. Then, pass the value to fill in. JDBC will handle the prevention of SQL injection attacks.

As for a regular **Statement**, you can call **executeQuery()** to perform a SQL query, or **executeUpdate()** to modify the database. The **executeUpdate()** method handles **INSERT**, **UPDATE**, and **DELETE SQL** statements.

In this example, **executeUpdate()** returns the number of rows in the table that was modified.

One of the primary benefits of using prepared statements is that JDBC will sanitize the input values so that you don't have to. The other primary benefit is improved performance. If you execute the same SQL statement again and again, or a nearly similar statement with just different values, then using a prepared statement will speed things up, mostly due to pre-compiling the statement.

Transactions and Rollback

In relational databases, transaction groups a set of SQL statements together. Either all the statements succeed, or the transaction will get rolled back, undoing the statements. In addition, databases treat all the statements within a transaction as happening at the same time, which helps to ensure that the data has integrity.

In JDBC, a transaction continues until you call **commit()** on the connection. If there is a failure, you should call **rollback()** on the connection to restore the data to the state it held prior to the transaction.

By default, a JDBC connection starts in auto-commit mode. This means that each JDBC connection gets committed one at a time. If you want to group a few statements together in a transaction, you first need to turn off auto-commit mode:

```
conn.setAutoCommit(false);
```

> **Note**
>
> After turning off auto-commit mode, you should turn it back on when done accessing the database.

When you want to end a transaction and commit the results to the database, call **commit()**:

```
conn.commit();
```

If an **SQLException** gets thrown, you'll want to roll back the transaction:

```
} catch (SQLException e) {
    e.printStackTrace();
    try {
        if (conn != null) {
            conn.rollback();
        }
    } catch (SQLException nested) {
        nested.printStackTrace();
    }
}
```

This code shows one of the most tedious parts of working with JDBC. In your exception handler for a **SQLException**, the calls made—**rollback()**, for instance—can also throw another **SQLException**, which you need to catch. You'll find that JDBC code is full of **try-catch-finally** blocks with nested **try-catch** blocks. *Exercise 7, Using Prepared Statements with Transactions* shows this technique in action.

Exercise 7: Using Prepared Statements with Transactions

In this exercise, we'll create another Java class that uses a JDBC **PreparedStatement** to update data in the email table and wrap that update in a JDBC transaction.

1. In IntelliJ, create a new class named **Prepared** and create a **main()** method.

2. Import the required libraries:

```
package com.packtpub.db;
import java.sql.Connection;
import java.sql.DriverManager;
import java.sql.PreparedStatement;
import java.sql.SQLException;
```

3. Enter the following code in the **Prepared** class.

```
public class Prepared {
    public static void main(String[] args) {
        Connection conn = null;
        PreparedStatement statement = null;
        String sql = "UPDATE email " +            "SET EMAIL_ADDRESS = ? " +
            "WHERE customer_id = ? " +
            "AND email_type = ? ";
```

The **Prepared** class starts by defining a **SQL UPDATE** statement using placeholders. This SQL statement will later get placed in a **PreparedStatement**.

4. In the first try-catch block, the program gets a **Connection** to the database and then calls **setAutoCommit()** with a parameter of **false** to turn off auto-commit mode. JDBC now expects the program to manage transactions.

Prepared.java

```
20          try {
21              conn = DriverManager.getConnection("jdbc:h2:~/test", "sa", "");
22              conn.setAutoCommit(false);
23
24              statement = conn.prepareStatement(sql);
25              statement.setString(1, "bob.marley@another_company.com");
26              statement.setLong(2, 1L);
27              statement.setString(3, "WORK");
28
29              int rowsChanged = statement.executeUpdate();
30
31              conn.commit();
32
33              System.out.println("Number rows changed: " + rowsChanged);
```

https://packt.live/2MSobyQ

When you run the **main()** method, you should see output like the following:

```
Number rows changed: 1
```

Just one row should be modified.

The program passes the SQL string to the connection's **prepareStatement()** method. This creates a **PreparedStatement** initialized with the given SQL. Next, the program fills in the placeholder values in the **PreparedStatement**.

When it's done, the program calls **executeUpdate()** on the statement, commits the transaction and then tells us the number of rows that were changed.

If any of the JDBC calls throws an **SQLException**, the catch block prints the stack trace and then calls **rollback()** on the connection. Calling **rollback()** can also throw **SQLException**, so the program catches that as well, printing the stack trace.

The **finally** block from the original try-catch-finally block restores auto-commit transaction mode, and then calls **close()** on the **PreparedStatement** and the connection, each of which might also result in an **SQLException**.

Simplifying JDBC Programming

As you can see from the examples, programming with JDBC is tedious. Because of that, a lot of projects have developed wrappers over the JDBC API in order to simplify making JDBC calls.

Java itself contains a number of utility classes, such as **JdbcRowSet**, which wrap **ResultSet** objects and provide a somewhat simpler API.

> **Note**
>
> The Spring framework provides a number of utilities to simplify JDBC programming. Refer to https://packt.live/35PalWP for more information.

By far the most popular way to access databases without the inconvenience of the JDBC API is to use object-relational mapping software.

Using Object-Relational Mapping Software

As the name suggests, **object-relational mapping**, or **ORM**, software maps between the world of objects and the world of relational tables. With an ORM, you typically write a Java class that represents one row of a table.

For example, the following class could represent a row in the customer table:

Customer.java

```
1   package com.packtpub.db;
2
3   public class Customer {
4       Long customerId;
5       String username;
6       String firstName;
7       String lastName;
8
9       public Customer(Long customerId, String username, String firstName, String
        lastName) {
10          this.customerId = customerId;
11          this.username = username;
12          this.firstName = firstName;
13          this.lastName = lastName;
14      }
```

`https://packt.live/2pvQhYT`

The **Customer** class is what is often called a **Plain Old Java Object** (**POJO**). ORM software then allows you to use query tables and get back a list of POJOs, or fill in data in a POJO and then persist that object to the database. In the majority of cases, ORM software uses reflection to discover the fields in the class and map those to columns in the table.

> **Note**
>
> *Chapter 19* covers reflection.

The **Java Persistence API**, or **JPA**, provides a standardized API to define the mapping between objects and database tables using annotations to describe the mapping. JPA also defines an API for persisting POJOs to database tables.

Underneath the standard Java Persistence API, you need to use a JPA provider, a library that implements the JPA. The most commonly used JPA provider is called **Hibernate**.

> **Note**
>
> For more information on JPA, refer to https://packt.live/2OZjHsP. JPA is part of the **Java Enterprise Edition (JavaEE)**.

Database Connection Pooling

The `DriverManager.getConnection()` method can take a good bit of time to establish a connection to a database. To help with this, you can use a database connection pool.

Connection pools set up multiple and managed connections to a database. Your application can then request a free connection from the pool. Your code uses the connection and then returns it to the pool.

Some of the main connection pool software libraries are:

- HikariCP, from https://packt.live/2Bw7gg5
- Apache Commons DBCP, from https://packt.live/31p4xQg
- C3p0, from https://packt.live/2pw1vN0
- The Tomcat connection pool, from https://packt.live/31pGgcJ

Non-Relational, or NoSQL, Databases

Relational databases work well when you have data that works well with the columns and rows in SQL database tables. In the real world, not all data fits neatly into this model. This has led to the creation of NoSQL databases, database management software that does not support relational tables.

> **Note**
>
> Oddly enough, some NoSQL databases support a SQL-like language for accessing data.

NoSQL databases all differ, and some of the categories to describe these databases overlap. Terrastore, https://packt.live/2P23i7e, and MongoDB, https://packt.live/31qJVY0, are considered document storage databases. In these systems, you store a full document, typically a structured document.

Cassandra, https://packt.live/2MtDtej, and HBase, https://packt.live/2VWebsp, are sometimes referred to as column-store or column family databases, which store data in columns as opposed to storing data in rows, as is done with most SQL databases. If you organize the columns properly, these databases can very quickly retrieve data. You can also store a huge number of columns.

Neo4j, https://packt.live/2o51EXm, is a graph database. In a graph database, you retrieve data by following relationships between elements. These relationships form a graph.

Activity 1: Track Your Progress

In this activity, we will set up database tables in the H2 database to track your progress through this course. These steps will help us complete this activity:

1. Create a table called **student**, where each record holds information on a student, such as you. Define the ID, first name, and last name columns.

2. Create a table called **chapter**, where each record holds information on a chapter. Define columns for an ID (use the chapter number) and chapter title. For simplicity, you can just enter the chapters up to and including this one.

3. Create a table to relate students to chapters, called **student_progress**. This table should have columns for the ID of a student, the ID of a chapter, and a date for when the chapter was completed. Use the **SQL DATE** type and pass the data as **yyyy-MM-dd**. This table should have a composite primary key.

   You can use the H2 web console to create the tables and insert records.

4. Create two Java programs that use JDBC.

   Create the first to query all the chapters a given student has completed, and when. Take as inputs the student's first and last name. This should generate output like the following:

```
BOB MARLEY
2019-03-01   2 Learning the Basics
2019-03-01   7 Databases and JDBC
```

Create the second program to insert chapter completion. Take as inputs the student's first and last name, along with a chapter number. The program should mark that chapter as having been completed today.

Because both programs take in user input, be sure to use a **PreparedStatement** in each to handle potentially malicious input data. You can create these programs as part of the customer's project created previously in this chapter.

> **Note**
>
> The solution for the activity can be found on page 548.

Summary

This chapter introduced relational database management systems (RDBMSs) and the SQL language, which is used for working with relational databases. We used an all-Java database called H2. SQL is a language that's used to retrieve and modify data stored in a relational database. JDBC is a Java API that communicates with a relational database. You can use SQL commands to retrieve and modify data.

There is a lot more to databases than can be presented in a single chapter, but after working through the exercises, you should be able to start working with databases using SQL and JDBC. A book or training course on SQL can help you delve into advanced database topics.

> **Note**
>
> The Packt video SQL Beginner to Guru: MySQL Edition - Master SQL with MySQL: https://packt.live/33Kli8S will help you advance your SQL skills.

In the next chapter, you'll learn about networking and files using Java.

8

Sockets, Files, and Streams

Overview

This chapter will teach you to work with external data storage systems. In the early sections, you will be taken through how to list the contents of directories—the logical first step to learning to create, open, read, and write to external files using Java. From there, you will study different methods, buffered and unbuffered, and how to distinguish between them. You will then learn to identify two main **application programming interfaces** (**API**s), `java.io` and `java.nio`, their respective relationship to the aforementioned methods, and when and where to use them. In this chapter's final activity, you will be asked to use all these Java skills and tools in order to communicate between two different programs running on remote computers, in preparation for the chapters to come.

Introduction

On an operating system level, files and directories are kind of similar. They are names representing a link to something in storage, whether it is your hard drive, somewhere in the cloud, or the USB drive in your pocket. However, at a conceptual level, they are inherently different. Files contain information, while directories link to other directories and files.

There are two main **Application Programming Interface** (APIs) that deal with the data: **java.io** and **java.nio**. Both APIs can be used to navigate directories and manipulate files. The information about the location of a file is called a pathname. It contains the full information of the directory in your hard drive in which the file resides, all the way to the file's name and extension. It should have the following form:

```
/folder_1/folder_2/[...]/folder_n/file.extension
```

Different operating systems refer to files and folder structures differently. In Unix systems (such as Linux or macOSX), the **/** symbol represents the separation between folders. Having one at the beginning of the pathname indicates an absolute positioning against the root folder of the system. Not having that symbol will indicate a relative positioning against the **classpath** or the path where our program is being executed from. In Windows computers, the folder separator is \, and the root is determined by a hard drive label. By default, the root folder in Windows is **C:**, but you can also store files in any other drive, such as **D:**.

The main difference between the two APIs mentioned previously (that is, **java.io** and **java.nio**) is in the way they read and write data. The first one, **java.io**, can work with streams (this is a concept that we will explore later in the chapter) and carries data byte to byte in a blocking manner from one point to another. The second one, **java.nio**, works with buffers. This means that data is read and written in chunks into a part of the memory (a buffer) and not directly from the stream. This allows non-blocking communication, which will, for example, allow your code to continue doing something else without having to wait until all the data is sent—you simply start copying the information into the buffer and move on to doing other things.

When it comes to files, the big difference is how using one method or the other will translate into faster or slower programs when trying to perform the same task in different ways. We will mainly focus on using **java.nio**, since it is easier to use files with it, and then refer to **java.io** occasionally. The **java.nio.file** (note the difference from **java.io.File**) API defines classes and interfaces for the JVM—which makes use of files, their attributes, and filesystems—is more recent, and offers an easier way to use interfaces. However, this is not true for all cases, as we will see in this chapter.

Listing Files and Directories

We are going to examine how to list files and directories in different ways. These techniques can come in handy when checking whether a certain file exists, which will allow you to give more sensitive information to users when, for example, trying to find a properties file. If you detect that the file you're looking for doesn't exist and, at the same time, you notice that you are not in the right directory, you could make your program locate the actual folder in which the file resides, or you could simply inform the user about this situation.

> **Note**
>
> There are different techniques to list the files and directories at any location on your computer. You must choose wisely depending on the circumstances. While the latest API seems more complex at first sight, as you will see in the following examples, it is a lot more powerful than any of the previous versions.

Let's start with the old way of listing the contents of a directory. In the next exercise, we will only use **java.io**. It requires making a call to **File(dir).list()**, where **dir** is a string representing the name of the folder you want to access. To ensure the code in this book works with your operating system, we have chosen to check your operating system's temporary folder. Java stores that in a JVM property, which is labeled **java.io.tmpdir**. Therefore, the call to **getProperty()** at the beginning of the method extracts the name of the folder. For example, for any Unix OS, that property points to the **/tmp** folder.

Your temporary folder is going to be filled up with a lot of files and folders created by the different programs running in your computer. Therefore, we have chosen to display only the first five listed by the OS – the order is determined by the OS. Unless you sort the results of calling **list()**, you will most likely not find any logic in how the output is sorted:

```java
import java.io.*;
import java.util.*;
public class Example01 {
    public static void main(String[] args) throws IOException {
        String pathString = System.getProperty("java.io.tmpdir");
        String [] fileNames = new File(pathString).list();
        for (int i = 0; i < 5; i++ ) {
```

```
            System.out.println(fileNames[i]);
        }
    }
}
```

The output of this example will be as follows:

```
Slack Crashes
+~JF8916325484854780029.tmp
gnome-software-CAXF1Z
.XIM-unix
.X1001-lock
Process finished with exit code 0
```

> **Note**
>
> Since the contents of computers are different for every one of us—even within specific folders—the kind of information you will see as output to the code listings in this chapter will look different from what you will see in your terminal.

In the previous example, we have been intentionally hiding the part of the APIs that take care of each block of code to simplify the code listing. If you remove the three import statements from the code and follow the instructions from the IDE to add the more granular APIs to handle this code, you will get the following instead:

```java
import java.io.File;
import java.io.IOException;
import java.util.ArrayList;
import java.util.List;
```

You have learned about almost all these APIs throughout the book up to now. Even **java.io.File** was briefly presented in the chapter on exceptions to catch **IOException**. In the following examples, we will follow the same principle, just to keep the program headers as short as possible. However, it is better to reduce the lines of code.

Let's explore another way to list the contents of a directory, but this time using **java. nio**:

```java
import java.io.IOException;
import java.nio.file.*;
import java.util.*;
public class Example02 {
    public static void main(String[] args) throws IOException {
```

```
        String pathString = System.getProperty("java.io.tmpdir");
        List<String> fileNames = new ArrayList<>();
        DirectoryStream<Path> directoryStream;
        directoryStream = Files.newDirectoryStream(Paths.get(pathString));
        for (Path path : directoryStream) {
            fileNames.add(path.toString());
        }
        for (int i = 0; i < 5; i++ ) {
            System.out.println(fileNames.get(i));
        }
    }
}
```

The output of this listing is different from the previous example, as you can see here:

```
/tmp/Slack Crashes
/tmp/+~JF8916325484854780029.tmp
/tmp/gnome-software-CAXF1Z
/tmp/.XIM-unix
/tmp/.X1001-lock
Process finished with exit code 0
```

Here, the full path to the directories and files are shown. This has to do with the way **DirectoryStream** captures information from the OS. The **for** loop in this example might look new for you. This has to do with how we work with streams. We haven't explained them yet, and we will not do so until later in this chapter. But you can see what it is doing: it creates a buffer that stores the information about the different directories inside. Then, it is possible to iterate through the buffer using the **for(Path path : directoryStream)** statement if there is data in it. Since we don't know about its size from the start, we will need a list to store the string containing the contents of the directory. However, at this point, we are still not calling the **java.util.stream** API yet, since **DirectoryStream** belongs to the **java.nio** API.

Another code listing that uses streams properly is shown here. Note that we do not show its output because it's the same as the previous example:

```
import java.io.IOException;
import java.nio.file.*;
import java.util.stream.Stream;
public class Example03 {
    public static void main(String[] args) throws IOException {
        String pathString = System.getProperty("java.io.tmpdir");
        Path path = Paths.get(pathString);
        Stream<Path> fileNames = Files.list(path);
```

```
                fileNames.limit(5).forEach(System.out::println);
        }
}
```

Separating Directories from Files

Imagine that you want to mark files differently from directories when listing a folder's contents. In order to do so, you can use a method from **java.nio** called **isDirectory()**, as shown in the following example:

Example04.java

```
17          for (int i = 0; i < 5; i++ ) {
18              String filePath = fileNames.get(i);
19              String fileType = Files.isDirectory(Paths.get(filePath)) ? "Dir" :
                    "Fil";
20              System.out.println(fileType + " " + filePath);
21          }
```

https://packt.live/2o43Yhe

We have highlighted the part of the code that is new compared with the previous example in which we accessed the directory using the java.nio API. **Files.isDirectory()** requires an object of the **Paths** class. **Paths.get()** transforms the path from a directory item, passed as a string to the actual instance of the Paths class. With that, **Files.isDirectory()** will answer with a Boolean that is **true** if the item is a directory and **false** if not. We used an inline **if** statement to assign the string **Dir** or **Fil**, depending on whether we are dealing with a directory or with a file. The result of this code listing is as follows:

```
Dir /tmp/Slack Crashes
Fil /tmp/+~JF8916325484854780029.tmp
Dir /tmp/gnome-software-CAXF1Z
Dir /tmp/.XIM-unix
Fil /tmp/.X1001-lock
Process finished with exit code 0
```

As you can see, in the temporary directory, there are both files and subdirectories. The next question is how to list the content of the subdirectories. We will approach that question as an exercise, but before we do that, try one more example that will list only those items that are directories. This is a more advanced technique, but it will give us an excuse to step back and try to implement our own solution with the knowledge we have gained so far:

```java
import java.io.IOException;
import java.nio.file.*;
import java.util.*;
import java.util.stream.Collectors;
public class Example05 {
    public static void main(String[] args) throws IOException {
        String pathString = System.getProperty("user.home");
        List<Path> subDirectories = Files.walk(Paths.get(pathString), 1)
                    .filter(Files::isDirectory)
                    .collect(Collectors.toList());
        for (int i = 0; i < 5; i++ ) {
            Path filePath = subDirectories.get(i);
            String fileType = Files.isDirectory(filePath) ? "Dir" : "Fil";
            System.out.println(fileType + " " + filePath);
        }
    }
}
```

First, to show that there is the possibility of using other environment variables (that's what we call the system properties as defined for your OS), we changed the folder to user home, which corresponds to your user space, or the directory where you will typically store your files. Please be careful from now on to avoid any kind of accidents with your files.

Files.walk() will extract the directory structure up to a certain depth, in our case, one. The depth represents how many levels of subdirectories your code will be digging into. **filter(Files::isDirectory)** is going to exclude anything that is not a directory. We have not seen filters yet, but it is a clear enough concept to not need any further explanation at this point. The final part of the call, **collect(Collectors.toList())**, will be creating a list of the output. This means that the **subDirectories** object will contain a list of paths to directories. That is why in this example, unlike the previous one, we do not have to make a call to **Paths.get(filePath)**. The output of that call will depend on what your OS is and whatever you have in your home folder. The result on my computer, which runs a version of Linux, is as follows:

```
Dir /home/<userName>
Dir /home/<userName>/.gnome
Dir /home/<userName>/Vídeos
Dir /home/<userName>/.shutter
Dir /home/<userName>/opt
Process finished with exit code 0
```

Here, **<userName>** corresponds to the user's nickname on the computer. As you can see, this is only representing the contents of the directory initialized at **pathString**. The question is, can we represent the content of the nested subdirectories to the initial **pathString** in our program?

Exercise 1: Listing the Contents of Subdirectories

Let's make a program to navigate through subdirectories using the knowledge we have gained so far. It might not be the most optimal way of solving this challenge, but it will work:

1. Let's start with the latest example, where we used a call to **Files.walk()** with a depth of 1 and a filter to list the contents—just the directories—of a certain directory, **pathString**. The depth in a directory search determines how many levels of subdirectories our will program navigate into. Level 1 is the same level as where the search is initiated. Level 2 indicates that we should also represent the contents of the directories inside the main directory. In principle, it should be as easy as giving the call a higher value for depth, like this:

```
List<Path> subDirectories = Files.walk(Paths.get(pathString), 2)
                .filter(Files::isDirectory)
                .collect(Collectors.toList());
```

2. But there is the catch. When running a call like that, it is likely that there are directories or files that your program is not allowed to access. An exception regarding permissions will be fired and your program will stop:

```
Exception in thread "main" java.io.UncheckedIOException: java.nio.file.
AccessDeniedException: /home/<userName>/.gvfs
        at java.nio.file.FileTreeIterator.fetchNextIfNeeded(FileTreeIterator.java:88)
        at java.nio.file.FileTreeIterator.hasNext(FileTreeIterator.java:104)
[...]
        at java.util.stream.ReferencePipeline.collect(ReferencePipeline.java:499)
        at Example04.main(Example04.java:13)
Caused by: java.nio.file.AccessDeniedException: /home/<userName>/.gvfs
        at sun.nio.fs.UnixException.translateToIOException(UnixException.java:84)
```

```
        at sun.nio.fs.UnixException.rethrowAsIOException(UnixException.java:102)
    [...]
        at java.nio.file.FileTreeIterator.fetchNextIfNeeded(FileTreeIterator.java:84)
        ... 9 more
Process finished with exit code 1
```

3. Accessing any directory or file that is contained in any of these subdirectories, which are under strict administrative user permissions, will make this program crash. It is of no use to catch this exception because the result will still be a non-functional directory listing. There is a pretty advanced technique to get this to work, but you have not been introduced to everything you need to know in order to do so. Instead, let's focus on the tools you have gained so far to create your own method to dig into subdirectories and extract their contents.

4. Let's go back to *Example 03* and modify it to just display directories inside user. home:

```
String pathString = System.getProperty("user.home");
Path path = Paths.get(pathString);
Stream<Path> fileNames = Files.list(path).filter(Files::isDirectory);
fileNames.limit(5).forEach(System.out::println);
```

5. As you can see, we have applied the **filter()** method we saw earlier. We could have also implemented the alternative of checking with **isDirectory()**, as we saw in *Example 04*, but this is cleaner, and simplicity is key.

6. Based on the idea that **list()** can give you the contents of any folder, let's call it again for each filename. This means we will have to modify the **forEach()** statement we are using so that we can access the second level of nested directories:

```
fileNames.limit(5).forEach( (item) -> {
    System.out.println(item.toString());
    try {
        Stream<Path> fileNames2 = Files.list(item).filter(Files::isDirectory);
        fileNames2.forEach(System.out::println);
    } catch (IOException ioe) {}
});
```

7. As you can see, the highlighted code is a repetition of the code we had earlier, with the name of the object changed to **fileNames2**. This time, we removed the limit, which means it will print the output of any subdirectories each directory has. The real novelty is how we have gone from calling just **System.out::print** to writing more complex code where we first print out the path we are at, and then we print the paths to the subfolders of that path. We are anticipating something called a lambda expression here. They will be explained in a later chapter. However, the code here is easy enough for you to understand. For each **(item)** in the **fileNames** buffer, we will perform the operations just mentioned. The result looks like this:

```
/home/<userName>/.gnome
/home/<userName>/.gnome/apps
/home/<userName>/Videos
/home/<userName>/Videos/technofeminism
/home/<userName>/Videos/Webcam
/home/<userName>/Videos/thumbnail
/home/<userName>/.shutter
/home/<userName>/.shutter/profiles
/home/<userName>/opt
/home/<userName>/opt/Python-3.4.4
/home/<userName>/.local
/home/<userName>/.local/share
/home/<userName>/.local/bin
/home/<userName>/.local/lib
Process finished with exit code 0
```

8. Also, **IOException** must be caught at the time of generating the list, otherwise the code will not compile. **throw IOException** in the declaration of the **main** method doesn't apply to the **forEach()** expression because it is one level deeper in the program's scope. We are looking at an inline definition of a method in this case. But the question is, how can we get around the idea of having an arbitrary depth in the directory exploration?

9. Digging deeper in the **java.nio** API, we find the **walkFileTree()** method, which can browse through directory structures up to a certain depth – two in the following example – and offers the possibility of overriding some of its methods to decide what happens when reaching a directory item and trying to access it. A call to this method could look like this:

```
Path path = Paths.get(System.getProperty("user.home"));
Files.walkFileTree(path, Collections.emptySet(), 2, new SimpleFileVisitor<Path>() {
```

```
        @Override
        public FileVisitResult preVisitDirectory(Path dir, BasicFileAttributes
          attrs) {
            System.out.println(dir.toString());
            return FileVisitResult.CONTINUE;
        }
    });
```

10. Here, you can see how the **preVisitDirectory()** method is called at the time of trying to open a directory item in a folder. A program including that line will run until, for example, a permissions-related exception arrives. If there is no exceptional situation, the overridden method will print out all directory names up to two levels of depth. In the case of the home directory we are experimenting with, we know that there is a folder that Java's default user permissions are not enough for our program to gain access to. Therefore, if we run this program, we will see it operate normally until an exception is reached:

```
/home/<userName>/.gnome/apps
/home/<userName>/Vídeos/technofeminism
/home/<userName>/Vídeos/Webcam
[...]
/home/<userName>/.local/lib
Exception in thread "main" java.nio.file.AccessDeniedException: /home/<userName>/.
gvfs
        at sun.nio.fs.UnixException.translateToIOException(UnixException.
          java:84)
        at sun.nio.fs.UnixException.rethrowAsIOException(UnixException.
          java:102)
        at sun.nio.fs.UnixException.rethrowAsIOException(UnixException.
          java:107)
        at sun.nio.fs.UnixFileSystemProvider.
          newDirectoryStream(UnixFileSystemProvider.java:427)
        at java.nio.file.Files.newDirectoryStream(Files.java:457)
        at java.nio.file.FileTreeWalker.visit(FileTreeWalker.java:300)
        at java.nio.file.FileTreeWalker.next(FileTreeWalker.java:372)
        at java.nio.file.Files.walkFileTree(Files.java:2706)
        at Exercise01.main(Exercise01.java:11)
Process finished with exit code 1
```

11. The **preVisitDirectory()** method will tell the **walkFileTree** method that it should continue to work through its return. The issue here is that because of the **AccessDeniedException**, our program will not enter **preVisitDirectory()**. We need to override yet another method called **visitFileFailed()** to see how to handle any kind of exception that occurs when trying to access an item in the directory:

```
@Override
public FileVisitResult visitFileFailed(Path file, IOException exc)
        throws IOException {
    System.out.println("visitFileFailed: " + file);
    return FileVisitResult.CONTINUE;
}
```

The output of this will be the desired result, as follows:

```
/home/<userName>/.gnome/apps
/home/<userName>/Vídeos/technofeminism
[...]
/home/<userName>/.local/lib
visitFileFailed: /home/<userName>/.gvfs
/home/<userName>/.config/Atom
[...]
/home/<userName>/drive_c/Program Files
/home/<userName>/drive_c/Program Files (x86)
/home/<userName>/drive_c/users
/home/<userName>/drive_c/windows
/home/<userName>/.swt/lib
Process finished with exit code 0
```

We can conclude from this process that, even though there are many ways to perform the same task, the way those solutions are implemented will allow us to have control. In this case, the **walk()** method is not enough for us to handle exceptions easily, so we had to explore an alternative that, in the end, turned out to be easier to understand.

For reference, the final code resulting from this exercise should be as follows:

Exercise01.java

```
1   import java.io.IOException;
2   import java.nio.file.*;
3   import java.nio.file.attribute.BasicFileAttributes;
4   import java.util.Collections;
5
6   public class Exercise01 {
7       public static void main(String[] args) throws IOException {
8           Path path = Paths.get(System.getProperty("user.home"));
9
10          Files.walkFileTree(path, Collections.emptySet(), 2,
new             SimpleFileVisitor<Path>() {
11
12                  @Override
13                  public FileVisitResult preVisitDirectory(Path dir,
                        BasicFileAttributes attrs) {
14                      System.out.println(dir.toString());
15                      return FileVisitResult.CONTINUE;
16                  }
```

https://packt.live/35MN9Zd

Creating and Writing to a File

Once we are familiar with how to list the contents of directories, the next logical step is to proceed with the creation of files and folders. Let's start by creating and writing data into a file by using **java.nio**. The easiest way to create a file using this API requires calling the following:

```
Files.createFile(newFilePath);
```

At the same time, creating a directory is as simple as this:

```
Files.createDirectories(newDirPath);
```

As a good practice, you should check whether directories and/or files exist prior to creating any with the same name. There is a simple method that will look into any objects of the Path class to see whether any can be found in the folder our program is exploring:

```
Files.exists(path);
```

Let's put all of this together into a single example that will create a folder, and then a file inside the folder:

Example06.java

```
1   import java.io.IOException;
2   import java.nio.file.Files;
3   import java.nio.file.Path;
4   import java.nio.file.Paths;
5
6   public class Example06 {
7       public static void main(String[] args) {
8           String pathString = System.getProperty("user.home") + "/javaTemp/";
9           Path pathDirectory = Paths.get(pathString);
10          if(Files.exists(pathDirectory)) {
11              System.out.println("WARNING: directory exists already at: " +
                    pathString);
12          } else {
13              try {
14                  // Create the directory
15                  Files.createDirectories(pathDirectory);
16                  System.out.println("New directory created at: " + pathString);
17              } catch (IOException ioe) {
18                  System.out.println("Could not create the directory");
19                  System.out.println("EXCEPTION: " + ioe.getMessage());
20              }
21          }
```

https://packt.live/2MSEPhX

The result of this code listing, the first time you execute it, should be as follows:

```
New directory created at: /home/<userName>/javaTemp/
New file created at: /home/<userName>/javaTemp/temp.txt
Process finished with exit code 0
```

Any subsequent executions should give us the following result:

```
WARNING: directory exists already at: /home/<userName>/javaTemp/
WARNING: file exists already at: /home/<userName>/javaTemp/temp.txt
Process finished with exit code 0
```

This created a file that is essentially empty. Making use of the terminal, you could list the size of the file by calling the `ls -lah ~/javaTemp/temp.txt` command, which will throw a result like the following:

```
-rw-r--r--  1 userName dialout   0 maj 15 13:57 /[...]/temp.txt
```

This means that the file takes zero bytes of hard drive space. This means that the file is there, but it is empty. Writing text to the file can easily be done using a method from the **java.nio.file.Files** API: **write()**. The only issue is that it is not trivial passing arguments to this method. In its easiest interface, you must pass two arguments: the **Path** object and a **List** containing a text. On top of that, there is a risk that the file may not exist, which requires handling the classic **IOException**. It could be something like this:

```
try {
    Files.write(pathFile, Arrays.asList("hola"));
    System.out.println("Text added to the file: " + pathFile);
} catch (IOException ioe) {
    System.out.println("EXCEPTION: " + ioe.getMessage());
}
```

> **Note**
>
> When calling **write()** to write text to a file, you don't have to add the end-of-line symbol at the end of the string. It will be added automatically by the method as one would expect when using commands such as println().

Once you have added the last code snippet to the latest example, the program will give the following result:

```
WARNING: directory exists already at: /home/<userName>/javaTemp/
WARNING: file exists already at: /home/<userName>/javaTemp/temp.txt
Text added to the file: /home/<userName>/javaTemp/temp.txt
Process finished with exit code 0
```

The previous example just writes text to the file but also deletes everything that was there before. In order to append text instead, you need to modify the call to the write command:

```
Files.write(pathFile, Arrays.asList("hola"), StandardOpenOption.APPEND);
```

The highlighted part of the call is responsible for determining what text will be added at the end of the file instead of erasing everything and writing everything from scratch. The following example simply appends text to an existing file:

Example07.java

```
8   public class Example07 {
9       public static void main(String[] args) {
10          String pathString = System.getProperty("user.home") +
                "/javaTemp/temp.txt";
11          Path pathFile = Paths.get(pathString);
12          String text = "Hola,\nme da un refresco,\npor favor?";
13
14          if(Files.exists(pathFile))
15              try {
16                  Files.write(pathFile, Arrays.asList(text),
                        StandardOpenOption.APPEND);
17                  System.out.println("Text added to the file: " + pathFile);
18              } catch (IOException ioe) {
19                  System.out.println("EXCEPTION: " + ioe.getMessage());
20              }
21      }
```

https://packt.live/2MrBV4B

This program appended a whole sentence to the example text file. The final content of the file will read is as follows:

```
hola
Hola,
me da un refresco,
por favor?
```

This is asking for a soda in Spanish. In the next section, let's examine how to read the file we just created.

Activity 1: Writing the Directory Structure to a File

The goal of this activity is to program an application that will read the directory structure, starting from a directory that is stored in a variable. The results will be written to a text file so that, for each nesting level, you will include either a tab space or four white spaces to indent nested folders visually from their respective parents. Also, you will have to show only the name of the folder and not the full path to it. In other words, the content of the file should correspond to the following structure:

```
Directory structure for folder: /folderA/folderB/.../folderN
folderN
    folderN1
        folderN11
        folderN12
        ...
    folderN2
```

```
        folderN21
        folderN22
          . . .
    folderN3
        folderN31
        folderN32
          . . .
      . . .
    folderNN
```

1. The program that you will have to create will need to have a certain depth of directories as a parameter, but we recommend you don't go too deep with this–a maximum of 10 is fine:

    ```
    Files.walkFileTree(path, Collections.emptySet(), 10, new SimpleFileVisitor<Path>()
    . . .
    ```

2. When working with the obtained paths to the directories, you need to split the resulting string using the / symbol as a separator and then take the last item. Additionally, you will have to print the number of indents based on the depth, which will require having some code that can estimate the current depth given the initial path. A trick for solving those problems could be by making the content of **preVisitDirectory()** like the following:

    ```
    // get the path to the init directory
    String [] pathArray = path.toString().split("/");
    int depthInit = pathArray.length;
    // get the path to the current folder
    String [] fileArray = dir.toString().split("/");
    int depthCurrent = fileArray.length;
    // write the indents
    for (int i = depthInit; i < depthCurrent; i++) {
        System.out.print("    ");
        // HINT: copy to list or write to file here
    }
    // write the directory name
    System.out.println(fileArray[fileArray.length - 1]);
    // HINT: copy to list or write to file here
    ```

    > **Note**
    >
    > The solution for this activity can be found on page 552.

Reading an Existing File

Reading a file can be done in a simple way. The question is about where you will store the data once you have it. We will work with lists, iterate through the lists, and then print out the results to **System.out**. The next example uses **readAllLines()** to open the existing file and reads the contents into the computer's memory, putting them into the **fileContent** list. After that, we use an iterator to go through each line and send them to the Terminal:

```java
import java.io.IOException;
import java.nio.file.*;
import java.util.List;
public class Example08 {
    public static void main(String[] args) {
        String pathString = System.getProperty("user.home") + "/javaTemp/temp.txt";
        Path pathFile = Paths.get(pathString);
        try {
            List<String> fileContent = Files.readAllLines(pathFile);
            // this will go through the buffer containing the whole file
            // and print it line by one to System.out
            for (String content:fileContent){
                System.out.println(content);
            }
        } catch (IOException ioe) {
            System.out.println("WARNING: there was an issue with the file");
        }
    }
}
```

The **temp.txt** file is the one where we saved a message earlier; therefore, the result will be as follows:

```
hola
Hola,
me da un refresco,
por favor?
Process finished with exit code 0
```

If the file wasn't there (you may have deleted it after the previous exercise), you would instead get the following:

```
WARNING: there was an issue with the file
Process finished with exit code 0
```

A different approach that gets the same result, but avoids Lists and uses Streams instead, is as follows:

```
import java.io.IOException;
import java.nio.file.*;
public class Example09 {
    public static void main(String[] args) {
        String pathString = System.getProperty("user.home") + "/javaTemp/temp.txt";
        Path pathFile = Paths.get(pathString);
        try {
            Files.lines(pathFile).forEach(System.out::println);
        } catch (IOException ioe) {
            System.out.println("WARNING: there was an issue with the file");
        }
    }
}
```

Reading a Properties File

Property files store key-value (also called key-map) pairs in a standard format. An example of the content of such a file is:

```
#user information
name=Ramiro
familyName=Rodriguez
userName=ramiroz
age=37
bgColor=#000000
```

This is a made-up example of the properties file for an imaginary user. Note how the comment is marked using a hashtag symbol, #. You will use properties files to store the configurable parameters of applications or even for localization strings.

Let's try reading a properties file. You can create a text file in the same temporary folder that we created in the user's space earlier in the chapter. Name it **user.properties** and write to it the contents of the preceding example. This follows an example of a program using **java.io** to read and print out the contents of a properties file. Given the way Java works, there is no better alternative to performing this task than using **java.nio**.

> ### Note
>
> Reading the contents of a properties file consists not just in getting each line of the file, but also parsing the key-value pairs and being able to extract data from them.

The first thing you will notice is that reading the properties file requires opening a file as a stream – again, a concept we will explore later in the chapter – using **FileInputStream**. From there, the **Properties** class contains a method called **load()** that can extract the key-value pairs from the data stream. To clean up the code listing, we have separated the loading and printing aspects of the code from the ones handling the opening of the file. Additionally, we have made sure that all exceptions are handled in the main class, just to have a single point where we can manage them, which makes for more readable code.

Example10.java

```
17      public static void main(String[] args) throws IOException {
18          String pathString = System.getProperty("user.home") +
                "/javaTemp/user.properties";
19
20          FileInputStream fileStream = null;
21          try {
22              fileStream = new FileInputStream(pathString);
23              PrintOutProperties(fileStream);
24          } catch (FileNotFoundException fnfe) {
25              System.out.println("WARNING: could not find the properties file");
26          } catch (IOException ioe) {
27              System.out.println("WARNING: problem processing the properties
                  file");
28          } finally {
29              if (fileStream != null) {
30                  fileStream.close();
31              }
32          }
33      }
```

https://packt.live/2Bry4OK

There is also an aspect that we have not yet discussed in this chapter. Streams must be closed once you are done working with them. This means that they will be unavailable for further data handling after you close them. This step is important for avoiding any kind of JVM memory issues during runtime. Therefore, the example code calls **fileStream.close()** once we are done loading the properties file. If you remember the *Good Practices* section in *Chapter 5, Exceptions*, it was mentioned that you should close streams inside the **finally** statement. This is also the reason why this program must throw **IOException** in the main method. If you wanted to handle this in a clean way (by avoiding nested try-catch statements or using **throws IOException** in the main method), you can wrap the whole **try** block in a method that you would, in turn, call from the main method where you could catch the **IOException**. Look at the forthcoming exercise to see how this is done.

The output of the previous example is as follows:

```
name: Ramiro
family name: Rodriguez
nick: ramiroz
age: 37
background color: #000000
Process finished with exit code 0
```

There are interesting methods within the **Properties** class for you to explore. For example, **properties.keys()** will return an enumeration of all the keys in the file, in our case name, familyName, userName, and so on. This specific method is inherited by **Properties** because of its relation to the **Hashtable** class. It is recommended that you read through the API's documentation for this class to discover the other interesting methods you can make use of.

When it comes to the properties files location, they could be stored inside the classpath, sometimes even inside the actual JAR file, which provides a very compact way to distribute applications with properties files inside.

The next aspect to explore is how to programmatically make your own properties files. Let's look into this topic through a step-by-step exercise.

Exercise 2: Creating a Properties File from the CLI

In this exercise, you will be making an application capable of creating a properties file (or modifying an existing one) from input on the CLI. You will pass the properties file's name and key-value pairs as arguments to your program. This will allow you to create any kind of properties file easily. An example of the expected call to the application will be as follows:

```
usr@localhost:~/[...]/Exercise02$ java Exercise02 myProperties.properties name=Petra
```

The process of operations in such a program is simple. First, you need to check whether the file exists. If so, load the properties. Then, add the new properties or modify the existing ones with the data handed over as an argument. Later, write the information to the file and give feedback to the user on the final content sent to the file. In that way, the user will be able to see that the modifications they made are working without having to open the file.

Let's see how to make such a program step by step:

1. Open IntelliJ and create a new Java CLI project called **Exercise02**.

2. First, we need to check whether the properties file we are defining in the CLI already exists. The program we are going to implement will check whether the file exists. If that is the case, it will open it and load the existing properties. The rest of the arguments in the CLI will be used to either modify existing key-value pairs or add new ones. To see whether a properties file exists and load it, we will need to execute the following:

```
if (Files.exists(pathFile)) {
    properties = LoadProperties(pathString);
}
```

3. Loading the properties is done reusing the code from *Example 10*, but wrapping it into the **LoadPoperties()** method that we called in the previous step. Let's implement it to return an object of the **Properties** class (note what we did to implement the **finally** statement to make sure that the stream is closed after a possible exception. We had to initialize the stream as null):

```
public static Properties LoadProperties (String pathString)
    throws IOException {
        Properties properties = new Properties();
        FileInputStream fileInputStream = null;
        try {
            fileInputStream = new FileInputStream(pathString);
            properties.load(fileInputStream);
        } catch (FileNotFoundException fnfe) {
            System.out.println("WARNING: could not find the properties file");
```

```
        } catch (IOException ioe) {
            System.out.println("WARNING: problem processing the properties
                file");
        } finally {
            if (fileInputStream != null) {
                fileInputStream.close();
            }
        }
    }
    return properties;
}
```

4. If the file doesn't exist, it will be created when calling the **store()** method later—there is no need to create an empty file at this point.

5. Next, we need to read the remaining arguments at the CLI from the **arg[]** array and push them, one by one, into the properties object. The properties object inherits its behavior from the **Hashtable** class, which handles key-value pairs. The **setProperty()** method will be used to either modify an existing property or to write a new one. Since the arguments are expressed as a string formatted as key=value, we can use **split()** to separate the arguments we need to pass to **setProperty()**:

```
for (int i = 1; i < args.length; i++) {
    String [] keyValue = args[i].split("=");
    properties.setProperty(keyValue[0], keyValue[1]);
}
```

6. We are going to be writing to a file, but instead of using a stream that will be inputting data, we will use one that will be outputting data. Its name is simple to infer, **FileOutputStream**. The declaration of a variable of that class will be as follows:

```
FileOutputStream fileOutputStream = new FileOutputStream(pathString);
```

7. To add some comments to the properties file, we simply need to add a parameter to the **store()** method. In this case, just to add some contextual information, let's add a timestamp by calling the following:

```
java.time.LocalDate.now()
```

8. We call the **store()** method, which will send the properties into the file. We will be overwriting whatever existed in it before. This call uses, as an argument, the output **Stream** and whatever comment we have chosen:

```
properties.store(fileOutputStream, "# modified on: " + java.time.LocalDate.now());
```

9. To improve the program's usability, make a method that will iterate through the whole properties set and print it out. In that way, the user can see whether they wrote things properly:

```
public static void PrintOutProperties(Properties properties) {
    Enumeration keys = properties.keys();
    for (int i = 0; i < properties.size(); i++) {
        String key = keys.nextElement().toString();
        System.out.println( key + ": " + properties.getProperty(key) );
    }
}
```

10. Run the code with, for example, the following call in the CLI. In this case, we are intentionally modifying the file we have been working with throughout the chapter. The program will print out the modified set. Please note that there is no clear order to the key-value pairs:

```
[...]/Exercise02$ java Exercise02 user.properties name=Pedro
age: 37
familyName: Rodriguez
name: Pedro
bgColor: #000000
userName: ramiroz
```

11. Open the resulting file in a text editor and see whether your changes took effect or not. Also note that the comments, as well as the \ sign added by the **store()** method to avoid the color parameter (which is expressed in HEX format using the hashtag symbol) being misunderstood as a comment.

12. You could now consider making other modifications to the program so it can clear up an existing file, append several files, and more. You could do that using different commands as arguments. The code for the full exercise is available on GitHub: https://packt.live/2JjUHZL

What are Streams?

Streams in Java are sequences of bytes and eventually, by extension, also objects. You can understand a stream as a flow of data between two places. Creating a variable of the stream type is like opening a peephole to look into a pipe carrying water between two containers and seeing the water passing through. What we are trying to say is that data inside a stream is always changing.

As we have seen before, we have two different ways of looking at things in this chapter: one through the lens of the `java.io` API and one through the `java.nio` API. While the second one works at a more abstract and therefore easier level, the first one is extremely powerful and low-level. Continuing with the water analogy, `java.io` would allow you to see the drops, while `java.nio` would let you play only with 1-liter bottles at a time. Each one of them has its advantages.

Streams in `java.io` can be as granular as going down to the level of the byte. If we were, for example, to look at a stream of sound data coming from the computer's microphone input, we would see the different bytes representing the sound, one by one. The other API, `java.nio` is buffer-oriented, and not so much stream-oriented. While this is true, there is a way to work with streams in `java.nio`. Because of its simplicity, in this section, we will see an example relating to `java.nio`, while in the following section, we will deal with streams using the API that is best prepared is to handle them: `java.io`.

Streams in `java.nio` are sequences of objects (not arbitrary unsorted data). Since those objects belong to specific classes, streams offer the possibility of applying the objects' corresponding methods to the stream directly. The result of applying a method to a stream is yet another stream, which means that methods can, therefore, be pipelined.

We have seen different streams in this chapter, mainly because streams play such a big role in Java that it is almost impossible to do any kind of file-related example without using them. Now you will see how they work in more depth. This will help you understand some of the aspects that may not have been so clear to you so far.

The nature of streams is typically hard to grasp in the first place. As mentioned, they are not plain data structures. Information is arranged in the form of objects. Input is taken from `Arrays`, I/O channels in the program, or `Collections`. The kinds of operation we can perform on streams are as follows:

- `map` (intermediate): This will let you map objects following a predicate that you can give as an argument.
- `filter` (intermediate): This is used to exclude some elements from the whole stream.
- `sorted` (intermediate): This will sort the stream.

- **collect** (terminal): This will put the results of the different operations into an object a form, for example, a list.

- **forEach** (terminal): This will iterate through all of the objects in the stream.

- **reduce** (terminal): This operates the stream to answer a single value.

We have marked each one of the operations with either intermediate or terminal. The former means that the operation that will be performed will give another stream as a result, and therefore it should be possible to chain another operation onto it afterward. The latter means that there cannot be further operations performed after that one has finished.

Until now, you have seen some of those operations in action in this chapter. You can go back to the examples where those operations showed up and revisit them. It will make it a lot clearer what **filter()**, **collect()**, and **forEach()** are doing. Let's see the other three operations in action:

```java
import java.io.IOException;
import java.nio.file.*;
import java.util.*;
public class Example11 {
    public static void main(String[] args) {
        String pathString = System.getProperty("user.home") + "/javaTemp/numbers.txt";
        Path pathFile = Paths.get(pathString);
        // if the numbers file doesn't exist, create a file with 10 random numbers
        // between 0 and 10, so that we can make something with them
        if (Files.notExists(pathFile)) {
            int [] numbers = new int[10];
            for (int i = 0; i < 10; i++) {
                numbers[i] = (int) (Math.random() * 10);
            }
```

The complete code of **Example11.java** is available at **Chapter 1/Code.java**.

This example is divided into two parts. The first half of the program checks whether a file called **numbers.txt** exists in the **javaTemp** folder that we have been using throughout the chapter. If this file doesn't exist, the program creates it with **Files.createFile(pathFile)** and then populates it with 10 random numbers previously stored in an array of **int** called **numbers**. The call to **Files.write(pathFile, Arrays.asList("" + n), StandardOpenOption.APPEND)** is responsible for adding each number in the array as separate lines in the file. The resulting file will look like this:

```
<contents of javaTemp/numbers.txt>
5
3
1
3
6
2
6
2
7
8
```

The idea of having one number per line is that we can then read the file as a list, transform the list into a stream, and then start making different operations. The simplest operation consists of calling **fileContent.forEach(System.out::print)**, which will print the raw data as the output:

```
Raw data
5313626278
```

Before applying other operations, such as **sorted()**, we need to transform the data into a stream, something that is done with the **stream()** method. This is done using the following:

```
fileContent.stream().sorted().forEach(System.out::print)
```

The result of this operation will be sorted. Equal values will show up side by side, repeated:

```
Sorted data
1223356678
```

With **map()**, we will be able to handle the data and perform different operations on it. For example, here, we multiply it by 2 and print it to the terminal:

```
fileContent.stream().map( x -> Integer.parseInt(x)*2).forEach(System.out::print):
```

The result is as follows:

```
Mapped data
106261241241416
```

Finally, there are different terminations that can be used. To do this, we will use lambda expressions, which are not introduced until a much later chapter. However, the following is easy enough to not need any further explanation. To perform the sum of all the numbers, we need to do the following operation:

```
System.out.println(
                fileContent
                    .stream()
                    .map(x -> Integer.parseInt(x))
                    .reduce(Integer::sum));
```

The following is the result:

```
Sum of data
Optional[43]
```

Note that, when reading the file, we have read it as a **List** of **String**, and therefore, the numbers are stored as strings. This means that, in order to operate them as numbers, we need to cast them back into integers, which is done through the call to **Integer. parseInt(x)**.

The Different Streams of the Java Language

To discuss types of streams, we need to take one step back and move away from **java.nio** and into **java.io**. This API is the one that has the best support for streams. Depending on the situation, streams can either go into the program or out from the program. This gives us two main interfaces for streams: **InputStream** and **OutputStream**.

Within each of those two main categories, there are four ways to look at streams from the perspective of the type of data they are dealing with: **File**, **ByteArray**, **Filter**, or **Object**. In other words, there is a **FileInputStream** class, a **FileOutputStream** class, a **ByteArrayInputStream** class, and more.

According to Javadocs, it is important to understand that there is a hierarchy of streams. All streams are built on top of byte streams. But we should try, as much as possible, to use the kind of stream type that is the closest in the hierarchy to the kind of data we are using. For example, if we were to deal with a series of images coming from the internet, we should avoid working at a low level with byte streams to store the images, and we should use object streams instead.

> **Note**
>
> Read more about streams in the official Java documentation at https://docs.oracle.
> com/javase/tutorial/essential/io/bytestreams.html.

How would it then open and print out a file using java.io and **FileInputStream**? We saw a bit of this when dealing with the properties files. Let's do the lowest-level example possible that will read a file and print out its contents byte by byte:

```java
import java.io.FileInputStream;
import java.io.IOException;
public class Example12 {
    public static void main(String[] args) throws IOException {
        FileInputStream inStream = null;
        try {
            inStream = new FileInputStream(
                    System.getProperty("user.home") + "/javaTemp/temp.txt");
            int c;
            while ((c = inStream.read()) != -1) {
                System.out.print(c);
            }
        } finally {
            if (inStream != null) {
                inStream.close();
            }
        }
    }
}
```

This example opens the temp.txt file we created earlier in the chapter and prints out its contents. Remember that it contained some plain text in the lines of **hola\nHola,\nme da un** .... When looking at the terminal, what you will read will be something like this:

```
10411110897107211110897441010910132100973211711032114101102114101115991114410112111114321
029711811111146310
Process finished with exit code 0
```

You might be wondering – what happened to the text? As you know, every symbol of the English alphabet is represented by a standard called ASCII. This standard represents each symbol with a number. It differentiates uppercase from lowercase, different symbols such as exclamation marks or hashtags, numbers, and more. An excerpt of the ASCII table representing the lowercase symbols is as follows:

97	a	107	k	117	u
98	b	108	l	118	v
99	c	109	m	119	w
100	d	110	n	120	x
101	e	111	o	121	y
102	f	112	p	122	z
103	g	113	q		
104	h	114	r		
105	I	115	s		
106	j	116	t		

If you start taking the stream of numbers you get and parse it using the table for the ASCII symbols, you will see that **104** corresponds to **h**, **111** to **o**, **108** to **l**, and **97** to **a**. If you had a full ASCII table (including capitals, symbols, and numbers) you would be able to decode the whole message. We did get the content of the file, but we didn't interpret the data we got in our program, which rendered the output unreadable. This is the reason why you should try to use a higher-level kind of stream, which will stop you having to decode the information at such a low level, which for characters – as in this example – is not such a big deal. But data transfers between software entities can get complex very quickly.

Let's examine another way of performing the same operation of opening the file, but with a different type of stream. In this case, we will use **FileReader**, which is a different type of stream, on top of **FileInputStream**. To get the stream in the form of characters and pass it over to **BufferedReader**, which is a stream class that includes the possibility of reading full lines of a text. Since we know that our file contains text arranged in lines, this will probably be the best way to see the contents of the file in a neat way:

Example13.java

```
5   public class Example13 {
6       public static void main(String[] args) throws IOException {
7           BufferedReader inStream = null;
8
9           try {
10              FileReader fileReader = new FileReader(
11                      System.getProperty("user.home") + "/javaTemp/temp.txt");
12              inStream = new BufferedReader(fileReader);
13              String line;
14              while ((line = inStream.readLine()) != null) {
15                  System.out.println(line);
16              }
```

https://packt.live/2BsKIgh

The output of this example will be what we expected to see in the first place:

```
hola
Hola,
me da un refresco,
por favor?
Process finished with exit code 0
```

In a nutshell, the information is the same, but it matters how we look at it. Using a higher-level class from the stream family will offer us better methods to handle the same information in a different yet more usable way.

There is another concept that we haven't introduced yet, and that is the difference between buffered streams and unbuffered streams. When working at a low level with java.io, you will be most likely working in an unbuffered way. This means that you will be addressing the OS directly from your code. Those exchanges are computationally hungry, especially in comparison with loading any information into a buffer inside the JVM and operating directly there instead (it doesn't mean that it will not be accessing the OS directly – it will, but it will optimize its use.

This example is clearly using **BufferedReader**, which differs from the previous one. We mentioned earlier in the chapter how **java.nio** works with buffers – this means that, unlike **java.io**, it doesn't offer the possibility of doing those direct calls to the OS. In a way, it is better because it is less prone to errors. If you have a properly constructed API with all the methods needed to perform whatever you want to do, you should avoid using other less optimal tools.

What are Sockets?

A socket is the endpoint of a bidirectional communication channel between two programs operating over a network. It is as if a virtual cable was connecting those two programs, offering the possibility of sending data back and forth. Java's APIs have classes to easily construct programs at both ends of the communication. The exchanges on, for example, the internet happen over a TCP/IP network, where we distinguish between the roles of those that participate in the communication. There are servers and clients. The former can be implemented using the ServerSocket class, while the latter can use the socket class.

The way the communication process works involves both parties. The client will send a request to the server asking for a connection. This is done through one of the available TCP/IP ports on your computer. If the connection is accepted, the socket is opened at both ends. The endpoints at the server and the client will be uniquely identifiable. This means that you will be able to use that port for multiple connections.

Knowing how to deal with sockets, together with streams, will allow you to work with information coming directly from the internet, which will bring your programs to the next level. In the following sections, we are going to see how to implement a client and a server to prototype this communication.

> **Note**
>
> While working with these examples, make sure your computer's security system (firewalls and the like) allow communicating over whatever port you decide to use. It wouldn't be the first time someone has wasted several hours thinking their code is wrong when the issue is somewhere else.

Creating a SocketServer

Trying to read data from sockets requires a little involvement from existing networked resources. If you want to have a program that connects to a server, you will require a known server before you can even try the connection. On the internet, there are servers offering the possibility of connecting, opening a socket, sending data, and receiving it back. These servers are called EchoServers—a name that leaves little doubt about what they do.

On the other hand, you can implement your own server and play it safe. Oracle offers a simple example of an EchoServer for you to test. This is going to be a new kind of challenge because you are going to need to run two programs on your computer at once: the EchoServer and whatever client you will implement.

Let's start by implementing the EchoServer that you can get from https://packt. live/33LmH0k. The code for you to analyze is included in the next example. Note that we have removed the opening disclaimer and code comments to keep it short:

Example14.java

```
14          try (
15              ServerSocket serverSocket =
16                  new ServerSocket(Integer.parseInt(args[0]));
17              Socket clientSocket = serverSocket.accept();
18              PrintWriter out =
19                  new PrintWriter(clientSocket.getOutputStream(),
                        true);
20              BufferedReader in = new BufferedReader(
21                  new InputStreamReader(clientSocket.getInputStream()));
22          ) {
23              String inputLine;
24              while ((inputLine = in.readLine()) != null) {
25                  out.println(inputLine);
26              }
27          } catch (IOException e) {
28              System.out.println("Exception caught when trying to listen on port "
29                  + portNumber + " or listening for a connection");
30              System.out.println(e.getMessage());
31          }
```

https://packt.live/2oLURSR

The first part of the code checks that you have selected a port for your server to be listening to. This port number is given as an argument on the CLI:

```
if (args.length != 1) {
    System.err.println("Usage: java EchoServer <port number>");
    System.exit(1);
}
```

If no port was chosen, this program will simply exit. Remember, as we mentioned earlier, to make sure that whatever port you use, it is not blocked by your computer's firewall.

The call to `ServerSocket(Integer.parseInt(args[0]))` will start the object of the `ServerSocket` class, configuring the port defined in the arguments to call the program as the one to listen to. Later, `serverSocket.accept()` will block the server and make it wait until a connection arrives. Once it arrives, it will be automatically accepted.

In the beginning code in this example, there are two different streams: `BufferReader in` for the input, and `PrinterWriter out` for the output. As soon as a connection is established, `in` will get the data, and `out` will send it – without any further processing– back to the socket. The server program will run until forcing an exit when pressing *Ctrl+C* on the terminal.

To get the server started, you will need to compile it using the build icon (the hammer) and call it from the terminal using a specific port name. Try port 8080, because that is typically used for experiments like the one, we are going to do now:

```
usr@localhost:~/IdeaProjects/[...]/Example14$ java Example14 8080
```

If everything goes as planned, the program will start running and will not print any messages. It is there just waiting for a connection to be made.

> **Note**
>
> Remember that, by default, your own computer always has the IP number 127.0.0.1, which allows you to figure out the IP number of your computer in the network. We will use this for the connection with the client.

Writing Data on and Reading Data from a Socket

While our server runs in the background, we will need to produce a simple program that will open a socket and send something to the server. To do this, you need to create a new project in the IDE but in a separate window. Remember that your server is currently running!

The simplest client that you can produce is Oracle's companion to the *EchoServer*. For obvious reasons, it is called *EchoClient*, and you can find it at https://packt. live/2PbLNBx.

Example15.java

```
15          try (
16                  Socket echoSocket = new Socket(hostName, portNumber);
17                  PrintWriter out =
18                    new PrintWriter(echoSocket.getOutputStream(), true);
19                  BufferedReader in =
20                    new BufferedReader(
21                        new InputStreamReader(echoSocket.getInputStream()));
22                  BufferedReader stdIn =
23                    new BufferedReader(
24                        new InputStreamReader(System.in))
25          ) {
26              String userInput;
27              while ((userInput = stdIn.readLine()) != null) {
28                  out.println(userInput);
29                  System.out.println("echo: " + in.readLine());
30              }
```

https://packt.live/33OrP3t

Note that, in this case, instead of creating a **SocketServer** object, we create a **Socket** object. This second program introduces the idea of using one of the system streams to capture data and send it to the socket: **System.in**. This program will run for as long as the input in **System.in** is **not null**. This is something that cannot really be achieved through direct interaction with System.in, because we will be just pressing keys on the keyboard. Therefore, you will need to call *Ctrl + C* to stop the client, just as was the case with the server.

Note how sending data to the server is done with **out.println()**, where out is a **PrinterWriter** object, a stream, that is constructed on top of the **Socket**. On the other hand, to read the incoming **Socket**, we have implemented a **BufferedReader** object called **in**. Since it is buffered, we can poll the object whenever we want. The call to **out. readLine()** and **in.readLine()** is blocking. It will not stop reading from **System.in** or from the socket until the end of the line has been reached.

This makes this reader synchronous because it waits for the user to type, sends the data, and, finally, waits until getting an answer from the socket.

> **Note**
>
> Every operating system makes three different system streams available to the JVM: System.in, System.out, and System.err. As they are streams, you can use the full power of the Stream classes to read data from them, put them into buffers, parse them, and so on.

To get the client started, you will need to compile it using the build icon (the hammer) and call it from the terminal using a specific IP and port name. Try the IP 127.0.0.1 and port 8080. Remember that you need to start the server before you start the client:

```
usr@localhost:~/IdeaProjects/[...]/Example14$ java Example15 127.0.0.1 8080
```

From that moment on, and until you issue the Ctrl + C command, for as long as the server is connected, you will be able to type whatever you want on the terminal, and when you press Enter, it will be sent to and from the server. Upon arrival, the client will write it to the terminal by adding the message echo before it. We highlight the response coming from the server by making the typeface bold:

```
Hello
echo: Hello
```

Also, when forcing an exit on the client, it will force an exit on the server.

Activity 2: Improving the EchoServer and EchoClient Programs

In this activity, you will have to make improvements to the programs in the last two sections. First, you will have to add some text to the data relayed on the server. This will make it easier for the user to understand that the data was sent back from the server. Let's make it a counter that will act as a sort of unique ID for the exchange. In this way, the answer from the server will be shown with a number added to the message:

```
Hello
echo: 37-Hello
```

On the other hand, you should add a command in the client that will send a termination signal to the server. This command will exit the server, and then exit the client. To terminate any of the programs, you can call **System.exit()** after sending a message to the terminal informing the user that the program is ending. As a termination command, you could make something simple, such as a message that contains the word 'bye'.

1. The expected results will require you to modify both the server and the client in a very similar way. On the client-side, you will have to do something like the following:

```
while ((userInput = stdIn.readLine()) != null) {
    out.println(userInput);
    if (userInput.substring(0,3).equals("bye")) {
        System.out.println("Bye bye!");
        System.exit(0);
    }
    System.out.println("echo: " + in.readLine());
}
```

2. On the server, the modifications should look like the following:

```
int contID = 0;
while ((inputLine = in.readLine()) != null) {
    contID++;
    out.println(contID + "-" + inputLine);
    if (inputLine.substring(0,3).equals("bye")) {
        System.out.println("Bye bye!");
        System.exit(0);
    }
}
```

The expected interaction between the server and the client should be as follows:

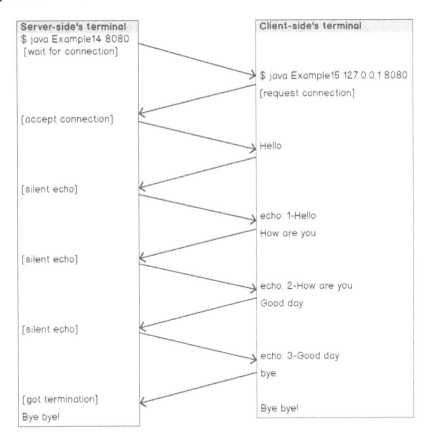

Figure 8.1: The interaction between the client and the server.

> **Note**
>
> The solution for this activity can be found on page 555.

Blocking and Non-Blocking Calls

This is a topic we have been covering in this chapter, but we have not addressed it directly. The **java.io** read and write operations are blocking. This means that the program will wait until the data is fully read or until the data has been fully written. However, working with buffered streams as implemented in **java.nio** allows you to check whether the data is ready to be read. When writing data, **java.nio** will copy the data to the buffer and let the API write the data to the channel by itself. This allows an entirely different programming style where we don't need to wait for the operations to happen. At the same time, this means that we will not have low-level control of the communication. A different part of the JVM performs that action for us.

Summary

In this chapter, you have been introduced to two main APIs in the Java language: java.io and java.nio. They have some overlapping functions, and they are needed to deal with streams and files. On top of that, you have seen how to work with sockets, a natural source of data that can only be handled with streams.

There have been a series of examples looking at how to capture data from the terminal, which in the end happened to be **stream (System.in)**. You then explored how to process it using streams with all sorts of high-level functions, such as filter, map, sorted, foreach, reduce, and collect. You have seen how to open files and properties files, and how java.nio is very capable with the former, but not with the latter.

From a more practical perspective, this chapter has introduced one important technique that was only explained in theory in an earlier chapter: how to use **finally** to close streams, and avoid potential memory issues during runtime. You have seen that, in order to handle exceptions cleanly, you may have to move blocks of code into methods. In this way, you can avoid throwing exceptions and can always process them with try-catch statements.

In order to play around with sockets, you have experimented with building an EchoServer and an EchoClient. You had two different programs interacting with one another and sending data over the internet. You saw how to run both the server and the client on your own computer, and it is now time to try those two programs running on different computers.

Finally, the two activities in this chapter introduced you to creating or modifying properties files on the fly by typing key-value pairs as arguments to a program, and remotely controlling another program via commands over the internet.

In the next chapter, you'll learn about HTTP and how to create a program that connects to a specific web server and downloads data.

9

Working with HTTP

Overview

In this chapter, we will examine the fundamentals of HTTP and create a program that connects to a specific web server and downloads data. We will begin with a study of HTTP request methods so that you can begin to practice making requests using Java's **HttpUrlConnection** class on your own. You will then learn to retrieve data using the GET and HEAD requests, and to send JSON-formatted data using the POST request. Towards the end of this chapter, you will learn to extract and parse HTML content using the open-source jsoup library, and explore the **java. net.http** module—a new HTTP class provided by Java 11—which supports both synchronous and asynchronous HTTP requests.

Introduction

The **Hypertext Transfer Protocol (HTTP)** forms the base for the **World Wide Web (WWW)**. Using HTTP's **request-response protocol**, a client, such as a web browser, can request data from a server. In the World Wide Web, a web browser requests content (HTML, JavaScript, images, and so on.), and then displays the results. In many cases, the content that is returned is fairly static.

Java applications typically differ. In most cases with Java, you will send requests to specialized backend web services for gathering data or updating systems. In both cases, though, the Java coding remains the same.

This chapter covers how to make HTTP requests from Java applications and parse the response data.

Exploring HTTP

With HTTP, a client application sends a specially formatted request to a server and then awaits a response. Technically, HTTP is a stateless protocol. This means that the server is not required to maintain any state information related to the client. Each client request can be treated individually as a new operation. The server does not need to store client-specific information.

Many servers do maintain some sort of state across multiple requests, though, such as when you make a purchase online, and the server needs to store the products you have selected; however, the basic protocol does not require this.

HTTP is a textual protocol (with allowances for compression). An HTTP request includes the following parts:

- An operation (called a **request method**), a resource identifier for the operation, and optional parameters on a line.

- Request headers; one per line.

- An empty line.

- A message body, which is optional.

- Each line ends with two characters: a carriage return and a line feed character.

HTTP uses the following two main concepts for identifying the resources that you are interested in:

- A resource identifier in the **Universal Resource Identifier** (**URI**) format identifies a resource on a server.

- A **Universal Resource Locator** (**URL**) includes a URI, along with the network protocol information, the server, and port number. URLs are what you type into the address bar of web browsers.

Java includes classes for both concepts: `java.net.URI` and `java.net.URL`.

For example, consider the following URL: `http://example.com:80/`.

In this example, the `http` identifies the protocol. The server is `example.com`, and the port number is `80` (the default HTTP port number). The trailing/character identifies the resource on the server, in this case, the top-level or root resource.

Most modern websites use the HTTPS protocol. This is a more secure version of HTTP because the data that is sent to and from the server is encrypted.

For example, consider the following URL: https://www.packtpub.com/.

In this case, the protocol is `https` and the server is `www.packtpub.com`. The port defaults to `443` (the default port for HTTPS). As before, the trailing/character identifies the resource on the server.

A URI can either have the full networking location or be relative to a server. The following are all valid URIs:

- `https://www.packtpub.com/tech/java`

- `http://www.example.com/docs/java.html`

- `/tech/java`

- `/docs/java.html`

- `file:///java.html`

URL is an older term, and generally represents the full specification of a resource on the internet. That said, like URIs, you can have relative URLs as well, such as `java.html`. In most cases, people talk about URIs.

In general, though, your Java applications will use the **URL** class to establish HTTP connections.

> **Note**
>
> You can read more about URIs at https://packt.live/32ATULO and URLs at https://packt.live/2JjIgNN.

HTTP Request Methods

Each HTTP request starts with a request method, such as GET. The method names come from the early days of the World Wide Web. These methods include the following:

- **GET:** This retrieves data from the server.

- **HEAD:** This is like a GET request but just retrieves the header information and does not include the response body.

- **POST:** This sends data to the server. Most HTML forms on web pages send the form data you fill in as a POST request.

- **PUT:** This also sends data to the server. A PUT request is often used to modify a resource, replacing the contents of the existing resource.

- **DELETE:** This requests the server to delete the given resource.

- **TRACE:** This echoes back the request data that is received by the server. This can be useful for debugging.

- **OPTIONS:** This lists the HTTP methods that the server supports for a given URL.

> **Note**
>
> There are other HTTP methods as well, notably **CONNECT** and **PATCH**. The **HttpUrlConnection** class, described in this chapter, only supports the ones listed here.

Representational State Transfer

Representational State Transfer (**REST**) is a term that is used to describe web services that use HTTP as a transport protocol. You can think of this as HTTP with objects. With a RESTful web service, for example, a GET request normally returns an object, formatted in the **JavaScript Object Notation** (**JSON**). JSON provides a way to encode an object as text in a manner that is independent of the programming language used. JSON formats data as name-value pairs or arrays using JavaScript syntax:

```
{
    "animal": "dog",
    "name": "biff"
}
```

In this example, the object has two properties: `animal` and `name`.

> **Note**
>
> Many RESTful web services send and receive data in JSON format. You can refer to *Chapter 19, Reflection,* for more information on JSON.

With web services, a **POST** request is typically used to create a new object, a **PUT** request is used to modify an existing object (by replacing it with the new data), and a **DELETE** request is used to delete an object.

> **Note**
>
> Some frameworks use different meanings for **POST** and **PUT** operations. The approach here is the approach that is used by the Spring Boot framework.

You'll find that Java is used a lot to create RESTful web services as well as web service clients.

> **Note**
>
> You can read the HTTP specification at https://packt.live/2MxDcHz or read an overview of HTTP at https://packt.live/35MM1od. You can refer to https://packt.live/2MYvHbq for more information on REST web services. Additionally, you can refer to https://packt.live/2P2Qz3W for more information on JSON.

Request Headers

A request header is a name-value pair that provides some information to the server. For example, the **User-Agent** request header identifies the application running on behalf of the user, typically the web browser. Almost all **User-Agent** strings start with **Mozilla/5.0** for historical reasons and because some sites will not render properly without mentioning the now-ancient Mozilla web browser. Servers do use the **User-Agent** header to guide browser-specific rendering. For example, consider the following:

```
Mozilla/5.0 (iPhone; CPU iPhone OS 12_1 like Mac OS X) AppleWebKit/605.1.15 (KHTML, like
Gecko) Version/12.0 Mobile/15E148 Safari/604.1
```

This **User-Agent** setting identifies an iPhone browser. The **Referer** header (spelled incorrectly for historical reasons) identifies the web page you are coming from. The **Accept** header lists the format for the data you'd like, such as **text/html**. The **Accept-Language** header lists a language code, such as **de** for German (Deutsch) if you'd like the response to be in German.

One important point about request headers is that each header can contain multiple values (which are comma separated), even if in most cases you will provide a single value.

> **Note**
>
> You can see a list of commonly used request headers at https://packt.live/2pFjIaH.

HTTP response messages also contain headers. These response headers can tell your application information about the remote resources.

Now that we've mentioned the highlights of HTTP, the next step is to start making network requests.

Using HttpUrlConnection

The **java.net.HttpUrlConnection** class provides the main way to access HTTP resources from Java. To establish an HTTP connection, you can use code like the following:

```
String path = "http://example.com";
URL url = new URL(path);
HttpURLConnection connection = (HttpURLConnection) url.openConnection();
connection.setRequestMethod("HEAD");
```

This code sets up a URL initialized with a link to example.com. The **openConnection()** method on the URL then returns **HttpUrlConnection**. Once you have **HttpUrlConnection**, you can set the HTTP method (**HEAD**, in this case). You can get data from the server, upload data to the server, and specify request headers.

With **HttpUrlConnection**, you can call **setRequestProperty()** to specify a request header:

```
connection.setRequestProperty("User-Agent", "Mozilla/5.0");
```

Each request generates a response, which may be successful or not. To check the response, get the response code:

```
int responseCode = connection.getResponseCode();
```

A code of 200 is a success. There are other codes in the 200 range that also indicate a success, but with conditions, such as 204, which indicates success but with no content. Codes in the 300s indicate redirects. Codes in the 400s point to client errors, such as the dreaded 404 Not Found error, and codes in the 500s point to server errors.

> **Note**
>
> You can see a list of HTTP response codes at https://packt.live/2OP9Rtr. These are also defined as constants in the **HttpUrlConnection** class.

Each response typically comes with a message, such as **OK**. You can retrieve this message by calling **getResponseMessage()**:

```
System.out.println( connection.getResponseMessage() );
```

To see the headers in the response, call **getHeaderFields()**. This method returns a map of headers, where the value is a list of strings:

```
Map<String, List<String>> headers = connection.getHeaderFields();
for (String key : headers.keySet()) {
    System.out.println("Key: " + key + " Value: " + headers.get(key));
}
```

> **Note**
>
> With HTTP, each header can have multiple values, which is why the value in the map is a list.

You can also retrieve headers one at a time. The next exercise puts all this together to show you how to write a short Java program that creates an **HTTP HEAD** request.

Exercise 1: Creating a HEAD Request

This exercise will send a HEAD request to **example.com**, which is an official practice domain you can use for testing:

1. Select **New** and then **Project** from the **File** menu in IntelliJ.

2. Select **Gradle** for the type of project. Click **Next**.

3. For the Group Id, enter **com.packtpub.net**.

4. For the Artifact Id, enter **chapter09**.

5. For the Version, enter **1.0**.

6. Accept the default setting on the next pane. Click **Next**.

7. Leave the project name as **chapter09**.

8. Click **Finish**.

9. Call up **build.gradle** in the IntelliJ text editor.

10. Change **sourceCompatibility** so that it is 12:

    ```
    sourceCompatibility = 12
    ```

11. In the **src/main/java** folder, create a new Java package.

12. Enter **com.packtpub.http** as the package name.

13. Right-click this package in the **Project** pane and create a new Java class named **HeadRequest**.

14. Enter the following code:

HeadRequest.java

```
1   package com.packtpub.http;
2
3   import java.io.IOException;
4   import java.net.HttpURLConnection;
5   import java.net.MalformedURLException;
6   import java.net.URL;
7   import java.util.List;
8   import java.util.Map;
9
10  public class HeadRequest {
11      public static void main(String[] args) {
12          String path = "http://example.com";
```

When you run this program, you will see an output like the following:

```
Code: 200
OK
Accept-Ranges: [bytes]
null: [HTTP/1.1 200 OK]
X-Cache: [HIT]
Server: [ECS (sec/96DC)]
Etag: ["1541025663+gzip"]
Cache-Control: [max-age=604800]
Last-Modified: [Fri, 09 Aug 2013 23:54:35 GMT]
Expires: [Mon, 18 Mar 2019 20:41:30 GMT]
Content-Length: [1270]
Date: [Mon, 11 Mar 2019 20:41:30 GMT]
Content-Type: [text/html; charset=UTF-8]
```

The code of **200** indicates our request was successful. You can then see the response headers. The square brackets in the output come from the default way that Java prints out lists.

You should feel free to change the initial URL to a site other than **example.com**.

Reading the Response Data with a GET Request

With a GET request, you will get **InputStream** from the connection to see the response. Call **getInputStream()** to get the data sent back by the server for the resource (URL) you requested. If the response code indicates an error, use **getErrorStream()** to retrieve information about the error, such as a Not Found page. If you expect textual data in the response, such as HTML, text, XML, etc., you can wrap **InputStream** in **BufferedReader**:

```
BufferedReader in = new BufferedReader(
        new InputStreamReader(connection.getInputStream())
    );
String line;
while ((line = in.readLine()) != null) {
    System.out.println(line);
}
in.close();
```

Exercise 2: Creating a GET Request

This exercise prints out the HTML content from example.com. You can change the URL if you wish to and experiment with other web sites:

1. In IntelliJ's Project pane, right-click on the **com.packtpub.http** package. Select **New** and then **Java Class**.

2. Enter **GetRequest** as the name of the Java class.

3. Enter the following code for **GetRequest.java**:

GetRequest.java

```
1  package com.packtpub.http;
2
3  import java.io.BufferedReader;
4  import java.io.IOException;
5  import java.io.InputStreamReader;
6  import java.net.HttpURLConnection;
7  import java.net.MalformedURLException;
8  import java.net.URL;
9
10 public class GetRequest {
11     public static void main(String[] args) {
12         String path = "http://example.com";
```

https://packt.live/2oLZrjZ

4. Run this program, and you will see the brief HTML content of **example.com**.

Using this technique, we can write a program to print out the content of a web page using a GET request.

Dealing with Slow Connections

HttpUrlConnection offers two methods to help with slow connections:

```
connection.setConnectTimeout(6000);
connection.setReadTimeout(6000);
```

Call **setConnectTimeout()** to adjust the timeout when establishing the network connection to the remote site. The value you give as input should be in milliseconds. Call **setReadTimeout()** to adjust the timeout when reading data on the input stream. Again, provide the new timeout input in milliseconds.

Requesting Parameters

With many web services, you'll have to input parameters when making a request. HTTP parameters are encoded as name-value pairs. For example, consider the following:

```
String path = "http://example.com?name1=value1&name2=value2";
```

In this case, **name1** is the name of a parameter, and so is **name2**. The value of the **name1** parameter is **value1**, and the value of **name2** is **value2**. Parameters are separated by an ampersand character, **&**.

> ### Note
>
> If the parameter values are simple alphanumeric values, you can enter them as shown in the example. If not, you need to encode the parameter data using URL encoding. You can refer to the **java.net.URLEncoder** class for more details on this.

Handling Redirects

In many cases, when you make an HTTP request to a server, the server will respond with a status indicating a redirect. This tells your application that the resource has moved to a new location, in other words; you should use a new URL.

HttpUrlConnection will automatically follow HTTP redirects. You can turn this off using the **setInstanceFollowRedirects()** method:

```
connection.setInstanceFollowRedirects(false);
```

Creating HTTP POST Requests

POST (and PUT) requests send data to the server. For a POST request, you need to turn on the output mode of **HttpUrlConnection** and set the content type:

```
connection.setRequestMethod("POST");
connection.setRequestProperty("Content-Type", "application/json");
connection.setDoOutput(true);
```

Next, to upload the data, here assumed to be a String, use code like the following:

```
DataOutputStream out =
        new DataOutputStream( connection.getOutputStream() );
out.writeBytes(content);
out.flush();
out.close();
```

With web browsing, most POST requests send form data. From Java programs, however, you are more likely to upload JSON or XML data with POST and PUT requests. Once you upload the data, your program should read the response, especially to see whether the request was successful.

Exercise 3: Sending JSON Data with POST Requests

In this exercise, we'll send a small JSON object to the https://packt.live/2oyJqxB test site. The site won't do anything with our data except echo it back, along with some **metadata** about the request:

1. In IntelliJ's Project pane, right-click on the **com.packtpub.http** package. Select **New** and then **Java** Class.

2. Enter **PostJson** as the name of the Java class.

3. Enter the following code for **PostJson.java**:

PostJson.java

```
1   package com.packtpub.http;
2
3   import java.io.BufferedReader;
4   import java.io.DataOutputStream;
5   import java.io.IOException;
6   import java.io.InputStreamReader;
7   import java.net.HttpURLConnection;
8   import java.net.MalformedURLException;
9   import java.net.URL;
10
11  public class PostJson {
12      public static void main(String[] args) {
13          /*
14          {
15              "animal": "dog",
16              "name": "biff"
17          }
18          */
```

https://packt.live/2MYwuZW

4. Run this program, and you should see an output like the following:

```
Code: 200
{
    "args": {},
    "data": "{ \"animal\": \"dog\", \"name\": \"biff\" }",
    "files": {},
    "form": {},
    "headers": {
        "Accept": "text/html, image/gif, image/jpeg, *; q=.2, */*; q=.2",
        "Content-Length": "35",
        "Content-Type": "application/json",
        "Host": "httpbin.org",
        "User-Agent": "Java/11.0.2"
    },
    "json": {
        "animal": "dog",
```

```
        "name": "biff"
    },
    "origin": "46.244.28.23, 46.244.28.23",
    "url": "https://httpbin.org/post"
}
```

> **Note**
>
> The Apache **HttpComponents** library can help simplify your work with HTTP. For more information, you can refer to https://packt.live/2BqZbtq.

Parsing HTML Data

An HTML document looks something like the following, but usually with a lot more content:

```
<!doctype html>
<html lang="en">
    <head>
        <title>Example Document</title>
    </head>
    <body>
        <p>A man, a plan, a canal. Panama.</p>
    </body>
</html>
```

HTML structures a document into a tree-like format, as shown in this example by indentation. The **<head>** element appears inside the **<html>** element. The **<title>** element appears inside the **<head>** element. An HTML document can have many levels of hierarchy.

> **Note**
>
> Most web browsers provide an option to view a page's source. Select that and you'll see the HTML for the page.

When you run a GET request from a Java application, you need to parse the returned HTML data. Typically, you parse that data into a tree structure of objects. One of the handiest ways to do this is with the open-source jsoup library.

jsoup provides methods to connect using HTTP, download the data, and parse that data into elements that reflect the hierarchy of HTML on the page.

Using jsoup, the first step is to download a web page. To do so, you can use code like the following:

```
String path = "https://docs.oracle.com/en/java/javase/12/";
Document doc = Jsoup.connect(path).get();
```

This code downloads the official Java 12 documentation start page, which contains a lot of links to specific Java documentation. The parsed HTML data gets placed into the **Document** object, which contains **Element** objects for each HTML element. This is purposely similar to Java's XML parsing API, which similarly parses XML documents into a tree structure of objects. Each element in the tree may have child elements. jsoup provides an API to access these child elements in a similar way to the Java XML parsing API.

> **Note**
>
> You can find a lot of useful documentation on the jsoup library at https://packt. live/2nZbmua.

On the Java 12 documentation page, you will see many links. In the underlying HTML, many of these links appear as follows:

```
<ul class="topics">
  <li>
    <a href="/en/java/javase/12/docs/api/overview-summary.html">API
      Documentation </a>
  </li>
</ul>
```

If we wanted to extract the URI link (https://packt.live/2VWd1x7, in this case) as well as the descriptive text (API Documentation), we would need to traverse the   to the **LI** list item tag, and then get the HTML link, which is held in an **A** tag, called an anchor.

One of the handy features of jsoup is that you can use select elements from the HTML using a selector syntax that is similar to the one that is offered by CSS and the jQuery JavaScript library.

To select all UL elements that have a CSS class of **topic**, you can use code like the following:

```
Elements topics = doc.select("ul.topics");
```

Once you have the selected elements, you can iterate over each one, as follows:

```
for (Element topic : topics) {
    for (Element listItem : topic.children()) {
        for (Element link : listItem.children()) {
            String url = link.attr("href");
            String text = link.text();
            System.out.println(url + " " + text);
        }
    }
}
```

This code starts at the **UL** level and goes down to the child elements under the **UL** tag, which would normally be **LI**, or list item, elements. Each **LI** element on the Java documentation page has one child—that is, an anchor tag with a link.

We can then pull out the link itself, which is held in the **href** attribute. We can also extract the English descriptive text used for the link.

> **Note**
>
> You can find a lot more information about HTML at https://packt.live/2o54P1e and https://packt.live/33L4akK.

Exercise 4: Using jsoup to Extract Data from HTML

This exercise demonstrates how to use the jsoup API to extract link URIs and descriptive text from an HTML document. Use this as an example of how to parse other HTML documents in your projects.

Go to https://packt.live/2MO4UOU in a web browser. You can see the official Java documentation.

We are going to extract the links in the main part of the page under section headings such as **Tools and Specifications**.

If you inspect the API Documentation link in the Specifications section, you will see the link to the documentation resides in a UL element with a CSS class name of **topics**. As shown previously, we can use the jsoup API to find all the UL elements with that CSS class name:

1. Edit the **build.gradle** file in IntelliJ.

2. Add the following to the dependencies block:

   ```
   // jsoup HTML parser from https://jsoup.org/
   implementation 'org.jsoup:jsoup:1.11.3'
   ```

3. Choose to Import Changes from the popup that appears after adding the new dependency.

4. In IntelliJ's Project pane, right-click on the **com.packtpub.http** package. Select **New** and then **Java Class**.

5. Enter **JavaDocLinks** as the name of the Java class.

6. Enter the following code for **JavaDocLinks.java**:

JavaDocLinks.java

```
1  package com.packtpub.http;
2
3  import org.jsoup.Jsoup;
4  import org.jsoup.nodes.Document;
5  import org.jsoup.nodes.Element;
6  import org.jsoup.select.Elements;
7
8  import java.io.IOException;
9
10 public class JavaDocLinks {
11     public static void main(String[] args) {
```

https://packt.live/2nYnBXS

In this exercise, we used the **jsoup** API to download an HTML document. Once downloaded, we extracted the link URIs and descriptive text associated with each link. This provides a good overview of the **jsoup** API, so you can use it in your projects.

Delving into the java.net.http Module

Java 11 adds a brand new **HttpClient** class in the new **java.net.http** module. The **HttpClient** class uses a modern **builder pattern** (also called a fluent API) to set up HTTP connections. It then uses a Reactive Streams model to support both synchronous and asynchronous requests.

> **Note**
>
> You can refer to *Chapter 16, Predicates and Other Functional Interfaces,* and *Chapter 17, Reactive Programming with Java Flow,* for more on Java's Stream API and Reactive Streams. See https://packt.live/32sdPfO for an overview of the **java.net.http** package in the module.

With the builder model, you can configure things such as timeouts and then call the **build()** method. The **HttpClient** class you get is immutable:

```
HttpClient client = HttpClient.newBuilder()
        .version(HttpClient.Version.HTTP_2)
        .followRedirects(HttpClient.Redirect.NORMAL)
        .connectTimeout(Duration.ofSeconds(30))
        .build();
```

In this example, we specify the following:

- HTTP version 2.

- The client should follow redirects normally, except if the redirect is from the more secure HTTPS to the less secure HTTP. This is the default behavior for **HttpClient. Redirect.NORMAL**.

- The connect timeout will be 30 seconds.

The **HttpClient** class can be used for multiple requests. The next step is to set up an HTTP request:

```
HttpRequest request = HttpRequest.newBuilder()
        .uri(URI.create("http://example.com/"))
        .timeout(Duration.ofSeconds(30))
        .header("Accept", "text/html")
        .build();
```

With this request:

- The URL is **http://example.com/**.

- The timeout on reading is 30 seconds.

- We set the **Accept** header to request the **text/html** content.

Once built, call **send()** on the client to send the request synchronously or call **sendAsync()** to send the request asynchronously. If you call **send()**, the call will block and your application will wait for the data to be returned. If you call **sendAsync()**, the call will return right away and your application can later check to see whether the data has arrived. Use **sendAsync()** if you want to process the data in a background thread. Refer to *Chapter 22, Concurrent Tasks* for more details on background threads and how to perform tasks concurrently:

```
HttpResponse<String> response =
        client.send(request, HttpResponse.BodyHandlers.ofString());
```

In this example, the request body handler specifies that we want the contents back as a string.

Exercise 5: Getting HTML Contents Using the java.net.http Module

In this exercise, we'll recreate *Exercise 2, Creating a GET Request* to get the contents of a web page. While it may seem like there is more code involved, this isn't necessarily the case. The **java.net.http** module can actually be quite flexible as you can introduce **lambda** expressions to handle the response. *Chapter 13, Functional Programming with Lambda Expressions* covers lambda expressions:

1. In IntelliJ's **Project** pane, right-click the **com.packtpub.http** package. Select **New** and then **Java Class**.

2. Enter **NetHttpClient** as the name of the Java class.

3. Enter the following code for **NetHttpClient.java**:

NetHttpClient.java

```
1   package com.packtpub.http;
2
3   import java.io.IOException;
4   import java.net.URI;
5   import java.net.http.HttpClient;
6   import java.net.http.HttpRequest;
7   import java.net.http.HttpResponse;
8   import java.time.Duration;
9
10  public class NetHttpClient {
11      public static void main(String[] args) {
12
13          HttpClient client = HttpClient.newBuilder()
14                  .version(HttpClient.Version.HTTP_2)
15                  .followRedirects(HttpClient.Redirect.NORMAL)
16                  .connectTimeout(Duration.ofSeconds(30))
17                  .build();
```

https://packt.live/2W33Ivy

When you run this program, you should see the same results as the **GetRequest** program created in *Exercise 2, Creating a GET Request.*

Activity 1: Using the jsoup Library to Download Files from the Web

With this activity, you will download the Java titles available through Packt. Go to https://www.packtpub.com/tech/Java in a web browser. Notice all the Java titles that are available. The activity will be to write a program to print all those titles:

1. Using the **jsoup** library, access https://packt.live/2J5dlEv.

2. Download the HTML content.

3. Find all the **DIV** elements with a CSS class of **book-block-title** and print the text within **DIV**.

4. When you run this, you should see the following output:

```
Hands-On Data Structures & Algorithms in Java 11 [Video]
Java EE 8 Microservices
Hands-On Object Oriented Programming with Java 11 [Video]
Machine Learning in Java - Second Edition
Java 11 Quick Start
Object-oriented and Functional Programming with Java 8 [Integrated Course]
Mastering Microservices with Java 9 - Second Edition
Design Patterns and Best Practices in Java
Java Interview Guide : 200+ Interview Questions and Answers [Video]
Ultimate Java Development and Certification Guide [Video]
Spring MVC For Beginners : Build Java Web App in 25 Steps [Video]
Java EE 8 and Angular
RESTful Java Web Services - Third Edition
Java EE 8 Application Development
Mastering Microservices with Java 9 - Second Edition
```

> **Note**
>
> The output is truncated.
>
> The solution for the activity can be found on page 557.

Summary

This chapter introduces HTTP networking, which is often used to connect to RESTful web services from within Java applications. HTTP is a textual request-response protocol. A client sends a request to a server and then gets a response. Each HTTP request has a method; for instance, you would use the GET request to retrieve data, POST to send data, and so on. In Java applications, you will often send and receive text in JSON format.

The `HttpUrlConnection` class provides the primary way to make HTTP requests. Your code writes to an output stream to send data, then reads the response from an input stream. The open-source jsoup library provides a convenient API to retrieve and parse HTML data. Starting with Java 11, you can use the `java.net.http` module for a more modern Reactive Streams approach to HTTP networking. In the next chapter, you'll learn about certificates and encryption—both commonly used with HTTP networking.

10

Encryption

Overview

This chapter discusses Java's support for encryption. It does this first, by defining symmetric and asymmetric key encryption, then teaching you to implement those encryptions **Advanced Encryption Standard (AES)** and **Rivest-Shamir-Adleman (RSA)**, respectively. You will further learn to differentiate between block and stream ciphers, so that you may utilize them appropriately when encrypting your files.

Introduction

Encryption is the process of scrambling data so that it can be sent in plain sight between two or more parties without anyone else being able to understand what was sent. Today, almost everything you do online is encrypted—be it reading an email, sending a photo to a popular social network, or downloading source code. Most serious websites today are also encrypted. Applying encryption to your software is vital for safeguarding your integrity, data, and business, as well as that of your customer.

> **Note**
>
> Encryption is a very complicated topic that gets more complex every year as we try to safeguard our applications from new malicious code and individuals. This chapter will not go into detail about how encryption should be implemented in software. Instead, we will explain how you can use the APIs that are available within Java.

In Java, we have a collection of classes and interfaces that have been specifically created for handling most security-related cases on the Java platform—they're all gathered in what is called the **Java Cryptography Architecture** (**JCA**). Within the JCA lies the foundation for building secure applications in Java. Several other secure libraries within Java use the JCA to implement their security. With the JCA, you can either create your own custom security providers or use the already available standard providers. In most cases, using the standard providers is enough.

Plaintext

In cryptographic terms, plaintext means the data that you wish to encrypt. Cleartext is another popular term that is used interchangeably with plaintext depending on who you ask.

Ciphertext

This is the encrypted version of plaintext. This is the data that is safe to send to the receiving party.

Ciphers

A cipher is a mathematical function, or algorithm, that is used to encrypt plaintext data into ciphertext. However, a cipher is not enough to create ciphertext from plaintext – you also require a key that defines the unique way your encryption will work. All keys are generated uniquely. Depending on the type of cipher you make, you'll have one or two keys to encrypt and decrypt your data.

To initialize a cipher in Java, you'll need to know three things about it: the algorithm used, the mode, and the type of padding. Different ciphers work in different ways, so defining the correct transformation is critical to avoid causing exceptions or creating insecure applications:

```
Cipher cipher = Cipher.getInstance(<transformation>);
cipher.init(Cipher.ENCRYPT_MODE, <key>);
```

The algorithms or ciphers are kept in what we call cryptographic providers (or just providers). Depending on the system in which the application is running, you may not have access to all kinds of ciphers out of the box. In some cases, you may even have to install additional providers to access the cipher you wish you use.

However, every **Java Virtual Machine** (**JVM**) does come with a set of available ciphers with different transformations. At the very least, you'll always find the following transformations available on any JVM today:

- AES/CBC/NoPadding
- AES/CBC/PKCS5Padding
- AES/ECB/NoPadding
- AES/ECB/PKCS5Padding
- AES/GCM/NoPadding
- DES/CBC/NoPadding
- DES/CBC/PKCS5Padding
- DES/ECB/NoPadding
- DES/ECB/PKCS5Padding
- DESede/CBC/NoPadding
- DESede/CBC/PKCS5Padding
- DESede/ECB/NoPadding

- DESede/ECB/PKCS5Padding

- RSA/ECB/PKCS1Padding

- RSA/ECB/OAEPWithSHA-1AndMGF1Padding

- RSA/ECB/OAEPWithSHA-256AndMGF1Padding

Keys

Every cipher requires at least one key to encrypt the plaintext and decrypt the ciphertext. Depending on the type of cipher, the key can be either symmetric or asymmetric. Usually, you'll work with keys stored in non-volatile memory, but you can also generate keys from code. In the JCA, there is a simple command that is used to generate a key for a specific cipher:

```
KeyPair keyPair = KeyPairGenerator.getInstance(algorithm).generateKeyPair();
```

Symmetric Key Encryption

Symmetric encryption is usually considered less safe than asymmetric encryption. This is not because the algorithms are less secure than asymmetric encryption, but because the key that is used to unlock the content must be shared by more than one party. The following diagram illustrates how symmetric encryption works, in general terms.

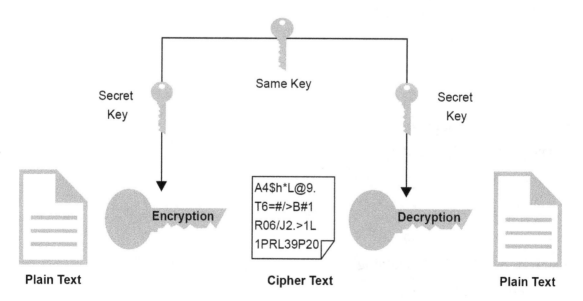

Figure 10.1: Symmetric encryption

You can create keys for symmetric encryption in this way:

```
Key key = KeyGenerator.getInstance(<algorithm>).generateKey();
```

One of the most popular symmetric encryption methods today is the **Advanced Encryption Standard (AES)**.

Exercise 1: Encrypting the String Using Advanced Encryption Standard

In this exercise, we will encrypt the "`My secret message`" string using AES:

1. If IntelliJ is already started but no project is open, then select `Create New Project`. If IntelliJ already has a project opened, then select `File` -> `New` -> `Project` from the menu.

2. In `New Project Dialog`, select a Java project. Click on `Next`.

3. Check the box to create the project from a template. Select `Command Line App`. Then, click on `Next`.

4. Give the new project the name `Chapter10`.

5. IntelliJ will give you a default project location; if you wish to select your own, you can enter it here.

6. Set the package name to `com.packt.java.chapter10`.

7. Click on `Finish`. IntelliJ will create your project called `Chapter10` with the standard folder structure. IntelliJ will also create the main entry point for your application, called `Main.java`.

8. Rename this file to `Exercise1.java`. When you're done, it should look like this:

```java
package com.packt.java.chapter10;

public class Exercise1 {

    public static void main(String[] args) {
    // write your code here
    }
}
```

9. Decide on the algorithm that you want to use for your encryption – in this example, we're using AES –then, generate the key for the encryption. Generating the key may cause an exception if the selected algorithm isn't supported by any of the providers on the system:

```java
package com.packt.java.chapter10;

import javax.crypto.KeyGenerator;
import java.security.Key;
import java.security.NoSuchAlgorithmException;

public class Exercise1{

    public static void main(String[] args) {
        try {
            String algorithm = "AES";
            Key privateKey = KeyGenerator.getInstance(algorithm)
                .generateKey();
        } catch (NoSuchAlgorithmException e) {
            e.printStackTrace();
        }
    }
}
```

> **Note**
>
> In this exercise, we're using a variable to store the key. However, in most real-life scenarios, you'll likely use a less volatile form of storage—such as a file or database.

10. The next step is to define the actual encryption transformation to use. As mentioned previously, the transformation contains information about how to handle the cipher. In this case, we're using AES, which is a block cipher, so we need to define how to apply the key to each block of the plaintext data. Additionally, we need to define whether there should be any padding, and what that padding should look like:

```java
package com.packt.java.chapter10;

import javax.crypto.KeyGenerator;
import java.security.Key;
```

```java
import java.security.NoSuchAlgorithmException;

public class Exercise1 {

    public static void main(String[] args) {
        try {
            String algorithm = "AES";
            Key privateKey = KeyGenerator.getInstance
                            (algorithm).generateKey();
            String transformation = algorithm + "/ECB/NoPadding";
        } catch (NoSuchAlgorithmException e) {
            e.printStackTrace();
        }
    }
}
```

We already chose AES as the algorithm, so we're starting the transformation with that. Following this, we've decided to go for the less-safe **Electronic Code Book (ECB)** transformation mode, which means we're applying the key in the same way for each block of plaintext data. Finally, we've defined that we'll use no padding if a block in the plaintext data is shorter than the cipher block length.

11. Query the system for the cipher with the suggested transformation. This method can throw both **NoSuchAlgorithmException** and **NoSuchPaddingException**. Make sure to handle this if that is the case:

```java
public static void main(String[] args) {
    try {
        String algorithm = "AES";
        Key privateKey = KeyGenerator.getInstance(algorithm)
            .generateKey();
        String transformation = algorithm + "/ECB/NoPadding";
        Cipher cipher = Cipher.getInstance(transformation);
    } catch (NoSuchAlgorithmException e) {
        e.printStackTrace();
    } catch (NoSuchPaddingException e) {
        e.printStackTrace();
    }
}
```

12. Encrypting and decrypting is almost identical when compared to the Java API. When encrypting a plaintext file, you initiate the cipher in encryption mode, and when decrypting a ciphertext file, you initiate the cipher in decryption mode. This may cause **InvalidKeyException** if the key is wrong:

```
public static void main(String[] args) {
    try {
        String algorithm = "AES";
        Key privateKey = KeyGenerator.getInstance(algorithm)
            .generateKey();
        String transformation = algorithm + "/ECB/NoPadding";
        Cipher cipher = Cipher.getInstance(transformation);
        cipher.init(Cipher.ENCRYPT_MODE, privateKey);
    } catch (NoSuchAlgorithmException e) {
        e.printStackTrace();
    } catch (NoSuchPaddingException e) {
        e.printStackTrace();
    } catch (InvalidKeyException e) {
        e.printStackTrace();
    }
}
```

13. In fact, encrypting your text is a two-step process, and you always need to adjust your work depending on the actual bytes of the data. Since we're working on a **String**, you will need to get the actual bytes of this **String**:

Exercise1.java

```
1 package com.packt.java.chapter10;
2
3 import javax.crypto.*;
4 import java.security.InvalidKeyException;
5 import java.security.Key;
6 import java.security.NoSuchAlgorithmException;
7
8 public class Exercise1 {
9
10     public static void main(String[] args) {
11         try {
12         String algorithm = "AES";
13         Key privateKey = KeyGenerator.getInstance(algorithm)
            .generateKey();
14         String transformation = algorithm + "/ECB/PKCS5Padding";
15         Cipher cipher = Cipher.getInstance(transformation);
16         cipher.init(Cipher.ENCRYPT_MODE, privateKey);
```

As you may have noticed, there are a lot of things that could go wrong when working with encryption. Usually, you should handle these exceptions gracefully, but in this case, we'll just print them.

14. Now, the last thing to do is print the encrypted version of the text to verify that you've encrypted the data. You should see gibberish in the terminal. That's fine; it just means you've succeeded in hiding the plaintext message in a ciphertext file:

    What happens if you change the transformation padding to `NoPadding`?

    What happens if you keep the `PKCS5Padding` but change the plaintext message to "`This is 16 bytes`"?

    Try to decrypt the message by instead initializing the cipher to `MODE_DECRYPT`, and then passing the ciphertext rather than the plaintext message. Remember, you need to use the same key for this process to work; otherwise, you'll see gibberish again.

Block Ciphers

AES is a block cipher, meaning that encryption is handled on one block of plaintext at a time. A block size depends on the key size; that is, a larger key means a larger block.

Initialization Vectors

Some of the transformation modes for block ciphers require you to work with an initialization vector – it's an improvement that handles the obvious repeat pattern of the ECB mode. This is easily visualized by an image showing the difference in encryption using AES/ECB and AES/CBC.

CBC refers to **Cipher Block Chaining** and, in short, it scrambles the current block of data based on the previous block of data. Or, if it was the first block, it scrambles the data based on the initialization vector.

Stream Ciphers

A stream cipher, on the other hand, works by encrypting each byte at a time. There is a theoretical discussion about what is known as "the one-time pad," which represents the ideal stream encryption. These are, in theory, extremely secure, but are also very impractical, as the key must be the same length as the plaintext data. With large plaintext data, such keys are impossible to use.

Asymmetric Key Encryption

In asymmetric key encryption, the private key is held by one party only—the receiver or owner of the data. The sender of the data, who is not considered the owner, uses what we call a public key to encrypt the data. The public key can be held by anyone without jeopardizing any previously encrypted messages. This is considered a more secure way of handling encryption, as only the receiver can decrypt the message.

Exercise 2: Encrypting the String Using the RSA Asymmetric Key Encryption

Encrypt the "My secret message" message using the **Rivest–Shamir–Adleman (RSA)** asymmetric key encryption. This is a public/private key combination:

1. Open the **Chapter10** project in IDEA if it's not already open.

2. Create a new Java class using the **File -> New -> Java Class** menu.

3. Enter **Exercise2** as **Name**, and then select **OK**. You should now have an empty class in your project:

```
package com.packt.java.chapter10;
public class Exercise2 {
}
```

4. Add a **main** method—you'll write all your code in that for this exercise:

```
package com.packt.java.chapter10;
public class Exercise2 {
    public static void main(String[] args) {
    }
}
```

5. Declare a plaintext **String** with the content "**My secret message**":

```
package com.packt.java.chapter10;
public class Exercise2 {
    public static void main(String[] args) {
        String plaintext = "My secret message";
    }
}
```

6. Add another string "RSA" in which you'll write the algorithm for this exercise:

```
package com.packt.java.chapter10;
public class Exercise2 {
    public static void main(String[] args) {
        String plaintext = "My secret message";
        String algorithm = "RSA";
    }
}
```

7. Because RSA is an asymmetric form of key encryption, you need to generate a key pair instead of a key. Catch the exception if the algorithm is not found:

```
public class Exercise2 {
    public static void main(String[] args) {
        try {
            String plaintext = "My secret message";
            String algorithm = "RSA";
            KeyPair keyPair = KeyPairGenerator.getInstance(algorithm)
                .generateKeyPair();
        } catch (NoSuchAlgorithmException e) {
            e.printStackTrace();
        }
    }
}
```

8. Define the transformation; we'll go with electronic code block and **PKCS1Padding** for this exercise:

```
public class Exercise2 {
    public static void main(String[] args) {
        try{
            String plaintext = "My secret message";
            String algorithm = "RSA";
            KeyPair keyPair = KeyPairGenerator.getInstance(algorithm)
                .generateKeyPair();
            String transformation = algorithm + "/ECB/PKCS1Padding";
        } catch (NoSuchAlgorithmException e) {
```

```
                    e.printStackTrace();
                }
            }
        }
```

9. Create a cipher for the algorithm and initialize it with the chosen transformation. Remember to always use the public key when encrypting with RSA:

```
        try{
            String plaintext = "My secret message";
            String algorithm = "RSA";
            KeyPair keyPair = KeyPairGenerator.getInstance(algorithm)
                .generateKeyPair();
            String transformation = algorithm + "/ECB/PKCS1Padding";
            Cipher cipher = Cipher.getInstance(transformation);
            cipher.init(Cipher.ENCRYPT_MODE, keyPair.getPublic());
        } catch (NoSuchAlgorithmException e) {
            e.printStackTrace();
        } catch (NoSuchPaddingException e) {
            e.printStackTrace();
        } catch (InvalidKeyException e) {
            e.printStackTrace();
        }
    }
```

10. Finally, encrypt the plaintext into ciphertext, you'll notice that the ciphertext is much larger when using RSA than AES. This is because of the key size.

Exercise2.java

```
1   package com.packt.java.chapter10;
2
3   import javax.crypto.*;
4   import java.security.InvalidKeyException;
5   import java.security.KeyPair;
6   import java.security.KeyPairGenerator;
7   import java.security.NoSuchAlgorithmException;
8
9   public class Exercise2 {
10
11      public static void main(String[] args) {
12          try {
13              String plaintext = "My secret message";
14              String algorithm = "RSA";
15              KeyPair keyPair = KeyPairGenerator.getInstance(algorithm)
                    .generateKeyPair();
16              String transformation = algorithm + "/ECB/PKCS1Padding";
17              Cipher cipher = Cipher.getInstance(transformation);
18              cipher.init(Cipher.ENCRYPT_MODE, keyPair.getPublic());
```

https://packt.live/2MvdL9x

You can also use the decrypt logic for RSA. Remember to use the private key when decrypting; otherwise, it will not work.

Encrypting Files

Encrypting files is very much like encrypting strings. However, with large files, it may be wise to empty the cipher streams. However, if the file is too large, or if there are multiple files, then it may be wise to apply **CipherStreams**–not to be confused with Stream Cipher.

CipherStreams inherit most of their behavior from **InputStream** and **OutputStream** of Java, with the modification that you can decrypt a file you read, or encrypt a file you write with the supplied cipher.

Exercise 3: Encrypting a File

The following exercise displays how to encrypt a file. You can find this file in the code repository.

1. Open the **Chapter10** project in IDEA if it's not already open.

2. Create a new Java class, using the **File | New | Java Class** menu.

3. Enter **Exercise3** as Name, and then select **OK**. You should now have an empty class in your project:

    ```
    package com.packt.java.chapter10;
    public class Exercise3 {
    }
    ```

4. Add a **main** method in which you'll write the code for this exercise:

    ```
    package com.packt.java.chapter10;

    public class Exercise3 {
        public static void main(String[] args) {
        }
    }
    ```

5. Define the algorithm to use for your encryption; we'll go back to AES for this exercise and generate the key:

```java
public static void main(String[] args) {
    try {
        String algorithm = "AES";
        Key secretKey = KeyGenerator.getInstance(algorithm)
            .generateKey();
    } catch (NoSuchAlgorithmException e) {
        e.printStackTrace();
    }
}
```

6. Get an instance of the cipher and initialize it for encryption:

```java
try{
    String algorithm = "AES";
    Key secretKey = KeyGenerator.getInstance(algorithm)
        .generateKey();
    String transformation = algorithm + "/CBC/NoPadding";
    Cipher cipher = Cipher.getInstance(transformation);
    cipher.init(Cipher.ENCRYPT_MODE, secretKey);
} catch (NoSuchAlgorithmException e) {
    e.printStackTrace();
} catch (NoSuchPaddingException e) {
    e.printStackTrace();
} catch (InvalidKeyException e) {
    e.printStackTrace();
}
```

7. Create a file for the encryption; you can download the **plaintext.txt** file from the book's GitHub repository if you wish. Alternatively, you can just create your own text file using lipsum—or even better, copy a document from your computer. We're placing these files in the "**res**" folder of your project:

```java
try {
    String algorithm = "AES";
    Key secretKey = KeyGenerator.getInstance(algorithm)
        .generateKey();
    String transformation = algorithm + "/CBC/NoPadding";
    Cipher cipher = Cipher.getInstance(transformation);
    cipher.init(Cipher.ENCRYPT_MODE, secretKey);
    Path pathToFile = Path.of("res/plaintext.txt");
    File plaintext = pathToFile.toFile();
```

```
        } catch (NoSuchAlgorithmException e) {
            e.printStackTrace();
        } catch (NoSuchPaddingException e) {
            e.printStackTrace();
        }catch (InvalidKeyException e){
            e.printStackTrace();
        }
    }
```

8. In addition to this, create a file that will hold the encrypted contents. Make sure the file doesn't already exist:

```
        File ciphertext = Path.of("res/ciphertext.txt").toFile();
        if (ciphertext.exists()) {
            ciphertext.delete();
        }
    } catch (NoSuchAlgorithmException e) {
        e.printStackTrace();
    } catch (NoSuchPaddingException e) {
        e.printStackTrace();
    } catch (InvalidKeyException e) {
        e.printStackTrace();
    }
```

9. Now it's time to add the cipher streams. In this instance, we need **FileInputStream** to read the contents of the **plaintext.txt** file, **FileOutputStream** to write an initialization vector, and **CipherOutputStream** to perform the encryption:

```
        try (FileInputStream fileInputStream = new
          FileInputStream(plaintext);
            FileOutputStream fileOutputStream = new
              FileOutputStream(ciphertext);
            CipherOutputStream cipherOutputStream = new
              CipherOutputStream(fileOutputStream, cipher)); {
    }
        } catch (NoSuchAlgorithmException e) {
            e.printStackTrace();
        } catch (NoSuchPaddingException e) {
            e.printStackTrace();
        } catch (InvalidKeyException e) {
```

```
            e.printStackTrace();
        } catch (FileNotFoundException e) {
            e.printStackTrace();
        } catch (IOException e) {
            e.printStackTrace();
        }
    }
}
```

10. Write the initialization vector; you will find it in the initialized cipher. Make sure to use **FileOutputStream** as we do not want to encrypt these bytes:

```
        try (FileInputStream fileInputStream = new
          FileInputStream(plaintext);
            FileOutputStream fileOutputStream = new
              FileOutputStream(ciphertext);
            CipherOutputStream cipherOutputStream =
              new CipherOutputStream(fileOutputStream,  cipher))  {
            fileOutputStream.write(cipher.getIV());

}

        } catch (NoSuchAlgorithmException e) {
            e.printStackTrace();
        } catch (NoSuchPaddingException e) {
            e.printStackTrace();
        } catch (InvalidKeyException e) {
            e.printStackTrace();
        } catch (FileNotFoundException e) {
            e.printStackTrace();
        } catch (IOException e) {
            e.printStackTrace();
        }
    }
```

11. Finally, write the contents of **FileInputStream** to **CipherOutputStream**, allowing the contents to be encrypted in the process:

Exercise3.java

```
1   package com.packt.java.chapter10;
2
3   import javax.crypto.Cipher;
4   import javax.crypto.CipherOutputStream;
5   import javax.crypto.KeyGenerator;
6   import javax.crypto.NoSuchPaddingException;
7   import java.io.*;
8   import java.nio.file.Path;
9   import java.security.InvalidKeyException;
10  import java.security.Key;
11  import java.security.NoSuchAlgorithmException;
12
13  public class Exercise3 {
14
15      public static void main(String[] args) {
```

https://packt.live/2J4nKjI

There are numerous ways of working with files in Java, and this is just one way of encrypting the contents. If you have larger files, perhaps **BufferedReader** would be a good option to use.

12. Instead of encrypting a file, use the cipher streams to encrypt a whole folder. Perhaps the best practice here is to first compress the folder into a ZIP archive and then encrypt that file.

Summary

The JCA contains everything you need to work with encryption. In this chapter, you've only really scratched the surface of this major framework. This is just enough to get you started, but if you intend to progress further into the complexities of this framework, you will first need to develop a greater understanding of cryptography.

In the next chapter, we will cover the launching of processes, as well as sending input and capturing the output of child processes.

11

Processes

Overview

In this chapter, we will quickly look at how Java handles processes. You will start by exploring the Runtime and **ProcessBuilder** classes, their functions, and how to launch them, in order to then create a process from either class. You'll then learn to send and receive data between parent and child, and how to store the outcomes of a process in a file. In this chapter's final activity, you will use these skills to create a parent process which will launch a child that will print an outcome (then captured by the parent) to the terminal.

Introduction

The **java.lang.Process** class is used to look for information about, and launch, runtime processes. If you want to understand how the **Process** class works, you can start by looking at the **Runtime** class. All Java programs include an instance of the **Runtime** class. It is possible to get information about the **Runtime** class by calling the **getRuntime()** method and assigning its outcome to a variable of the **Runtime** class. With that, it is possible to obtain information about the **JVM** environment that commands your program:

```
public class Example01 {
    public static void main(String[] args) {
        Runtime runtime = Runtime.getRuntime();
        System.out.println("Processors: " + runtime.availableProcessors());
        System.out.println("Total memory: " + runtime.totalMemory());
        System.out.println("Free memory: " + runtime.freeMemory());
    }
}
```

Processes carry the information relating to a program being launched on a computer. Each operating system handles processes differently. What the **JVM** offers with the **Process** class is an opportunity to control them in the same way. This is done through a single method of the **Runtime** class, called **exec()**, which returns an object of the **Process** class. **Exec** has different implementations that allow you to simply issue a command, or to do so by modifying the environmental variable and even the directory the program will run from.

Launching a Process

As mentioned earlier, a process is launched with **exec()**. Let's look at a simple example where we will call the Java compiler, something that is done the same way from the terminal on any operating system:

```
import java.io.IOException;
public class Example02 {
public static void main(String[] args) {
    Runtime runtime = Runtime.getRuntime();
    try {
        Process process = runtime.exec("firefox");
    } catch (IOException ioe) {
        System.out.println("WARNING: something happened with exec");
    }
  }
}
```

When running this example, if you happen to have Firefox installed, it will launch automatically. You could change that to be any other application on your computer. The program will exit with no error, but it will not do anything besides that.

Now, let's add a couple of lines to the previous example so that the program you just opened will be closed after 5 seconds:

```
import java.io.IOException;
import java.util.concurrent.TimeUnit;
public class Example03 {
    public static void main(String[] args) {
        Runtime runtime = Runtime.getRuntime();
        Process process = null;
        try {
            process = runtime.exec("firefox");
        } catch (IOException ioe) {
            System.out.println("WARNING: something happened with exec");
        }
        try {
            process.waitFor(5, TimeUnit.SECONDS);
        } catch (InterruptedException ie) {
            System.out.println("WARNING: interruption happened");
        }
        process.destroy();
    }
}
```

The `waitFor(timeOut, timeUnit)` method will wait for the process to end for 5 seconds. If it was `waitFor()` without parameters, it would wait for the program to end by itself. Following the 5-second timeout, the process variable will call the `destroy()` method, which will stop the process immediately. For this reason, opening and closing an application over a short period of time.

There is an alternative way of launching a process that doesn't require the creation of a **Runtime** object. This other method makes use of the **ProcessBuilder** class. The construction of a **ProcessBuilder** object will require the actual command to be executed as a parameter. The following example is a revision of the previous one, with the addition of this new constructor:

```
import java.io.IOException;
public class Example04 {
    public static void main(String[] args) {
        ProcessBuilder processBuilder = new ProcessBuilder("firefox");
        Process process = null;
```

```
    try {
        process = processBuilder.start();
    } catch (IOException ioe) {
        System.out.println("WARNING: something happened with exec");
    }
    try {
        process.waitFor(10, TimeUnit.SECONDS);
    } catch (InterruptedException ie) {
        System.out.println("WARNING: interruption happened");
    }
    process.destroy();
    }
}
```

There are a couple of things you should be aware of. First, the process includes the call to the command as an argument in the constructor. However, that does not launch the process until you call **processBuilder.start()**. The only issue is that the object resulting from **ProcessBuilder** does not include the same method as the one coming from the **Process** API. For example, methods such as **waitFor()** and **destroy()** are not available, therefore, if those were needed, you would have to instantiate an object of **Process** before you could call it in your program.

Sending Input to a Child Process

Once the process is running, it would be interesting to pass over some data to it. Let's make a small program that will **echo** whatever you type on the CLI back to it. Later, we will write a program that will launch the first application and that will send text for it to print. This simple **echo** program could be like the one in the following example:

```java
public class Example05 {
    public static void main(String[] args) throws java.io.IOException
    {
        int c;
        System.out.print ("Let's echo: ");
        while ((c = System.in.read ()) != '\n')
        System.out.print ((char) c);
    }
}
```

As you can see, this simple program will be reading from the **System.in** stream until you press *Enter*. Once that happens, it will exit gracefully:

```
Enter some text: Hello World
Hello World
Process finished with exit code 0
```

In the first line of the preceding output, we enter the string '**Hello World**' for this example, which is echoed on the next line. Next, you can make another program that will launch this example and send some text to it:

Example06.java

```
20      try {
21        process.waitFor(5, TimeUnit.SECONDS);
22      } catch (InterruptedException ie) {
23        System.out.println("WARNING: interrupted exception fired");
24      }
25
26      OutputStream out = process.getOutputStream();
27      Writer writer = new OutputStreamWriter(out);
28      writer.write("This is how we roll!\n"); // EOL to ensure the process sends
          back
29
30      writer.flush();
31      process.destroy();
32    }
33 }
```

https://packt.live/2pEJLiw

This example has two interesting tricks that you need to look into. The first is the call to the previous example. Since we have to launch a Java application, we need to call the **java** executable with the **cp** parameter, which will indicate the directory in which **JVM** should be looking for the example compiled. You just compiled and tried out *Example05*, which means that there is already a compiled class in your computer.

> **Note**
>
> After the call to the **cp** parameter, in Linux/macOS, you need to add a colon (:) before the name of the class, whereas in the case of Windows, you should use a semicolon (;).

Once you compile this example, its relative path to the previous example is **../../../** **Example05/out/production/Example05**. This might be completely different in your case, depending on how you named your project folders.

The second thing to note is also highlighted in the code listing. There, you can see the declaration of the **OutStream** that is linked to the one coming from the process. In other words, we are linking an outgoing stream from *Example06* to the **System.in** in the *Example05* application. In order to be able to write strings to it, we construct a **Writer** object that exposes a **write** method with the ability to send strings to the stream.

We can call this example from the CLI using:

```
usr@localhost:~/IdeaProjects/chapter11/[...]production/Example06$ java Example06
```

The result is nothing. The reason for this is that **System.out** on the echo example (*Example05*) is not made available to the application that initiated the process. If we want to use it, we need to capture it inside *Example06*. We will see how to do that in the following section.

Capturing the Output of a Child Process

We now have two different programs; one that can run by itself (*Example05*), and one that is executed from another one, which will also try to send information to it and capture its output. The purpose of this section is to capture the output from *Example05* and print it out to a terminal.

To capture whatever is being sent by the child process to **System.out**, we need to create a **BufferedReader** in the parent class that will be fed from the **InputStream** that can be instantiated from the process. In other words, we need to enhance *Example06* with the following:

```
InputStream in = process.getInputStream();
Reader reader = new InputStreamReader(in);
BufferedReader bufferedReader = new BufferedReader(reader);
String line = bufferedReader.readLine();
System.out.println(line);
```

The reason for needing a **BufferedReader** is that we are using the end of the line (**EOL** or "**\n**") as a marker for a message between processes. That allows the utilization of methods such as **readLine()**, which will block the program until it captures an EOL; otherwise, we could stick to the **Reader** object.

Once you have added that to the example, calling the previous program from the terminal will result in the following output:

```
usr@localhost:~/IdeaProjects/chapter11/[...]production/Example06$ java Example06
Let's echo: This is how we roll!
```

After this output, the program will end.

An important aspect to consider is that since **BufferedReader** is of a buffered nature, it requires the use of **flush()** as a way to force the data we sent to the buffer to be sent out to the child process. Otherwise, it will be waiting forever when **JVM** gives it a priority, which eventually could bring the program to a stall.

Storing the Output of a Child Process in a File

Wouldn't it be useful to store the data in a file? This is one of the reasons why you may be interested in having a process to run a program (or a series of programs) – capturing their output in a log file to study them. By adding a small modification to the process launcher, you could capture whatever it is that is sent to **System.out** by the other program. This is really powerful as you could make a program that could be used to launch any existing command in your operating system and capture all of its output, which could be used later to conduct some sort of forensic analysis of the outcomes:

Example07.java

```
26          // write to the child's System.in
27          OutputStream out = process.getOutputStream();
28          Writer writer = new OutputStreamWriter(out);
29          writer.write("This is how we roll!\n");
30          writer.flush();
31
32          // prepare the data logger
33          File file = new File("data.log");
34          FileWriter fileWriter = new FileWriter(file);
35          BufferedWriter bufferedWriter = new BufferedWriter(fileWriter);
36
37          // read from System.out from the child
38          InputStream in = process.getInputStream();
39          Reader reader = new InputStreamReader(in);
40          BufferedReader bufferedReader = new BufferedReader(reader);
41          String line = bufferedReader.readLine();
```

https://packt.live/33X3Wal

The outcome will be not just writing the result to the terminal, but also creating a **data.log** file that will contain the exact same sentence.

Activity 1: Making a Parent Process to Launch a Child Process

In this activity, we will create a parent process that will launch a child process that will print out an increasing series of numbers. The outcomes of the child process will be captured by the parent, which will print them to the terminal.

To stop the program from running forever to reach infinity, the child process should stop when a certain number is reached. Let's take **50** as a limit for this activity, at which point the counter will exit.

At the same time, the parent process will read the inputs and compare them with a certain number, for example, 37, after which the counter should restart. To ask the child process to restart, the parent should send a single-byte command to the child. Let's use an asterisk (*) for this activity. You should use the **sleep()** command so that printing on the terminal doesn't happen too quickly. A good configuration would be **sleep(200)**.

Given the abovementioned brief, the expected output from running the child program on its own is as follows:

```
0
1
2
3
[...]
49
50
```

But, when called from the parent program, the outcome should be:

```
0
1
2
[...]
36
37
0
1
[loops forever]
```

1. The child should have an algorithm that looks like the following:

```
int cont = 0;
while(cont <= 50) {
   System.out.println(cont++);
   sleep(200);
   if (System.in.available() > 0) {
     ch = System.in.read();
     if (ch == '*') {
     cont = 0;
     }
   }
 }
}
```

Here, there is a call to **System.in.available()** to check whether there is any data in the output buffer from the child program.

2. On the other hand, the parent program should consider including something along the lines of:

```
if (Integer.parseInt(line) == 37) {
  writer.write('*');
  writer.flush(); // needed because of the buffered output
}
```

This would detect whether the number that just arrived as a **String** will be converted to an **Integer**, and from there it would be compared to the limit we suggested for the counting to reset.

We didn't go in-depth in terms of all of the methods offered by the **Process** class. It is therefore recommended to wrap the work in this chapter in good old-school reference documentation and visit JavaDoc to see what else this class has to offer.

> **Note**
>
> The solution for this activity can be found at page 559. You can read more about the **Process** class on Oracle's official documentation: https://docs.oracle.com/javase/8/docs/api/java/lang/Process.html.

Summary

In this short chapter, you were introduced to the **Process** class in Java. You got to see how a process that outputs to **System.out** can be captured in the parent program. At the same time, you also saw how the parent can easily send data to the child. The examples showed that it is possible to launch not just your own programs, but also any other program, such as a web browser. The possibilities for building software automation with programs that include the **Process** API are endless.

We also saw the importance of streams in terms of intra-process communication. Basically, you have to create streams on top of streams to develop more complex data structures, which will allow the code to run a lot faster. The next chapter will cover regular expressions.

12

Regular Expressions

Overview

This chapter discusses regular expressions and considers both how and why they are so useful in Java. To begin, you will first explore how to construct these expressions in order to search for information in your program—a fundamental skill for any developer. When you have a firm understanding of the nature and function of these regular expressions, you will be able to use them to perform simple full-body matches in your search, and, later in the chapter, to extract substrings from a text using groups and non-capturing groups. In the final exercise, you have to employ all of these skills to perform recursive matches and extract a set of similar elements (i.e. a pattern) from a text.

Introduction

In your career as a developer, you will often find a search for information to be a logical first step to problem-solving: searching for documentation, searching for a specific line of code, or just making a program that extracts information from a given body of text into data that the program can understand.

A regular expression is a specific language for defining these search rules, much like Java is a language to construct programs. The syntax can be quite complex. When you see a regular expression for the first time, it can be daunting.

The following is a very basic pattern matcher for an email address construction, with many flaws:

```
/.+\@.+\..+/
```

If you're seeing this for the first time, you might think that it's a typographical error (or that a cat was involved). However, it's perfectly legitimate code. We'll dive deeper into the construction of this example shortly, but first, let's take a look at a more thorough pattern-matcher that validates an email address' construction:

```
/[a-zA-Z]+[a-zA-Z0-9]+\@[a-zA-Z0-9]{2,}\.[a-zA-Z]{2,}/
```

This looks like even more gibberish to the novice. Perhaps the same cat was making a nest on your keyboard.

In this chapter, we uncover the logic behind this madness. We will start with decrypting what regular expressions mean, then look at how this will come in handy in Java.

Decrypting Regular Expressions

The way regular expressions are constructed follows some basic rules that are the same on every platform and implementation; however, there are some implementation-specific rules that might vary depending on the platform and implementation the regular expression was constructed for.

Let's revisit our initial email pattern matching /.+\@.+\..+/ expression. We can see that it starts with a slash mark like this, / and ends with a /. These are the opening and closing markers for the expression; anything within these characters belongs to the actual expression.

Regular expressions are constructed from a few basic components; they are character classes, anchors, groups, and special escape characters. Then, we have the quantifiers that control how many of the preceding characters should be matched. Last but not least, we have the expression flags, which control certain behaviors for the whole expression. Let's look at them in more detail in the upcoming sections.

Character Classes

Character classes define the sets of characters that the pattern matcher will search for. The set is defined in square brackets.

The expression [xyz] will match an x, a y, or a z. These are case sensitive, so an X will not match. If you're matching characters that follow alphabetically, you can replace the expression with a range. Instead of [xyz], you can write [x-z]. This is very convenient if you want to cover many characters in your expression:

Regular Expression	String to be matched	Result
[xyz]	x	Matches
[xyz]	z	Matches
[xyz]	y	Matches
[xyz]	c	Does not match

Figure 12.1: Regular expressions for character classes

There are also predefined character classes. These allow you to search for specific sets of characters without having to type out the full character set. For example, the dot (.) shown earlier will match any character except for line breaks. Written out in full as a set, the expression for this search would look like [^\n\r], so you can see how just using . is quicker and easier. You can see in the following tables what the ^, \n, and \r symbols represent.

You can also search using negated sets. This will match everything that is not part of that set.

Character Sets

A character set matches any character defined in the set. The following figure shows a couple of examples:

[xyz]	In this example, any x, y, or z, would match.
[^xyz]	Negated character set; this matches any character that is not defined in the set. In this example, all characters except x, y, and z will match.
[x-z], [0-9]	A range covers all characters placed within the range specified, either in numerical or alphabetical order.

Figure 12.2: Regular expressions for character sets

Predefined character sets help you build quick expressions. The following figure lists predefined character sets, which are useful for building quick expressions:

.	Matches all characters, except line breaks.
\w, \W	Matches a word; a word can contain any alphabetical or numerical characters. The negated version is shown in uppercase (\w will match anything that's not a word)
\s, \S	Matches any whitespace, such as spaces, line breaks, and tabs. The negated version of this set is in uppercase.
\d, \D	Matches any numeric character between 0 and 9. The negated version is in uppercase

Figure 12.3: Regular expressions for predefined character sets

Quantifiers

Quantifiers are simple rules that allow you to define how the preceding character sets should be matched. Should only one of the characters be allowed, or a range between one and three? See the following figure for acceptable quantifiers:

+	At least one character in the preceding set must be present.
*	Zero or more characters must be found in the text.
{1}, {2,4}, {5,}	A range is defined in curly brackets. The range can match a defined allowed number of matches, a range of matches, or a range without an upper limit.
?	This means that the preceding character should match either 0 or 1 times.

Figure 12.4: Regular expressions for quantifiers

Anchors

Anchors give you one extra dimension of control so you can define the boundaries in a text rather than the text itself:

^xyz	The starting anchor lets you match the start of a text.
$	The end anchor lets you match the end of a text.
\b, \B	Word boundaries represent non-word characters in a text. They are similar to negated character sets, but they will include the beginning and end of a word.

Figure 12.5: Regular expressions for anchors

Capturing Groups

Capturing groups allow you to group tokens in an expression to form sub-strings. Any capturing token can be used within a group, including nesting other groups. They also allow for reuse in the expression using references:

(xyz), (x(y(z)))	A common application for groups is separating strings into substrings.
\1, \2, \3	References a specific group and performs a match on that group. Capturing groups are indexed based on opening parenthesis.
(?:xyz)	Using non-capturing groups, you can exclude matched groups from a result, but still keep them as part of the relevant matching expression.

Figure 12.6: Regular expressions for capturing groups

Escaped Characters

You can use the \ character to escape characters to match them in the string. It is useful for matching serialized data such as XML and JSON. It is also used to match non-text characters such as a tab and a newline.

Here are some common escaped characters:

\n	Newline
\t	Tab
\uFFFF	Unicode Character
\0	Null Character

Figure 12.7: Regular expressions for escaped characters

Flags

Any characters placed directly after the closing marker are called flags. There are five flags, which you may combine in any way, though you may avoid using flags altogether.

//g	The global flag will allow the matcher to store the indices of the last match so that it may continue searching for more matches in the text. In Java, however, the global flag is replaced by the find() method found in the Matcher object.
//i	This makes the expression match any text, ignoring case differences. The matcher would not consider the difference between Text and tEXT.
No flags	The expression will match the first occurrence of the expression. Technically, this means that the search index will never change. Any subsequent searches will always return the same result.

Figure 12.8: Regular expressions for flags

Now that you have a basic understanding of how these regular expressions work, let's look at a full-fledged example in the following exercise.

Exercise 1: Implementing Regular Expressions

Using an online regular expression checker, we'll build a regular expression that verifies whether a street address is correctly specified. The format that the address follows is the street name followed by the street number. The street name and the street number are separated by a single whitespace.

We will check if the following common Swedish addresses are valid or not:

- Strandvagen 1
- Storgatan 2
- Ringvagen3
- Storgatan

> **Note:**
>
> We will use https://packt.live/2MYzyFq for this exercise because of its easy-to-use interface and modern feel. However, the regular expression should work on other platforms as well.

To complete the exercise, perform the following steps:

1. Visit https://packt.live/2MYzyFq.

2. Enter three different local addresses of your choice in the space under the title **Text**, at least one should be incorrectly formatted. The addresses I've chosen are **Strandvagen 1**, **Storgatan 2**, and **Ringvagen3**. These are all very common street names in Sweden, the last of which is incorrectly formatted as it is lacking a whitespace between the street name and the number.

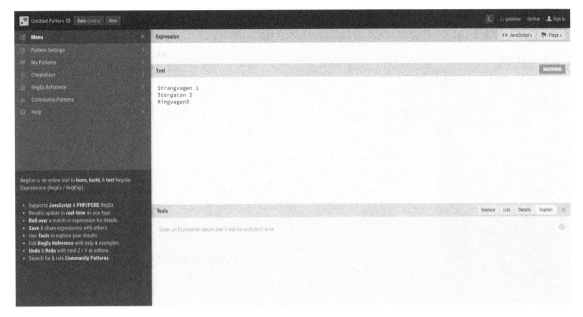

Figure 12.9: Inputting incorrectly formatted text

From the simple rules we defined, we can extract the following:

the street address must start with a name

the street address should have a number

3. Add the first rule. The name is an alphabetic-only word (i.e. contains only letters):

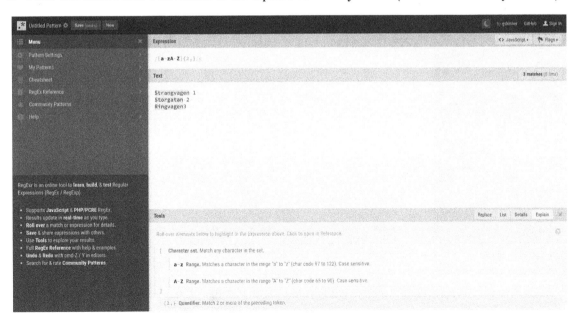

Figure 12.10: Adding the first rule

4. Let there be, at most, one empty space between the digit and the number. We can already see that one address is incorrectly formatted:

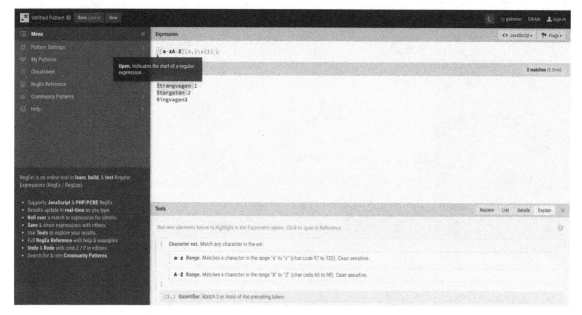

Figure 12.11: Modifying the rule to consider one empty space between digit and number

5. Add at least one digit to the address. Now one more address has disappeared:

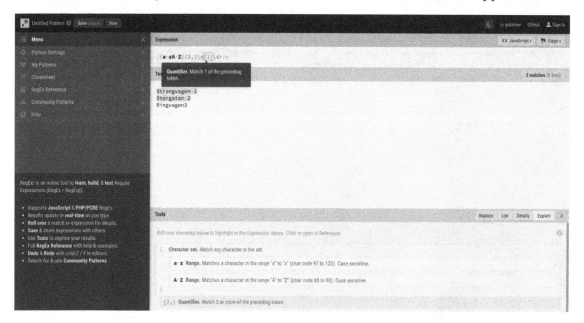

Figure 12.12: Modifying the rule to add one digit to the address

This example shows a simple procedure to construct a regular expression to validate an address.

Activity 1: Regular Expressions to Check If the Entrance is Entered in the Desired Format

Add one more rule to the preceding regular expression; allow for one optional character after the number. This will define which entrance to use at an address that has multiple entrances–for example, **Strandvagen 1a** or **Ringvagen 2b**.

> **Note**
>
> The solution for this activity can be found on page 560.

Regular Expressions in Java

Now that you have an idea of how regular expressions can be used to match patterns, this topic will focus on how regular expressions can be used within Java applications. To use regular expressions in Java, the **java.util.regex** package is available. The two main classes there are called **Pattern** and **Matcher**.

The **Pattern** class handles the actual pattern; it validates, compiles, and returns a **Pattern** object that you can store and reuse multiple times. It can also be used to perform quick validations against a supplied string.

The **Matcher** class allows us to extract more information, and to perform different kinds of matching on the supplied text.

Creating a **Pattern** object is as simple as using the static **compile** method.

For example, you would like to compile a pattern to ensure that a text contains at least one **a**. Your Java code should be as follows:

```
Pattern pattern = Pattern.compile("a+");
Matcher matcher = pattern.matcher("How much wood would a woodchuck chuck if a woodchuck
could chuck wood?");
Boolean matches = matcher.matches();
```

> **Note**
>
> In Java, we shouldn't supply the starting and ending token of the regular expression. With the **Pattern** object, then, you can perform a match on a given string.

Note that this method will attempt to match the entire string to the regular expression; if only part of the string matches the regular expression, it will return false.

If, instead, you just wish to make a quick validation, you can use the static **matches** method, which will return a Boolean; it is just a shorthand for doing exactly the same as the previous example:

```
boolean matches = Pattern.matches("a+", "How much wood would a woodchuck chuck if a
woodchuck could chuck wood?");
```

Exercise 2: Extracting the Domain Using Pattern Matching

In this exercise, you will extract every part of a URL and store them in variables, starting with the protocol, then the domain, and then finally the path:

1. If IntelliJ IDEA is already started, but no project is open, select **Create New Project**. If IntelliJ already has a project open, select **File** -> **New** -> **Project** from the menu.

2. In the **New Project** dialog, select a Java project. Click **Next**.

3. Check the box to create the project from a template. Select **Command Line App**. Click **Next**.

4. Give the new project the name **Chapter12**.

5. IntelliJ will provide a default project location. You can enter any other desired location as well.

6. Set the package name to **com.packt.java.chapter12**.

7. Click **Finish**. Your project will be created with the standard folder structure, and an entry point class for your program.

8. Rename this file **Exercise2.java**. When you're done, it should look like this:

```
package com.packt.java.chapter12;
public class Exercise2 {
    public static void main(String[] args) {
// write your code here
    }
}
```

9. Declare this book's website **url**, which we'll split into separate parts. If you haven't visited the website yet, you can find it at https://www.packtpub.com/application-development/mastering-java-9:

```
package com.packt.java.chapter12;
public class Exercise2 {
    public static void main(String[] args) {
        String url = "https://www.packtpub.com/application-
            development/mastering-java-9";
    }
}
```

10. We'll start by finding just the protocol using regular expressions. Declare a string to hold the regular expression and call it **regex**. It should contain at least the letters **http** and an optional **s**. Wrap the whole expression in a group to ensure you can extract it as a substring later:

```
package com.packt.java.chapter12;
public class Exercise2 {
    public static void main(String[] args) {
        String url = "https://www.packtpub.com/application-development/mastering-
java-9";
        String regex = "(http[s]?)";
    }
}
```

> **Note**
>
> This is, of course, just one example of extracting the protocol. You can experiment with finding strings before the first colon or other interesting expressions.

11. Compile the expression into a **pattern** object. Since we're not performing a global match, we'll not use the shorthand. Instead, we'll create the **Matcher** for later use:

```
package com.packt.java.chapter12;
import java.util.regex.Matcher;
import java.util.regex.Pattern;
public class Exercise2 {
    public static void main(String[] args) {
        String url = "https://www.packtpub.com/application-development/
            mastering-java-9";
        String regex = "(http[s]?)";
        Pattern pattern = Pattern.compile(regex);
        Matcher matcher = pattern.matcher(url);
    }
}
```

12. Attempt to find the first group, using the **find()** method:

```
package com.packt.java.chapter12;
import java.util.regex.Matcher;
import java.util.regex.Pattern;
public class Exercise2 {
    public static void main(String[] args) {
        String url = "https://www.packtpub.com/application
            development/mastering-java-9";
        String regex = "(http[s]?)";
        Pattern pattern = Pattern.compile(regex);
        Matcher matcher = pattern.matcher(url);
        boolean foundMatches = matcher.find();
    }
}
```

> **Note**
>
> You can find the number of available groups using the **groupCount()** method. This is very useful if you want to loop through all groups in order.

13. If any matches were found, start extracting the groups into variables. For now, simply print the variable:

```java
String url = "https://www.packtpub.com/application-
    development/mastering-java-9";
String regex = "(http[s]?)";
Pattern pattern = Pattern.compile(regex);
Matcher matcher = pattern.matcher(url);
boolean foundMatches = matcher.find();
if (foundMatches) {
    String protocol = matcher.group(1);
    System.out.println("Protocol: " + protocol);
}
    }
}
```

14. Before capturing the domain name, we need to ignore the useless characters between that and the protocol—the `://`. Add a non-capturing group for those characters:

```java
String url = "https://www.packtpub.com/application-
    development/mastering-java-9";
String regex = "(http[s])(?:://)";
Pattern pattern = Pattern.compile(regex);
Matcher matcher = pattern.matcher(url);
boolean foundMatches = matcher.find();
if (foundMatches) {
    String protocol = matcher.group(1);
    System.out.println("Protocol: " + protocol);
}
    }
}
```

15. Now, add a third group to the regular expression to find the domain. We'll try to find the whole domain, letting the **www** application notation be optional:

```java
String regex = "(http[s])(?::://)([w]{0,3}\\.?[a-zA-Z]+\\.[a-zA-
    Z]{2,3})";
Pattern pattern = Pattern.compile(regex);
Matcher matcher = pattern.matcher(url);
boolean foundMatches = matcher.find();
if (foundMatches) {
    String protocol = matcher.group(1);
    System.out.println("Protocol: " + protocol);
}
    }
}
```

16. Now, collect the domain group and print it:

```java
String regex = "(http[s])(?::://)([w]{0,3}\\.?[a-zA-Z]+\\.[a-zA-
    Z]{2,3})";
Pattern pattern = Pattern.compile(regex);
Matcher matcher = pattern.matcher(url);
boolean foundMatches = matcher.find();
if (foundMatches) {
    String protocol = matcher.group(1);
    String domain = matcher.group(2);
    System.out.println("Protocol: " + protocol);
    System.out.println("domain: " + domain);
}
    }
}
```

17. Finally, extract the **path** components and print them to the terminal:

Exercise2.java

```
1   package com.packt.java.chapter12;
2
3   import java.util.regex.Matcher;
4   import java.util.regex.Pattern;
5
6   public class Exercise2 {
7
8       public static void main(String[] args) {
9
10          String url = "https://www.packtpub.com/application-
                development/mastering-java-9";
11
12          String regex = "(http[s])(?::://)([w]{0,3}\\.?[a-zA-Z]+\\.[a-zA-
                Z]{2,3})(?:[/])(.*)";
13
14          System.out.println(regex);
```

https://packt.live/2J4qn57

When running this exercise, you should see the following text in the terminal:

```
(http[s])(?:://)([w]{0,3}\.?[a-zA-Z]+\.[a-zA-Z]{2,3})(?:[/])(.*)
Protocol: https
domain: www.packtpub.com
Path: application-development/mastering-java-9
```

This example shows how to use capturing groups to extract only the vital information from a small string. However, you'll notice that the match is only performed once. In Java, it's easy to do a recursive match on a large body of text using similar techniques to this.

Exercise 3: Extracting Links Using Pattern Matching

In this exercise, you'll perform a recursive matching on the Packt website to extract all links, then print these links in the terminal. For simplicity, we'll use an already saved dump of the Packt website; of course you can go ahead and download the website on your own using curl, wget, or similar tools depending on the platform you're using. You can also view the source of the website in your favorite browser and copy it to a file.

1. Open the **Chapter12** project in IntelliJ IDEA if it's not already open.

2. Create a new Java class by going to **File** -> **New** -> **Java Class**.

3. Enter **Exercise 3** as the name and click **OK**. IntelliJ IDEA will create a new class, which should look something like this:

```
package com.packt.java.chapter12;
public class Exercise3 {
}
```

4. Create the main entry point for your program – the **static main** method:

```
public class Exercise3 {
    public static void main(String[] args) {
    }
}
```

5. Copy the Packt website dump into your project's **res** folder. If the folder doesn't exist, create it as a sibling to **src**.

6. Read the contents of the file into a new string; call it **packtDump**:

```
public class Exercise3 {
    public static void main(String[] args) {
        String filePath = System.getProperty("user.dir") + File.separator
            +"res" + File.separator + "packt.txt";
        try {
            String packtDump = new
                String(Files.readAllBytes(Paths.get(filePath)));
        } catch (IOException e) {
            e.printStackTrace();
        }
    }
}
```

7. Start creating a regular expression for capturing links from a website. They usually look something like this. We need to look for the starting and the ending tokens of the link, and capture anything in between:

```
<a href="http://link.to/website">visible text</a>
```

Start by looking for the opening token, **`<a href=\"`**:

```
String filePath = System.getProperty("user.dir") + File.separator
  +"res" + File.separator + "packt.txt";
try {
    String packtDump = new
      String(Files.readAllBytes(Paths.get(filePath)));
    String regex = "(?:<a href=\")";
} catch (IOException e) {
    e.printStackTrace();
}

}
}
```

8. Add another non-capturing group for the ending token. The link ends with the next instance of double quotation marks ("):

```
String filePath = System.getProperty("user.dir") + File.separator
  +"res" + File.separator + "packt.txt";
try {
    String packtDump = new
      String(Files.readAllBytes(Paths.get(filePath)));
    String regex = "(?:<a href=\")(?:\"{1})";
} catch (IOException e) {
    e.printStackTrace();
}

}
}
```

9. Finally, add the only capturing group needed for this regular expression–the link group:

```
String filePath = System.getProperty("user.dir") + File.separator
  + "res" + File.separator + "packt.txt";
try {
    String packtDump = new
      String(Files.readAllBytes(Paths.get(filePath)));
    String regex = "(?:<a href=\")([^\"]+)(?:\"{1})";
} catch (IOException e) {
    e.printStackTrace();
}

}
}
```

10. Compile the pattern and match it against the **packtDump** string:

```
String filePath = System.getProperty("user.dir") + File.separator
    +  "res" + File.separator + "packt.txt";
try {
    String packtDump = new
        String(Files.readAllBytes(Paths.get(filePath)));
    String regex = "(?:<a href=\")([^\"]+)(?:\"{1})";
    Pattern pattern = Pattern.compile(regex);
    Matcher matcher = pattern.matcher(packtDump);
} catch (IOException e) {
    e.printStackTrace();
}
```

11. Create a list for storing the links:

```
String regex = "(?:<a href=\")([^\"]+)(?:\"{1})";
Pattern pattern = Pattern.compile(regex);
Matcher matcher = pattern.matcher(packtDump);
List<String> links = new ArrayList<>();
} catch (IOException e) {
    e.printStackTrace();
}
```

12. Finally, loop through all matches and add them to the list. We only have one capturing group here, so there's no need to check the number of groups and loop through them:

```
String regex = "(?:<a href=\")([^\"]+)(?:\"{1})";
Pattern pattern = Pattern.compile(regex);
Matcher matcher = pattern.matcher(packtDump);
List<String> links = new ArrayList<>();
while (matcher.find()) {
```

```
            links.add(matcher.group(1));
        }
    } catch (IOException e) {
        e.printStackTrace();
    }
  }
}
```

13. Now you can wrap the exercise up by printing the list to the terminal:

Exercise3.java

```
12 public class Exercise3 {
13
14     public static void main(String[] args) {
15         String filePath = System.getProperty("user.dir") + File.separator +
             "res" + File.separator + "packt.txt";
16         try {
17             String packtDump = new
                 String(Files.readAllBytes(Paths.get(filePath)));
18             String regex = "(?:<a href=\")([^\"]+)(?:\"{1})";
19             Pattern pattern = Pattern.compile(regex);
20             Matcher matcher = pattern.matcher(packtDump);
21             List<String> links = new ArrayList<>();
22             while (matcher.find()) {
23                 links.add(matcher.group(1));
24             }
25             System.out.println(links);
```

https://packt.live/35OorYo

Executing this exercise, you should see a long list of both relative and absolute links in your terminal.

```
[/account, #, /register, https://account.packtpub.com/, https://www.packtpub.com/account/
password, #, /, /all, /tech, /, /books/content/support, https://hub.packtpub.com, ... ]
```

You've successfully extracted the links from the Packt website. A real-world application may use this to build site-maps or otherwise document how websites are interconnected. The next step in this program is all up to you. The following steps will let you analyze the content of the Packt website more thoroughly:

1. Remove any non-functional links such as **#** and links back to **home** **/**.

2. Also, remove all links that start with **http**; only the relative links should remain.

3. The first path of the relative links represents the category of that book. Divide the books on the website into different categories and see which category is the most popular.

Summary

In this chapter, you've learned how to use regular expressions to search and extract information from large bodies of text. This can be very handy when parsing structured or semi-structured data. Regular expressions are not specific to Java. The Java implementation may differ slightly from other platforms and languages; however, the general syntax remains the same.

In the next chapter, you'll explore a programming paradigm that is growing in popularity. Functional programming, while not originally intended for Java, can help you to write programs that you can test more easily, which may limit the number of state-changing problems.

13

Functional Programming with Lambda Expressions

Overview

This chapter discusses how Java doubles up as a functional programming language. It also details the manner in which lambda expressions are used to perform pattern matching in Java. It accomplishes this, first, by explaining, in general terms, the difference between **Object-Oriented Programming** (**OOP**) and **Functional Programming** (**FP**). You will then learn the basic definition of a pure function, as well as the difference between functional and normal interfaces. And, finally, you practice employing lambda expressions as callbacks to events and using them to filter data.

Introduction

While Java has been around for over 20 years now, and **Functional Programming** (**FP**) has been around for even longer than Java, it's not been until recently that the topic of FP has caught traction in the Java community. This is probably due to Java being an inherently imperative programming language; when learning Java, you learn OOP.

However, the movements in the mainstream programming community have, in the past few years, shifted more toward FP. These days, you can see it on every platform—from the web to mobile to servers. FP concepts are everywhere.

Background

FP has been around for a very long time even though it is a relatively new topic in Java. In fact, it has been around even longer than the first personal computer; it has its origins in the lambda calculus study that Alonzo Church created in the 1930s.

The name "lambda" comes from the Greek symbol, which was the symbol Church decided to use when describing the rules and mathematical functions for his lambda calculus.

The lambda identity function is, quite simply, a function returning the input parameter—that is, the identity. In a more normal mathematical script.

As you can see, lambda calculus is a simple approach to use for expressing mathematical equations. However, it doesn't necessarily have to be mathematical. In its truest form, it's a function with one argument and a body where the arithmetic happens. In lambda calculus, the function is a first-class citizen – meaning it can be treated like any other variable. You can even combine multiple lambdas if you require multiple attributes in your function.

Functional Programming

FP boils down to two things: side effects and determinism. These concepts form the basis of what we call FP, and they are also the easiest things for newcomers to grasp in this paradigm because they don't introduce new, complex patterns.

Side Effects

When writing a program, we often strive to get some form of side effect – a program without side effects is a very dull program, as nothing would happen. However, side effects are also a common headache when trying to test a program reliably as its state may change unpredictably.

A very useful class in Java is the `Math` class; it contains all sorts of mathematical helpers and is likely to be used in all Java applications, either directly or indirectly. Here is an example of printing a pseudo-random number to the console:

```
public static void main(String[] args) {
    System.out.println(Math.random());
}
```

If we dig into the code of `Math.java` and review the details of the `random()` function, we will notice that it uses an object, **randomNumberGenerator**, that doesn't belong exclusively to the `random()` function:

```
public final class Math {
    public static double random() {
        return RandomNumberGeneratorHolder.randomNumberGenerator.nextDouble();
    }
}
```

It also calls `nextDouble()` on the **randomNumberGenerator** object. This is what we refer to as a side effect; the **random** function reaches outside its own home, or body, and performs changes on other variables or classes. These variables, in turn, can be by other functions or objects that may or may not produce their own side effects. This behavior is a red flag when you are trying to implement a program in FP fashion because it's unpredictable. It can also be more difficult to make it safe to use in a multithreaded environment.

> **Note**
>
> The `Math.random()` function, by design, delivers an unpredictable result. However, as an example, it serves us well to highlight the concept of side effects. The **random** function is also safe to use in multithreaded environments (for the most part)— Sun and Oracle have done their homework!

As the `Math.random()` function produces different results for the same arguments, it's defined as a non-deterministic function.

Deterministic Functions

A deterministic function is defined as a function that will always produce the same result for the same arguments, no matter how many times, or when, you execute the function:

```
public static void main(String[] args) {
    System.out.println(Math.random());
    System.out.println(Math.random());
}
```

In this example, `Math.random()` is called twice, and will always print two different values to the terminal. No matter how many times you call `Math.random()`, it will always give different results – as, by design, it's not deterministic:

```
public static void main(String[] args) {
    System.out.println(Math.toRadians(180));
    System.out.println(Math.toRadians(180));
}
```

Running this simple code, we can see that the `Math.toRadians()` function will give the same result for both functions, and doesn't seem to change anything else in the program. This is a hint that it is deterministic – let's dig into the function and review it:

```
public final class Math {
    private static final double DEGREES_TO_RADIANS = 0.017453292519943295;

    public static double toRadians(double angdeg) {
        return angdeg * DEGREES_TO_RADIANS;
    }
}
```

The function, as expected, will not change anything from the outside world and will always produce the same result. This means that we can consider it as a deterministic function. However, it does read a constant that lives outside of the function's scope; this is something of an edge case of what we can call a **pure function**.

Pure Functions

The purest of functions can be considered black boxes, meaning that what happens inside the function is not really of any interest to the programmer. They are only interested in what is put into the box, and what comes out of it as a result—that's because there will always be a result of a pure function.

The pure function takes arguments and produces a result based on these arguments. The pure function will never change the state of the outside world or rely on it. Everything that is required by the function should be available inside it, or as an input to it.

Exercise 1: Writing Pure Functions

A grocery store has a system for managing their stock; however, the company that built their software has gone bankrupt and has lost all the source code for their system. This is a system that only allows customers to buy one thing at a time. Because their customers want to buy two things at a time, never more or less, they have asked you to implement a function that takes the price of two products and returns the sum of those two prices. They want you to implement this without causing any side effects or incompatibilities with their current system. You'll implement this as a pure function:

1. If IntelliJ is already started but no project is open, then select **Create New Project**. If IntelliJ already has a project open, then select **File** -> **New** -> **Project** from the menu.

2. In **New Project** dialog, select the **Java project**. Then, click on **Next**.

3. Check the box to create the project from a template. Select **Command Line App**. Then, click on **Next**.

4. Give the new project the name **Exercise1**.

5. IntelliJ will give you a default project location; if you wish to select one, you can enter it here.

6. Set the package name to **com.packt.java.chapter13**.

7. Click on **Finish**. IntelliJ will create your project, called **Exercise1**, with the standard folder structure. IntelliJ will also create the main entry point for your application, called **Main.java**; it will look like the following code snippet:

```java
package com.packt.java.chapter13;
public class Main {
    public static void main(String[] args) {
    // write your code here
    }
}
```

8. Rename **Main.java** to **Exercise1.java**.

9. Create a new function in the **Main** class, placing it under the **main(String[] args)** function. Call the new function **sum** and let it return an integer value. This function should take two integers as input. For the simplicity of the code, we'll make the function a **static** utility function:

```
package com.packt.java.chapter13;
public class Exercise1 {
    public static void main(String[] args) {
    // write your code here
    }
    static int sum(int price1, int price2) {
    }
}
```

10. All this function should do is return the sum of the two arguments–**price1** and **price2**:

```
package com.packt.java.chapter13;
public class Exercise1 {
    public static void main(String[] args) {
    // write your code here
    }
    static int sum(int price1, int price2) {
        return price1 + price2;
    }
}
```

11. Call this new method a few times using the same parameters in your **main** function:

```
package com.packt.java.chapter13;
public class Exercise1 {
    public static void main(String[] args) {
        System.out.println(sum(2, 3));
        System.out.println(sum(2, 3));
        System.out.println(sum(2, 3));
```

```
        }
        static int sum(int price1, int price2) {
            return price1 + price2;
        }
    }
```

12. Now run your program and observe the output.

> **Note**
>
> The `System.out.println()` method is considered by many as an impure function because it manipulates the terminal – which is, of course, "the outside world" because, at some point in the call stack, the function will reach outside of its body to manipulate an `OutputStream` instance.

The function you just wrote takes two arguments and produces a whole new output, without modifying anything outside the function's scope. With this, you've successfully taken the first step toward writing applications in a more functional way.

Another important consideration when writing functional programs is how to handle the state in your application. In OOP, we attack the problem of handling state in large applications by using the divide-and-conquer strategy. Here, each object in the application contains a little piece of the state of the entire application.

An implicit attribute of this type of state handling is the ownership and mutability of the state. Each object often has a private state that is accessible using a public interface— the object's method. If, for example, we review the **ParseException.java** class from the OpenJDK source code, we'll find this pattern as well:

```
package java.text;
public class ParseException extends Exception {
    private static final long serialVersionUID = 2703218443322787634L;
    public ParseException(String s, int errorOffset) {
        super(s);
        this.errorOffset = errorOffset;
```

```
    }
    public int getErrorOffset() {
        return errorOffset;
    }
    private int errorOffset;
}
```

Here, we can see one private member variable called **errorOffset**. This member variable is writeable from the constructor and is accessible for other objects via the **getErrorOffest()** method. We can also imagine a class that has another method that changes the **errorOffset** value–that is, a setter.

One possible problem with this approach to state handling is multithreaded applications. If two or more threads were to either read or write to this member variable, we would usually see unpredictable changes. These changes can, of course, be mended in Java by using synchronization. However, synchronization comes at a cost; it's complicated to plan access accurately and, often, we end up with race conditions. It's also quite an expensive procedure in any language that supports it.

> **Note**
>
> Using synchronization is quite popular and is a safe way to build multithreaded applications. However, one of the downsides of synchronization—apart from it being very expensive—is that it effectively makes our application behave as a single-threaded application, as all threads accessing the synchronized data must wait their turn to handle the data.

In FP, we try to avoid using synchronization by instead saying that our state should always be immutable–effectively negating the need for synchronization.

Immutability of State

When the state is immutable, it essentially means that it cannot change, ever. There is a common way of writing this rule in FP that goes something like this: replace your data rather than editing it in place.

As we discussed in *Chapter 3, Object-Oriented Programming*, one of the core concepts of OOP is inheritance; that is, the ability to create child classes that build upon, or inherit, the functionality already present in parent classes, but also add new functionality to the child classes. In FP, this becomes relatively tricky because we're targeting data that should never change.

The easiest way of making data unchangeable in Java is by using the **final** keyword. There are three ways of using the **final** keyword in Java: locking variables for change, making methods impossible to override, and making classes impossible to extend. When building immutable data structures in Java, it's often not enough with just one of these methods; we need to use two or sometimes even all three.

Exercise 2: Creating an Immutable Class

A local carpenter has set up shop on your street and has asked you to build the storage mechanism for a simple shopping cart application, which they will use internally for people ordering furniture. The application should be able to safely handle multiple people editing it at the same time from different threads. The salespeople will take orders on the phone and the carpenters will be editing the price in hours spent and material used. The shopping cart must be immutable. To do this, perform the following steps:

1. In the **Project** pane in IntelliJ, right-click on the folder named **src**.

2. Choose **New** -> **Java Class** in the menu and enter **Exercise2**.

3. Define the **main** method in your new class:

```
package com.packt.java.chapter13;
public class Exercise2 {
    public static void main(String[] args) {

    }
}
```

4. Create a new inner class called **ShoppingCart**, and then make it **final** to ensure that it cannot be extended or its behavior changed. Your code should now look something like this:

```
package com.packt.java.chapter13;
public class Exercise2 {
    public static void main(String[] args) {

    }
    public static final class ShoppingCart {

    }
}
```

5. We also need items to put into this cart, so create a simple data object for **ShoppingItem**, give it a name and price attribute, and then make the class immutable. We'll later use this class to instantiate a few different objects to test the mutability of our **ShoppingCart** class:

```
public static final class ShoppingCart{
}
private static final class ShoppingItem {
    private final String name;
    private final int price;
    public ShoppingItem(String name, int price) {
        this.name = name;
        this.price = price;
    }
}
```

6. Add a list in which we will keep all the items for this immutable shopping cart. Make sure that you declare the list with the **final** keyword, keeping it unchangeable:

```
package com.packt.java.chapter13;
import java.util.ArrayList;
import java.util.List;
public class Exercise2 {

    public static final class ShoppingCart{
        private final List<ShoppingItem> mShoppingList = new ArrayList<>();
    }

}
```

Now we have a way to create items for our customers to purchase, and we also have a bag for our customers to put their selected items in. However, we lack a way for our customers to add items to the shopping cart.

7. In the object-oriented approach to solving this problem, we could add a method called **addItem(ShoppingItem shoppingItem)**:

```
package com.packt.java.chapter13;
import java.util.ArrayList;
import java.util.List;
public class Exercise2 {
```

```
private final class ShoppingCart{
    private final List<ShoppingItem> mShoppingList = new ArrayList<>();

    public void addItem(ShoppingItem item) {
        mShoppingList.add(item);
    }
}

}
```

Looking at this solution from an FP approach, we can already see that it will modify the collection. This is something that we're desperately trying to avoid as multiple people will be working on this shopping cart at the same time. In this case, using the **final** keyword has no impact since the contents of a final list can still change. One basic approach to solving this in a functional way is to return a new **ShoppingCart** when adding an item.

8. Add a new constructor to the **ShoppingCart** class and let it take a list as an argument. Then, pass this list to **mShoppingList** of the **ShoppingCart** class and make it unmodifiable with the **Collections.unmodifiableList()** method:

```
package com.packt.java.chapter13;
import java.util.ArrayList;
import java.util.Collections;
import java.util.List;
public class Exercise2 {
    public static final class ShoppingCart{
        public final List<ShoppingItem> mShoppingList;
        public ShoppingCart(List<ShoppingItem> list) {
            mShoppingList = Collections.unmodifiableList(list);
        }
        public void addItem(ShoppingItem item) {
            mShoppingList.add(item);
        }
    }
}
```

9. Rewrite the **addItem(ShoppingItem item)** method and let it return a new
    ShoppingCart item instead of **void**. Copy the list of the previous **ShoppingCart** items
    into a temporary list and add another item to it. Then, pass this temporary list to
    the constructor and return the newly created **ShoppingCart** object:

```
public static final class ShoppingCart{
    public final List<ShoppingItem> mShoppingList;
    public ShoppingCart(List<ShoppingItem> list) {
        mShoppingList = Collections.unmodifiableList(list);
    }
    public ShoppingCart addItem(ShoppingItem item) {
        List<ShoppingItem> newList = new ArrayList<>(mShoppingList);
        newList.add(item);
        return new ShoppingCart(newList);
    }
}
```

In this code, we can see that the constructor now accepts a list of **ShoppingItem**
classes; we can also see that the list is directly saved as an unmodifiable list. This is
a special type of list in Java—one that throws an exception whenever you attempt to
modify it in any way, either directly or through its iterator.

We can also see that the **addItem(ShoppingItem item)** function now returns a new
ShoppingCart, with a whole new list, but with the items from the previous shopping
list shared between the two **ShoppingCart** instances. This is an acceptable solution
even for a multithreaded environment as the **ShoppingItem** classes are final and,
therefore, may never change their state.

> **Note**
>
> Java 8 introduced the Stream API, which was a whole new way of working with
> collections, that is, a more FP-based approach. You can read more about the
> Stream API in *Chapter 15, Processing Data with Streams*. In this chapter, we'll focus
> on solutions that don't use the Stream API.

10. Now you need to use this new **ShoppingCart** in a program. Edit your **main** method, and then let it create an empty **ShoppingCart** first. Then, add a new shopping item to that cart, storing the newly created **ShoppingCart** in another variable. Finally, add another **ShoppingItem** to the second **ShoppingCart**, again storing the new **ShoppingCart** in a new variable:

Exercise2.java

```
7   public class Exercise2 {
8
9       public static void main(String[] args) {
10          ShoppingCart myFirstCart =
            new ShoppingCart(new ArrayList<ShoppingItem>());
11          ShoppingCart mySecondCart =
            myFirstCart.addItem(new ShoppingItem("Chair", 150));
12          ShoppingCart myThirdCart =
            mySecondCart.addItem(new ShoppingItem("Table",350));
13      }
```

https://packt.live/2Jdr101

11. Place a breakpoint on the last line and debug your code. You'll notice the carts that are created when calling **addItem** maintain their own unmodifiable list of **ShoppingItem**, but the immutable **ShoppingItem** are shared across the lists.

The **Collections.unmodifiableList()** method and other similar methods (such as **Set**, **Map**, and **SortedList**) are not providing any immutability to the list itself. They produce a view of the list that prohibits any change. However, anyone with a reference to the actual list will still be able to change the data.

In this exercise the lists are safe as the **main** method doesn't keep any reference to the lists, so no one outside can change it. However, this is not the recommended path when attempting to implement a program using a functional approach; don't trust anyone to follow rules unless they strictly must. Since Java 9, there are now real immutable collections that are available.

Activity 1: Modifying Immutable Lists

Add a new behavior to your **ShoppingCart**:

1. Create a **removeItem(ShoppingItem)** function.

2. Create a function that takes multiple **ShoppingItem** as arguments, either as a list or as variable arguments.

3. Modify your **ShoppingCart** to take multiple items of each **ShoppingItem**—for example, four chairs and one table. Additionally, modify the **addItem(ShoppingItem)** and **removeItem(ShoppingItem)** functions.

> **Note**
>
> The solution for this activity can be found on page 561.

Immutable Collections

Using **Collections.unmodifiableList** is a quick way to provide an unmodifiable version of an existing list. Another option available since Java 9 is to use the immutable collections with factory methods. These factory methods allow you to create three different immutable collection types: **List**, **Set**, and **Map**.

> **Note**
>
> There are a few libraries that provide more optimized immutable collections; one popular example is Guava with its **ImmutableArrayList** and other types.

If we were to use the **List** factory methods instead of the **Collections** class in our shopping cart, it could look something like this:

```java
public class Main {
    public static final class ShoppingCart {
        public final List<ShoppingItem> mShoppingList;
        public ShoppingCart(List<ShoppingItem> list) {
            mShoppingList = List.copyOf(list);
        }
        public ShoppingCart addItem(ShoppingItem item) {
            List<ShoppingItem> newList = new ArrayList<>(mShoppingList);
            newList.add(item);
            return new ShoppingCart(newList);
        }
    }
}
```

Here, we can see that there's very little difference to what we had before. Instead of using `Collections.unmodifiableList()` to create an unmodifiable view of the list, we create an immutable copy of this list with `List.copyOf()`. The difference in our example is invisible for the user. However, at the bottom, they're based on different implementations—the `UnmodifiableCollection` and `ImmutableCollections` classes, respectively.

Exercise 3: Overriding the String Method

In this exercise, we'll make a small technical proof of the difference between `UnmodifiableCollection` and `ImmutableCollection` classes. For this example, we'll need to override the `toString()` method for the `ShoppingItem` and `ShoppingCart` classes:

1. Add the `toString()` method to the `ShoppingItem` class, and then let it return the name:

    ```
    private static final class ShoppingItem {
        @Override
        public String toString() {
            return name + ", " + price;
        }
    }
    ```

2. Add the `toString()` method to the `ShoppingCart` class. Then, let it return a concatenated string for all the `ShoppingItem` in the list:

    ```
    public static final class ShoppingCart {
        public String toString() {
            StringBuilder sb = new StringBuilder("Cart: ");
            for (int i = 0; i < mShoppingList.size(); i++) {
                sb.append(mShoppingList.get(i)).append(", ");
            }
            return sb.toString();
        }
    }
    ```

3. Now we have a simple way of printing the contents of a **ShoppingCart** using the **toString()** method. To demonstrate the difference, replace the code in the **main** method. Add a few books to a standard list, and then copy this list into an unmodifiable version and an immutable version. Print the two copies:

```java
public static void main(String[] args) {
    List<ShoppingItem> books = new ArrayList<>();
    books.add(new ShoppingItem("Java Fundamentals", 100));
    books.add(new ShoppingItem("Java 11 Quick Start", 200));
    List<ShoppingItem> immutableCopy = List.copyOf(books);
    List<ShoppingItem> unmodifiableCopy =
        Collections.unmodifiableList(books);
    System.out.println(immutableCopy);
    System.out.println(unmodifiableCopy);

}
```

4. Now remove the first item, the **Java Fundamentals** book, from the original **books** list and print the two copies again:

```java
public static void main(String[] args) {
    List<ShoppingItem> books = new ArrayList<>();
    books.add(new ShoppingItem("Java Fundamentals", 100));
    books.add(new ShoppingItem("Java 11 Quick Start", 200));
    List<ShoppingItem> immutableCopy = List.copyOf(books);
    List<ShoppingItem> unmodifiableCopy =
        Collections.unmodifiableList(books);
    System.out.println(immutableCopy);
    System.out.println(unmodifiableCopy);
    books.remove(0);
    System.out.println(immutableCopy);
    System.out.println(unmodifiableCopy);

}
```

This simple example provides proof of the difference between an unmodifiable view and an immutable copy. In the unmodifiable version, the list can still be changed, and the unmodifiable view will pick up on that change, whereas the immutable version will ignore that change because it contains a new list of items.

Functional Interfaces

Functional interfaces are declared as standard Java interfaces, except they're only allowed to contain one abstract function, but can contain any number of default or static functions.

The **Comparator** interface is one of the older interfaces of Java. It has been with us since version 1.2 and has seen many several over the years. However, the biggest change yet is probably the move to become a functional interface in Java 8.

Reviewing the changes on the **Comparator** interface in Java 8, you'll notice some interesting changes. First, the interface has grown from 4 lines of code to 80 lines, excluding package declaration and comments. Then, you'll notice that there's a new annotation at the top:

```
@FunctionalInterface
```

This annotation marks that this is now a functional interface. Its main purpose is to tell the reader that this interface is intended to follow the functional interfaces specification as defined in Java 8. If it fails to follow those guidelines, the Java compiler should print an error.

After the two original abstract function declarations, you'll find no less than seven default functions. These default functions were introduced in Java 8 to add new functionality to interfaces without breaking backward compatibility. The default functions are always public and will always contain a code block. They can return a value, but this is not required by the specification.

Finally, we'll find a total of nine **static** functions. Since Java 8, the functional interface can contain any number of **static** methods, they work very much like the static methods found in normal classes. You will explore more details about building and using functional interfaces in a later chapter in this book.

Lambda Expressions

Along with the functional improvements in Java 8, there also came **Lambda** expressions. One of the primary improvements with lambdas is the code readability—most of the boilerplate code for interfaces is now gone.

A very commonly used interface is the **Runnable interface**; it's used in multithreaded applications to perform any type of task in the background, such as downloading a large file from a network. In Java 7 and earlier versions, you'd often see the Runnable interface used as an anonymous instance:

```
new Thread(new Runnable() {
    @Override
    public void run() {
    }
}).start();
```

Since Java 8, the preceding five lines of code can now be simplified by using a lambda expression instead:

```
new Thread(() -> {}).start();
```

As you can see, the code becomes much more readable when we remove a lot of the boilerplate code.

The lambda expression consists of two main components: the arguments and the body. Additionally, between these two components, there is always an arrow operator (which is also known as a lambda operator). The body also contains the optional return value. The parentheses contain the optional arguments for the lambda expression. Because it's an FP component, though, you'll want to use arguments:

```
(int arg1, int arg2) -> { return arg1 + arg2; }
```

You can also omit the type of the arguments as those will be inferred by the functional interface that the lambda expression implements:

```
(arg1, arg2) -> { return arg1 + arg2; }
```

If you have only one argument, you can omit the parentheses:

```
arg1 -> { return arg1; }
```

However, if you have no arguments in your lambda, then you must include the parentheses:

```
() -> { return 5; }
```

Then there is the function body; if you have many lines of code in your lambda logic, you must use the curly brackets to enclose the body:

```
(arg1, arg2) -> {
    int sum = arg1 + arg2;
    return sum;
}
```

However, if you only have one single line of code, you can omit the curly brackets and immediately return the value:

```
(arg1, arg2) -> return arg1 + arg2;
```

Finally, you can also omit the **return** keyword if all you have is a single line of code:

```
(arg1, arg2) -> arg1 + arg2;
```

If we were to write the lambda calculus identity function in Java, assuming we have a functional interface called **Identity**, it would look something like this:

```
Identity identity = x -> x;
```

One commonly used interface is the **Comparator** interface, which is used in almost any object you wish to order, specifically in a collection of some form.

Exercise 4: Listing Spare Tires

A racing team has contacted you to organize their stock of spare tires because it's in a mess. They've asked you to write an application that will show the list of available tires in order of size, starting with the biggest tire.

To do this, you'll build a lambda function that implements the **Comparator** functional interface. For reference, this is the base view of the **Comparator** interface, excluding the default and static functions:

```
@FunctionalInterface
public interface Comparator<T> {
    int compare(T o1, T o2);
}
```

1. In the **Project** pane in IntelliJ, right-click on the folder named **src**.

2. Choose **New** -> **Java Class** in the menu, and then enter **Exercise4**.

3. Define the **main** method in your new class:

    ```
    package com.packt.java.chapter13;
    public class Exercise4 {
        public static void main(String[] args) {
        }
    }
    ```

4. Create a new inner class called **Tire**. It should have a size variable that is the diameter of the tire in inches. Make sure that the class and size are declared as **final** to adhere to the FP guidelines:

```java
package com.packt.java.chapter13;
public class Exercise4 {
    public static void main(String[] args) {
    }
    public static final class Tire {
        private final int size;
    }
}
```

5. Create the **Tire** constructor, taking one argument–the **size**–and passing that to the member variable. Additionally, override the **toString()** method to print the size of the tire:

```java
    public static void main(String[] args) {
    }
    public static final class Tire {
        private final int size;
        public Tire(int size) {
            this.size = size;
        }
        @Override
        public String toString() {
            return String.valueOf(size);
        }
    }
}
```

6. Create a list of tires that need to be sorted into your **main** method:

```java
    public static void main(String[] args) {
        List<Tire> tires = List.of(
            new Tire(17),
            new Tire(16),
            new Tire(18),
            new Tire(14),
            new Tire(15),
            new Tire(16));
    }
```

7. Create the actual lambda expression, using the **Comparator** functional interface, that you will use to sort the immutable list of tires. It should take two arguments, and return the difference in size. Remember that the lambda expression infers a lot of the structure; you won't need to specify the types or return a keyword in this simple example. The lambda expression is a first-class citizen, so it's fine to store it in a variable for later use:

```
public static void main(String[] args) {
    List<Tire> tires = List.of(
        new Tire(17),
        new Tire(16),
        new Tire(18),
        new Tire(14),
        new Tire(15),
        new Tire(16));
    Comparator<Tire> sorter = (t1, t2) -> t2.size - t1.size;
}
```

> **Note**
>
> You can, of course, also apply the lambda expression as an anonymous instance—that way, you can save a few lines of code while keeping the code very readable.

8. Apply the lambda expression in the **sort** method. The **List.sort()** method modifies the content of the list, so you need to copy your immutable list of tires before sorting it:

```
public static void main(String[] args) {
    List<Tire> tires = List.of(
        new Tire(17),
        new Tire(16),
        new Tire(18),
        new Tire(14),
        new Tire(15),
        new Tire(16));
    Comparator<Tire> sorter = (t1, t2) -> t2.size - t1.size;
    List<Tire> sorted = new ArrayList<>(tires);
    sorted.sort(sorter);
}
```

9. Finally, print the result:

```
public static void main(String[] args) {
    List<Tire> tires = List.of(
        new Tire(17),
        new Tire(16),
        new Tire(18),
        new Tire(14),
        new Tire(15),
        new Tire(16));
    Comparator<Tire> sorter = (t1, t2) -> t2.size - t1.size;
    List<Tire> sorted = new ArrayList<>(tires);
    sorted.sort(sorter);
    System.out.println(sorted);
}
```

10. To make this program functional, you could move the sorting intelligence to a pure function that takes a list as an argument, then performs the sorting on a copy of that list and returns the immutable sorted list. This way, you will avoid keeping a reference of the mutable list in your main program:

> **Note**
>
> The complete code snippet can be referred at: https://packt.live/35OxQiJ.

You've just created your first lambda expression, based on an already present **Functional** interface, and you've then used it to sort a list of tires. There are lots of functional interfaces available since Java 8, and you've probably already been using most of them; we'll explore this in more detail later in the book.

Summary

It shouldn't matter the order in which different threads act on your data, and you should be able to easily add functionality that doesn't affect older parts of your application. Following these FP concepts allows you to build code that can easily be used in multithreaded applications, as well as to build code that can be tested very easily for problems and regression bugs. It also often makes your code much more readable.

Using the core concepts of FP that you've learned about in this chapter—pure functions and immutability—can lead to performance issues in some cases, specifically when modifying large datasets. There are ways to get around these, as we'll explore in later chapters.

Because Java was designed for an OOP approach, it can be a bit daunting to get into FP at first, but if you "go functional" in only certain parts of your code, the transition from OOP may become easier.

In the next chapter, we'll focus on how to navigate larger datasets and repeat code without using loops.

14

Recursion

Overview

In this chapter, we will see how using recursion can help you to write effective code. The chapter begins with an initial exercise illustrating one of the simplest mistakes you can make with recursion: forgetting to code a termination condition. The first step, then, is learning how to salvage your program when the Java stack has blown away. From there, you will learn to write recursive methods in order to handle mathematical formulas and other recurrent processing needs. Finally, with these techniques (and those further defined by this chapter), you will practice creating and processing XML files with the **Document Object Model (DOM)** API.

Introduction

Recursion is where a method calls itself, over and over again. Recursion, when used carefully, can be a useful programming technique; but the key is to use it correctly.

An important point is that recursion is just a programming technique. You can often avoid it, if you want, by writing some form of an iterative loop. However, if the problem you need to solve is truly recursive, the iterative approach will likely be much more complex than the comparatively simpler and more elegant recursion code which corresponds.

This chapter delves into this handy programming technique.

Delving into Recursion

Recursion is useful for many mathematical problems, such as when working with cellular automata, Sierpinski triangles, and fractals. In computer graphics, recursion can be used to help generate realistic-looking mountains, plants, and other natural phenomena. Classic problems, such as the Tower of Hanoi, work well with recursion.

In Java applications, you will often use recursion when traversing tree data structures, including XML and HTML documents.

> **Note**
>
> You can refer to https://packt.live/2Jalre8 for more information on the Tower of Hanoi problem.

A simple example of recursion looks like the following:

```
public int add(int num) {
    return add(num + 1);
}
```

In this example, each call to the **add()** method will call itself with a number that is one greater than the one used for the current call.

> **Note**
>
> You always need a termination condition to stop the recursion. This example does not have one.

Exercise 1: Using Recursion to Overflow the Stack

This example demonstrates what happens when you don't provide a way for a recursive method to stop. Bad things happen to your program. Follow these steps to perform the exercise:

1. Select **New** and then select **Project...** from the **File** menu in IntelliJ.

2. Select **Gradle** for the type of project. Click on **Next**.

3. For **Group Id**, enter **com.packtpub.recursion**.

4. For **Artifact Id**, enter **chapter14**.

5. For **Version**, enter **1.0**.

6. Accept the default on the next pane. Click on **Next**.

7. Leave the project name as **chapter14**.

8. Click on **Finish**.

9. Call up **build.gradle** in the IntelliJ text editor.

10. Change **sourceCompatibility** so that it is set to **12** as shown here:

    ```
    sourceCompatibility = 12
    ```

11. In the **src/main/java** folder, create a new Java package.

12. Enter **com.packtpub.recursion** as the package name.

13. Right-click on this package in the **Project** pane and create a new Java class named **RunForever**.

14. Enter the recursive method as follows:

    ```java
    public int add(int num) {
        return add(num + 1);
    }
    ```

15. Enter a **main()** method as follows:

    ```java
    public class RunForever {
        public static void main(String[] args) {
            RunForever runForever = new RunForever();
            System.out.println(runForever.add(1));
        }
    }
    ```

16. Run this program; you will see it fail with an exception:

```
Exception in thread "main" java.lang.StackOverflowError
at com.packtpub.recursion.RunForever.add(RunForever.java:11)
```

The full code will look as follows:

```
package com.packtpub.recursion;
public class RunForever {
    public int add(int num) {
        return add(num + 1);
    }
    public static void main(String[] args) {
        RunForever runForever = new RunForever();
        System.out.println(runForever.add(1));
    }
}
```

We can fix this problem by providing a terminating condition to stop the recursion, as shown in the following **RunAndStop.java** file:

```
package com.packtpub.recursion;
public class RunAndStop {
    public int add(int num) {
        if (num < 100) {
            return add(num + 1);
        }
        return num;
    }
    public static void main(String[] args) {
        RunAndStop runAndStop = new RunAndStop();
        System.out.println( runAndStop.add(1) );
    }
}
```

When you run this program, you will see the following output:

```
100
```

Trying Tail Recursion

Tail recursion is when the last executable statement of the recursive method is a call to itself. Tail recursion is important because the Java compiler could—but doesn't at this time—jump back to the start of the method. This helps because the compiler wouldn't have to store the stack frame for the method call, making it more efficient and using less memory on the call stack.

Exercise 2: Using Recursion to Calculate Factorials

Factorials are great examples for demonstrating how recursion works.

You can calculate the factorial of an integer by multiplying the number with all the positive numbers that are less than itself. For example, the factorial of 4, also written as 4!, is calculated as 4 * 3 * 2 * 1. Carry out the following steps to perform the exercise:

1. Right-click on the `com.packtpub.recursion` package name.

2. Create a new Java class named `Factorial`.

3. Enter the recursive method:

```java
public static int factorial(int number) {
    if (number == 1) {
        return 1;
    } else {
        return number * factorial(number - 1);
    }
}
```

Since a factorial is a number multiplied by all positive numbers less than itself, in each call to the `factorial()` method, it returns the number multiplied by the factorial of the number minus one. If the passed-in number is 1, it returns simply the number 1.

4. Enter the `main()` method, which launches the factorial calculation:

```java
public static void main(String[] args) {
    System.out.println( factorial(6) );
}
```

This code will calculate the factorial of 6, which is also represented as 6 factorial or 6!.

5. When you run this program, you will see the following output:

```
720
```

The full code will look as follows:

```java
package com.packtpub.recursion;
public class Factorial {
    public static int factorial(int number) {
        if (number == 1) {
            return 1;
        } else {
```

```
            return number * factorial(number - 1);
        }
    }
    public static void main(String[] args) {
        System.out.println( factorial(6) );
    }
}
```

Factorials and many other mathematical concepts work well with recursion. Another common task that fits with this programming technique is processing a hierarchical document, such as XML or HTML.

Processing an XML Document

XML documents have nodes. Each node may have child nodes; for example, consider the following:

cities.xml

```
1  <?xml version="1.0" encoding="UTF-8" standalone="no"?>
2  <cities>
3    <city>
4      <name>London</name>
5      <country>United Kingdom</country>
6      <summertime-high-temp>20.4 C</summertime-high-temp>
7      <in-year-2100>
8        <with-moderate-emission-cuts>
9          <name>Paris</name>
10         <country>France</country>
11         <summertime-high-temp>22.7 C</summertime-high-temp>
12       </with-moderate-emission-cuts>
```

https://packt.live/2N4X4Rl

In this XML snippet, the **<cities>** element has one child element, **<city>**. The **<city>** child element, in turn, has four child elements.

> **Note**
>
> This data comes from https://packt.live/33lrCyR and was used in an exercise in *Chapter 6, Libraries, Packages, and Modules.*

Now, consider how you would write code to process the above XML data. Java comes with classes to parse the XML file. The only issue is what to do with the XML document once you have parsed it into Java objects. That's where recursion can be useful.

You could write code to process each **`<city>`** element, such as the data for **London**. In that element, the code would extract the data from the child elements, such as the name of the city, the name of the country, and the summertime high temperature.

Note how the two additional cities, **Paris** and **Milan**, are shown. This data could be processed in a similar way to how the **London** data was processed. Once you see the similarity, you may find that recursion proves useful.

Exercise 3: Creating an XML File

To demonstrate how to parse and then recursively traverse XML documents, we need some XML data:

1. Right-click on **src/main/resources** and select **New** and then **File**.

2. Enter **cities.xml** as the name of the file.

3. Enter the following XML data into the file:

cities.xml

```
2   <cities>
3     <city>
4       <name>London</name>
5       <country>United Kingdom</country>
6       <summertime-high-temp>20.4 C</summertime-high-temp>
7       <in-year-2100>
8          <with-moderate-emission-cuts>
9             <name>Paris</name>
10            <country>France</country>
11            <summertime-high-temp>22.7 C</summertime-high-temp>
12         </with-moderate-emission-cuts>
```

https://packt.live/2N4X4Rl

Java includes more than one API for processing XML data. With the **Simple API for XML (SAX)**, you can process an XML document one event at a time. Events include starting an element, getting some text from within an element, and ending an element.

With the **Document Object Model (DOM)**, the API reads in an XML document. From this point your code can traverse the elements in the tree of DOM elements. The API that fits best with recursive processing is the DOM API.

> **Note**
>
> You can find more information about the Java XML APIs at https://packt.live/31yBoSL and https://packt.live/2BvD2tJ.

Introducing the DOM XML API

With the DOM API, you can use a **DocumentBuilder** class to parse an XML file into a tree of objects in memory. These objects all implement the **org.w3c.Node** interface. The node interface allows you to extract data from each XML element and then retrieve all the child nodes under a node.

Regular XML elements, such as **<city>** in our example, implement the **Element** interface, which extends the **Node** interface. Additionally, textual items implement the **Text** interface. And, the overall document is represented by the **Document** interface.

The entire DOM is hierarchical. For example, consider the following:

```
<city>
    <name>London</name>
</city>
```

In this short snippet, **<city>** is an element, and has a child element for **<name>**. The **London** text is a child of the **<name>** element. The **London** text will be held in an object that implements the **Text** interface.

> **Note**
>
> The DOM API needs to load the entire XML document into a hierarchy of nodes. The DOM API would not be appropriate for a large XML document, as you could run out of memory.

When using the DOM API, the first step is to load an XML file and parse it into the hierarchy of objects.

To do that, you need a **DocumentBuilder** class:

```
DocumentBuilderFactory factory = DocumentBuilderFactory.newInstance();
DocumentBuilder builder = factory.newDocumentBuilder();
```

Once you have a **DocumentBuilder** class, you can parse an XML file to get a **Document** interface:

```
File xmlFile = new File("src/main/resources/cities.xml");
Document document = builder.parse(xmlFile);
```

Since a **Document** is a **Node**, you can start processing all the child nodes. Typically, you start with the first child of the **Document** interface (**<cities>** in our earlier example):

```
Node node = document.getFirstChild();
NodeList children = node.getChildNodes();
for (int i = 0; i < children.getLength(); i++) {
    Node child = children.item(i);
}
```

The call to **getFirstChild()** returns the first child of the **document**, which is the top-level XML element. You can then call **getChildNodes()** to retrieve all the immediate child elements. Unfortunately, the **NodeList** object returned is not a **List** and not a **Collection** interface, which makes iterating over the child nodes more difficult.

You can then use recursion to get the child nodes of any given node, and the children of those children, and so on. For example, look at the following:

```
if (node.hasChildNodes()) {
    indentation += 2;
    NodeList children = node.getChildNodes();
    for (int i = 0; i < children.getLength(); i++) {
        Node child = children.item(i);
        if (child.getNodeType() == Node.TEXT_NODE) {
            printText(child.getTextContent() );
        } else {
            traverseNode(child, indentation);
        }
    }
}
```

In this example, we first check whether a given node has child nodes. If not, we have nothing to do. If there are child nodes, we'll use the same technique shown previously to get each child node.

Once we have a node, the code checks whether the node is a **Text** node by using the **getNodeType()** method. If the node is a **Text** node, we'll print out the text. If not, we'll make a recursive call with the child node. This will retrieve all the children of the child node.

Exercise 4: Traversing an XML Document

In this exercise, we'll write code to traverse the tree of node objects parsed from the **cities.xml** file we created in *Exercise 3, Creating an XML File*. The code will print out the XML elements as text. Carry out the following steps to complete the exercise:

1. Edit the **build.gradle** file. Add new dependency for the **Apache Commons Lang** library:

```
dependencies {
        testCompile group: 'junit', name: 'junit', version: '4.12'
        // https://mvnrepository.com/artifact/org.apache.commons/commons-lang3
        implementation group: 'org.apache.commons', name: 'commons-lang3', version:
'3.8.1'
        }
```

   This library has a few helpful utility methods that we will use when generating the output.

2. Right-click on the **com.packtpub.recursion** package name.

3. Create a new Java class named **XmlTraverser**.

4. Enter the following method to load an XML file into the DOM tree:

XmlTraverser.java

```
17 public Document loadXml() {
18    Document document = null;
19
20    DocumentBuilderFactory factory = DocumentBuilderFactory.newInstance();
21    try {
22      DocumentBuilder builder = factory.newDocumentBuilder();
23
24      File xmlFile = new File("src/main/resources/cities.xml");
25      document = builder.parse(xmlFile);
26
27    }
```

https://packt.live/33MDhN2

Note how this code catches all the possible exceptions from reading in the file and parsing the XML content.

5. Next, enter in a method to print the **Text** node content:

```java
public void printText(String text) {
    if (StringUtils.isNotBlank(text)) {
        System.out.print(text);
    }
}
```

This method uses the Apache **StringUtils** class to check whether the text is blank or not. You'll find that the DOM API populates a lot of blank **Text** nodes.

6. To help represent the hierarchical nature of XML documents, enter a utility method for indenting:

```java
public void indent(int indentation) {
    System.out.print( StringUtils.leftPad("", indentation));
}
```

Again, we use the **StringUtils** class to do the tedious work of padding an empty string with a given number of spaces.

7. Next, we create the main recursive method:

```java
public void traverseNode(Node node, int indentation) {
    indent(indentation);
    System.out.print(node.getNodeName() + " ");
    if (node.hasChildNodes()) {
        indentation += 2;
        NodeList children = node.getChildNodes();
        for (int i = 0; i < children.getLength(); i++) {
            Node child = children.item(i);
            if (child.getNodeType() == Node.TEXT_NODE) {
                printText( child.getTextContent() );
            } else {
                System.out.println();         // previous line
                traverseNode(child, indentation);
            }
        }
    }
}
```

8. This method prints out the name of the input node (which will be the city, country, or something similar). It then checks for child nodes. If the child node is a **Text** node, it prints out the text. Otherwise, this method calls itself recursively to process all the children of the child node.

9. To get going, create a short method to start the recursive calls from the first child of the XML document:

```
public void traverseDocument(Document document) {
    traverseNode(document.getFirstChild(), 0);
}
```

10. Next, we need a **main()** method to load the XML file and traverse the document:

```
public static void main(String[] args) {
    XmlTraverser traverser = new XmlTraverser();
    Document document = traverser.loadXml();
    // Traverse XML document.
    traverser.traverseDocument(document);
}
```

11. When you run this program, you will see the following output:

```
cities
  city
    name London
    country United Kingdom
    summertime-high-temp 20.4 C
    in-year-2100
      with-moderate-emission-cuts
        name Paris
        country France
        summertime-high-temp 22.7 C
      with-no-emission-cuts
        name Milan
        country Italy
        summertime-high-temp 25.2 C
```

> **Note**
>
> The preceding output is truncated. The full source code of this exercise can be found at: https://packt.live/33VDygZ.

Activity 1: Calculating the Fibonacci Sequence

The Fibonacci sequence is a series of numbers where each number is the sum of the previous two numbers. Write a recursive method to generate the first 15 numbers of the Fibonacci sequence. Note that the Fibonacci value for 0 is 0, and the Fibonacci value for 1 is 1.

The Fibonacci sequence goes 0, 1, 1, 2, 3, 5, 8, 13, 21, 34, 55, and so on.

So, you can use the following as a guide:

```
fibonacci(4) =
fibonacci(3) + fibonacci(2) =
{fibonacci(2) + fibonacci(1)} + {fibonacci(1) + fibonacci(0)} =
{fibonacci(1) + fibonacci(0) + fibonacci(1) + fibonacci(0)} + {fibonacci(1) + fibonacci(0)} =
1 + 0 + 1 + 0 + 1 + 0 = 3
```

We'll use a recursive method to calculate the Fibonacci value for a given input, and then create a loop to display the sequence. To do so, perform the following steps:

1. Create the **fibonacci** method.

2. Check if the value passed to the **fibonacci** method is 0, if yes then return 0.

3. Also, check if the value passed to the **fibonacci** method is 1, if yes then return 1.

4. Else, add the fibonacci values of the previous two numbers.

5. In the main method, create a for loop that initializes from 0 to 15 and call the **fibonaci** method.

When you run your program, you should see an output like the following:

```
0
1
1
2
3
5
8
13
21
34
55
89
144
233
377
```

> **Note**
>
> The solution for this activity can be found on page 562.

Summary

Recursion is a handy programming technique that is used for a few complex problems. You'll commonly find recursion in mathematical formulas, as well as when traversing hierarchical data structures such as binary trees or XML documents. With recursion, a Java method or a class calls itself. But do not forget to code a terminating condition, or you'll find your application quickly runs out of memory on the Java call stack. you'll find your application quickly runs out of memory on the Java call stack.

In the next chapter, you'll learn about predicates and functional programming with Java.

15

Processing Data with Streams

Overview

This chapter discusses the Stream API in Java that allows you to write effectively, with fewer lines of code. Once you have a firm grasp of the differences between parallel and sequential streams (defined and outlined in the early sections), you will be able to practice using the Java Stream API to work with arrays and collections by first learning how to create and close those streams. The next step is to explore the different types of operations available to you in Java, their definitions and their respective functions. The first you will encounter are terminal operations and reducers which you will use to extract data from a stream of elements. You will then move on to intermediate operations to filter, map, and otherwise mutate stream structures. And, finally, in this chapter's final exercise and activity, you will learn to apply different types of collectors to wrap stream elements in new containers.

Introduction

Java 8 introduced the new Stream API. With streams, Java programmers can now use a more declarative style of writing programs that you have previously only seen in functional programming languages or functional programming libraries.

Using streams, you can now write more expressive programs with fewer lines of code, and easily chain multiple operations on large lists. Streams also make it simple to parallelize your operations on lists–that is, should you have very large lists or complex operations. One thing that is important to remember about streams is that, while it might appear as though they're an improved collection, they're actually not. Streams do not have any storage of their own; instead, they use the storage of the supplied source.

In Java, there are four types of streams: **Stream**, which is used for streaming objects; **IntStream**, which is for streaming integers; **LongStream**, which streams longs; and finally, **DoubleStream**, which, of course, streams doubles. All of these streams work in exactly the same way, except they're specialized to work with their respective types.

> **Note**
>
> Diving into the code, you'll find that each of these types is just an interface with static methods pointing back to the **StreamSupport** class. This is the core API for anyone wanting to write stream-specific libraries. However, when building an application, you're usually fine to use the four standard stream interfaces and static generator functions.

The source of a stream can be either single elements, collections, arrays, or even files. Following the stream source is a number of intermediate operations that form the core pipeline. The pipeline ends with a terminal operation that, usually, either loops through the remaining elements to create a side effect or reduces them to a specific value–for example, counting how many elements there are left in the last stream.

> **Note**
>
> Streams are lazily constructed and executed. This means that a stream is not run until the terminal operation has been executed. Source elements are also only read as needed; that is, only the required elements are carried through to the next operation.

Creating Streams

There are multiple ways of creating streams in Java; the simplest of these is by using the **Stream.of()** function. This function can take either a single object or multiple objects in **varargs**:

```
Stream<Object> objectStream = Stream.of(new Object());
```

If you have multiple objects in your stream, then use the **varargs** version:

```
Stream<Object> objectStream = Stream.of(new Object(), new Object(), new Object());
```

The primitive versions of these streams work in an identical fashion; just replace the **Object** instances with integers, longs, or doubles.

You can also create streams from different collections—for example, lists and arrays. Creating a stream from a list will look like this:

```
List<String> stringList = List.of("string1", "string2", "string3");
Stream<String> stringStream = stringList.stream();
```

To create a stream from an array of items, you can use the **Arrays** class, just like the primitive versions of streams do:

```
String[] stringArray = new String[]{"string1", "string2", "string3"};
Stream<String> stringStream = Arrays.stream(stringArray);
```

There is one special type of stream that covers the dreaded null type gracefully, and is detailed as follows:

```
Stream<Object> nullableStream = Stream.ofNullable(new Object());
```

This stream will take one single object that can be null. If the object is null, then it will generate an empty stream; alternatively, if the object is not null, it will generate a stream of that one object. This can, of course, be very handy in situations where we're unsure about the state of sources.

Another way to generate a stream of elements is by using the **Stream.iterate()** generator function. This function will generate an infinite number of elements in your stream until you tell it to stop, starting at the seed element:

```
Stream<Integer> stream = Stream.iterate(0, (i) -> {
    return i + 1;
}).limit(5);
```

In this example, we're creating a stream of five elements, starting with index 0. This stream will contain the elements 0, 1, 2, 3, and 4:

> **Note**
>
> The **Stream.iterate()** generator function can be quite hazardous if you do not provide the proper limits. There are a number of ways to create infinite streams— usually by placing operations in the wrong order or forgetting to apply a limit to the stream.

There is also a special **Builder** class, which is embedded in the **Stream** type. This **Builder** class allows you to add elements as you create them; it removes the need to keep an **ArrayList**—or other collection—as a temporary buffer for elements.

The **Builder** class has a very simple API; you can **accept()** an element into the builder, which is perfect when you want to generate elements from a loop:

```
Stream.Builder<String> streamBuilder = Stream.builder();
for (int i = 0; i < 10; i++) {
    streamBuilder.accept("string" + i);
}
```

You can also **add()** elements to the builder. The **add()** method allows chaining, which is perfect for when you don't want to generate elements from a loop, but instead add them in a single line:

```
Stream.Builder<String> streamBuilder = Stream.builder();
streamBuilder.add("string1").add("string2").add("string3");
```

To create the stream using a builder, you can call the **build()** method when all the methods have been added. However, note that if you try to add elements to the builder after the **build()** method has been called, it will throw an **IllegalStateException**:

```
Stream<String> stream = streamBuilder.build();
```

All these simple ways of creating streams use the same underlying helper class, called **StreamSupport**. This class has a number of helpful and advanced methods for creating streams with different properties. The common denominator for all of these streams is **Spliterator**.

Parallel Streams

Streams are either sequential or parallel in the Java Stream API. Sequential streams use just a single thread in order to perform any operation. Usually, you'll find that this stream is more than enough to solve most problems; however, sometimes, you may require multiple threads running on multiple cores.

Parallel streams are operated on in parallel by multiple threads on multiple cores. They utilize **ForkJoinPool** in the JVM to launch multiple threads. They can be a very powerful tool when you find yourself in a performance hotspot. However, as parallel streams utilize multiple threads, you should be wary of using them unless needed; the overhead of parallel streams may very well create more problems than they solve.

> ### Note
> Parallel streams are a double-edged sword. They can be extremely useful in certain situations, however, at the same time, they can completely lock your program down. As parallel streams utilize the common **ForkJoinPool**, they spawn threads that may block your application and other system components to such a degree that the user will be affected.

To create a parallel stream, you can use the **Collections.parallelStream()** method, which will attempt to create a parallel stream:

```
List.of("string1", "string2", "string3").parallelStream()
```

Alternatively, you can make a stream parallel by using the **BaseStream.parallel()** intermediate operation:

```
List.of(1, 2, 3).stream().parallel()
```

Note that, at any point between the source and the terminal operation, you can change the type of the stream, using the **BaseStream.parallel()** or **BaseStream.sequential()** operations. These operations will only have an impact on the stream if they need to change the underlying state of the stream; if the stream already has the correct state, it will simply return itself. Calling **BaseStream.parallel()** multiple times will have no impact on performance:

```
List.of(1, 2, 3).stream().parallel().parallel().parallel()
```

Encounter Order

Depending on the type of the source for the stream, it may have a different encounter order. Lists, for example, have a built-in ordering of elements—also called the index. The ordering of the source also means that elements will be encountered in that order; however, you can change this encounter order using the **BaseStream.unordered()** and **Stream.sorted()** intermediate operations.

The **unordered()** operation doesn't change the ordering of a stream; instead, it only attempts to remove a specific attribute and informs us whether a stream is ordered or not. The elements will still have a specific order. The whole point of unordered streams is to make other operations more performant when applied to parallel streams. Applying the **unordered()** operation to a sequential stream will make it non-deterministic.

Closing Streams

Much like the streams of previous Java versions, **InputStream** and **OutputStream**, the Stream API includes a **close()** operation. However, in most cases, you'll never actually need to worry about closing your streams. The only time you should worry about closing your streams is when the source is a system resource—such as files or sockets—which need to be closed to avoid hogging resources from the system.

The **close()** operation returns void, meaning that after you call **close()**, the stream is unavailable for any other intermediate or terminal operations; although it is possible to register **close** handlers that will be informed when the stream has been closed. The **close** handler is a **Runnable** functional interface; preferably, you'll register them using a lambda function:

```java
Stream.of(1, 2, 3, 4).onClose(() -> {
    System.out.println("Closed");
}).close();
```

You can register any number of **close** handlers in your pipeline. The **close** handlers will always run even if any one of them renders an exception in their code. Additionally, it is worth noting that they will always be called in the same order in which they're added to the pipeline, regardless of the encounter order of the stream:

```
Stream.of(1, 2, 3, 4).onClose(() -> {
    System.out.println("Close handler 1");
}).onClose(() -> {
    System.out.println("Close handler 2");
}).onClose(() -> {
    System.out.println("Close handler 3");
}).close();
```

> **Note**
>
> Even if it's possible to register a close handler on any stream, it might not actually run if the stream doesn't need to be closed.

Since Java 7, there is an interface called **AutoCloseable**, which will attempt to automatically close held resources in a **try-with-resources** statement. The **BaseStream** interface, which all streams inherit from, extends this **AutoCloseable** interface. This means that any stream will attempt to release resources automatically if wrapped in a try-with-resources statement:

```
try (Stream<Integer> stream = Stream.of(6, 3, 8, 12, 3, 9)) {
    boolean matched = stream.onClose(() -> {
        System.out.println("Closed");
    }).anyMatch((e) -> {
        return e > 10;
    });
    System.out.println(matched);
}
```

While the preceding example does work, there's rarely any reason to wrap a basic stream in a try-with-resources statement, other than if you explicitly need to run logic when the stream has finished running. This example will first print **true** to the terminal, and after that print **Closed**.

Terminal Operations

Every pipeline needs to end with a terminal operation; without this, the pipeline will not be executed. Unlike intermediate operations, terminal operations may have various return values as they mark the end of the pipeline. You cannot apply another operation after a terminal operation.

> **Note**
>
> When a terminal operation is applied to a stream, you cannot use that stream again. Therefore, storing references to streams in code can cause confusion as to how that reference might be used – you're not allowed to "split" a stream into two different use cases. If you attempt to apply operations on a stream that already had the terminal operation executed, then it will throw an `IllegalStateException` with the message `stream has already been operated upon or closed`.

There are 16 different terminal operations in the Stream API—each of them with their own specific use cases. The following is an explanation of each of them:

- **forEach**: This terminal operator acts like a normal **for** loop; it will run some code for each element in the stream. This is not a thread-safe operation, so you'll need to provide synchronization should you find yourself using shared state:

```
Stream.of(1, 4, 6, 2, 3, 7).forEach((n) -> { System.out.println(n); });
```

If this operation is applied on a parallel pipeline, the order in which elements are acted on will not be guaranteed:

```
Stream.of(1, 4, 6, 2, 3, 7).parallel().forEach((n) -> { System.out.println(n); });
```

If the order in which the elements are acted on matters, you should use the **forEachOrdered()** terminal operation instead.

- **forEachOrdered**: Much like the **forEach()** terminal operation, this will allow you to perform an action for each element in the stream. However, the **forEachOrdered()** operation will guarantee the order in which elements are processed, regardless of how many threads they're processed on:

```
Stream.of(1, 4, 6, 2, 3, 7).parallel().forEachOrdered((n) -> { System.out.
println(n); });
```

Here, you can see a parallel stream with a defined encounter order. Using the **forEachOrdered()** operation, it will always encounter elements in the natural, indexed order.

- **toArray**: These two terminal operations will allow you to convert the elements of the stream into an array. The basic version will generate an **Object** array:

```
Object[] array = Stream.of(1, 4, 6, 2, 3, 7).toArray();
```

If you need a specific type of array, you can supply a constructor reference for the type of array you need:

```
Integer[] array = Stream.of(1, 4, 6, 2, 3, 7).toArray(Integer[]::new);
```

A third option is to also write your own generator for the **toArray()** operation:

```
Integer[] array = Stream.of(1, 4, 6, 2, 3, 7).toArray(elements -> new
Integer[elements]);
```

- **reduce**: To perform a reduction on a stream means to only extract the interesting parts of the elements of that stream and reduce them to a single value. There are two generic **reduce** operations available. The first, simpler one, takes an accumulator function as an argument. It is usually used after a map operation is applied on a stream:

```
int sum = Stream.of(1, 7, 4, 3, 9, 6).reduce(0, (a, b) -> a + b);
```

The second, more complex version takes an identity that also acts as the initial value of the reduction. It also requires an accumulator function where the reduction takes place, as well as a combining function to define how two elements are reduced:

```
int sum = Stream.of(1, 7, 4, 3, 9, 6).reduce(0, (total, i) -> total + i, (a, b) -> a
+ b );
```

In this example, the accumulator adds up the result of the combining function to the identity value, which, in this case, is the total sum of the reduction.

- **sum**: This is a more specific reduction operation, which will sum all elements in the stream. This terminal operation is only available for **IntStream**, **LongStream**, and **DoubleStream**. To use this functionality in a more generic stream, you would have to implement a pipeline using the **reduce()** operation, usually preceded by a **map()** operation. The following example illustrates the use of **IntStream**:

```
int intSum = IntStream.of(1, 7, 4, 3, 9, 6).sum();
System.out.println(intSum);
```

This will print the result as **30**. The following example illustrates the use of **LongStream**:

```
long longSum = LongStream.of(7L, 4L, 9L, 2L).sum();
System.out.println(longSum);
```

This will print the result as **22**. The following example illustrates the use of
DoubleStream:

```
double doubleSum = DoubleStream.of(5.4, 1.9, 7.2, 6.1).sum();
System.out.println(doubleSum);
```

This will print the result as **20.6**.

- **collect**: The collection operation is like the reduce operation, in that it takes
  the elements of a stream and creates a new result. However, instead of reducing
  the stream to a single value, **collect** can take the elements and generate a new
  container or collection that holds all the remaining elements; for example, a list.
  Usually, you would use the **Collectors help** class, as it contains a lot of ready-to-use
  collect operations:

```
List<Integer> items = Stream.of(6, 3, 8, 12, 3, 9).collect(Collectors.toList());
System.out.println(items);
```

This would print **[6, 3, 8, 12, 3, 9]** to the console. You can review more usages
of **Collectors** in the *Using Collectors* section. Another option is to write your own
supplier, accumulator, and combiner for the **collect()** operation:

```
List<Integer> items = Stream.of(6, 3, 8, 12, 3, 9).collect(
        () -> { return new ArrayList<Integer>(); },
        (list, i) -> { list.add(i); },
        (list, elements) -> { list.addAll(elements); });
System.out.println(items);
```

This can, of course, be simplified in this example by using method references:

```
List<Integer> items = Stream.of(6, 3, 8, 12, 3, 9).collect(ArrayList::new,
List::add, List::addAll);
System.out.println(items);
```

- **min**: As the name suggests, this terminal operation will return the minimum value,
  wrapped in an **Optional**, of all elements in the stream specified according to a
  Comparator. In most cases, you'd use the **Comparator.comparingInt()**, **Comparator.
  comparingLong()**, or **Comparator.comparingDouble()** static helper functions when
  applying this operation:

```
Optional min = Stream.of(6, 3, 8, 12, 3, 9).min((a, b) -> { return a - b;});
System.out.println(min);
```

This should write **Optional[3]**.

- **max**: The opposite of the **min()** operation, the **max()** operation returns the value of the element with the maximum value according to a specified **Comparator**, wrapped in an **Optional**:

```
Optional max = Stream.of(6, 3, 8, 12, 3, 9).max((a, b) -> { return a - b;});
System.out.println(max);
```

This will print **Optional[12]** to the terminal.

- **average**: This is a special type of terminal operation that is only available on **IntStream**, **LongStream**, and **DoubleStream**. It returns an **OptionalDouble** containing the average of all elements in the stream:

```
OptionalDouble avg = IntStream.of(6, 3, 8, 12, 3, 9).average();
System.out.println(avg);
```

This will give you an **Optional** with the containing value **6.833333333333333**.

- **count**: This is a simple terminal operator returning the number of elements in the stream. It's worth noting that, sometimes, the **count()** terminal operation will find more efficient ways of calculating the size of the stream. In these cases, the pipeline will not even be executed:

```
long count = Stream.of(6, 3, 8, 12, 3, 9).count();
System.out.println(count);
```

- **anyMatch**: The **anyMatch()** terminal operator will return true if any of the elements in the stream match the specified predicate:

```
boolean matched = Stream.of(6, 3, 8, 12, 3, 9).anyMatch((e) -> { return e > 10; });
System.out.println(matched);
```

As there is an element with a value above 10, this pipeline will return **true**.

- **allMatch**: The **allMatch()** terminal operator will return **true** if all the elements in the stream match the specified predicate:

```
boolean matched = Stream.of(6, 3, 8, 12, 3, 9).allMatch((e) -> { return e > 10; });
System.out.println(matched);
```

Since this source has elements whose values are below 10, it should return **false**.

- **noneMatch**: Opposite to **allMatch()**, the **noneMatch()** terminal operator will return **true** if none of the elements in the stream match the specified predicate:

```
boolean matched = Stream.of(6, 3, 8, 12, 3, 9).noneMatch((e) -> { return e > 10; });
System.out.println(matched);
```

Because the stream has elements of values above 10, this will also return **false**.

- **findFirst**: This retrieves the first element of the stream, wrapped in an **Optional**:

```
Optional firstElement = Stream.of(6, 3, 8, 12, 3, 9).findFirst();
System.out.println(firstElement);
```

This will print **Optional[6]** to the terminal. If there were no elements in the stream, it would instead print **Optional.empty**.

- **findAny**: Much like the **findFirst()** terminal operation, the **findAny()** operation will return an element wrapped in an **Optional**. This operation, however, will return any one of the elements that remain. You should never really assume which element it will return. This operation will, usually, act faster than the **findFirst()** operation, especially in parallel streams. It's ideal when you just need to know whether there are any elements left but don't really care about which remain:

```
Optional firstElement = Stream.of(7, 9, 3, 4, 1).findAny();
System.out.println(firstElement);
```

- **iterator**: This is a terminal operator that generates an iterator that lets you traverse elements:

```
Iterator<Integer> iterator = Stream.of(1, 2, 3, 4, 5, 6)
        .iterator();
while (iterator.hasNext()) {
    Integer next = iterator.next();
    System.out.println(next);
}
```

- **summaryStatistics**: This is a special terminal operation that is available for **IntStream**, **LongStream**, and **DoubleStream**. It will return a special type—for example, **IntSummaryStatistics**—describing the elements of the stream:

```
IntSummaryStatistics intStats = IntStream.of(7, 9, 3, 4, 1).summaryStatistics();
System.out.println(intStats);
LongSummaryStatistics longStats = LongStream.of(6L, 4L, 1L, 3L, 7L).summaryStatistics();
```

```
System.out.println(longStats);
DoubleSummaryStatistics doubleStats = DoubleStream.of(4.3, 5.1, 9.4, 1.3, 3.9).
summaryStatistics();
System.out.println(doubleStats);
```

This will print all the summaries of the three streams to the terminal, which should look like this:

```
IntSummaryStatistics{count=5, sum=24, min=1, average=4,800000, max=9}
LongSummaryStatistics{count=5, sum=21, min=1, average=4,200000, max=7}
DoubleSummaryStatistics{count=5, sum=24,000000, min=1,300000, average=4,800000,
max=9,400000}
```

Intermediate Operations

A stream can take any number of intermediate operations following the creation of the stream. An intermediate operation is often a filter or mapping of some type, but there are other types as well. Every intermediate operation returns another stream; that way, you can chain any number of intermediate operations to your pipeline.

The order of intermediate operations is very important as the stream returned from an operation will only reference the remaining or required elements of the previous stream.

There are several different types of intermediate operations. The following is an explanation of each of them:

- **filter**: As the name suggests, this intermediate operation will return a subset of elements from the stream. It uses a predicate when applying the matching pattern, which is a functional interface that returns a **Boolean**. The easiest and most common way to implement this is using a lambda function:

```
Stream.of(1, 2, 3, 4, 5, 6)
        .filter((i) -> { return i > 3; })
        .forEach(System.out::println);
```

In this example, the **filter** method will filter away any elements that have a value that is 3 or lower. The **forEach()** terminal operation will then take the remaining elements and print them all in a loop.

- **map**: The **map** operation will apply a special function to every element of the stream and return the modified elements:

```
Stream.of("5", "3", "8", "2")
        .map((s) -> { return Integer.parseInt(s); })
        .forEach((i) -> { System.out.println(i > 3); });
```

This pipeline will take the strings, convert them to integers using the `map()` operation, and then print either **true** or **false** depending on whether the parsed string value is more than 3. This is just one simple example of `map`; this method is incredibly versatile in transforming your stream into something very different.

There are also special versions of this intermediate operation that will return integer values, long values, and double values. They're called `mapToInt()`, `mapToLong()`, and `mapToDouble()`, respectively:

```
Stream.of("5", "3", "8", "2")
        .mapToInt((i) -> { return Integer.parseInt(i); })
        .forEach((i) -> { System.out.println(i > 3); });
```

Note that these special case `map` operations will return **IntStream**, **LongStream**, or **DoubleStream** rather than **Stream<Integer>**, **Stream<Long>**, or **Stream<Double>**.

- **flatMap**: This gives you an easy way of flattening a multidimensional data structure into one single stream—for example, a stream of objects that themselves contain objects or arrays. With **flatMap()**, you can take these sub elements and concatenate them into a single stream:

```
Stream.of(List.of(1, 2, 3), List.of(4, 5, 6), List.of(7, 8, 9))
        .flatMap((l) -> { return l.stream(); })
        .forEach((i) -> { System.out.print(i); });
```

In this example pipeline, we're creating a stream from multiple lists; then, in the **flatMap** operation, we're extracting streams of each list. The **flatMap** operation then concatenates them into a single stream, which we loop through with **forEach**. The terminal will print out the full stream: **123456789**.

The **flatMap** function also exists as an integer, long, and double special operations—**flatMapToInt**, **flatMapToLong**, and **flatMapToDouble**—which, of course, will return the respective typed stream:

- **distinct**: This will return all the unique elements in the stream. If there are duplicate elements in the stream, the first item will be returned:

```
Stream.of(1, 2, 2, 2, 2, 3)
        .distinct()
        .forEach((i) -> { System.out.print(i); });
```

Here, we're starting with a stream of six elements, however, four of them are identical in value. The **distinct()** operation will filter these elements and the remaining three will be printed to the terminal.

- **sorted**: The **sorted** intermediate operation exists in two versions. The first version, without arguments, assumes that the elements of the **map** can be sorted in the natural order–implementing the **Comparable** interface. If they can't be sorted, then an exception will be thrown:

```
Stream.of(1, 3, 6, 4, 5, 2)
        .sorted()
        .forEach((i) -> { System.out.print(i); });
```

The second version of the **sorted** operation takes a **Comparator** as an argument, and will return the sorted elements accordingly:

```
Stream.of(1, 3, 6, 4, 5, 2)
        .sorted((a, b) -> a - b)
        .forEach((i) -> { System.out.print(i); });
```

- **unordered**: The opposite of **sorted**, the **unordered** intermediate operation will impose an unordered encounter order on the streams elements. Using this operation on parallel streams can, sometimes, improve the performance, as certain intermediate and terminal stateful operations perform better with a more relaxed ordering of elements:

```
Stream.of(1, 2, 3, 4, 5, 6)
        .unordered()
        .forEach((i) -> { System.out.print(i); });
System.out.println();
Stream.of(1, 2, 3, 4, 5, 6)
        .parallel()
        .unordered()
        .forEach((i) -> { System.out.print(i); });
```

- **limit**: This returns a new stream with **n** number of elements. If the number of elements is fewer than the requested limit, it has no effect:

```
Stream.of(1, 2, 3, 4, 5, 6)
        .limit(3)
        .forEach((i) -> { System.out.print(i); });
```

The result of running this example will be **123**, ignoring any elements beyond the third element.

- **skip**: This skips the first **n** elements of this stream and returns the remaining elements in a new stream:

```
Stream.of(1, 2, 3, 4, 5, 6)
        .skip(3)
        .forEach((i) -> { System.out.print(i); });
```

This will print **456** to the terminal, skipping the first three elements.

- **boxed**: The special primitive streams, **IntStream**, **LongStream**, and **DoubleStream**, all have access to the **boxed()** operation. This operation will "box" each primitive element in the class version of said type, and return that stream. **IntStream** will return **Stream<Integer>**, **LongStream** will return **Stream<Long>**, and **DoubleStream** will return **Stream<Double>**:

```
IntStream.of(1, 2)
        .boxed()
        .forEach((i) -> { System.out.println(i + i.getClass().getSimpleName()); });
System.out.println();
LongStream.of(3, 3)
        .boxed()
        .forEach((l) -> { System.out.println(l + l.getClass().getSimpleName()); });
System.out.println();
DoubleStream.of(5, 6)
        .boxed()
        .forEach((d) -> { System.out.println(d + d.getClass().getSimpleName()); });
```

This example will take each primitive stream, box it in the corresponding object type, and then print the value together with the class name of the type:

```
1Integer
2Integer
3Long
4Long
5.0Double
6.0Double
```

- **takeWhile**: This is a special type of operation that acts differently depending on whether the stream is ordered or not. If the stream is ordered—that is, it has a defined encounter order—it will return a stream containing the longest streak of matching elements that match the predicate, starting with the first element in the stream. This stream of elements, which always starts with the first element, is also sometimes called a prefix:

```
Stream.of(2, 2, 2, 3, 1, 2, 5)
        .takeWhile((i) -> { return i == 2; })
        .forEach((i) -> { System.out.println(i); });
```

This pipeline will print **222** to the terminal. You should note, however, that this operation will return an empty stream if the first element doesn't match the predicate. This is because of the inner workings of **takeWhile()**; that is, it will start at the first element and continue until the first element fails to match—giving you an empty stream:

```
Stream.of(1, 2, 2, 3, 1, 2, 5)
        .takeWhile((i) -> { return i == 2; })
        .forEach((i) -> { System.out.println(i); });
```

If the stream is unordered—that is, it has no defined encounter order—the **takeWhile()** operation may return any matching subset of elements, including the empty subset. In this use case, a **filter()** operation might be more suitable.

- **dropWhile**: The **dropWhile()** operation is the opposite of **takeWhile()**. Just like **takeWhile()**, it will act differently depending on whether the stream is ordered or not. If the stream is ordered, it will drop the longest prefix matching the predicate, instead of returning the prefix like **takeWhile()** does:

```
Stream.of(2, 2, 2, 3, 1, 2, 5)
        .dropWhile((i) -> { return i == 2; })
        .forEach((i) -> { System.out.print(i); });
```

This pipeline will print **3125** to the terminal, dropping the matching prefix, which is the first three 2's. If the stream is unordered, the operation may drop any subset of elements, or drop an empty subset, effectively returning the whole stream. Be careful when using this operation on unordered streams.

- **Parallel**: This returns a parallel stream. By default, the operations in a parallel stream run on threads from the common **ForkJoinPool**. Most streams are sequential unless specifically created as parallel, or turned into parallel using this intermediate operation.

- **Sequential**: This returns a sequential stream and is the opposite of parallel.

- **peek**: This intermediate operation is mainly used to examine the stream after other intermediate operations have been applied. Usually, the goal is to understand how the operations have affected the elements. In the following example, we're printing how each element traverses each stream operation in the pipeline:

```
long count = Stream.of(6, 5, 3, 8, 1, 9, 2, 4, 7, 0)
        .peek((i) -> { System.out.print(i); })
        .filter((i) -> { return i < 5; })
        .peek((i) -> { System.out.print(i); })
        .map((i) -> { return String.valueOf(i); })
        .peek((p) -> { System.out.print(p); })
        .count();
System.out.println(count);
```

The terminal will read **653338111922244470005** in this example. What we can quickly deduce is that any elements with a value of 5 or above will only be printed once. **Peek** will follow each element in turn through the whole stream; that's why the order may seem odd. 6 and 5 will only be printed once, as they're filtered after the first **peek** operation. 3, however, will be triggered on all three **peek()** operations, hence there are three 3's in a row. The last number 5 in the output is just the count of the remaining elements.

While the **peek()** operation is most commonly used to examine elements as they traverse the pipeline, it is also possible to mutate the elements of the stream using these operations. Consider the following class definition:

```
class MyItem {
    int value;
    public MyItem(int value) {
        this.value = value;
    }
}
```

Then, consider adding a number of these values to a stream that has a mutating **peek** operation applied to it:

```
long sum = Stream.of(new MyItem(1), new MyItem(2), new MyItem(3))
        .peek((item) -> {
            item.value = 0;
        })
        .mapToInt((item) -> { return item.value; })
        .sum();
System.out.println(sum);
```

The sum of these objects should have been, if we disregard the **peek()** operation, 6. However, the **peek** operation is mutating each object to have a value of zero–effectively making the sum zero. While this is possible, it was never designed to be used like this. Using **peek()** to mutate is not recommended as it is not thread-safe, and accessing any shared state might cause exceptions. The different **map()** operations are usually a better option.

Exercise 1: Using the Stream API

An online grocery shop that allows customers to collect, and save, multiple different shopping carts at the same time has asked you to implement a joint checkout for their multiple-shopping cart system. The checkout procedure should concatenate the price for all items in all shopping carts, and then present that to the customer. To do this, perform the following steps:

1. If IntelliJ is already started but no project is open, then select **Create New Project**. If IntelliJ already has a project opened, then select **File** | **New** | **Project** from the menu.

2. In the **New Project** dialog box, select the **Java project**, and then click **Next**.

3. Check the box to create the project from a template. Select **Command Line App**, and then click **Next**.

4. Give the new project the name **Chapter15**.

5. IntelliJ will give you a default project location. If you wish to select one, you may enter it here.

6. Set the package name to **com.packt.java.chapter15**.

7. Click **Finish**.

   IntelliJ will create your project, called **Chapter15**, with the standard folder structure. IntelliJ will also create the main entry point for your application, called **Main.java**.

8. Rename this file to **Exercise1.java**. When you're done, it should look like this:

```
package com.packt.java.chapter15;
public class Exercise1 {
    public static void main(String[] args) {
    // write your code here
    }
}
```

9. Create a new inner class, called **ShoppingArticle**. Make it static so that we can easily access it from the main entry point for our program. This class should contain the name of the article and the price of that article. Let the **price** be a double variable:

```java
private static final class ShoppingArticle {
    final String name;
    final double price;
    public ShoppingArticle(String name, double price) {
        this.name = name;
        this.price = price;
    }
}
```

10. Now create a simple **ShoppingCart** class. In this version, we will only allow one item per article in the cart, so a list will be enough to keep the articles in **ShoppingCart**:

```java
private static final class ShoppingCart {
    final List<ShoppingArticle> mArticles;
    public ShoppingCart(List<ShoppingArticle> list) {
        mArticles = List.copyOf(list);
    }
}
```

11. Create your first shopping cart, **fruitCart**, and add three fruit articles to it – **Orange**, **Apple**, and **Banana**—one of each type. Set the per-unit price to **1.5**, **1.7**, and **2.2** **Java-$** each:

```java
public class Exercise1 {
    public static void main(String[] args) {
        ShoppingCart fruitCart = new ShoppingCart(List.of(
                new ShoppingArticle("Orange", 1.5),
                new ShoppingArticle("Apple", 1.7),
                new ShoppingArticle("Banana", 2.2)
        ));
    }
}
```

12. Create another **ShoppingCart**, but this time with vegetables—**Cucumber**, **Salad**, and **Tomatoes**. Set a price in Java-$ for them as well, as **0.8**, **1.2**, and **2.7**:

```
ShoppingCart vegetableCart = new ShoppingCart(List.of(
        new ShoppingArticle("Cucumber", 0.8),
        new ShoppingArticle("Salad", 1.2),
        new ShoppingArticle("Tomatoes", 2.7)
    ));
}
```

13. Wrap up the test shopping carts with a third and final **shoppingCart** containing some meat and fish. They're usually a little more expensive than fruit and vegetables:

```
ShoppingCart meatAndFishCart = new ShoppingCart(List.of(
        new ShoppingArticle("Cod", 46.5),
        new ShoppingArticle("Beef", 29.1),
        new ShoppingArticle("Salmon", 35.2)
    ));
}
```

14. Now it's time to start implementing the function that will calculate the total price of all the items in the shopping carts. Declare a new function that takes a **ShoppingCart vararg** as an argument and returns a double. Let it be static so that we can easily use it in the **main** function:

```
private static double calculatePrice(ShoppingCart... carts) {
}
```

15. Build a pipeline starting with a stream of all of the carts:

```
private static double calculatePrice(ShoppingCart... carts) {
    return Stream.of(carts)
}
```

16. Add a **flatMap()** operation to extract a single stream of **ShoppingArticles** for all **ShoppingCarts**:

```
private static double calculatePrice(ShoppingCart... carts) {
    return Stream.of(carts)
        .flatMap((cart) -> { return cart.mArticles.stream(); })
}
```

17. Extract the price for each **ShoppingArticle** using the **mapToDouble()** operation; this will create a **DoubleStream**:

```
private static double calculatePrice(ShoppingCart... carts) {
    return Stream.of(carts)
        .flatMap((cart) -> { return cart.mArticles.stream(); })
        .mapToDouble((item) -> { return item.price; })
}
```

18. Finally, reduce the prices of all **ShoppingArticle** to a sum, using the **sum()** method that is available in **DoubleStream**:

```
private static double calculatePrice(ShoppingCart... carts) {
    return Stream.of(carts)
            .flatMap((cart) -> { return cart.mArticles.stream(); })
            .mapToDouble((item) -> { return item.price; })
            .sum();
}
```

19. Now you have a function that will reduce a list of **ShoppingCart** to a unified sum in Java-$. All you have to do now is to apply this function to your **ShoppingCart** class, and then print out the resulting sum to the terminal, rounding it to two decimals:

```
double sum = calculatePrice(fruitCart, vegetableCart, meatAndFishCart);
System.out.println(String.format("Sum: %.2f", sum));
}
```

> **Note**
>
> You can refer the complete code at: https://packt.live/2qzLaHx.

You've now created your first complete piece of code using the functional Java Stream API. You've created a stream of complex objects, applying a mapping operation to the elements of the stream to transform them, and then another mapping operation to transform the elements yet again, changing the stream type twice. Finally, you reduced the whole stream to a single primitive value that was presented to the user.

Activity 1: Applying Discount on the Items

Improve the preceding example by adding a function that applies a discount for certain items in the shopping carts, before calculating the final price. Ensure the price calculation is still correct.

> **Note**
>
> The solution for this activity can be found on page 563.

Using Collectors

Collectors in Java are a very powerful tool when you need to extract certain data points, descriptions, or elements from large data structures. They offer a very understandable way of describing what you want to do with a stream of elements, without needing to write complex logic.

There are a number of helpful default implementations of the **Collector** interface that you can start using easily. Most of these collectors will not allow null values; that is, if they find a null value in your stream, they will throw a **NullPointerException**. Before using a collector to reduce your elements in any of these containers, you should take care to handle null elements in the stream.

The following is an introduction to all default Collectors:

- **toCollection**: This generic collector will allow you to wrap your elements in any known class implementing the **Collection** interface; examples include **ArrayList**, **HashSet**, **LinkedList**, **TreeSet**, and others:

```
List.of("one", "two", "three", "four", "five")
        .stream()
        .collect(Collectors.toCollection(TreeSet::new));
```

- **toList**: This will reduce your elements into an **ArrayList** implementation. If you need a more specific type of list, you should use the **toCollection()** collector:

```
List.of("one", "two", "three", "four", "five")
        .stream()
        .collect(Collectors.toList());
```

- **toUnmodifiableList**: This is essentially the same as the **toList()** collector, with the one difference that it uses the **List.of()** generator function to make the list unmodifiable:

```
List.of("one", "two", "three", "four", "five")
        .stream()
        .collect(Collectors.toUnmodifiableList());
```

- **toSet**: This wraps the elements in a **HashSet**:

```
List.of("one", "two", "three", "four", "five")
        .stream()
        .collect(Collectors.toSet());
```

- **toUnmodifiableSet**: This is just like the **toSet()** collector, with the difference being that it will use the **Set.of()** generator to create an unmodifiable set:

```
List.of("one", "two", "three", "four", "five")
        .stream()
        .collect(Collectors.toUnmodifiableSet());
```

- **joining**: This collector will use a **StringBuilder** to concatenate the elements of the stream into a string without any separating characters:

```
String joined = List.of("one", "two", "three", "four", "five")
        .stream()
        .collect(Collectors.joining());
System.out.println(joined);
```

This will print **onetwothreefourfive** to the terminal. If you need the elements to be separated by a comma, for example, use **Collectors.joining(",")**:

```
String joined = List.of("one", "two", "three", "four", "five")
        .stream()
        .collect(Collectors.joining(","));
System.out.println(joined);
```

In this example, you get **one,two,three,four,five** printed to the terminal. Finally, you have the option of adding a prefix and a suffix to the generated string as well:

```
String joined = List.of("one", "two", "three", "four", "five")
        .stream()
        .collect(Collectors.joining(",", "Prefix", "Suffix"));
System.out.println(joined);
```

The prefix and suffix are added to the string, not each element. The generated string will look like: **Prefixone,two,three,four,fiveSuffix**.

- **mapping**: This is a special type of collector that allows you to apply a mapping to each element of the stream before applying a defined collector:

```
Set<String> mapped = List.of("one", "two", "three", "four", "five")
        .stream()
        .collect(Collectors.mapping((s) -> { return s + "-suffix"; }, Collectors.
toSet()));
System.out.println(mapped);
```

Here, we're starting with a source of **List<String>** and collecting to a **Set<String>**. But before we collect, we're concatenating a **-suffix** string to each element using the **mapping()** collector.

- **flatMapping**. Just like the **flatMap()** intermediate operation, this collector will allow you to apply a flat mapping to the stream elements, before collecting them to a new container. In the following example, we start with a source, **List<Set<String>>**, then we flatten it out to a **Stream<Set<String>>** and apply **Collector.toList()**–effectively turning all the sets into a single list instead:

```
List<String> mapped = List.of(
        Set.of("one", "two", "three"),
        Set.of("four", "five"),
        Set.of("six")
)
        .stream()
        .collect(Collectors.flatMapping(
                (set) -> { return set.stream(); },
                Collectors.toList())
        );
System.out.println(mapped);
```

- **filtering**: Just like the **filter()** intermediate operation, here, you're allowed to apply a filtering before you implement operations on the stream.

```
Set<String> collected = List.of("Andreas", "David", "Eric")
        .stream()
        .collect(Collectors.filtering(
                (name) -> { return name.length() < 6; },
                Collectors.toSet())
        );
System.out.println(collected);
```

- **collectingAndThen**: This special collector will allow you to finish the collection off with a special function; for example, turning your collection into an immutable collection:

```
Set<String> immutableSet = List.of("Andreas", "David", "Eric")
        .stream()
        .collect(Collectors.collectingAndThen(
                Collectors.toSet(),
                (set) -> { return Collections.unmodifiableSet(set); })
        );
System.out.println(immutableSet);
```

- **counting**: This produces the same result as the **count()** intermediate operation:

```
long count = List.of("Andreas", "David", "Eric")
        .stream()
        .collect(Collectors.counting());
System.out.println(count);
```

- **minBy**: This collector is equivalent to using the **min()** terminal operator. The following example will print **Optional[1]** to the terminal:

```
Optional<Integer> smallest = Stream.of(1, 2, 3)
        .collect(Collectors.minBy((a, b) -> { return a - b; });
System.out.println(smallest);
```

- **maxBy**: You'll get the same result using this collector as you would with the **max()** terminal operator:

```
Optional<Integer> biggest = Stream.of(1, 2, 3)
        .collect(Collectors.maxBy((a, b) -> { return a - b; }));
System.out.println(biggest);
```

- **summingInt**: This is an alternative to the **reduce()** intermediate operation, and is used to calculate the sum of all elements in the stream:

```
int sum = Stream.of(1d, 2d, 3d)
        .collect(Collectors.summingInt((d) -> { return d.intValue(); }));
System.out.println(sum);
```

- **summingLong**: This is the same as **Collector.summingInt()**, but will instead produce a sum in the **long** type:

```
long sum = Stream.of(1d, 2d, 3d)
        .collect(Collectors.summingLong((d) -> { return d.longValue(); }));
System.out.println(sum);
```

- **summingDouble**: This is the same as `Collector.summingLong()`, but will instead produce a sum in the **double** type:

```
double sum = Stream.of(1, 2, 3)
        .collect(Collectors.summingDouble((i) -> { return i.doubleValue(); }));
System.out.println(sum);
```

- **averagingInt**: Returns the average the integers passed:

```
double average = Stream.of(1d, 2d, 3d)
        .collect(Collectors.averagingInt((d) -> { return d.intValue(); }));
System.out.println(average);
```

- **averagingLong**: Returns the average the longs passed:

```
double average = Stream.of(1d, 2d, 3d)
        .collect(Collectors.averagingLong((d) -> { return d.longValue(); }));
System.out.println(average);
```

- **averagingDouble**: Returns the average of the numbers passed in the argument:

```
double average = Stream.of(1, 2, 3)
        .collect(Collectors.averagingDouble((i) -> { return i.doubleValue(); }));
System.out.println(average);x§
```

- **Reducing**: This is a collector that reduces the element of the stream to an optional. This is best utilized when used in combination with other collectors; otherwise, you are probably better off using the normal **reduce()** terminal operator, which this collector inherits its name and operation from.

- **groupingBy**: This collector will group elements according to a given function and collect them according to a given collection type. Consider the following example class, describing a car:

```
private static class Car {
    String brand;
    long enginePower;
    Car(String brand, long enginePower) {
        this.brand = brand;
        this.enginePower = enginePower;
    }
    public String getBrand() {
```

```
        return brand;
    }
    @Override
    public String toString() {
        return brand + ": " + enginePower;
    }
}
```

If you would like to sort a few cars according to their brand and collect them into new containers, then it's simple with the **groupingBy()** collector:

```
Map<String, List<Car>> grouped = Stream.of(
        new Car("Toyota", 92),
        new Car("Kia", 104),
        new Car("Hyundai", 89),
        new Car("Toyota", 116),
        new Car("Mercedes", 209))
    .collect(Collectors.groupingBy(Car::getBrand));
System.out.println(grouped);
```

Here, we have four different cars. Then, we apply the **groupingBy()** collector based on the brand of cars. This will produce a **Map<String, List<Car>>** collection, where **String** is the brand of the car, and the **List** contains all the cars for said brand. This will always return **Map**; however, it is possible to define what kind of collection to gather the grouped elements in. In the following example, we've grouped them into **Set** instead of the default list:

```
Map<String, Set<Car>> grouped = Stream.of(
        new Car("Toyota", 92),
        new Car("Kia", 104),
        new Car("Hyundai", 89),
        new Car("Toyota", 116),
        new Car("Mercedes", 209))
    .collect(Collectors.groupingBy(Car::getBrand, Collectors.
        toSet()));
System.out.println(grouped);
```

The **groupingBy** collector becomes even more powerful if you combine it with another collector—for example, the **reducing** collector:

```
Map<String, Optional<Car>> collected = Stream.of(
        new Car("Volvo", 195),
        new Car("Honda", 96),
        new Car("Volvo", 165),
```

```
        new Car("Volvo", 165),
        new Car("Honda", 104),
        new Car("Honda", 201),
        new Car("Volvo", 215))
    .collect(Collectors.groupingBy(Car::getBrand, Collectors.
      reducing((carA, carB) -> {
        if (carA.enginePower > carB.enginePower) {

            return carA;

        }
        return carB;
    })));
System.out.println(collected);
```

In this example, we group the cars by brand and then reduce them to only show the car of each brand with the most powerful engine. This kind of combination, of course, also works with other collectors, such as filtering, counting, and others:

- **GroupingByConcurrent**: This is a concurrent and unordered version of the **groupingBy** collector, and has the exact same API.

- **partitioningBy**: The **partitioningBy** collector works in a similar way to the **groupingBy** collector, with the difference being that it will group elements into two collections that either matches a predicate or doesn't match a predicate. It will wrap these two collections into **Map**, where the **true** keyword will reference the collection of elements that matches the predicate, and the **false** keyword will reference the elements that don't match the predicate:

```
Map<Boolean, List<Car>> partitioned = Stream.of(
        new Car("Toyota", 92),
        new Car("Kia", 104),
        new Car("Hyundai", 89),
        new Car("Toyota", 116),
        new Car("Mercedes", 209))
    .collect(Collectors.partitioningBy((car) -> { return car.
      enginePower > 100; }));
System.out.println(partitioned);
```

You can also select which kind of collection the elements should be wrapped in, just like the **groupingBy** collector:

```
Map<Boolean, Set<Car>> partitioned = Stream.of(
        new Car("Toyota", 92),
        new Car("Kia", 104),
        new Car("Hyundai", 89),
        new Car("Toyota", 116),
        new Car("Mercedes", 209))
```

```
        .collect(Collectors.partitioningBy((car) -> { return car.
            enginePower > 100; }, Collectors.toSet())));
System.out.println(partitioned);
```

- **toMap**: This collector will allow you to create a **map** from your stream elements by defining a mapping function, where you provide a key and value to put into the **map**. Often, this is just a unique identifier in the element and the element itself.

This can be a little bit tricky because if you provide a duplicate element, then your pipeline will throw an **IllegalStateException** since **Map** is not allowed duplicate keys:

```
Map<String, Integer> mapped = List.of("1", "2", "3", "4", "5")
        .stream()
        .collect(Collectors.toMap((s) -> {
            return s;
        }, (s) -> {
            return Integer.valueOf(s);
        }));
System.out.println(mapped);
```

This simple example demonstrates how to map a string representation of an integer to the actual integer. If you know you may have duplicate elements, then you can supply a **merge** function to resolve that conflict:

```
Map<String, Integer> mapped = List.of("1", "2", "3", "4", "5", "1", "2")
        .stream()
        .collect(Collectors.toMap((s) -> {
            return s;
        }, (s) -> {
            return Integer.valueOf(s);
        }, (a, b) -> {
            return Integer.valueOf(b);
        }));
System.out.println(mapped);
```

You also have the option of generating your own type of **Map** by applying a **factory** function at the very end of the collector. Here, we're telling the collector to generate a fresh **TreeMap** for us:

```
TreeMap<String, Integer> mapped = List.of("1", "2", "3", "4", "5", "1", "2")
        .stream()
        .collect(Collectors.toMap((s) -> {
            return s;
        }, (s) -> {
            return Integer.valueOf(s);
```

```
    }, (a, b) -> {
        return Integer.valueOf(b);
    }, () -> {
        return new TreeMap<>();
    }));
System.out.println(mapped);
```

- **toUnmodifiableMap**: This is essentially the same as **toMap**, with the same API; however, it returns unmodifiable versions of **Map** instead. This is perfect for when you know you will never mutate the data in **Map**.

- **toConcurrentMap**: Because of the way **Map** is implemented, it can be a bit hazardous to performance when using it in parallel streams. In this case, it's recommended that you use the **toConcurrentMap()** collector instead. This has a similar API to the other **toMap** functions, with the difference being that it will return instances of **ConcurrentMap** rather than **Map**.

- **Summarizing**: This is a collector that enables summary statistics for non-primitive streams. It is perfect if you need to display some statistics about complex objects without having to first apply other intermediate operations. Considering the **Car** class from previous collectors, you could produce a summary of all car engines like this:

```
LongSummaryStatistics statistics = Stream.of(
        new Car("Volvo", 165),
        new Car("Volvo", 165),
        new Car("Honda", 104),
        new Car("Honda", 201)
).collect(Collectors.summarizingLong((e) -> {
    return e.enginePower;
}));
System.out.println(statistics);
```

I/O Streams

Apart from collections and other primitives, you can use files and I/O streams as sources in your pipelines. This makes writing tasks against servers very descriptive.

Because these types of resources generally need to be closed properly, you should use a try-with-resources statement to ensure the resources are handed back to the system when you're done with them.

Consider having a CSV file called **authors.csv** with these contents:

```
Andreas, 42, Sweden
David, 37, Sweden
Eric, 39, USA
```

You can put this file into a stream using a try-with-resources statement:

```
String filePath = System.getProperty("user.dir") + File.separator +  "res/authors.csv";
try (Stream<String> authors = Files.lines(Paths.get(filePath))) {
    authors.forEach((author) -> {
        System.out.println(author);
    });
} catch (IOException e) {
    e.printStackTrace();
}
```

In I/O streams, you can add **onClose** handlers to receive a notification when the stream is closed. Unlike other streams, this will be closed automatically when the resources for the stream have been closed. In this example, that's handled automatically by the try-with-resources statement. In the following example, we've added an **onClose** handler that will print the word **Closed** when the stream has been closed:

```
try (Stream<String> authors = Files.lines(Paths.get(filePath))) {
    authors.onClose(() -> {
        System.out.println("Closed");
    }).forEach((author) -> {
        System.out.println(author);
    });
} catch (IOException e) {
    e.printStackTrace();
}
```

Here is the same example written with an **InputStream** instead. Notice that the code is now more verbose, having three nested object creations:

```
try (Stream<String> authors = new BufferedReader(
        new InputStreamReader(new FileInputStream(filePath))).lines()
) {
    ...
} catch (FileNotFoundException e) {
    e.printStackTrace();
}
```

Exercise 2: Converting CSV to a List

A web-based grocery shop has implemented its very own database based on a standard Java **List** collection, and has also implemented a backup system where the database is backed up to CSV files. However, they still haven't built a way of restoring that database from a CSV file. They have asked you to build a system that will read such a CSV file, inflating its contents to a list.

The database backup CSV file contains one single type of object: **ShoppingArticle**. Each article has a **name**, a **price**, a **category**, and finally, a **unit**. The name, category, and unit should each be a **String**, and the price a **double**:

1. Open the **Chapter15** project in IDEA if it's not already open.

2. Create a new Java class, using **File| New | Java**.

3. Enter **Exercise2** as the name, and then select **OK**.

   IntelliJ will create your new class; it should look something like the following snippet:

   ```
   package com.packt.java.chapter15;
   public class Exercise2 {
   }
   ```

4. Add a **main** method to this class. This is where you'll write the bulk of your application. Your class should now look like this:

   ```
   package com.packt.java.chapter15;
   public class Exercise2 {
       public static void main(String[] args) {
       }
   }
   ```

5. Create a **ShoppingArticle** inner class and make it static so that you can easily use it in the main method. Override the **toString** method to make it easy to print articles to the terminal later:

   ```
   private static class ShoppingArticle {
       final String name;
       final String category;
       final double price;
       final String unit;
       private ShoppingArticle(String name, String category, double price,
           String unit) {
           this.name = name;
           this.category = category;
           this.price = price;
   ```

```
            this.unit = unit;
        }
        @Override
        public String toString() {
            return name + " (" + category + ")";
        }
    }
```

6. Create a new folder in your project called **res** if it doesn't already exist. Then, place it in the root, next to the **src** folder.

7. Copy the **database.csv** file from GitHub to your project and place it in the **res** folder.

8. Back in your **Exercise2.java** class, add a function that produces **List<ShoppingArticle>**. This will be our function to load the database into a list. Since the function will be loading a file, it needs to throw an I/O exception (**IOException**):

```
private static List<ShoppingArticle> loadDatabaseFile() throws IOException {
    return null;
}
```

9. Call this function from your **main** method:

```
public static void main(String[] args) {
    try {
        List<ShoppingArticle> database = loadDatabaseFile();
    } catch (IOException e) {
        e.printStackTrace();
    }
}
```

10. Start by loading the database file with a try-with-resources block. Use **Files.lines** to load all the lines from the **database.csv** file. It should look something like this:

```
private static List<ShoppingArticle> loadDatabaseFile() throws IOException {
    try (Stream<String> stream = Files.lines(Path.of("res/database.csv"))) {
    }
    return null;
}
```

11. Let's peek into the stream in order to look at the state of it right now. Intermediate operations will only run when there's a terminal operation defined, so add a **count()** at the end just to force it to execute the whole pipeline:

```
private static List<ShoppingArticle> loadDatabaseFile() throws IOException {
    try (Stream<String> stream = Files.lines(Path.of("res/database.csv"))) {
        return stream.peek((line) -> {
            System.out.println(line);
        }).count();
    } catch (IOException e) {
        e.printStackTrace();
    }
    return null;
}
```

This should print every single line of the file. Notice that it also prints the header line–which we're not concerned with when converting to **ShoppingArticles**.

12. Since we're not really interested in the first row, add a **skip** operation just before the **count()** method:

```
private static List<ShoppingArticle> loadDatabaseFile() throws IOException {
    try (Stream<String> stream = Files.lines(Path.of("res/database.csv"))) {
        return stream.peek((line) -> {
            System.out.println(line);
        }).skip(1).count();
    } catch (IOException e) {
        e.printStackTrace();
    }
    return null;
}
```

13. Now you have every single line of the database file loaded as elements in the stream, except for the header. It's time to extract every piece of data from those lines; a suitable operation for this is **map**. Split every line into **String** arrays using the **split()** function:

```
private static List<ShoppingArticle> loadDatabaseFile() throws IOException {
    try (Stream<String> stream = Files.lines(Path.of("res/database.csv"))) {
        return stream.peek((line) -> {
            System.out.println(line);
        }).skip(1).map((line) -> {
            return line.split(",");
        }).count();
    } catch (IOException e) {
        e.printStackTrace();
    }
    return null;
}
```

14. Add another **peek** operation to find out how the **map** operation changed the stream; your stream type should now be **Stream<String[]>**:

```
private static List<ShoppingArticle> loadDatabaseFile() throws IOException {
    try (Stream<String> stream = Files.lines(Path.of("res/database.csv"))) {
        return stream.peek((line) -> {
            System.out.println(line);
        }).skip(1).map((line) -> {
            return line.split(",");
        }).peek((arr) -> {
            System.out.println(Arrays.toString(arr));
        }).count();
    } catch (IOException e) {
        e.printStackTrace();
    }
    return null;
}
```

15. Add another **map** operation, but this time to turn the stream into
    Stream<ShoppingArticle>:

```
private static List<ShoppingArticle> loadDatabaseFile() throws IOException {
    try (Stream<String> stream = Files.lines(Path.of("res/database.csv"))) {
        return stream.peek((line) -> {
            System.out.println(line);
        }).skip(1).map((line) -> {
            return line.split(",");
        }).peek((arr) -> {
            System.out.println(Arrays.toString(arr));
        }).map((arr) -> {
            return new ShoppingArticle(arr[0], arr[1],
                Double.valueOf(arr[2]), arr[3]);
        }).count();
    } catch (IOException e) {
        e.printStackTrace();
    }
    return null;
}
```

16. Now you can peek again to ensure the articles were created properly:

```
private static List<ShoppingArticle> loadDatabaseFile() throws IOException {
    try (Stream<String> stream = Files.lines(Path.of("res/database.csv"))) {
        return stream.peek((line) -> {
            System.out.println(line);
        }).skip(1).map((line) -> {
            return line.split(",");
        }).peek((arr) -> {
            System.out.println(Arrays.toString(arr));
        }).map((arr) -> {
```

```
            return new ShoppingArticle(arr[0], arr[1],
                Double.valueOf(arr[2]), arr[3]);
        }).peek((art) -> {
            System.out.println(art);
        }).count();
    } catch (IOException e) {
        e.printStackTrace();
    }
    return null;
}
```

17. Collect all the articles in a list. Use an unmodifiable list to protect the database from unwanted modifications:

```
private static List<ShoppingArticle> loadDatabaseFile() throws IOException {
    try (Stream<String> stream = Files.lines(Path.of("res/database.csv"))) {
        return stream.peek((line) -> {
            System.out.println(line);
        }).skip(1).map((line) -> {
            return line.split(",");
        }).peek((arr) -> {
            System.out.println(Arrays.toString(arr));
        }).map((arr) -> {
            return new ShoppingArticle(arr[0], arr[1],
                Double.valueOf(arr[2]), arr[3]);
        }).peek((art) -> {
            System.out.println(art);
        }).collect(Collectors.toUnmodifiableList());
    } catch (IOException e) {
        e.printStackTrace();
    }
    return null;
}
```

This may seem verbose, as some operations could have been applied together to make it shorter. However, there's a point to keeping every single operation small, and that's to make the whole logic very transparent. If you find a problem with the pipeline, you can simply move a single operation in the pipeline, and that should sort all problems.

If you combine multiple steps in an operation, it's more difficult to move the operations around in the pipeline or to replace it fully.

Activity 2: Searching for Specifics

With the database loaded, apply some searching logic:

1. Build a function that will find the cheapest fruit from a list of `ShoppingArticles`.

2. Build a function that will find the most expensive vegetable from a list of `ShoppingArticles`.

3. Build a function that will gather all fruits in a separate list.

4. Build a function that will find the five least expensive articles in the database.

5. Build a function that will find the five most expensive articles in the database.

> **Note**
>
> The Solution for this Activity can be found on page 564.

Summary

Descriptive code is always an ideal to strive for when writing programs. The simpler the code is, the easier it will be to communicate your intentions to colleagues and other interested parties.

The Java Streams API allows you to construct simple, and highly descriptive functions. Quite often they'll be pure functions since the Streams API makes it very easy to avoid manipulating state.

In the next chapter, we'll delve further into functional programming topics, exploring the different functional interfaces available.

16

Predicates and Other Functional Interfaces

Overview

This chapter explores all the valid use cases of functional interfaces. It will first define what these interfaces are (beginning with the predicate interface), as well as how best to employ them in your code. You will then learn how to build and apply predicates, studying their composition and how to use this to model complex behavior. You will practice creating consumer interfaces to change the state of your program, and, eventually, use functions to extract useful constructs.

Introduction

Alongside the many other improvements in Java 8 (such as the streaming API, method references, optionals, and collectors) there are interface improvements that allow default and static methods known as functional interfaces. These are interfaces with one single abstract method, which enables their transformation into lambdas. You can read more about this in *Chapter 13, Functional Programming with Lambda Expressions*.

There are a total of 43 unique functional interfaces in the `java.util.function` package; most of them are variants of the same kind of interface, albeit with different data types. In this chapter, we'll introduce you to the **predicate functional interface**, along with a few other selected interfaces.

Here, you'll find that many of the functional interfaces operate in very similar ways, often just replacing the type of data that the interface can operate on.

Predicate Interface

The predicate interface is a quite simple, yet surprisingly elegant and complex, functional interface that allows you, as a programmer, to define functions that describe the state of your program in the shape of Booleans. In Java, speech predicates are one-argument functions that return a Boolean value.

The predicate API looks like this:

```
boolean test(T t);
```

However, the predicate API also utilizes the new interface features of Java 8. Its sports default and static functions to enrich the API, allowing more complex descriptions of your program's state. Here, three functions are important:

```
Predicate<T> and(Predicate<T>);
Predicate<T> or(Predicate<T>);
Predicate<T> not(Predicate<T>);
```

With these three functions, you can chain predicates to describe more complex queries on your program's state. The **and** function will combine two or more predicates, ensuring that every predicate supplied returns true.

The **or** function is equivalent to a logical OR, letting you short-circuit the predicate chain when required.

Finally, the **not** function returns the negated version of the predicate supplied, and it has the exact same effect as calling **negate()** on the supplied predicate.

There is also a **helper** function to build a predicate that checks whether two objects are identical according to the **equals** method on said objects. We can use the static **isEqual(Object target)** method to build that predicate for two objects The following exercise will serve as an example of defining a predicate.

Exercise 1: Defining a predicate

Defining a predicate is quite simple. Consider building the backend server of a home alarm system. This system needs to easily understand the state of numerous different sensors at the same time—instances such as: Is the door open or closed? Is the battery healthy or not? Are the sensors connected?

Building such a system is a complex task. We'll try simplifying the process in this exercise:

1. If IntelliJ is already started, but no project is open, select **Create New Project**. If IntelliJ already has a project open, select **File** -> **New** -> **Project** from the menu.

2. In **New Project** dialog, select a Java project. Click **Next**.

3. Check the box to create the project from a template. Select **Command Line App**. Click **Next**.

4. Give the new project the name **Chapter16**.

5. IntelliJ will give you a default project location. If you wish to select one, you may enter it here.

6. Set the package name to **com.packt.java.chapter16**.

7. Click **Finish**.

   Your project will be created with the standard folder structure, and with an entry point class for your program. It will look something like this:

   ```java
   package com.packt.java.chapter16;
   public class Main {
       public static void main(String[] args) {
       // write your code here
       }
   }
   ```

8. Rename this file to **Exercise1.java**, making sure to use the **Refactor | Rename** menu. When you're done, it should look like this:

```
package com.packt.java.chapter16;
public class Exercise1 {
    public static void main(String[] args) {
    // write your code here
    }
}
```

9. The alarm system will have three different kinds of sensors – a **Gateway sensor**, a **Movement sensor**, and a **Fire sensor**. They will all have the same basic qualities but may differ in certain aspects. Create the **Base** sensor interface and let it have two getter/setter pairs. The first pair should be called **batteryHealth** and will return an integer between 0 and 100, and the second pair will be a Boolean value called **triggered**:

```
package com.packt.java.chapter16;
public interface Sensor {
    int batteryHealth();
    void batteryHealth(int health);
    boolean triggered();
    void triggered(boolean state);
}
```

10. Create the **Gateway Sensor** class, and allow it to implement the **Sensor** interface and return instance variables:

```
package com.packt.java.chapter16;
public class Gateway implements Sensor {
    private int batteryHealth;
    private boolean triggered;
    @Override
    public int batteryHealth() {
        return batteryHealth;
    }
    @Override
    public void batteryHealth(int health) {
        this.batteryHealth = health;
```

```
            }
            @Override
            public boolean triggered() {
                return triggered;
            }
            @Override
            public void triggered(boolean state) {
                triggered = state;
            }
    }
```

11. Do the same thing for the **Movement** and **Fire** sensor classes, except the **Fire** sensor will also have the current **temperature**, and the **movement sensor** will return the strength of the ambient light in the room:

```
package com.packt.java.chapter16;
public class Fire implements Sensor {
    private int batteryHealth;
    private boolean triggered;
    private int temperature;
    @Override
    public int batteryHealth() {
        return batteryHealth;
    }
    @Override
    public void batteryHealth(int health) {
    }
    @Override
    public boolean triggered() {
        return triggered;
    }
    @Override
    public void triggered(boolean state) {
    }
    public int temperature() {
        return temperature;
    }
    }
}
```

The code for **Movement** class is as follows:

```java
package com.packt.java.chapter16;
public class Movement implements Sensor {
    private int batteryHealth;
    private boolean isTriggered;
    private int ambientLight;
    @Override
    public int batteryHealth() {
        return batteryHealth;
    }
    @Override
    public void batteryHealth(int health) {
    }
    @Override
    public boolean triggered() {
        return isTriggered;
    }
    @Override
    public void triggered(boolean state) {
    }
    public int ambientLight() {
        return ambientLight;
    }
}
```

12. Add constructors to all three sensor classes, utilizing IntelliJ helpers to this end. Open the **Fire** class, use the **Code | Generate** menu, and select **Constructor**.

13. Select all three variables and click **OK**. Your **Fire** class should now look something like this:

```java
package com.packt.java.chapter16;
public class Fire implements Sensor {
    private int batteryHealth;
    private boolean triggered;
    private int temperature;
    public Fire(int batteryHealth, boolean isTriggered, int temperature) {
        this.batteryHealth = batteryHealth;
        this.triggered = isTriggered;
        this.temperature = temperature;
    }
}
```

```
    @Override
    public int batteryHealth() {
        return batteryHealth;
    }
    @Override
    public void batteryHealth(int health) {
    }
    @Override
    public boolean triggered() {
        return triggered;
    }
    @Override
    public void triggered(boolean state) {
    }
    public int temperature() {
        return temperature;
    }
}
```

14. Generate constructors for the **Gateway** and **Movement** sensors as well.

15. You should now have three functioning classes representing sensor states in your program.

16. It's now time to describe your first predicate class, the predicate that describes whether a sensor has a triggered alarm. Create a new class, and call it **HasAlarm**:

```
package com.packt.java.chapter16;
public class HasAlarm {
}
```

17. Implement the **Predicate** interface, using **Sensor** as the type definition. In the **test** function, return the trigger status of the sensor:

```
package com.packt.java.chapter16;
import java.util.function.Predicate;
public class HasAlarm implements Predicate<Sensor> {
    @Override
    public boolean test(Sensor sensor) {
        return sensor.triggered();
    }
}
```

18. Back in your program's entry point, the **main** method, create a list of sensors and add a few **Gateway** sensors to it:

```java
package com.packt.java.chapter16;
import java.util.ArrayList;
import java.util.List;
public class Exercise1 {
    public static void main(String[] args) {
        List<Sensor> sensors = new ArrayList<>();
        sensors.add(new Gateway(34, false));
        sensors.add(new Gateway(14, true));
        sensors.add(new Gateway(74, false));
        sensors.add(new Gateway(8, false));
        sensors.add(new Gateway(18, false));
        sensors.add(new Gateway(9, false));
    }
}
```

19. Use a **for** loop in the main method to iterate through the list. In the **for** loop, add an **if** statement that uses the predicate to check whether an alarm was triggered:

```java
package com.packt.java.chapter16;
import java.util.ArrayList;
import java.util.List;
import java.util.function.Predicate;
public class Exercise1 {
    public static void main(String[] args) {
        List<Sensor> sensors = new ArrayList<>();
        sensors.add(new Gateway(34, false));
        sensors.add(new Gateway(14, true));
        sensors.add(new Gateway(74, false));
        sensors.add(new Gateway(8, false));
        sensors.add(new Gateway(18, false));
        sensors.add(new Gateway(9, false));
        for (Sensor sensor : sensors) {
```

```
            if (new HasAlarm().test(sensor)) {
                System.out.println("Alarm was triggered");
            }
        }
    }
}
```

> **Note**
>
> You may very well ask yourself what the point of this is. This is no different from using the sensor's **public triggered()** function. This is also an uncommon way of applying predicates, but it illustrates how predicates work. A much more common approach involves using streams and lambdas.

20. Now, create another predicate and call it **HasWarning**. In this class, we'll simply check whether the battery status is below a threshold of **10**, which will symbolize 10% in our example:

```
package com.packt.java.chapter16;
import java.util.function.Predicate;
public class HasWarning implements Predicate<Sensor> {
    public static final int BATTERY_WARNING = 10;
    @Override
    public boolean test(Sensor sensor) {
        return sensor.batteryHealth() < BATTERY_WARNING;
    }
}
```

21. Use the **HasAlarm** and **HasWarning** predicates to generate a newly composed predicate. Instantiate the **HasAlarm** predicate and apply the default **or()** function to chain the **HasWarning** predicate as well:

```
package com.packt.java.chapter16;
import java.util.ArrayList;
import java.util.List;
import java.util.function.Predicate;
public class Exercise1 {
    public static void main(String[] args) {
        List<Sensor> sensors = new ArrayList<>();
        sensors.add(new Gateway(34, false));
        sensors.add(new Gateway(14, true));
        sensors.add(new Gateway(74, false));
```

```
                sensors.add(new Gateway(8, false));
                sensors.add(new Gateway(18, false));
                sensors.add(new Gateway(9, false));
                Predicate<Sensor> hasAlarmOrWarning = new HasAlarm().or(new
                    HasWarning());
                for (Sensor sensor : sensors) {
                    if (new HasAlarm().test(sensor)) {
                        System.out.println("Alarm was triggered");
                    }
                }
            }
        }
    }
```

22. Add a new **if** statement in the **for** loop using the newly composed predicate:

Exercise1.java

```
1   package com.packt.java.chapter16;
2
3   import java.util.ArrayList;
4   import java.util.List;
5   import java.util.function.Predicate;
6
7   public class Exercise1 {
8
9       public static void main(String[] args) {
10          List<Sensor> sensors = new ArrayList<>();
11          sensors.add(new Gateway(34, false));
12          sensors.add(new Gateway(14, true));
13          sensors.add(new Gateway(74, false));
14          sensors.add(new Gateway(8, false));
15          sensors.add(new Gateway(18, false));
16          sensors.add(new Gateway(9, false));
```

https://packt.live/2P9njsy

As mentioned earlier, applying predicates—or any other functional interface, for that matter—directly on objects in loops like this is uncommon. Instead you will primarily use the Java streams API.

Activity 1: Toggling the Sensor States

Rewrite the program once more, adding a scanner to your program to toggle sensor states from the command line. Each sensor should be capable of at least toggling the battery health and triggered status. When a sensor has updated, you should check the system for changes and generate a proper response on the command line if a warning or alarm has been triggered.

> **Note**
>
> The solution to this Activity can be found on page 565.

Consumer Interface

In functional programming, we're often told to avoid side effects in our code. The consumer functional interface, however, is an exception to this rule. Its only purpose is to produce a side effect based on the state of the argument. The consumer has quite a simple API, the core function of which is called **accept()** and doesn't return anything:

```
void accept(T);
```

This can also be used for chaining multiple consumers by using the **andThen()** function, which returns the newly chained consumer:

```
Consumer<T> andThen(Consumer<T>);
```

Exercise 2: Producing Side Effects

Continuing the previous exercise, consider the following example wherein we will add functionality for reacting to warnings and alarms in the system. You can use consumers to produce side effects and to store the current state of the system in variables:

1. Copy the **Exercise1.java** class, and call it **Exercise2**. Remove the whole **for** loop, but leave the instantiated predicate.

2. Create a new static Boolean variable in **Exercise2**, and call it **alarmServiceNotified**:

```
package com.packt.java.chapter16;
import java.util.ArrayList;
import java.util.List;
import java.util.function.Predicate;
public class Exercise2 {
    static boolean alarmServiceNotified;
    public static void main(String[] args) {
        List<Sensor> sensors = new ArrayList<>();
```

```
            sensors.add(new Gateway(34, false));
            sensors.add(new Gateway(14, true));
            sensors.add(new Gateway(74, false));
            sensors.add(new Gateway(8, false));
            sensors.add(new Gateway(18, false));
            sensors.add(new Gateway(9, false));
            Predicate<Sensor> hasAlarmOrWarning = new HasAlarm().or(new
                HasWarning());
        }
    }
```

> **Note**
>
> This is, of course, not the manner in which you'd commonly apply static variables
> (if you ever really should use static variables). However, in this example, it makes it
> a lot easier to illustrate side effects.

3. Create a new class, call it **SendAlarm**, and allow it to implement the consumer
   interface. It should look something like this:

```
package com.packt.java.chapter16;
import java.util.function.Consumer;
public class SendAlarm implements Consumer<Sensor> {
    @Override
    public void accept(Sensor sensor) {

    }
}
```

4. Inside the **accept(Sensor sensor)** function, check whether the sensor has been
   triggered. If it has been triggered, set the static variable to **true**:

```
package com.packt.java.chapter16;
import java.util.function.Consumer;
public class SendAlarm implements Consumer<Sensor> {
    @Override
    public void accept(Sensor sensor) {
        if (sensor.triggered()) {
            Exercise2.alarmServiceNotified = true;
        }
    }
}
```

5. Back in the **main** method, instantiate a new **SendAlarm** consumer:

```
package com.packt.java.chapter16;
import java.util.ArrayList;
import java.util.List;
import java.util.function.Predicate;
public class Exercise2 {
    static boolean alarmServiceNotified;
    public static void main(String[] args) {
        List<Sensor> sensors = new ArrayList<>();
        sensors.add(new Gateway(34, false));
        sensors.add(new Gateway(14, true));
        sensors.add(new Gateway(74, false));
        sensors.add(new Gateway(8, false));
        sensors.add(new Gateway(18, false));
        sensors.add(new Gateway(9, false));
        Predicate<Sensor> hasAlarmOrWarning = new HasAlarm().or(new
    HasWarning());
        SendAlarm sendAlarm = new SendAlarm();
    }
}
```

6. Using streams, first, filter the list of sensors based on the previously defined composed predicate. Then, use **forEach** to apply the **SendAlarm** consumer to each of the sensors that have an alarm or warning triggered:

```
sensors.stream().filter(hasAlarmOrWarning).forEach(sendAlarm);
```

7. Now, add an **if** statement, checking whether the alarm service was notified, and print a message if it was:

```
if (alarmServiceNotified) {
    System.out.println("Alarm service notified");
}
```

8. Build one more consumer, and this time call it **ResetAlarm**:

```
package com.packt.java.chapter16;
import java.util.function.Consumer;
public class ResetAlarm implements Consumer<Sensor> {
    @Override
    public void accept(Sensor sensor) {
    }
}
```

9. Add logic to the **ResetAlarm accept()** function to set **batteryHealth** to **50** and **Triggered** to **false**. Also, set the static notification variable to **false**:

```
package com.packt.java.chapter16;
        import java.util.function.Consumer;
public class ResetAlarm implements Consumer<Sensor> {
    @Override
    public void accept(Sensor sensor) {
        sensor.triggered(false);
        sensor.batteryHealth(50);
        Exercise2.alarmServiceNotified = false;
    }
}
```

10. Instantiate the new **ResetAlarm** consumer, and then apply it after the **SendAlarm** consumer using the **andThen()** function:

```
package com.packt.java.chapter16;
import java.util.ArrayList;
import java.util.List;
import java.util.function.Consumer;
import java.util.function.Predicate;
public class Exercise2 {
    static boolean alarmServiceNotified;
    public static void main(String[] args) {
        List<Sensor> sensors = new ArrayList<>();
        sensors.add(new Gateway(34, false));
        sensors.add(new Gateway(14, true));
        sensors.add(new Gateway(74, false));
        sensors.add(new Gateway(8, false));
        sensors.add(new Gateway(18, false));
        sensors.add(new Gateway(9, false));
        Predicate<Sensor> hasAlarmOrWarning = new HasAlarm().or(new
        HasWarning());
        if (sensors.stream().anyMatch(hasAlarmOrWarning)) {
            System.out.println("Alarm or warning was triggered");
        }
        SendAlarm sendAlarm = new SendAlarm();
```

```
            ResetAlarm resetAlarm = new ResetAlarm();
            sensors.stream().filter(hasAlarmOrWarning)
        .forEach(sendAlarm.andThen(resetAlarm));
            if (alarmServiceNotified) {
                System.out.println("Alarm service notified");
            }
        }
    }
}
```

11. Finally, a bonus. At the very end of *Exercise 2, Producing Side Effects* 's **main** method, apply the negated version of the **hasAlarmOrWarning** predicate, and print out an **Everything okay** message:

Exercise2.java

```
21          Predicate<Sensor> hasAlarmOrWarning = new HasAlarm().or(new
        HasWarning());
22
23          if (sensors.stream().anyMatch(hasAlarmOrWarning)) {
24              System.out.println("Alarm or warning was triggered");
25          }
26
27          SendAlarm sendAlarm = new SendAlarm();
28
29          ResetAlarm resetAlarm = new ResetAlarm();
30
31          sensors.stream().filter(hasAlarmOrWarning)
        .forEach(sendAlarm.andThen(resetAlarm));
32
33          if (alarmServiceNotified) {
34              System.out.println("Alarm service notified");
35          }
36
37          if (sensors.stream().anyMatch(hasAlarmOrWarning.negate())) {
38              System.out.println("Nothing was triggered");
39          }
```

https://packt.live/2JqD7n9

Function

The function, functional interface (yes, it's called a function) was introduced mainly to translate one value into another. It is often used in mapping scenarios. It also contains default methods to combine multiple functions into one, and chain functions after one another.

The main function in the interface is called **apply**, and it looks like this:

```
R apply(T);
```

It defines a return value, **R**, and an input to the function. The idea is that the return value and input don't have to be of the same type.

The composition is handled by the **compose** function, which also returns an instance of the interface, which means that you can chain compositions. The order is right to left; in other words, the argument function is applied before the calling function:

```
Function<V, R> compose(Function<V, T>);
```

Finally, the **andThen** function allows you to chain functions after one another:

```
Function<T, V> andThen(Function<R, V>);
```

In the following exercise, you will practice using these functions.

Exercise 3: Extracting Data

Extract all of the alarm system data as integers—battery percentages, temperatures, triggered status, and others, depending on how far you've taken your alarm system. Start by extracting the battery health data:

1. Copy the **Exercise2** class and call it **Exercise3**.

2. Remove everything except the list of sensors. Your class should look something like this:

```
package com.packt.java.chapter16;
import java.util.ArrayList;
import java.util.List;
public class Exercise3 {
    public static void main(String[] args) {
        List<Sensor> sensors = new ArrayList<>();
        sensors.add(new Gateway(34, false));
        sensors.add(new Gateway(14, true));
        sensors.add(new Gateway(74, false));
        sensors.add(new Gateway(8, false));
        sensors.add(new Gateway(18, false));
        sensors.add(new Gateway(9, false));
    }
}
```

3. Create a new class, call it **ExtractBatteryHealth**, and let it implement the **Function<T, R>** functional interface. Override the **apply** function. Your class should look like this:

```
package com.packt.java.chapter16;
import java.util.function.Function;
public class ExtractBatteryHealth implements Function<Sensor, Integer> {
```

```
        @Override
        public Integer apply(Sensor sensor) {
            return null;
        }
    }
```

4. In the **apply** function, make it return the battery health, as follows:

```
package com.packt.java.chapter16;
import java.util.function.Function;
public class ExtractBatteryHealth implements Function<Sensor, Integer> {
    @Override
    public Integer apply(Sensor sensor) {
        return sensor.batteryHealth();
    }
}
```

5. Instantiate your new **ExtractBatteryHealth** function and add a few more sensors to the list if you haven't already done so:

```
package com.packt.java.chapter16;
import java.util.ArrayList;
import java.util.List;
public class Exercise3 {
    public static void main(String[] args) {
        List<Sensor> sensors = new ArrayList<>();
        sensors.add(new Gateway(34, false));
        sensors.add(new Gateway(14, true));
        sensors.add(new Fire(78, false, 21));
        sensors.add(new Gateway(74, false));
        sensors.add(new Gateway(8, false));
        sensors.add(new Movement(87, false, 45));
        sensors.add(new Gateway(18, false));
        sensors.add(new Fire(32, false, 23));
        sensors.add(new Gateway(9, false));
        sensors.add(new Movement(76, false, 41));
        ExtractBatteryHealth extractBatteryHealth = new ExtractBatteryHealth();
    }
}
```

6. Finally, use the java streams **map** operation and apply your new instance of **ExtractBatteryHealth**. Terminate the stream with a **toArray** operation. You should now have an array of all your battery health:

```java
package com.packt.java.chapter16;
import java.util.ArrayList;
import java.util.List;
public class Exercise3 {
    public static void main(String[] args) {
        List<Sensor> sensors = new ArrayList<>();
        sensors.add(new Gateway(34, false));
        sensors.add(new Gateway(14, true));
        sensors.add(new Fire(78, false, 21));
        sensors.add(new Gateway(74, false));
        sensors.add(new Gateway(8, false));
        sensors.add(new Movement(87, false, 45));
        sensors.add(new Gateway(18, false));
        sensors.add(new Fire(32, false, 23));
        sensors.add(new Gateway(9, false));
        sensors.add(new Movement(76, false, 41));
        ExtractBatteryHealth extractBatteryHealth = new
            ExtractBatteryHealth();
        Integer[] batteryHealths =
            sensors.stream().map(extractBatteryHealth)
            .toArray(Integer[]::new);
    }
}
```

7. Print your battery health to the terminal:

```java
package com.packt.java.chapter16;
import java.util.ArrayList;
import java.util.Arrays;
import java.util.List;
public class Exercise3 {
    public static void main(String[] args) {
        List<Sensor> sensors = new ArrayList<>();
        sensors.add(new Gateway(34, false));
        sensors.add(new Gateway(14, true));
        sensors.add(new Fire(78, false, 21));
```

```
            sensors.add(new Gateway(74, false));
            sensors.add(new Gateway(8, false));
            sensors.add(new Movement(87, false, 45));
            sensors.add(new Gateway(18, false));
            sensors.add(new Fire(32, false, 23));
            sensors.add(new Gateway(9, false));
            sensors.add(new Movement(76, false, 41));
            ExtractBatteryHealth extractBatteryHealth = new ExtractBatteryHealth();
            Integer[] batteryHealths =
              sensors.stream().map(extractBatteryHealth)
              .toArray(Integer[]::new);
            System.out.println(Arrays.toString(batteryHealths));
        }
    }
```

Activity 2: Using a Recursive Function

Calculate the average battery health in your alarm system–either through a loop, a stream, or a recursive function.

> **Note**
>
> The solution for this activity can be found on page 566.

Activity 3: Using a Lambda Function

Instead of instantiating the **ExtractBatteryHealth** functional interface, use a lambda and store a reference to that.

> **Note**
>
> The solution for this activity can be found on page 567.

Summary

In this chapter, you've explored how to use the functional interfaces provided by Java 8. You've used them both in loops, on single instances, and in streams—all of which are valid use cases for functional interfaces. However, you'll quickly find that these instances of functional interfaces (lamdas, for short) are more commonly used together with streams.

There are many pre-defined functional interfaces in Java, but only a few of them are unique in the way they work. Most are just primitive versions of the different functions, such as **IntPredicate**, **LongPredicate**, **DoublePredicate**, and **Predicate**.

In the next chapter, you'll learn more about the Reactive Streams initiative, the Flow API, and what Java does to build good foundational interfaces for reactive programming.

17

Reactive Programming with Java Flow

Overview

This chapter covers the Java Flow API and the advantages of the Reactive Streams specification. It will first define, in general terms, the motivation for Flow and Reactive Streams, as well as the respective functions of Publishers, Subscribers, and Processors in Java. You will then learn to use the basic **SubmissionPublisher** to build a reactive application and, in the final sections, practice implementing a simple Subscriber and Processor using Flow.

Introduction

The Reactive Streams specification presents an ongoing development within software architecture, referred to as Reactive Systems. These systems, ideally, have the following advantages:

- A faster response

- More controlled responses in relation to one another

- Increased reliability

A natively supported API for developing Reactive Systems or applications was introduced in Java 9, called Flow.

The Java 9 Flow API was not intended to compete with the already developed, highly adopted, and appreciated reactive libraries or APIs available out there. The biggest reason for the advent of the Flow API was the need for a common denominator amongst these libraries; to ensure that the core of reactive programming would be the same regardless of which implementation you use. That way, you can easily translate from one implementation to another.

To achieve this, the Java Flow API adheres to the Reactive Streams specification–the specification that most of the libraries available use as a blueprint for their design. The Reactive Streams initiative, which designed the specification, was started in 2013 by Netflix and several other large corporations with a vested interest in delivering content reliably.

> **Note**
>
> While they may share a lot of the same lingo, the Flow API is not in any way related to the Streams API of Java 8. They are focused on solving different kinds of problems.

In simple terms, reactive programming is a way to write programs using components that communicate with each other by streaming events. These events are often asynchronous in nature and should never overwhelm the receiving party. Within a reactive system, there are two main components–publishers and subscribers. This is similar to a networked pub/sub system, but on a micro-scale.

The Java Flow API (or rather Reactive Streams, which Flow adheres to) has three main actors:

- The Publisher has the knowledge of the available data and pushes it on-demand to any interested subscriber.

- The Subscriber is the one demanding the data.

- The Processor may sit between a publisher and a subscriber. Processors can intercept and transform the published data before releasing it to a subscriber or another processor. Thus, the processor can act as both a subscriber and a publisher.

Communication between these components is of both a push and pull nature. The subscriber first asks the publisher to send, at most, **n** messages. That's the pull part of the communication. Following that request, the publisher will begin to send messages to the subscriber, but it will never exceed **n** messages.

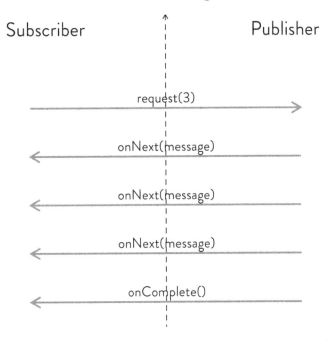

Figure 17.1: Communication between the Subscriber and the Publisher

When the publisher has sent the final message, it will provide a notification that the sending of messages is complete, and the subscriber may then act as needed–probably requesting more messages or aborting the communication entirely.

The entire Flow API, which we will look into further in this chapter, is defined in a single Java class. It contains one interface for each of the actors, and an extra interface describing the subscription object, which is the messaging link between the publisher and subscriber.

Publisher

The publisher holds the data that other components are interested in getting. The publisher will wait until a subscriber who is interested in the data requests n-number of items to be sent, and will only then start sending those items to the subscriber.

Asking for a specific number of items, rather than asking for everything, is called backpressure, and is very important in the Reactive Streams specification. This backpressure lets listeners request only as many items as they can handle at a time, ensuring that the application will not stall or crash.

The interface for **Publisher** in Flow, and Reactive Streams looks like this:

```
@FunctionalInterface
public static interface Publisher<T> {
    public void subscribe(Subscriber<? super T> subscriber);
}
```

You'll notice that it's a functional interface, which can be implemented as a lambda, should you wish.

SubmissionPublisher

Creating a fully functional Publisher can be quite a complicated endeavor. Luckily, Flow includes a complete implementation called **SubmissionPublisher**. We'll use this class in several examples in this chapter.

You can use **SubmissionPublisher** either directly, as a component, or as a superclass for your extended **Publisher**. **SubmissionPublisher** requires an **Executor** and a buffer size. By default, it will use the common **ForkJoinPool** and a buffer size of 256:

```
SubmissionPublisher<?> publisher = new SubmissionPublisher<>();
SubmissionPublisher<?> publisher = new SubmissionPublisher<>(ForkJoinPool.commonPool(),
Flow.defaultBufferSize());
```

The choice of executor should be based on how your application is designed and the tasks it is supposed to handle. In some cases, the common **ForkJoinPool** is the best choice, while in other situations, a scheduled thread pool may work better. You may need to try different executors and buffer sizes to find the combination that best suits your needs:

```
SubmissionPublisher<?> publisher = new SubmissionPublisher<>(Executors.
newCachedThreadPool(), 512);
```

You may also use **SubmissionPublisher** as a superclass for your own implementation.

In the following example, `MyPublisher` extends `SubmissionPublisher`, but defines a fixed `threadpool` executor rather than the common `ForkJoinPool` executor:

```
public class MyPublisher extends SubmissionPublisher<String> {
    public MyPublisher() {
        super(Executors.newFixedThreadPool(1), Flow.defaultBufferSize());
    }
}
```

Subscriber

The subscriber represents the end-user. It receives the data at the very end of the stream and acts on it. The action may include updating a user interface, pushing it to another component, or transforming it in any way.

The interface of the subscribers contains four different callbacks, each of which represents a message of some type from the publisher or the subscriber itself:

- **onSubscribe:** The `onSubscribe` method is invoked as soon as the subscriber has a valid subscription. Generally, this is used to kick-start the delivery of items from the publisher. The `Subscriber` will typically inform the `Publisher` here, by requesting another item.

- **onNext:** The `onNext` method is invoked when another item is made available from the `Publisher`.

- **onError:** The `onError` method is invoked when an error occurs. This usually means that the subscriber will no longer receive any more messages and should be closed down.

- **onComplete:** The `onComplete` method is invoked by the publisher when the final item has been sent.

The following example illustrates all of these callbacks:

```
public static interface Subscriber<T> {
    public void onSubscribe(Subscription subscription);
    public void onNext(T item);
    public void onError(Throwable throwable);
    public void onComplete();
}
```

Subscription

A **Subscriber** may use the Subscription API to control a publisher, either by requesting more items, or by canceling the subscription altogether:

```
public static interface Subscription {
    public void request(long n);
    public void cancel();
}
```

It is the **Publisher** who creates the subscriptions. It does this whenever a **Subscriber** has subscribed to that **Publisher**. If a **Subscriber** happens to subscribe twice to one publisher, it will fire the **onError()** callback with **IllegalStateException**.

Exercise 1: A Simple Application with a Single Publisher and a Single Subscriber

In this exercise, we will build an application with a single **Publisher** and a single **Subscriber**. The **Publisher** will send a string of messages to the **Subscriber**, which will then print it to the terminal. The messages are found in the **lipsum.txt** file, which should be placed in your **projects /res** folder. For this exercise, we will use the common **ForkJoinPool** to generate the executor:

1. If IntelliJ is already started, but no project is open, select **Create New Project**. If IntelliJ already has a project opened, select **File** à **New** à **Project** from the menu.

2. In **New Project** dialog, select a Java project, and then click **Next**.

3. Check the box to create the project from a template. Select **Command Line App**, and then click **Next**.

4. Name the new project **Chapter17**.

5. IntelliJ will give you a default project location. If you wish to select a different one, you may enter it here.

6. Set the package name to **com.packt.java.chapter17**.

7. Click **Finish**.

    IntelliJ will create your project, called **Chapter17**, with the standard folder structure. IntelliJ will also create a main entry point called **Main.java**.

8. Rename this file to **Exercise1.java**. When you're done, it should look like this:

```
package com.packt.java.chapter17;
public class Exercise1 {
    public static void main(String[] args) {
    // write your code here
    }
}
```

9. We will use **SubmissionPublisher** in this exercise. This is a fully functional implementation of the **Publisher** interface, which you can use to demonstrate the basic functionality of a reactive application. Declare a default **SubmissionPublisher**, as shown here, and then initialize it:

```
package com.packt.java.chapter17;
import java.util.concurrent.SubmissionPublisher;
public class Exercise1 {
    public static void main(String[] args) {
        SubmissionPublisher<String> publisher = new SubmissionPublisher<>();
    }
}
```

10. Flow doesn't come with any already available implementations of **Subscriber**, so we will need to implement our own **Subscriber**. Create a new class called **LipsumSubscriber**, and allow it to implement the **Flow.Subscriber** interface. Your new class should look something like the following example:

```
    @Override
    public void onSubscribe(Flow.Subscription subscription) {
    }
    @Override
    public void onNext(String item) {
    }
    @Override
    public void onError(Throwable throwable) {
    }
    @Override
    public void onComplete() {
    }
}
```

11. The subscriber has four methods to implement. The **onSubscribe** method will be called by the publisher when the **Subscription** object has been created. Usually, you'll store a reference to that subscription so that you can issue requests to the publisher, create a **Flow.Subscription** member variable in your **LipsumSubscriber** class, and store the reference from the **onSubscribe** method:

```java
private Flow.Subscription subscription;
@Override
public void onSubscribe(Flow.Subscription subscription) {
    this.subscription = subscription;
}
@Override
public void onNext(String item) {

}
@Override
public void onError(Throwable throwable) {

}
@Override
public void onComplete() {

}
}
```

12. Usually, you'll also request at least one item when the subscription has been created. Use the **request** method to ask for one item from the publisher:

```java
@Override
public void onSubscribe(Flow.Subscription subscription) {
    this.subscription = subscription;
    this.subscription.request(1);
}
@Override
public void onNext(String item) {

}
@Override
public void onError(Throwable throwable) {

}
@Override
public void onComplete() {

}
}
```

13. Looking at the next method in the class, called **onNext**, this is the callback executed by the **Publisher** whenever an item is issued to all subscribers. In this example, we will simply print the contents of the item:

```java
@Override
public void onNext(String item) {
    System.out.println(item);
}
@Override
public void onError(Throwable throwable) {

}
@Override
public void onComplete() {

}
}
```

14. To keep getting more items from the publisher, we need to keep requesting them; this is what is called backpressure. It's the subscriber who is in control in terms of how many items it can handle at a time. In this exercise, we'll handle one item at a time and then request another. Request another item after you've printed the current item to the console:

```java
@Override
public void onNext(String item) {
    System.out.println(item);
    this.subscription.request(1);
}
@Override
public void onError(Throwable throwable) {

}
@Override
public void onComplete() {

}
}
```

15. The subscriber can use the methods **onError** and **onComplete** to perform a cleanup and make sure that no resources are kept in vain. In this example, we will simply print the error and a completion message:

```
@Override
public void onError(Throwable throwable) {
    System.out.println(throwable.getMessage());
}
@Override
public void onComplete() {
    System.out.println("completed");
}
}
```

16. Back in the **main** method, create a new subscriber and allow it to subscribe to the publisher:

```
package com.packt.java.chapter17;
import java.util.concurrent.SubmissionPublisher;
public class Exercise1 {
    public static void main(String[] args) {
        SubmissionPublisher<String> publisher = new SubmissionPublisher<>();
        LipsumSubscriber lipsumSubscriber = new LipsumSubscriber();
        publisher.subscribe(lipsumSubscriber);
    }
}
```

17. However, this will not actually do anything. The publisher still has no data to send, so we need to provide the data to the publisher as well. We'll use the **lipsum.txt** file as the source. Copy the file to the **res/** folder in your project. Create the folder if it doesn't already exist:

```
package com.packt.java.chapter17;
import java.util.concurrent.SubmissionPublisher;
public class Exercise1 {
    public static void main(String[] args) {
        SubmissionPublisher<String> publisher = new SubmissionPublisher<>();
        LipsumSubscriber lipsumSubscriber = new LipsumSubscriber();
        publisher.subscribe(lipsumSubscriber);
        String filePath = "res/lipsum.txt";
    }
}
```

18. To send the words from the **lipsum.txt** file to the **Publisher**, you need to load the file into some kind of container. We will use the **Stream** API to load the words, and then push them to the publisher immediately. Wrap the stream in a try-with-resources block to enable the JVM to auto-close the resource after loading it:

```java
package com.packt.java.chapter17;
import java.io.IOException;
import java.nio.file.Files;
import java.nio.file.Paths;
import java.util.Arrays;
import java.util.concurrent.SubmissionPublisher;
import java.util.stream.Stream;
public class Exercise1 {
    public static void main(String[] args) {
        SubmissionPublisher<String> publisher = new SubmissionPublisher<>();
        LipsumSubscriber lipsumSubscriber = new LipsumSubscriber();
        publisher.subscribe(lipsumSubscriber);
        String filePath = "res/lipsum.txt";
        try (Stream<String> words = Files.lines(Paths.get(filePath))) {
            words.flatMap((l) -> Arrays.stream(l.split("[\\s.,\\n]+")))
                .forEach(publisher::submit);
        } catch (IOException e) {
            e.printStackTrace();
        }
    }
}
```

Here, we are loading the file as a stream of strings. It will load the lines from the file into one string each. Since every line may contain multiple words, we need to apply a flat mapping to each line to extract the words. We are using a simple regular expression to split the lines into words, looking for one or more whitespaces, punctuation items, or a new line.

> **Note**
>
> You can read more about the Streams API, and the different methods used here, in *Chapter 15, Processing Data with Streams*.

19. At this point, the program will execute and print all the words available in the file. However, you may notice that it does not print any completion messages. That is because we haven't actually notified the subscribers that the stream has ended. Send the completion signal, as seen here:

```
package com.packt.java.chapter17;
import java.io.IOException;
import java.nio.file.Files;
import java.nio.file.Paths;
import java.util.Arrays;
import java.util.concurrent.SubmissionPublisher;
import java.util.stream.Stream;
public class Exercise1 {
    public static void main(String[] args) {
        SubmissionPublisher<String> publisher = new SubmissionPublisher<>();
        LipsumSubscriber lipsumSubscriber = new LipsumSubscriber();
        publisher.subscribe(lipsumSubscriber);
        String filePath = "res/lipsum.txt";
        try (Stream<String> words = Files.lines(Paths.get(filePath))) {
            words.flatMap((l) -> Arrays.stream(l.split("[\\s.,\\n]+")))
                .forEach(publisher::submit);
            publisher.close();
        } catch (IOException e) {
            e.printStackTrace();
        }
    }
}
```

Running this program should yield the following output in the console:

```
Lorem
ipsum
dolor
sit
amet
consectetur
adipiscing
elit
```

```
Pellentesque
malesuada
ultricies
ultricies
Curabitur
...
```

Having built your first reactive application, you may notice that it doesn't really make much sense to use this extra logic in a very simple program, as shown in this example. Applying the Reactive Streams concept to a simple example makes very little sense as it is meant to be used in asynchronous applications, where you may not be sure when, or if, a Subscriber can currently receive messages.

Processor

The Processor is something of a chameleon in Flow; it may act as both a **Subscriber** and a **Publisher**.

There are several different reasons for adding an interface such as the Processor. One reason may be that you have a stream of data that you do not fully trust. Imagine an asynchronous flow of data from a server, where data is delivered over a UDP connection that lacks promises of delivery; this data will eventually be corrupted and you need to handle that. A simple way would be to inject a filter of some kind between the publisher and subscriber. This is where a **Processor** excels.

Another reason for using a Processor could be to separate a polymorphic data stream between different subscribers so that alternative actions may be taken based on the data type.

Exercise 2: Using a Processor to Convert a Stream of Strings to Numbers

In this exercise, we will first build a Publisher that periodically publishes a string from a text file. Then, we will use a scheduler to control the timer. The Subscriber should then attempt to transform a certain string to a number. The **numbers.txt** file will be used to build this application. In this example, we will also show how to clean up the handling of the data using a Supplier implementation to make the data source abstract.

The **numbers.txt** file contains intentional errors that we will handle by applying a processor before the subscriber:

1. Open the **Chapter17** project in IDEA if it's not already opened.

2. Create a new Java class, using the **File | New |Java Class** menu.

3. In the **Create New Class** dialog, enter **Exercise2** as **Name**, and select **OK**.

IntelliJ will create your new class. It should look something like the following snippet:

```
package com.packt.java.chapter17;
public class Exercise2 {
}
```

4. Add a **main** method to this class:

```
package com.packt.java.chapter17;
public class Exercise2 {
    public static void main (String[] args) {
    }
}
```

5. We will continue using the basic **SubmissionPublisher** supplied in the Flow library, but in this exercise, we'll create our own subclass. Create a new class called **NumberPublisher**. This should extend **SubmissionPublisher**, as shown in the following code block:

```
package com.packt.java.chapter17;
import java.util.concurrent.SubmissionPublisher;
public class NumberPublisher extends SubmissionPublisher<String> {
}
```

6. Our new **NumberPublisher** should publish numbers periodically to any interested **Subscriber**. There are several different options in terms of how to accomplish this, but probably the easiest solution is to use a **Timer**. Add a **Timer**, and a **TimerTask** to your publisher:

```
package com.packt.java.chapter17;
import java.util.Timer;
import java.util.TimerTask;
import java.util.concurrent.SubmissionPublisher;
public class NumberPublisher extends SubmissionPublisher<String> {
    final Timer timer = new Timer();
```

```
    final TimerTask timerTask = new TimerTask() {
        @Override
        public void run() {
        }
    };
    public NumberPublisher() {
    }
}
```

7. When the publisher is shutting down, so should **Timer**. Override the publisher's **close()** method, and add a call to the **cancel()** method of **Timer** just before the publisher is about to shut down:

```
@Override
public void close() {
    timer.cancel();
    super.close();
}
```

8. There are two different ways to let the publisher send items to the connected subscribers. Using either **submit()** or **offer()**. **submit()** works in a fire-and-forget fashion, while **offer()** lets the publisher retry sending the item once using a handler. In our case, **submit()** would work just fine. But, before you can submit, you need some data. Add a **Supplier** to the **Publisher** using dependency injection:

```
package com.packt.java.chapter17;
import java.util.Timer;
import java.util.TimerTask;
import java.util.concurrent.SubmissionPublisher;
import java.util.function.Supplier;
public class NumberPublisher extends SubmissionPublisher<String> {
    final Timer timer = new Timer();
    final TimerTask timerTask = new TimerTask() {
        @Override
        public void run() {
        }
```

```
    };
    final Supplier<String> supplier;
    public NumberPublisher(Supplier<String> supplier) {
        this.supplier = supplier;
    }
    @Override
    public void close() {
        timer.cancel();
        super.close();
    }
}
```

> **Note**
>
> A supplier is a functional interface that is often used to deliver results – to anyone and anything.

9. Now that we know how to get the data we need using **Supplier**, we can actually send it to the subscribers. Inside the **run()** method of **TimerTask**, add a call to **submit()** and get the data from the supplier:

```
        @Override
        public void run() {
            submit(supplier.get());
        }
    };
    final Supplier<String> supplier;
    public NumberPublisher(Supplier<String> supplier) {
        this.supplier = supplier;
    }
    @Override
    public void close() {
        timer.cancel();
        super.close();
    }
}
```

10. One last thing remains, because the publisher may run into trouble when attempting to either get items from the supplier or send items onward. We need to catch any exception when attempting to execute the **submit()** method. Add a try-catch clause, and use a **closeExceptionally()** method to inform any subscriber that we ran into difficulty. Executing **closeExceptionally()** will force the publisher into a state where it cannot send anything else out:

```
        @Override
        public void run() {
            try {
                submit(supplier.get());
            } catch (Exception e) {
                closeExceptionally(e);
            }
        }
    };
    final Supplier<String> supplier;
    public NumberPublisher(Supplier<String> supplier) {
        this.supplier = supplier;
    }
    @Override
    public void close() {
        timer.cancel();
        super.close();
    }
}
```

11. Now, **TimerTask** is fully implemented. The data is injected into **Publisher** using **Supplier**, and shutdown handling is ready. All that remains to do is to actually schedule periodic publishing. Using **Timer**, schedule **TimerTask** for repeat execution every 1 second. Since **TimerTask** accepts only milliseconds, we need to remember to multiply the delay by **1000**. We're also setting the initial delay to **1000** milliseconds:

```
package com.packt.java.chapter17;
import java.util.Timer;
import java.util.TimerTask;
import java.util.concurrent.SubmissionPublisher;
import java.util.function.Supplier;
public class NumberPublisher extends SubmissionPublisher<String> {
    final Timer timer = new Timer();
    final TimerTask timerTask = new TimerTask() {
        @Override
        public void run() {
```

```java
            try {
                submit(supplier.get());
            } catch (Exception e) {
                closeExceptionally(e);
            }
        }
    };
    final Supplier<String> supplier;
    public NumberPublisher(Supplier<String> supplier) {
        this.supplier = supplier;
        this.timer.schedule(timerTask, 1000, 1000);
    }
    @Override
    public void close() {
        timer.cancel();
        super.close();
    }
}
```

12. Now that our **NumberPublisher** is ready, we need to start feeding it data, but in order to feed it the data that should be published, we need to load the data. The data we're going to send is located in the **numbers.txt** file. Copy the **numbers.txt** file to the **/res** folder, creating the folder if it doesn't already exist.

13. In the **Exercise2** class, create a new method called **getStrings()**, which will return the numbers from the **numbers.txt** file as **Strings**:

```java
package com.packt.java.chapter17;
public class Exercise2 {
    public static void main(String[] args) {
    }
    private static String[] getStrings() {
    }
}
```

14. In this new method, create a variable called **filePath**. Let it point to the **numbers. txt** file, located in the **/res** folder. We will use this **filePath** variable to load the file contents in the next step:

```
package com.packt.java.chapter17;
public class Exercise2 {
    public static void main(String[] args) {
    }
    private static String[] getStrings() {
        String filePath = "res/numbers.txt";
    }
}
```

15. Load the file contents into a **String** stream, and then wrap the load in a try-with-resources block so that we don't need to care about releasing the file resources when we're done:

```
package com.packt.java.chapter17;
import java.io.IOException;
import java.nio.file.Files;
import java.nio.file.Paths;
import java.util.stream.Stream;
public class Exercise2 {
    public static void main(String[] args) {
    }
    private static String[] getStrings() {
        String filePath = "res/numbers.txt";
        try (Stream<String> words = Files.lines(Paths.get(filePath))) {

        } catch (IOException e) {
            e.printStackTrace();
        }
    }
}
```

16. The **numbers.txt** file contains lots of numbers and some other characters that might cause trouble later on. But, in order to actually decode the file to single words, we need to review the structure of the file. Let's open it, and you should see something like this—multiple rows with a column-like structure:

6	2e	22	4	11	59	73	41	60	8
42	91	99	89	17	96	54	24	77	36
12	9	64	0a	31	75	1	14	34	56
67	78	37	87	93	92	100	28	47	5

52	85	29	38	21	88	65	81	25	70
95	3	74	2	35	84	32	66	86	69
58	45	48	10	26	53	40	13	49	94
98	71	39	68	76	43	63	7g	72	80
61	46	57	18	79	27	20	83	82	33
97	2h	50	44	15	16	55	30	19	51

17. The stream of strings we've just loaded will not be of much help. Each item in the stream will represent a whole line, and we need to transform the stream before it will be useful to us. First of all, apply a **flatMap** operator to create a new stream for each item in the original stream. This will let us split each line up into multiple items, and return them to the main stream:

```java
package com.packt.java.chapter17;
import java.io.IOException;
import java.nio.file.Files;
import java.nio.file.Paths;
import java.util.Arrays;
import java.util.stream.Stream;
public class Exercise2 {
    public static void main(String[] args) {
    }
    private static String[] getStrings() {
        String filePath = "res/numbers.txt";
        try (Stream<String> words = Files.lines(Paths.get(filePath))) {
            return words.flatMap((line) ->
                Arrays.stream(line.split("[\\s\\n]+")))
        } catch (IOException e) {
            e.printStackTrace();
        }
    }
}
```

> **Note**
>
> You can read more about processing data with Streams in *Chapter 15, Processing Data with Streams*, and regular expressions in *Chapter 12, Regular Expressions*.

18. The stream now contains items representing each column for each line. But, in order to use the data, we need to filter it based on length as we don't want any 0 length words, and then we need to turn the stream into an array of strings. Filter the items of the stream, allowing only words with a length in excess of 0 to pass:

```
package com.packt.java.chapter17;
import java.io.IOException;
import java.nio.file.Files;
import java.nio.file.Paths;
import java.util.Arrays;
import java.util.stream.Stream;
public class Exercise2 {
    public static void main(String[] args) {
    }
    private static String[] getStrings() {
        String filePath = "res/numbers.txt";
        try (Stream<String> words = Files.lines(Paths.get(filePath))) {
            return words.flatMap((line) -> Arrays.stream(line.split("[\\s\\n]+")))
                    .filter((word) -> word.length() > 0)
        } catch (IOException e) {
            e.printStackTrace();
        }
    }
}
```

19. Now, turn the whole stream into an array of strings. This will return an array of strings to the caller of the method. However, if we do have an error in reading the file, we need to return something too. Return **null** at the very end of the **getStrings()** method. The publisher will interpret **null** as an error and throw **NullPointerException**, closing the connection to the subscriber:

```
package com.packt.java.chapter17;
import java.io.IOException;
import java.nio.file.Files;
import java.nio.file.Paths;
import java.util.Arrays;
import java.util.stream.Stream;
public class Exercise2 {
    public static void main(String[] args) {
    }
    private static String[] getStrings() {
        String filePath = "res/numbers.txt";
        try (Stream<String> words = Files.lines(Paths.get(filePath))) {
```

```
                return words.flatMap((line) ->
                    Arrays.stream(line.split("[\\s\\n]+")))
                        .filter((word) -> word.length() > 0)
                        .toArray(String[]::new);
        } catch (IOException e) {
            e.printStackTrace();
        }
        return null;
    }
}
```

20. The data for our little program is ready for pushing into the publisher so that it can send it to any interested subscriber. Now, we need to build a supplier that will take these strings and send them to the publisher, one by one, when the publisher requests them. Create a supplier in the **main** method of the **Exercise2** class:

```
package com.packt.java.chapter17;
import java.io.IOException;
import java.nio.file.Files;
import java.nio.file.Paths;
import java.util.Arrays;
import java.util.function.Supplier;
import java.util.stream.Stream;
public class Exercise2 {
    public static void main(String[] args) {
        Supplier<String> supplier = new Supplier<String>() {
            @Override
            public String get() {
                return null;
            }
        };
    }
}
```

21. Let the Supplier call **getStrings()** to retrieve the full array:

```
public class Exercise2 {
    public static void main(String[] args) {
        Supplier<String> supplier = new Supplier<String>() {
            @Override
            public String get() {
                String[] data = getStrings();
                return null;
            }
        };
    }
}
```

22. The supplier, however, cannot return the entire dataset; it is designed to return one string at a time. For this to work, we need to keep an index of the last string sent to **Supplier**:

```
public class Exercise2 {
    public static void main(String[] args) {
        Supplier<String> supplier = new Supplier<String>() {
            int index;
            @Override
            public String get() {
                String[] data = getStrings();
                return data[index];
            }
        };
    }
}
```

23. This will constantly return the first number in the file, and that's not what we want. So, we need to increment the index every time someone asks the supplier for a string:

```
public class Exercise2 {
    public static void main(String[] args) {
        Supplier<String> supplier = new Supplier<String>() {
            int index;
            @Override
```

```
                public String get() {
                    String[] data = getStrings();
                    return data[index++];
                }
            };
        }
    }
```

24. This, however, will throw an exception when we reach the final number in the file. So, we need to protect against that. In this case, we'll return **null** when we reach the end. Add an **if** statement, checking that we haven't gone too far:

```
public class Exercise2 {
    public static void main(String[] args) {
        Supplier<String> supplier = new Supplier<String>() {
            int index;
            @Override
            public String get() {
                String[] data = getStrings();
                if (index < data.length - 1) {
                    return data[index++];
                } else {
                    return null;
                }
            }
        };
    }
}
```

25. The supplier is now ready to be used by our **NumberPublisher**. Create an instance of **NumberPublisher** in the **main()** method of **Exercise2**, passing the supplier as an argument:

```
public class Exercise2 {
    public static void main(String[] args) {
        Supplier<String> supplier = new Supplier<String>() {
            int index;
            @Override
            public String get() {
                String[] data = getStrings();
                if (index < data.length - 1) {
                    return data[index++];
                } else {
```

```
                    return null;
                }
            }
        };
        NumberPublisher publisher = new NumberPublisher(supplier);
    }
}
```

26. Create a Subscriber and allow it to request an item on subscription success. Then, request a new item every time it receives an item—backpressure. While implementing the subscriber, add printouts for every method so that we can easily see what's happening:

```java
package com.packt.java.chapter17;
import java.io.IOException;
import java.nio.file.Files;
import java.nio.file.Paths;
import java.util.Arrays;
import java.util.concurrent.Flow;
import java.util.function.Supplier;
import java.util.stream.Stream;
public class Exercise2 {
    public static void main(String[] args) {
        Supplier<String> supplier = new Supplier<String>() {
            int index;
            @Override
            public String get() {
                String[] data = getStrings();
                if (index < data.length - 1) {
                    return data[index++];
                } else {
                    return null;
                }
            }
        };
        NumberPublisher publisher = new NumberPublisher(supplier);
        publisher.subscribe(new Flow.Subscriber<>() {
            Flow.Subscription subscription;
            @Override
            public void onSubscribe(Flow.Subscription subscription) {
                this.subscription = subscription;
                subscription.request(1);
            }
```

```java
        @Override
        public void onNext(String item) {
            System.out.println("onNext: " + item);
            subscription.request(1);
        }
        @Override
        public void onError(Throwable throwable) {
            System.out.println("onError: " + throwable.getMessage());
        }
        @Override
        public void onComplete() {
            System.out.println("onComplete()");
        }
    });
  }
}
```

Running this code, you should get an output to the console, and the entire file should print:

```
onNext: 6
onNext: 2e
onNext: 22
onNext: 4
onNext: 11
onNext: 59
onNext: 73
. . .
```

27. However, in the subscriber, we expect to get data we can easily transform into integers. If we apply simple integer parsing to the text, we'll end up in trouble:

```java
publisher.subscribe(new Flow.Subscriber<>() {
        Flow.Subscription subscription;
        @Override
        public void onSubscribe(Flow.Subscription subscription) {
            this.subscription = subscription;
            subscription.request(1);
        }
        @Override
        public void onNext(String item) {
            System.out.println("onNext: " + Integer.valueOf(item));
            subscription.request(1);
        }
```

```
    @Override
    public void onError(Throwable throwable) {
        System.out.println("onError: " + throwable.getMessage());
    }
    @Override
    public void onComplete() {
        System.out.println("onComplete()");
    }
});
```

This will stop, with a parse exception, when reaching the second item, **2e**, which, of course, is not an integer:

```
onNext: 6
onError: For input string: "2e"
```

To rectify the problem with the broken subscriber, you can, of course, catch the exception right there. But, in this exercise, we will involve a filter processor in the mix. **Processor** will subscribe to **Publisher**, and **Subscriber** will subscribe to **Processor**. In essence, **Processor** is both a Publisher and a Subscriber. To make this simple for us, allow **NumberProcessor** to extend **SubmissionPublisher**, just like **NumberPublisher** does.

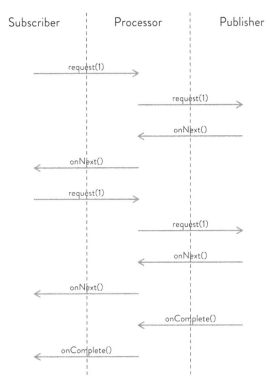

Figure 17.2: Communication between the Subscriber, the Processor, and the Publisher

28. Create a class called **NumberProcessor**, allow it to extend **SubmissionPublisher**, and implement the **Flow.Processor** interface:

```
package com.packt.java.chapter17;
import java.util.concurrent.Flow;
import java.util.concurrent.SubmissionPublisher;
public class NumberProcessor extends SubmissionPublisher<String> implements Flow.
Processor<String, String> {
    @Override
    public void onSubscribe(Flow.Subscription subscription) {
    }
    @Override
    public void onNext(String item) {
    }
    @Override
    public void onError(Throwable throwable) {
    }
    @Override
    public void onComplete() {
    }
}
```

29. **NumberProcessor** will subscribe to **NumberPublisher**, and, just like the subscriber, it needs to store a reference to the publisher so that it can control when to request new items. Store the reference received in **onSubscribe()** as a private field in the processor. Also, take this opportunity to request the first item from the publisher:

```
package com.packt.java.chapter17;
import java.util.concurrent.Flow;
import java.util.concurrent.SubmissionPublisher;
public class NumberProcessor extends SubmissionPublisher<String> implements
  Flow.Processor<String, String> {
    private Flow.Subscription subscription;
    @Override
    public void onSubscribe(Flow.Subscription subscription) {
        this.subscription = subscription;
        this.subscription.request(1);
```

```
        }
        @Override
        public void onNext(String item) {

        }
        @Override
        public void onError(Throwable throwable) {

        }
        @Override
        public void onComplete() {

        }
    }
```

30. Whenever you receive an item from the publisher, you need to also request the next item, just like the subscriber would:

```
package com.packt.java.chapter17;
import java.util.concurrent.Flow;
import java.util.concurrent.SubmissionPublisher;
public class NumberProcessor extends SubmissionPublisher<String> implements Flow.
Processor<String, String> {
    private Flow.Subscription subscription;
    @Override
    public void onSubscribe(Flow.Subscription subscription) {
        this.subscription = subscription;
        this.subscription.request(1);
    }
    @Override
    public void onNext(String item) {
        this.subscription.request(1);
    }
    @Override
    public void onError(Throwable throwable) {

    }
    @Override
    public void onComplete() {

    }
}
```

31. If the subscription to **NumberPublisher** is closed, we also need to inform the subscriber that there was a problem. Likewise, we need to inform the subscriber when the subscription ended. In the **onError()** callback, add a call to **closeExceptionally()**, and, in **onComplete()**, add a call to **close()**:

```java
package com.packt.java.chapter17;
import java.util.concurrent.Flow;
import java.util.concurrent.SubmissionPublisher;
public class NumberProcessor extends SubmissionPublisher<String> implements
    Flow.Processor<String, String> {
    private Flow.Subscription subscription;
    @Override
    public void onSubscribe(Flow.Subscription subscription) {
        this.subscription = subscription;
        this.subscription.request(1);
    }
    @Override
    public void onNext(String item) {
        this.subscription.request(1);
    }
    @Override
    public void onError(Throwable throwable) {
        closeExceptionally(throwable);
    }
    @Override
    public void onComplete() {
        close();
    }
}
```

32. The processor is almost done. The one thing that is missing is communicating the received items back to the subscriber. We will do this in the **onNext()** callback method. However, since we know that there may be invalid values, we want to filter those. We'll use a predicate for this, declaring a predicate to the **NumberProcessor** class:

```java
package com.packt.java.chapter17;
import java.util.concurrent.Flow;
import java.util.concurrent.SubmissionPublisher;
import java.util.function.Predicate;
public class NumberProcessor extends SubmissionPublisher<String> implements
    Flow.Processor<String, String> {
    private Flow.Subscription subscription;
    private Predicate<String> predicate = new Predicate<String>() {
```

```
            @Override
            public boolean test(String s) {
                return false;
            }
        };
    @Override
    public void onSubscribe(Flow.Subscription subscription) {
        this.subscription = subscription;
        this.subscription.request(1);
    }
    @Override
    public void onNext(String item) {
        this.subscription.request(1);
    }
    @Override
    public void onError(Throwable throwable) {
        closeExceptionally(throwable);
    }
    @Override
    public void onComplete() {
        close();
    }
}
```

33. The predicate is a simple functional interface that is used to verify the input using a **test()** method. The **test()** method should always return **true** if the value was acceptable, or **false** if it was faulty. In our predicate, we will attempt to parse the string supplied. If the parsing is successful, we will return true; otherwise, we will return **false**:

```
package com.packt.java.chapter17;
import java.util.concurrent.Flow;
import java.util.concurrent.SubmissionPublisher;
import java.util.function.Predicate;
public class NumberProcessor extends SubmissionPublisher<String> implements
    Flow.Processor<String, String> {
    private Flow.Subscription subscription;
    private Predicate<String> predicate = new Predicate<String>() {
        @Override
        public boolean test(String s) {
            try {
                Integer.valueOf(s);
                return true;
```

```
            } catch (NumberFormatException e) {
                return false;
            }
        }
    };
    @Override
    public void onSubscribe(Flow.Subscription subscription) {
        this.subscription = subscription;
        this.subscription.request(1);
    }
    @Override
    public void onNext(String item) {
        this.subscription.request(1);
    }
    @Override
    public void onError(Throwable throwable) {
        closeExceptionally(throwable);
    }
    @Override
    public void onComplete() {
        close();
    }
}
```

34. Back in the **onNext()** callback, we can now use our predicate to verify the value
    supplied before we submit it to the subscribers:

```
package com.packt.java.chapter17;
import java.util.concurrent.Flow;
import java.util.concurrent.SubmissionPublisher;
import java.util.function.Predicate;
public class NumberProcessor extends SubmissionPublisher<String> implements Flow.
Processor<String, String> {
    private Flow.Subscription subscription;
    private Predicate<String> predicate = new Predicate<String>() {
        @Override
        public boolean test(String s) {
```

```
            try {
                Integer.valueOf(s);
                return true;
            } catch (NumberFormatException e) {
                return false;
            }
        }
    }
};
@Override
public void onSubscribe(Flow.Subscription subscription) {
    this.subscription = subscription;
    this.subscription.request(1);
}
@Override
public void onNext(String item) {
    if (predicate.test(item)) {
        submit(item);
    }
    this.subscription.request(1);
}
@Override
public void onError(Throwable throwable) {
    closeExceptionally(throwable);
}
@Override
public void onComplete() {
    close();
}
}
```

Note

You can read more about predicates and how to use them in *Chapter 16, Predicates and Other Functional Interfaces.*

35. Now that your **Processor** is ready, inject it between **NumberPublisher** and **Subscriber**:

```java
package com.packt.java.chapter17;
import java.io.IOException;
import java.nio.file.Files;
import java.nio.file.Paths;
import java.util.Arrays;
import java.util.concurrent.Flow;
import java.util.function.Supplier;
import java.util.stream.Stream;
public class Exercise2 {
    public static void main(String[] args) {
        Supplier<String> supplier = new Supplier<String>() {
            int index;
            @Override
            public String get() {
                String[] data = getStrings();
                if (index < data.length - 1) {
                    return data[index++];
                } else {
                    return null;
                }
            }
        };
        NumberPublisher publisher = new NumberPublisher(supplier);
        NumberProcessor processor = new NumberProcessor();
        publisher.subscribe(processor);
        processor.subscribe(new Flow.Subscriber<>() {
            Flow.Subscription subscription;
            @Override
            public void onSubscribe(Flow.Subscription subscription) {
                this.subscription = subscription;
                subscription.request(1);
            }
            @Override
            public void onNext(String item) {
                System.out.println("onNext: " + Integer.valueOf(item));
                subscription.request(1);
            }
```

```java
            @Override
            public void onError(Throwable throwable) {
                System.out.println("onError: " + throwable.getMessage());
            }
            @Override
            public void onComplete() {
                System.out.println("onComplete()");
            }
        });
    }
    private static String[] getStrings() {
        String filePath = "res/numbers.txt";
        try (Stream<String> words = Files.lines(Paths.get(filePath))) {
            return words.flatMap((line) -> Arrays.stream(line.split("[\\s\\n]+")))
                    .filter((word) -> word.length() > 0)
                    .toArray(String[]::new);
        } catch (IOException e) {
            e.printStackTrace();
        }
        return null;
    }
}
```

After running this example, you should see that the processor filters the faulty number values from the file before they reach the subscriber:

```
onNext: 6
onNext: 22
onNext: 4
onNext: 11
onNext: 59
onNext: 73
onNext: 41
onNext: 60
onNext: 8
...
```

This example shows how to take content from a publisher and pass it through a processor to ensure that the values are valid.

Activity 1: Let NumberProcessor Format Values as Integers

Improve **NumberProcessor** further. Let it not only verify that the values can be parsed as integers, but also publish them to the subscriber as integers. The subscriber should only accept integer values, and no longer need to parse the received values.

1. Change the processors published item type to Integer. Make the necessary changes in the implementation to match the new type.

2. Change the subscriber for the processor, it should accept only Integer values in the **onNext** method.

> **Note**
>
> The solution for this activity can be found on page 568.

Summary

In this chapter, you've learned the basics of Reactive Streams components, how they communicate, and their respective roles in a reactive application.

In most cases, you should avoid using the Flow API to build reactive applications as there are much more advanced and user-friendly reactive libraries available out there. The Flow API provides only the basic building blocks for reactive applications, while implementations such as Akka or RxJava will give you a richer experience, providing essential functionality such as throttling, filtering, and debouncing, to name a few. If you're interested in delving further into reactive programming, there are entire books devoted to the subject.

As mentioned before, Flow provides the basis for building your own Reactive Streams library, however complex that may be. Should you wish to implement a Reactive Streams library of your own, you should start by reviewing the Reactive Streams Technology Compatibility Kit. This test-based kit will help you to ensure that your implementation follows the Reactive Streams rules.

After the next chapter, which focuses on unit testing, you should be all set to start looking at the compatibility kit and build your own Reactive Streams library.

18

Unit Testing

Overview

This chapter focuses on testing with JUnit, one of the primary testing frameworks for Java. In its earliest sections and exercises, you will learn to write a successful unit test with JUnit to test your code, using assertions to verify that your code is correct. You will then be introduced to parameterized tests—a type of unit test which allows you to run the same test on a set of data inputs—which you will also learn to write. Finally, the chapter will define mocking, which is the technique whereby you will practice how to 'mock out' external dependencies so that you can concentrate on testing a single Java class.

Introduction

Testing allows you to make sure your Java code performs correctly. For example, if you were calculating employees' pay, you would want the code to be accurate; otherwise, your organization may face legal consequences. While not every programming issue leads to legal doom, it is still a good idea to test your code.

Writing tests while you code, as opposed to when you are done, can speed up your work. This is because you won't be spending time trying to figure out why things don't seem to work. Instead, you will know exactly what part of the code isn't correct. This is especially useful for any code that requires complex logic.

In addition to this, as new enhancements are added to the code, you will want to make sure that nothing in the new code breaks the old functionality. Having a suite of well-written unit tests can really help in this regard. If you are a new developer hired into a team that has been working on an application for some time, a good suite of tests is a sign that your team follows engineering best practices.

Getting Started with Unit Tests

A unit test tests one unit of code. In Java terms, this usually means that a unit test tests a single Java class. The test should run quickly, so you know whether there are any problems as soon as possible.

A unit test is a separate Java class designed just for testing. You should write separate test methods for each part of the original class you want to test. Typically, the more fine-grained the test, the better.

Sometimes, due to necessity, a unit test will test more than one class. That's OK and not something to worry about. In general, though, you want to concentrate on writing separate tests for each class in your Java application.

> **Note**
>
> Writing your Java classes so that they are easy to test will improve your code. You'll have better code organization, clearer code, and better quality as a result.

Integration tests, on the other hand, test a part of the entire system, including external dependencies. For example, a unit test should not access a database. That's the job of integration tests.

Functional tests go further and test an entire system all in one, such as an online banking application or a retail store application. This is sometimes called end-to-end testing.

> **Note**
>
> Software development job interviews tend to go badly if you say you do not believe in writing tests.

Introducing JUnit

JUnit provides the most widely used test framework for Java code. Now on version 5, JUnit has been around for years.

With JUnit, your tests reside in test classes, that is, classes that use JUnit's framework to validate your code. These test classes reside outside of the main application code. That's why both Maven and Gradle projects have two subdirectories under the **src** directory: main, for your application code, and test, for the tests.

Typically, tests are not part of your built application. So, if you build a JAR file for your application, the tests will not be part of that JAR file.

JUnit has been around for a long time, and you will find the official documentation at https://packt.live/2J9seWE and the official site at https://packt.live/31xFtXu.

> **Note**
>
> Another popular test framework is called Spock. Spock uses the Groovy language, which is a JVM language that is similar to Java. You can refer to https://packt.live/2P4fPqG for more information about Spock. TestNG is another Java unit testing framework. You can refer to https://packt.live/33X2nct for more information about TestNG.

Writing Unit Tests with JUnit

Oozie is a workflow scheduler for the Hadoop big data clusters. Oozie workflows are jobs that perform tasks on potentially massive amounts of data stored in Hadoop clusters. Oozie coordinator jobs run workflow jobs on a schedule.

When defining a schedule, you typically set three values:

- The starting timestamp, which defines when the coordinator should start a workflow job.

- The ending timestamp, which defines when the coordinator should end.

- A frequency, in minutes, at which the coordinator should launch jobs. For example, a frequency of 60 specifies launching a workflow job every 60 minutes (that is, each hour), from the starting timestamp to the ending timestamp.

> **Note**
>
> You can refer to https://packt.live/2BzqIOJ for more information about Oozie coordinators and even more scheduling options. For now, we'll just concentrate on validating the coordinator scheduling information.

Here, we're going to define a simple JavaBean class that holds the scheduling information and then write a JUnit test to validate a coordinator schedule.

The basic bean looks like the following (with the getters, setters, and constructors not shown):

```
public class CoordSchedule {
    private String startingTimestamp;
    private String endingTimestamp;
    private int frequency;

}
```

The starting and ending timestamps are **String** values based on an assumption that this bean would hold data read in from a configuration file. It also allows us to validate the **String** format for the timestamps.

> **Note**
>
> Remember that IntelliJ can generate constructors along with the getter and setter methods.

Now, consider what you would want to test, along with how you would write those tests. Testing edge cases is a good idea.

For a coordinator, here are the rules:

- The ending timestamp must be after the starting timestamp.
- Both timestamps must be in UTC in the format of **yyyy-MM-ddTHH:mmZ** (this is the ISO 8601 format).
- The frequency must be less than 1,440 (that is, the number of minutes in a normal day). Oozie provides alternative configuration settings to go beyond this limitation. For now, we'll just test against this limit.
- The frequency should be greater than 5 (this is an arbitrary rule designed to prevent new workflows starting while another workflow is still running).

To create a test, you create a separate test class. Test classes should have a single no-argument constructor. Test classes cannot be abstract classes.

> **Note**
>
> If you work with the Maven build tool (refer to *Chapter 6, Libraries, Packages, and Modules*), then your test classes should all have names that end in **Test**, **Tests**, or **TestCase**. All test classes in this chapter have names ending in **Test**.

JUnit uses the **@Test** annotation to identify a test method. You can add a **@DisplayName** annotation to specify the text to be displayed should the test fail. This can make your test reports easier to read:

```
@Test
@DisplayName("Frequency must be less than 1440")
void testFrequency() {
}
```

Inside your test methods, use the **Assertions** class methods to validate the results:

```
Assertions.assertTrue(schedule.getFrequency() < 1440);
```

> **Note**
>
> JUnit provides a few other assertion methods, such as **assertEquals()** and **assertAll()**.

Exercise 1: Writing a First Unit Test

This example will show the basics of writing a JUnit unit test. For this exercise, we will simply test whether the properties are correct; though, typically, you would also test program logic:

1. Select **New** and then **Project...** from the **File** menu in IntelliJ.

2. Select **Gradle** for the type of project. Click on **Next**.

3. For **Group Id**, enter **com.packtpub.testing**.

4. For **Artifact Id**, enter **chapter18**.

5. For **Version**, enter **1.0**.

6. Accept the default settings on the next pane. Click on **Next**.

7. Leave the project name as **chapter18**.

8. Click on **Finish**.

9. Call up **build.gradle** in the IntelliJ text editor.

10. Change **sourceCompatibility** so that it is set to **12**:

    ```
    sourceCompatibility = 12
    ```

11. Remove the JUnit dependency defined in the **build.gradle** file (it is for an older version). Replace that dependency with the following dependencies:

    ```
    testImplementation('org.junit.jupiter:junit-jupiter-api:5.4.2')
    testImplementation('org.junit.jupiter:junit-jupiter-engine:5.4.2')
    ```

    This brings in JUnit 5 to our project, rather than JUnit 4.

    Add the following to **build.gradle** after the dependencies section:

    ```
    test {
        useJUnitPlatform()
    }
    ```

    This ensures that you use the JUnit 5 test platform for running tests.

12. In the **src/main/java** folder, create a new Java package.

13. Enter **com.packtpub.testing** as the package name.

14. In the **src/test/java** folder, create a new Java package.

15. Enter the same name, **com.packtpub.testing**.

    The **src/test/java** folder is where you will place your test classes. The **src/main/java** folder is where the application classes are located.

16. Right-click on this package in the **src/main/java** folder and create a new Java class named **CoordSchedule**.

17. Enter two constants that we'll use to validate the data:

    ```
    public static final int MAX_FREQUENCY = 1440;
    public static final int MIN_FREQUENCY = 5;
    ```

18. Enter the properties of this class:

    ```
    private String startingTimestamp;
    private String endingTimestamp;
    private int frequency;
    ```

19. With the editor cursor inside the class (that is, between the starting and ending curly braces), right-click and choose **Generate…**.

20. Select **Constructor** and then select all three properties. You should see a constructor like the following:

    ```
    public CoordinatorSchedule(String startingTimestamp,
        String endingTimestamp, int frequency) {
        this.startingTimestamp = startingTimestamp;
        this.endingTimestamp = endingTimestamp;
        this.frequency = frequency;
    }
    ```

21. Again, with the editor cursor inside the class (that is, between the starting and ending curly braces), right-click and choose **Generate…**.

22. Select **Getter** and **Setter** and then select all three properties. You will then see the **get** and **set** methods for each of the three properties.

23. Enter the following method to parse the **String** timestamp value:

```java
private Date parseTimestamp(String timestamp) {
    Date date = null;
    SimpleDateFormat format =
      new SimpleDateFormat("yyyy-MM-dd'T'HH:mm'Z'",Locale.getDefault());
    format.setTimeZone(TimeZone.getTimeZone("UTC"));
    try {
        date = format.parse(timestamp);
    } catch (ParseException e) {
        e.printStackTrace();
    }
    return date;
}
```

24. Enter the following two utility methods to return the **Date** objects for the two timestamps:

```java
public Date getStartingTimestampAsDate() {
    return parseTimestamp(startingTimestamp);
}
public Date getEndingTimestampAsDate() {
    return parseTimestamp(endingTimestamp);
}
```

These methods allow other code to get the timestamps in date format, rather than as a string.

We now have the Java class that we are going to test.

The next step is to create a unit test class.

25. Right-click on this package in the **src/test/java** folder and create a new Java class named **CoordScheduleTest**.

26. Enter the following test method:

```java
@Test
@DisplayName("Frequency must be less than 1440")
void testFrequency() {
    CoordSchedule schedule = new CoordSchedule(
            "2020-12-15T15:32Z",
            "2020-12-30T05:15Z",
```

```
                60
        );
        Assertions.assertTrue(schedule.getFrequency() < 50);
    }
```

Note that this test should fail because we use a maximum value of **50** instead of the actual requirement, which is a maximum of **1,440**. It is good to see what failure will look like first.

27. Click on the **Gradle** pane. Expand **Tasks** and then expand **verification**.

28. Double-click on **Test**. This runs the Gradle **test** task. This will show an output like the following (with most of the stack trace omitted for clarity):

```
> Task :compileJava UP-TO-DATE
> Task :processResources NO-SOURCE
> Task :classes UP-TO-DATE
> Task :compileTestJava UP-TO-DATE
> Task :processTestResources NO-SOURCE
> Task :testClasses UP-TO-DATE
> Task :test FAILED
expected: <true> but was: <false>
org.opentest4j.AssertionFailedError: expected: <true> but was: <false>
at com.packtpub.testing.CoordScheduleTest.testFrequency(CoordScheduleTest.java:19)
com.packtpub.testing.CoordScheduleTest > testFrequency() FAILED
      org.opentest4j.AssertionFailedError at CoordScheduleTest.java:19
1 test completed, 1 failed
FAILURE: Build failed with an exception.
```

29. This isn't a very nice test report. Luckily, JUnit provides a much nicer report. Click on the Gradle elephant icon and the test report will appear in your web browser:

Figure 18.1: The IntelliJ Run pane with the Gradle icon shown

30. Switch to your web browser and you will see the test report:

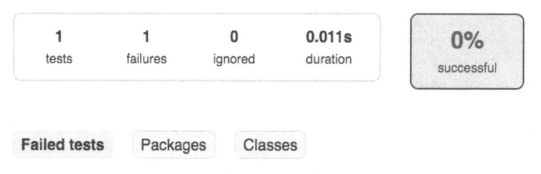

You will see a list of failed tests with the text from the **DisplayName** annotation. For each failed test, you can drill down into the test. This provides a much better format with which to display the test results.

Next, we'll fix the broken test and validate the other rules.

Exercise 2: Writing a Successful Test

Now that we have a test that fails, we'll need to fix the test and add test methods to verify the starting and ending timestamps:

1. Edit **CoordScheduleTest** in IntelliJ.

2. Replace the **testFrequency()** method with the following code:

```
@Test
@DisplayName("Frequency must be less than 1440")
void testFrequency() {
    CoordSchedule schedule = new CoordSchedule(
            "2020-12-15T15:32Z",
            "2020-12-30T05:15Z",
            60
    );
```

```
        int frequency = schedule.getFrequency();
        Assertions.assertTrue(frequency
                < CoordSchedule.MAX_FREQUENCY);
        Assertions.assertTrue(frequency
                > CoordSchedule.MIN_FREQUENCY);
    }
```

3. Add a test method to check for an incorrectly formatted date:

```
    @Test
    @DisplayName("Timestamp will be null if not formatted correctly")
    void testStartingTimestamps() {
        CoordSchedule schedule = new CoordSchedule(
                "2020/12/15T15:32Z",
                "2020-12-15T15:35Z",
                60
        );
        Date starting = schedule.getStartingTimestampAsDate();
        // Timestamp is not formatted properly.
        Assertions.assertNull(starting);
    }
```

4. Add a test method to verify that the ending timestamp is later than the starting timestamp:

```
    @Test
    @DisplayName("Ending timestamp must be after starting")
    void testTimestamps() {
        CoordSchedule schedule = new CoordSchedule(
                "2020-12-15T15:32Z",
                "2020-12-15T15:35Z",
                60
        );
        Date starting = schedule.getStartingTimestampAsDate();
        Assertions.assertNotNull(starting);
        Date ending = schedule.getEndingTimestampAsDate();
        Assertions.assertNotNull(ending);
        Assertions.assertTrue(ending.after(starting));
    }
```

5. Click on the **Gradle** pane. Expand **Tasks** and then expand **verification**.

6. Double-click on **Test**. This runs the Gradle **test** task. This will show an output like the following (with most of the stack trace omitted for clarity):

```
Testing started at 14:59 ...

14:59:33: Executing tasks ':cleanTest :test --tests "com.packtpub.testing.
CoordScheduleTest"'...
> Task :cleanTest

> Task :compileJava

> Task :processResources NO-SOURCE

> Task :classes

> Task :compileTestJava

> Task :processTestResources NO-SOURCE

> Task :testClasses

> Task :test

java.text.ParseException: Unparseable date: "2020/12/15T15:32Z"

at java.base/java.text.DateFormat.parse(DateFormat.java:395)

at com.packtpub.testing.CoordSchedule.parseTimestamp(CoordSchedule.java:64)

at com.packtpub.testing.CoordSchedule.getStartingTimestampAsDate(CoordSchedule.
java:49)

at com.packtpub.testing.CoordScheduleTest.testStartingTimestamps(CoordScheduleTest.
java:41)

...

BUILD SUCCESSFUL in 0s

4 actionable tasks: 4 executed

14:59:34: Tasks execution finished ':cleanTest :test --tests "com.packtpub.testing.
CoordScheduleTest"'.
```

Notice that the incorrectly formatted timestamp shows an exception stack trace (truncated here for length). This was expected (the input timestamp was not correct), so it is not an error. These tests should succeed.

Deciding What to Test

You can always write more tests, so, sooner or later, you need to decide on what you really do need to test.

It is normally a good idea to focus on:

- What code, if in error, would cause the greatest impact?

- What code is depended on the most by other code? This code should get extra tests.

- Are you checking for edge cases, such as maximum and minimum values?

In order to simplify writing better tests, and especially to deal with a few edge cases, you may want to use parameterized tests.

Writing Parameterized Tests

A parameterized test is a unit test that accepts parameters. Instead of all the test values being set in the **test** method, you can pass parameters. This makes it much easier to test multiple cases. For example, when processing string data, you may want to test multiple strings, including null and empty strings.

With a parameterized test, you need to specify the parameters you want to pass to the test. JUnit will pass these parameters as actual method parameters to your test. For example, look at the following:

```
@ParameterizedTest
@ValueSource(ints = { 10000, 11000 })
public void testMetStepGoal(int steps) {
    DailyGoal dailyGoal = new DailyGoal(DAILY_GOAL);
    Assertions.assertTrue(dailyGoal.hasMetGoal(steps));
}
```

In this example, you use a **@ParameterizedTest** annotation instead of **@Test**. This tells JUnit to look for the parameters.

The **@ValueSource** annotation defines two values to get passed to the **test** method: **10000** and **11000**. In both cases, this test assumes that the passed-in parameters will each result in the **hasMetGoal()** method returning **true**.

> **Note**
>
> Parameterized tests make JUnit much more acceptable to someone who uses Spock.

JUnit will call the **test** method once for each value in the **@ValueSource** list, so two times in this example.

The **@ValueSource** annotation expects a list of values to pass to the test method. If you have more complex values, you can use the **@CsvSource** annotation instead.

The **@CsvSource** annotation takes a comma-separated set of values. For example, look at the following:

```
@ParameterizedTest
@CsvSource({
    "10,     false",
    "9999,   false",
    "10000,  true",
    "20000,  true"
})
public void testHasMetStepGoal(int steps, boolean expected) {
    // …
}
```

In this example, the first call to **testHasMetStepGoal()** will return **10** for the **steps** parameter and **false** for the **expected** parameter. Note that JUnit converts the types for you. Similar to **@ValueSource**, each data line results in a separate call to the **test** method.

@CsvSource is very handy if you want to pass in a number of values to be compared against each other, or in the case here, where you would want to pass both good and bad values, along with a parameter that indicates whether the test is expected to be **true** or not.

Because the values within **@CsvSource** are stored as strings, you need some special syntax to handle empty strings, null strings, and strings with spaces:

```
@CsvSource({
    "'A man, a plan, a canal. Panama',   7",
    "'Able was I ere I saw Elba',   7",
    ",  0",
    "'',  0"
})
```

The first line has a string with spaces. Use single quote characters (') to delimit strings with spaces.

The third line has just a comma for the first parameter. JUnit will pass **null** for this construct.

The fourth line has two single quotes used to generate an empty string.

In addition to **@CsvSource**, you can load the data from an external comma-separated value (CSV) file using the **@CsvFileSource** annotation.

> **Note**
>
> JUnit supports a few other ways to get the parameter values, including from a separate file, from a method you write, and more. You can refer to https://packt. live/2J8oXGU for more information about parameterized tests.

Exercise 3: Writing a Parameterized Test

Let's assume that you are writing code that accesses a wearable fitness device. One of the things the device tracks is the number of steps the wearer takes on a given day. You can then compare the number of steps taken against a daily goal. Has the wearer met this goal?

This example demonstrates how to write a parameterized test, based on the daily step goal from *Chapter 6, Libraries, Packages, and Modules*:

1. Edit **build.gradle**.

2. Add the following to the dependencies block:

```
testImplementation('org.junit.jupiter:junit-jupiter-params:5.4.2')
```

3. This dependency brings in support for the parameterized tests.

4. Right-click on the **com.packtpub.testing** package in the **src/main/java** folder. Select **New** and **Java Class**.

5. Enter **DailyGoal** as the class name.

6. Enter the following code for this class:

```
int dailyGoal = 10000;
public DailyGoal(int dailyGoal) {
    this.dailyGoal = dailyGoal;
}
public boolean hasMetGoal(int steps) {
    if (steps >= dailyGoal) {
        return true;
    }
    return false;
}
```

This is the class we will test.

7. Right-click on the `com.packtpub.testing` package in the `src/test/java` folder. Select **New** and **Java Class**.

8. Enter **DailyGoalTest** as the class name.

9. Enter the following constant for the device wearer's daily step goal:

```
public static final int DAILY_GOAL = 10000;
```

10. Next, enter a **test** method for step counts that meet or exceed the daily goal:

```
@ParameterizedTest
@ValueSource(ints = { 10000, 11000 })
public void testMetStepGoal(int steps) {
    DailyGoal dailyGoal = new DailyGoal(DAILY_GOAL);
    Assertions.assertTrue(dailyGoal.hasMetGoal(steps));
}
```

With a daily step goal of **10000** steps, **10000** and **11000** both meet this goal.

11. Next, we'll test the result when the step count is lower than the daily step goal:

```
@ParameterizedTest
@ValueSource(ints = { 10, 9999 })
public void testNotMetStepGoal(int steps) {
    DailyGoal dailyGoal = new DailyGoal(DAILY_GOAL);
    Assertions.assertFalse(dailyGoal.hasMetGoal(steps));
}
```

Notice how **9999** is just one step below the goal.

Next, enter a test method using the **@CsvSource** values for the test parameters:

```
@ParameterizedTest
@CsvSource({
    "10,     false",
    "9999,   false",
    "10000,  true",
    "20000,  true"
})
public void testHasMetStepGoal(int steps, boolean expected) {
    DailyGoal dailyGoal = new DailyGoal(DAILY_GOAL);
    // Using a lambda will lazily evaluate the expression
    Assertions.assertTrue(
```

```
            dailyGoal.hasMetGoal(steps) == expected,
            () -> "With " + steps +
                " steps, hasMetGoal() should return " +
                expected);
    }
```

This test method is a bit more complicated. Each call to the test passes two parameters.

The lambda expression in the call to **Assertions.assertTrue()** is the error message. Using a lambda expression means that the error message won't get evaluated unless the test assertion fails.

When you run this test class, it should succeed.

When Tests Won't Work—Disabling Tests

The **@Disabled** annotation allows you to disable a test. Normally, it is not good practice to simply disable any test that fails. This defeats the whole idea of testing. However, you may come across times where, due to some condition outside of your control, you just must disable tests. For example, if you are using the code from another group, and that group has broken an expectation or introduced a bug in its code, you may need to–temporarily–disable tests that depend on that code:

```
@Disabled("Until platform team fixes issue 5578")
@Test
public void testThatShouldNotFail() {
    // …
}
```

You can add the **@Disabled** annotation to an entire test class, or just to a test method, as shown in the preceding code block.

Test Setup

In many tests, you may need to perform some setup work, as well as cleanup work after the test. For example, you may want to initialize the objects that are needed for the test. JUnit provides a number of life cycle annotations to support such work.

If you annotate a method with **@BeforeEach**, JUnit will run that method before running each test method. Similarly, methods annotated with **@AfterEach** are run after each test method. If you want to run the setup or clean up the code just once for a test class, you can use **@BeforeAll** and **@AfterAll**. These two methods come with some restrictions, though.

JUnit creates a new instance of your test class for each test method. This ensures your tests run in isolation and avoid what is called test pollution, where one test impacts another test. Normally, this is a good thing, because tracking down test failures that depend on the order of the test execution is particularly frustrating.

Because JUnit creates a new instance of the test class for each test method, the @ BeforeAll and @AfterAll methods must be **static**. Additionally, the data that these methods initialize or clean up should also be **static**.

If you don't want to create **static** methods, you can change JUnit's policy of creating a new instance of the test class for each test method.

If you annotate your test class with the following, JUnit will create just one instance of the test class shared by all the test methods:

```
@TestInstance(TestInstance.Lifecycle.PER_CLASS)
```

You'll see an example of this in the *Mocking* section.

Exercise 4, Using Test Setup and Cleanup Methods demonstrates how to code these setup and cleanup methods.

Exercise 4: Using Test Setup and Cleanup Methods

This exercise demonstrates a simple unit test with placeholder methods for both setting up and cleaning up. The test will verify a simple class that converts Celsius temperature values to Fahrenheit:

1. Right-click on the **com.packtpub.testing** package in the **src/main/java** folder. Select **New** and **Java Class**.

2. Enter **TempConverter** as the class name.

3. Enter the following method:

```
public static double convertToF(double degreesC) {
    double degreesF = (degreesC * 9/5) + 32;
    // Round to make nicer output.
    return Math.round(degreesF * 10.0) / 10.0;
}
```

4. Right-click on the **com.packtpub.testing** package in the **src/test/java** folder. Select **New** and **Java Class**.

5. Enter **TempConverterTest** as the class name.

6. Enter the following test method that checks for **-40.0** degrees on both temperature scales:

```
@Test
public void testFahrenheitWhenCold() {
    // -40 C == -40 F
    double degreesC = -40.0;
    double degreesF = TempConverter.convertToF(degreesC);
    Assertions.assertEquals(degreesC, degreesF);
}
```

This temperature is unpleasant regardless of the temperature scale used.

Notice how this test uses the **assertEquals()** assertion.

7. Enter another test method to ensure the conversion works when the temperature is **100.0** degrees Celsius:

```
@Test
public void testFahrenheitWhenHot() {
    // 100 C == 212 F
    double degreesC = 100.0;
    double degreesF = TempConverter.convertToF(degreesC);
    Assertions.assertEquals(212.0, degreesF);
}
```

8. Next, enter a method to be run before all the tests:

```
@BeforeAll
public static void runBeforeAllTests() {
    System.out.println("Before all tests");
}
```

Note that this method must be static (or you must use the class-level annotation listed previously).

Normally, you would use this method to set up complex test data instead of just printing a value.

9. Enter a method to be run after all the tests:

```
@AfterAll
public static void runAfterAllTests() {
    System.out.println("After all tests");
}
```

Again, this method must be static.

10. Now, enter a method to be run before each of the two test methods:

```
@BeforeEach
public void runBeforeEachTest() {
    System.out.println("Before each test");
}
```

11. Similarly, enter a method to be run after each test method:

```
@AfterEach
public void runAfterEachTest() {
    System.out.println("After each test");
}
```

12. Click on the green arrow by the class statement and select **Run 'TempConverterTest'**. The test should run without errors.

    You will see an output like the following:

```
Before all tests
Before each test
After each test
Before each test
After each test
After all tests
BUILD SUCCESSFUL in 0s
4 actionable tasks: 2 executed, 2 up-to-date
```

Note that the **@BeforeAll** method is only run once. Then, with each test method, the **@BeforeEach** and **@AfterEach** methods are executed. Finally, the **@AfterAll** method is executed.

Mocking

A unit test is supposed to test just one Java class. There are times, however, where a class is heavily dependent on other classes, and perhaps even external systems such as databases or handheld devices. In these cases, a technique called mocking proves useful. Mocking is where you mock out the other dependencies so that you can test just the class you want to look at.

A **mock** is a class used just for testing that pretends to be some external dependency. With a mocking framework, you can examine a mocked class to ensure that the right methods were called the right number of times with the right parameters.

Mocking works great when you have code that queries for data in a database or external system. What you do is create an instance that is a mock for a particular class. Then, when the query method gets called, you have the mock return arbitrary test data. This avoids the dependency on the external system.

Mocking also works great when you want to verify that a particular method was called, without actually calling that method. Think of an email notifier that sends email messages on some kind of failure. In a unit test, you don't want actual email messages to get sent. (In an integration or functional test, however, you should verify that the messages do get sent.)

Testing with Mocks Using Mockito

Mockito is a great framework for adding mocks to your testing. Say that you have an application that monitors workflows running in a big data cluster; these could be Oozie workflows mentioned previously, or any other type of workflows.

Your application gets the status of the workflows by calling a remote web service. In your unit tests, you don't want to call the remote web service. Instead, you just want to mock out the external system.

The code we want to test will look something like the following:

```
WorkflowStatus workflowStatus = workflowClient.getStatus(id);
if (!workflowStatus.isOk()) {
    emailNotifier.sendFailureEmail(workflowStatus);
}
```

First, the code calls a remote web service to get the status of a workflow, based on the workflow ID. Then, if the workflow status is not OK, the code sends an email message. For unit tests, we need to mock both the call to **getStatus()** and the call to **sendFailureEmail()**.

The **WorkflowClient** class manages the HTTP communication to the remote web service.

A call to the **getStatus()** method with a workflow ID returns the status of that given workflow:

```
WorkflowStatus workflowStatus = workflowClient.getStatus(id);
```

> **Note**
>
> You can refer to *Chapter 9, Working with HTTP*, for more information about HTTP and web services.

With Mockito, the first thing you need to do is to create a mock of the **WorkflowClient** class:

```
import static org.mockito.Mockito.*;
workflowClient = mock(WorkflowClient.class);
```

The next step is to stub out the call to **getStatus()**. In Mockito terminology, when something happens, then a particular result is returned. In this case, the stubbed code should return a prebuilt **WorkflowStatus** object with the desired status of a test:

```
String id = "WORKFLOW-1";
WorkflowStatus workflowStatus =
    new WorkflowStatus(id, WorkflowStatus.OK);
when(workflowClient.getStatus(id)).thenReturn(workflowStatus);
```

In this code, we first set up a string of the workflow ID and then construct a **WorkflowStatus** object with a successful status (**OK**). The crucial code starts with **when()**. Read this code when the **getStatus** call is made with the given ID on the mock **WorkflowClient** class, and then return our prebuilt **WorkflowStatus** object.

In this case, Mockito is looking for an exact match. The passed-in workflow ID must match, or the mock will not return the specified result. You can also specify that the mock should return the result with any input workflow ID, as shown in the following:

```
when(workflowClient.getStatus(anyString())).thenReturn(workflowStatus);
```

In this case, the **anyString()** call means any string value passed in will match. Note that Mockito has other calls, such as **anyInt()**.

> **Note**
>
> Mockito includes very good documentation at https://packt.live/2P6ogl9. You can do a lot more with mocks than the examples shown here, but you should avoid the temptation to mock everything.

With the call to the external web service mocked out, the next step is to check whether a failure email gets sent. To do this, mock the class that sends email failure messages:

```
import static org.mockito.Mockito.*;
EmailNotifier emailNotifier = mock(EmailNotifier.class);
```

In the code we want to test, the email message is sent only on failures. So, we will want to test two things:

- The email is not sent if the status is OK.

- The email is sent if the status is *not* OK.

In both cases, we will use Mockito to check the number of times the **sendFailureEmail()** method gets called. If it is zero times, then no email is sent. If it is one or more times, then an email message is sent.

To ensure that no email message was sent, use code like the following:

```
verify(emailNotifier, times(0)).sendFailureEmail(workflowStatus);
```

This code checks that the **sendFailureEmail()** method was called zero times, that is, not called at all.

To verify that the email message was sent, you can specify the number of times as **1**:

```
verify(emailNotifier, times(1)).sendFailureEmail(workflowStatus);
```

You can also use Mockito's shortcut, which assumes the method gets called just once:

```
verify(emailNotifier).sendFailureEmail(workflowStatus);
```

In more complex tests, you may want to ensure a method gets called a few times.

As mentioned previously, JUnit creates a new instance of your test class for each test method. When mocking, you may want to set up the mocks once, instead of every time a test method runs.

To tell JUnit to create just one instance of the test class and share it among all test methods, add the following annotation to the class:

```
@TestInstance(TestInstance.Lifecycle.PER_CLASS)
public class WorkflowMonitorTest {
    private EmailNotifier emailNotifier;
    private WorkflowClient workflowClient;
    private WorkflowMonitor workflowMonitor;
    @BeforeAll
    public void setUpMocks() {
```

```
        emailNotifier = mock(EmailNotifier.class);
        workflowClient = mock(WorkflowClient.class);
        workflowMonitor =
                new WorkflowMonitor(emailNotifier, workflowClient);
    }
}
```

The **setUpMocks()** method will get called once before all the test methods run. It sets up the two mock classes and then passes the mock objects to the constructor for the **WorkflowMonitor** class.

The following exercise shows all these classes together, using Mockito-based mocks in the unit test.

Exercise 5: Using Mocks when Testing

This exercise creates a **WorkflowMonitor** class and then uses mock objects to handle external dependencies:

1. In the **src/main/java** folder in the IntelliJ **Project** pane, create a new Java package.

2. Enter **com.packtpub.workflow** as the package name.

3. In the **src/test/java** folder, create a new Java package.

4. Enter the same name, **com.packtpub.workflow.**

5. Edit **build.gradle.**

6. Add the following to the dependencies block:

    ```
    testImplementation("org.mockito:mockito-core:2.+")
    ```

7. Right-click on the **com.packtpub.workflow** package in the **src/main/java** folder. Select **New** and **Java Class.**

8. Enter **WorkflowStatus** as the class name.

9. Enter the following code for this simple value object class:

    ```
    public static final String OK = "OK";
    public static final String ERROR = "ERROR";
    private String id;
    private String status = OK;
    ```

```
public WorkflowStatus(String id, String status) {
    this.id = id;
    this.status = status;
}
public boolean isOk() {
    if (OK.equals(status)) {
        return true;
    }
    return false;
}
```

In a real system, this class would hold additional values, such as when the workflow started, when it stopped, and other information on the workflow. The status information was simplified for this exercise.

10. Right-click on the **com.packtpub.workflow** package in the **src/main/java** folder. Select **New** and **Java Class**.

11. Enter **EmailNotifier** as the class name.

12. Enter the following method:

```
public void sendFailureEmail(WorkflowStatus workflowStatus) {
    // This would have actual code...
}
```

In a real application, this would send email messages. For simplicity, we'll leave that blank.

13. Right-click on the **com.packtpub.workflow** package in the **src/main/java** folder. Select **New** and **Java Class**.

14. Enter **WorkflowClient** as the class name.

15. Enter the following method:

```
public WorkflowStatus getStatus(String id) {
    // This would use HTTP to get the status.
    return new WorkflowStatus(id, WorkflowStatus.OK);
}
```

Again, this is simplified.

16. Right-click on the **com.packtpub.workflow** package in the **src/main/java** folder. Select **New** and **Java Class**.

17. Enter **WorkflowMonitor** as the class name.

18. Enter the following properties:

```
private EmailNotifier emailNotifier;
private WorkflowClient workflowClient;
```

19. Right-click on the class, choose **Generate...** and then choose **Constructor**.

20. Select both properties and then click on **OK**.

21. Enter the following method:

```
public void checkStatus(String id) {
    WorkflowStatus workflowStatus = workflowClient.getStatus(id);
    if (!workflowStatus.isOk()) {
        emailNotifier.sendFailureEmail(workflowStatus);
    }
}
```

This is the method we will test using mock objects.

22. Right-click on the **com.packtpub.workflow** package in the **src/test/java** folder. Select **New** and **Java Class**.

23. Enter **WorkflowMonitorTest** as the class name.

24. Annotate the class so that we can create a **@BeforeAll** method:

```
@TestInstance(TestInstance.Lifecycle.PER_CLASS)
```

25. Enter the following properties and set up the **@BeforeAll** method:

```
private EmailNotifier emailNotifier;
private WorkflowClient workflowClient;
private WorkflowMonitor workflowMonitor;
@BeforeAll
public void setUpMocks() {
    emailNotifier = mock(EmailNotifier.class);
    workflowClient = mock(WorkflowClient.class);
    workflowMonitor =
      new WorkflowMonitor(emailNotifier, workflowClient);
}
```

This sets up the mock objects and then instantiates a **WorkflowMonitor** object using the mocked dependencies.

26. Enter the following test method to test a case when the workflow is successful:

```
@Test
public void testSuccess() {
    String id = "WORKFLOW-1";
    WorkflowStatus workflowStatus =
        new WorkflowStatus(id, WorkflowStatus.OK);
    when(workflowClient.getStatus(id)).thenReturn(workflowStatus);
    workflowMonitor.checkStatus(id);
    verify(emailNotifier, times(0)).sendFailureEmail(workflowStatus);
}
```

We should also test a case where the workflow status is not OK.

27. Enter the following test method:

```
@Test
public void testFailure() {
    String id = "WORKFLOW-1";
    WorkflowStatus workflowStatus =
        new WorkflowStatus(id, WorkflowStatus.ERROR);
    when(workflowClient.getStatus(anyString()))
        .thenReturn(workflowStatus);
    workflowMonitor.checkStatus(id);
    verify(emailNotifier).sendFailureEmail(workflowStatus);
}
}
```

28. Click on the green arrow by the class statement and select **Run 'WorkflowMonitorTest'**. The test should run without errors.

Activity 1: Counting the Words in the String

Word count is of paramount value in the publishing industry. Write a class that, given a string, will count all the words in the string.

1. You can use the **split()** method to break up the string into words, using the **\s+** regular expression to separate the words, which matches whitespace characters(that is, spaces and tabs). Name this class **WordCount**.

2. Trim the input string to remove any spaces at the beginning or end.

   Note that an empty string should generate zero for the word count; so should a **null** string. Input strings that are all spaces should generate zero as well.

3. Once you have the class written, write a parameterized unit test for that class. Use the parameters and **@CsvSource** to pass in a string along with the expected word count. Be sure to include punctuation such as commas and periods in your input strings. In addition to this, be sure to include input strings with null strings and empty strings in the input parameters.

> **Note**
>
> The solution for this activity can be found on page 569.

Summary

This chapter introduced unit testing. Testing is good and you want to write tests for all your Java code. If you write successful tests, then you can feel confident your code was written correctly.

JUnit provides the most popular testing framework for writing Java unit tests, though there are other frameworks you can try as well. The **@Test** annotation on a method tells JUnit that the given code is considered a test. JUnit will execute the test and see whether it succeeds. The JUnit assertions class contains a few **static** methods that you can use to verify the test results.

A parameterized test is a test into which you pass a few parameters. This is very useful when writing tests for code that you want to ensure can handle a variety of inputs. Mocking is a technique where you mock out external dependencies so that a unit test can concentrate on testing just one class.

Appendix

About

This section is included to assist the students to perform the activities present in the book. It includes detailed steps that are to be performed by the students to complete and achieve the objectives of the book.

Chapter 1: Getting Started

Activity 1: Obtaining the Minimum of Two Numbers

Solution

1. Declare **3** double variables: **a**, **b**, and **m**. Initialize them with the values **3**, **4** and **0** respectively

    ```
    double a = 3;
    double b = 4;
    double m = 0; // variable for the minimum
    ```

2. Create a **String** variable **r**, it should contain the output message to be printed.

    ```
    // string to be printed
    String r = "The minimum of numbers: " + a + " and " + b + " is ";
    ```

3. Use the **min()** method to obtain the minimum of the two numbers and store the value in **m**.

    ```
    // mathematical operation
    m = Math.min(a,b);
    ```

4. Print the results.

    ```
    System.out.println(r + m); // print out the results
    ```

> **Note**
>
> The complete code for this activity can be found here: https://packt.live/2MFtRNM

Chapter 2: Learning the Basics

Activity 1: Taking Input and Comparing Ranges

Solution

1. In **main()**, introduce an **if** statement to check if the arguments entered are of the right length:

```java
public class Activity1 {
    public static void main(String[] args) {
        if (args.length < 2) {
            System.err.println("Error. Usage is:");
            System.err.println("Activity1 systolic diastolic");
            System.exit(-1);
        }
```

2. Parse these arguments as **int** values and save them in variables:

```java
int systolic  = Integer.parseInt(args[0]);
int diastolic = Integer.parseInt(args[1]);
```

3. Check the different values entered to see whether the blood pressure is in the desired range using the following code:

```java
System.out.print(systolic + "/" + diastolic + " is ");
if ((systolic <= 90) || (diastolic <= 60)) {
    System.out.println("low blood pressure.");
} else if ((systolic >= 140) || (diastolic >= 90)) {
    System.out.println("high blood pressure.");
} else if ((systolic >= 120) || (diastolic >= 80)) {
    System.out.println("pre-high blood pressure.");
} else {
    System.out.println("ideal blood pressure.");
}
    }
}
```

Chapter 3: Object-Oriented Programming

Activity 1: Adding the Frequency-of-Symbol Calculation to WordTool

Solution

Add a method to the previously created **WordTool** class to calculate the frequency of a certain symbol. To do so, perform the following steps:

1. Add a method to count the number of words in a string.

```
public int wordCount ( String s ) {
    int count = 0;  // variable to count words
    // if the entry is empty or is null, count is zero
    // therefore we evaluate it only otherwise
    if ( !(s == null || s.isEmpty()) ) {
        // use the split method from the String class to
        // separate the words having the whitespace as separator
        String[] w = s.split("\\s+");
        count = w.length;
    }
    return count;
}
```

2. Add a method to count the number of letters in a string and add the possibility of separating the case of having whitespaces or not.

```
public int symbolCount ( String s, boolean withSpaces ) {
    int count = 0;  // variable to count symbols
    // if the entry is empty or is null, count is zero
    // therefore we evaluate it only otherwise
    if ( !(s == null || s.isEmpty()) ) {
        if (withSpaces) {
            // with whitespaces return the full length
            count = s.length();
        } else {
            // without whitespaces, eliminate whitespaces
            // and get the length on the fly
            count = s.replace(" ", "").length();
        }
    }
    return count;
}
```

3. Add a method to calculate the frequency of a certain symbol.

```
public int getFrequency ( String s, char c ) {
    int count = 0;
    // if the entry is empty or is null, count is zero
    // therefore we evaluate it only otherwise
    if ( !(s == null || s.isEmpty()) ) {
        count = s.length() - s.replace(Character.toString(c), "").length();
    }
    return count;
}
```

4. In the main class, create an object of the **WordTool** class and add a string variable containing a line of text of your choice.

```
WordTool wt = new WordTool();
String text = "The river carried the memories from her childhood.";
```

5. Add a variable to contain the symbol to look for in the text, and choose a symbol, in this case '**e**'. As it is a character, use single quotes to delimit it.

```
char search = 'e';
```

6. Add code inside the main method to print out the calculations made by **WordTool**.

```
System.out.println( "Analyzing the text: \n" + text );
System.out.println( "Total words: " + wt.wordCount(text) );
System.out.println( "Total symbols (w. spaces): " + wt.symbolCount(text, true) );
System.out.println( "Total symbols (wo. spaces): " + wt.symbolCount(text, false) );
System.out.println( "Total amount of " + search + ": " + wt.getFrequency(text,
search) );
```

Activity 2: Adding Documentation to WordTool

Solution

Make sure you document each one of the examples and add enough metadata for people to know how to handle the different methods.

1. Include an introduction comment to the class, you should at least include a short text, the **@author**, **@version**, and **@since** parameters.

```
/**
 * <H1>WordTool</H1>
 * A class to perform calculations about text.
 *
 * @author Joe Smith
 * @version 0.1
 * @since 20190305
 */
```

2. Add an explanation to the **wordCount** method, remember including the parameters and the expected outcome to the method as **@param** and **@return**.

```
/**
 * <h2>wordCount</h2>
 * returns the amount of words in a text, takes a string as parameter
 *
 * @param s
 * @return int
 */
public int wordCount ( String s ) { [...]
```

3. Do the same for **symbolCount**.

```
/**
 * <h2>symbolCount</h2>
 * returns the amount of symbols in a string with or without counting spaces
 *
 * @param s
 * @param withSpaces
 * @return int
 */
public int symbolCount ( String s, boolean withSpaces ) { [...]
```

4. Do not forget the last method in the class, **getFrequency**.

```
/**
 * <h2>getFrequency</h2>
 * returns the amount of occurrences of a symbol in a string
 *
 * @param s
 * @param c
 * @return int
 */
public int getFrequency ( String s, char c ) { [...]
```

5. You are now ready to export the documentation file from this example.

   The documentation site resulting from this activity should look like the one displayed in the following screenshot:

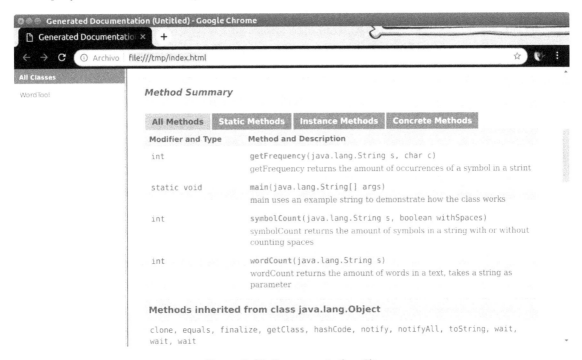

Figure 3.12: Documentation Site

Chapter 4: Collections, List, and Java's Built-In APIs

Activity 1: Searching for Multiple Occurrences in an Array

Solution

1. Create the **text** array.

```
String[] text = {"So", "many", "books", "so", "little", "time"};
```

2. Create the variable that contains the word to be searched for: so

```
String searchQuery = "so";
```

3. Initialize the variable occurrence to **-1**.

```
int occurrence = -1;
```

4. Create a **for** loop to iterate through the array to check for the occurrence.

```
for(int i = 0; i < text.length; i++) {
    occurrence = text[i].compareToIgnoreCase(searchQuery);
    if (occurrence == 0) {
        System.out.println("Found query at: " + i);
    }
}
```

> **Note**
>
> The complete code for this activity can be found here: https://packt.live/35RQ9Ud

Activity 2: Iterating through Large Lists

Solution

1. To start, you should create a randomly sized list containing random numbers. Create the list that you will use to contain the numbers later. You will store numbers of the type **Double**.

    ```
    List <Double> numbers = new ArrayList <Double> ();
    ```

2. Define next the size of the list using a variable that we name **numNodes**. Make the variable of type **long**. Since the random method does NOT generate that type, you need to cast the outcome.

    ```
    long numNodes = (long) Math.round(Math.random() * 10000);
    ```

3. Use a **for** loop to iterate through the list and create each one of the elements in it.

    ```
    for (int i = 0; i < numNodes; i++) {
        numbers.add(Math.random() * 100);
    }
    ```

4. To compute the average, you could create an iterator that will go through the list of values and add the weighted value corresponding to each element.

    ```
    Iterator iterator = numbers.iterator();
    ```

5. The value coming from the **iterator.next()** method must be cast into a **Double** before it can be weighed against the total number of elements.

    ```
    Double average = 0.0;
    while(iterator.hasNext()) {
        average += (Double) iterator.next() / numNodes;
    }
    ```

6. Do not forget to print out the results.

    ```
    System.out.println("Average: " + average);
    ```

> **Note**
>
> The complete code for this activity can be found here: https://packt.live/35Yvo9m

Chapter 5: Exceptions

Activity 1: Designing an Exception Class Logging Data

Solution

1. Import the relevant classes needed for this program to work: **NoSuchFileException** and **logging**.

   ```
   import java.nio.file.NoSuchFileException;
   import java.util.logging.*;
   ```

2. Make your own methods for issuing exceptions, start by creating one for the **NullPointerException** case.

   ```
   public static void issuePointerException() throws NullPointerException {
       throw new NullPointerException("Exception: file not found");
   }
   ```

3. You will also need a method for the case the file is not found: **NoSuchFileException**.

   ```
   public static void issueFileException() throws NoSuchFileException {
       throw new NoSuchFileException("Exception: file not found");
   }
   ```

4. Back to the **Main** method, create the **logger** object that will be reporting the exceptions and their severity level.

   ```
   Logger logger = Logger.getAnonymousLogger();
   ```

5. Capture the argument passed to the script via the CLI and store it in a variable.

   ```
   int exceptionNum = Integer.valueOf(args[0]);
   ```

6. Discriminate among the possible exceptions to log using a switch-case statement. Remember catching the exceptions with try-catch.

Activity01.java

```
1   switch (exceptionNum) {
2       case 1:
3           try {
4               issuePointerException();
5           } catch (NullPointerException ne) {
6               logger.log(Level.SEVERE, "Exception happened", ne);
7           }
8           break;
9       case 2:
10          try {
11              issueFileException();
12          } catch (NoSuchFileException ne) {
13              logger.log(Level.WARNING, "Exception happened", ne);
14          }
15          break;
```

https://packt.live/33SEL8B

Chapter 6: Libraries, Packages, and Modules

Activity 1: Tracking Summer High Temperatures

Solution

1. Create an IntelliJ Gradle project. Modify **settings.gradle** as follows:

```
rootProject.name = 'temps'
```

2. Modify **build.gradle** as follows:

build.gradle

```
1  buildscript {
2      repositories {
3          jcenter()
4      }
5      dependencies {
6          classpath 'com.github.jengelman.gradle.plugins:shadow:2.0.1'
7      }
8  }
```

https://packt.live/2pJJJFY

3. Create a **class** named **City**. Add the following fields and constructor:

```
package com.packtpub.temps;
public class City {
    private String name;
    private String country;
    double summertimeHigh;        // In degrees C
    public City(String name, String country, double summertimeHigh) {
        this.name = name;
        this.country = country;
        this.summertimeHigh = summertimeHigh;
    }
}
```

4. Right-click inside the class. Choose **Generate**, and then **Getter and Setter**. Select all the fields and click **OK**. This will generate the getter and setter methods:

```
public String getName() {
    return name;
}
public void setName(String name) {
    this.name = name;
```

```
    }
    public String getCountry() {
        return country;
    }
    public void setCountry(String country) {
        this.country = country;
    }
    public double getSummertimeHigh() {
        return summertimeHigh;
    }
    public void setSummertimeHigh(double summertimeHigh) {
        this.summertimeHigh = summertimeHigh;
    }
```

5. Add a method to convert degrees to Fahrenheit. This method uses the **TempConverter** class:

```
public String format(boolean fahrenheit) {
    String degrees = summertimeHigh + " C";
    if (fahrenheit) {
        degrees = TempConverter.convertToF(summertimeHigh) + " F";
    }
    return name + ", " + country + " " + degrees;
}
```

6. Create a **class** named **SummerHigh** to hold the city information for summer high temperatures. Enter the following properties and constructor:

```
package com.packtpub.temps;
public class SummerHigh {
    private City base;
    private City moderateCuts;
    private City noCuts;
    public SummerHigh(City base, City moderateCuts, City noCuts) {
        this.base = base;
        this.moderateCuts = moderateCuts;
        this.noCuts = noCuts;
    }
}
```

7. Right-click inside the class. Choose **Generate**, and then **Getter and Setter**. Select all the fields and click **OK**. This will generate the getter and setter methods:

```
public City getBase() {
    return base;
}
public void setBase(City base) {
    this.base = base;
}
public City getModerateCuts() {
    return moderateCuts;
}
public void setModerateCuts(City moderateCuts) {
    this.moderateCuts = moderateCuts;
}
public City getNoCuts() {
    return noCuts;
}
public void setNoCuts(City noCuts) {
    this.noCuts = noCuts;
}
```

8. Enter a format method in order to render the output readable:

```
public String format(boolean fahrenheit) {
    StringBuilder builder = new StringBuilder();
    builder.append("In 2100, ");
    builder.append(base.format(fahrenheit));
    builder.append(" will be like\n    ");
    builder.append(noCuts.format(fahrenheit));
    builder.append(" with no emissions cuts,");
    builder.append("\n    ");
    builder.append(moderateCuts.format(fahrenheit));
    builder.append(" with moderate emissions cuts");
    return builder.toString();
}
```

This code makes use of the **City class format()** method.

9. Create a class called **SummerHighs**. This class holds a table of **SummerHigh** objects. Enter the following field and constructor to initialize the table:

```
package com.packtpub.temps;
import com.google.common.collect.HashBasedTable;
import com.google.common.collect.Table;
import java.util.Map;
public class SummerHighs {
    private Table<String, String, SummerHigh> data;
    public SummerHighs() {
        data = HashBasedTable.create();
    }
}
```

10. Enter a method to get summer high temperature information by **city**:

```
public SummerHigh getByCity(String city) {
    Map<String, SummerHigh> row = data.row(city.toLowerCase());
    SummerHigh summerHigh = null;
    for ( String key : row.keySet()) {
        summerHigh = row.get(key);
    }
    return summerHigh;
}
```

This method uses the **Guava** library Table class.

11. Enter a method to get summer high temperature information by **country**:

```
public SummerHigh getByCountry(String country) {
    Map<String, SummerHigh> column = data.column(country.toLowerCase());
    SummerHigh summerHigh = null;
    for ( String key : column.keySet()) {
        summerHigh = column.get(key);
    }
    return summerHigh;
}
```

This method also uses the **Guava** library's Table class.

12. Now create a number of convenience methods to make adding cities easier:

```
// Convenience methods to help initialize data.
public void addSummerHigh(SummerHigh summerHigh) {
    City baseCity = summerHigh.getBase();
    data.put(baseCity.getName().toLowerCase(),
            baseCity.getCountry().toLowerCase(), summerHigh);
}
public SummerHigh createSummerHigh(City base, City moderateCuts,
                                   City noCuts) {
    return new SummerHigh(base, moderateCuts, noCuts);
}
public City createCity(String name, String country, double summertimeHigh) {
    return new City(name, country, summertimeHigh);
}
```

13. Then, create a method to initialize the summer high temperature data described previously:

SummerHighs.java

```
67    addSummerHigh(
68        createSummerHigh(
69            createCity("Tokyo", "Japan", 26.2),
70            createCity("Beijing", "China", 29.0),
71            createCity("Wuhan", "China", 31.2)
72        )
73    );
```

https://packt.live/2qELV2d

14. Create a class named **Main** to run our program. Then, create a **main()** method as follows:

Main.java

```
6           SummerHighs summerHighs = new SummerHighs();
7           summerHighs.initialize();
8
9           boolean fahrenheit = false;
10          // Handle inputs
11          if (args.length < 2) {
12              System.err.println("Error: usage is:");
13              System.err.println(" -city London");
14              System.err.println(" -country United Kingdom");
15          }
16
17          String searchBy = args[0];
18          String name = args[1];
19          SummerHigh high = null;
20          if ("-city".equals(searchBy)) {
21              high = summerHighs.getByCity(name);
22          } else if ("-country".equals(searchBy)) {
23              high = summerHighs.getByCountry(name);
24          }
```

https://packt.live/2BBF2AO

15. Finally, create a class named **TempConverter** to convert from degrees Celsius to degrees Fahrenheit:

```
package com.packtpub.temps;
public class TempConverter {
    public static double convertToF(double degreesC) {
        double degreesF = (degreesC * 9/5) + 32;
        // Round to make nicer output.
        return Math.round(degreesF * 10.0) / 10.0;

    }
}
```

Chapter 7: Databases and JDBC

Activity 1: Track Your Progress

Solution

1. The **student** table holds information on the **student**:

```
CREATE TABLE IF NOT EXISTS student
(
STUDENT_ID long,
FIRST_NAME varchar(255),
LAST_NAME varchar(255),
PRIMARY KEY (STUDENT_ID)
);
```

2. The **chapter** table has a **chapter number** and a **name**:

```
CREATE TABLE IF NOT EXISTS chapter
(
CHAPTER_ID long,
CHAPTER_NAME varchar(255),
PRIMARY KEY (CHAPTER_ID)
);
```

Note that the **chapter ID** is the **chapter number**.

3. The **student_progress** table maps a **student ID** to a **chapter ID**, indicating that a particular student completed a particular chapter:

```
CREATE TABLE IF NOT EXISTS student_progress
(
STUDENT_ID long,
CHAPTER_ID long,
COMPLETED date,
PRIMARY KEY (STUDENT_ID, CHAPTER_ID)
);
```

Note that by using both **student ID** and **chapter ID** as the composite **primary key**, each student can complete each chapter just once. There are no do-overs.

4. Here is a hypothetical student:

```
INSERT INTO student
(STUDENT_ID, FIRST_NAME, LAST_NAME)
VALUES (1, 'BOB', 'MARLEY');
```

Note that in order to make it easier to match the names, we insert all of them in uppercase.

5. The following **INSERT** statements provide data for the first seven chapters:

```
INSERT INTO chapter
(CHAPTER_ID, CHAPTER_NAME)
VALUES (1, 'Getting Started');
INSERT INTO chapter
(CHAPTER_ID, CHAPTER_NAME)
VALUES (2, 'Learning the Basics');
INSERT INTO chapter
(CHAPTER_ID, CHAPTER_NAME)
VALUES (3, 'Object-Oriented Programming: Classes and Methods');
INSERT INTO chapter
(CHAPTER_ID, CHAPTER_NAME)
VALUES (4, 'Collections, Lists, and Java's Built-In APIs');
INSERT INTO chapter
(CHAPTER_ID, CHAPTER_NAME)
VALUES (5, 'Exceptions');
INSERT INTO chapter
(CHAPTER_ID, CHAPTER_NAME)
VALUES (6, 'Modules, Packages, and Libraries');
INSERT INTO chapter
(CHAPTER_ID, CHAPTER_NAME)
VALUES (7, 'Databases and JDBC');
```

Note the two single quotes used to insert text with a quote.

6. To add a record of **student_progress**, generate an **INSERT** statement like the following:

```
INSERT INTO student_progress
(STUDENT_ID, CHAPTER_ID, COMPLETED)
VALUES (1, 2, '2019-08-28');
```

This should be done within a Java program using a **PreparedStatement**.

7. To query for a student's progress, use a query such as the following:

```
SELECT first_name, last_name, chapter.chapter_id, chapter_name, completed
FROM student, chapter, student_progress
WHERE first_name = 'BOB'
AND last_name = 'MARLEY'
AND student.student_id = student_progress.student_id
AND chapter.chapter_id = student_progress.chapter_id
ORDER BY chapter_id;
```

Note that the **first name** and **last name** will be input by the user. This should be placed in **PreparedStatement**.

The **ORDER BY** clause ensures that the output will appear in chapter order.

8. The **ShowProgress** program outputs the chapters a given student has completed:

ShowProgress.java

```
1  package com.packtpub.db;
2  import java.sql.*;
3  public class ShowProgress {
4      public static void main(String[] args) {
5          if (args.length < 2) {
6              System.err.println("Error: please enter the first and last
                 name.");
7              System.exit(-1);
8          }
9          // Get student first and last name as inputs.
10         String firstName = args[0].toUpperCase();
11         String lastName = args[1].toUpperCase();
```

https://packt.live/31EPNg4

Note how the input first and last names are forced to uppercase prior to searching the database. Also, note that we do not allow two students to have the same name. This is not realistic.

After querying, the program outputs the student's name and then one line for each chapter completed.

9. To run this program, build the **shadowJar** task in Gradle, and then run a command such as the following in the IntelliJ **Terminal** window:

```
java -cp customers-1.0-all.jar com.packtpub.db.ShowProgress bob marley
```

The jar file is located in the **libs** subdirectory of the build directory.

The output will appear as follows:

```
BOB MARLEY
2019-03-01  2 Learning the Basics
2019-03-01  3 Object-Oriented Programming: Classes and Methods
2019-03-01  7 Databases and JDBC
```

10. The **RecordProgress** program adds a **student_progress** record:

RecordProgress.java

```
1   package com.packtpub.db;
2
3   import java.sql.*;
4
5   public class RecordProgress {
6       public static void main(String[] args) {
7
8           // Get input
9           if (args.length < 3) {
10              System.err.println("Error: please enter first last chapter.");
11              System.exit(-1);
12          }
13
14          // Get student first and last name and chapter number.
15          String firstName = args[0].toUpperCase();
```

https://packt.live/362QaF1

11. To run this program, use a command such as the following:

```
java -cp customers-1.0-all.jar com.packtpub.db.RecordProgress bob marley 4
```

You will see output like the following:

```
Number rows added: 1
```

As before, the input names are forced to uppercase prior to searching the database.

Chapter 8: Sockets, Files, and Streams

Activity 1: Writing the Directory Structure to a File

Solution

1. Import the relevant classes to get this example to work. Basically you will be working with collections, files, and the associated exceptions.

    ```
    import java.io.IOException;
    import java.nio.file.*;
    import java.nio.file.attribute.BasicFileAttributes;
    import java.util.Collections;
    ```

2. Determine the folder you will start looking for directories from. Let's assume you start from **user.home**. Declare a Path object linking to that folder.

    ```
    Path path = Paths.get(System.getProperty("user.home"));
    ```

3. Next you will call **File.walkFileTree**, which will allow you iterate through a folder structure up to a certain depth. In this case, you can set whatever depth you want, for example **10**. This means the program will dig up to **10** levels of directories looking for files.

    ```
    Files.walkFileTree(path, Collections.emptySet(), 10, new SimpleFileVisitor<Path>() {
    [...]
    ```

4. The approach in this case consists in overriding a couple of methods from **SimpleFileVisitor** to extract the path information and return it as a string making the file structure easy to read. The first method to override is **preVisitDirectory**, that is triggered in the class when an item in a directory happens to be a nested directory.

    ```
    @Override
    public FileVisitResult preVisitDirectory(Path dir, BasicFileAttributes attrs) {
    ```

5. Inside **preVisitDirectory**, there is a couple of operations you will need to perform. First you need to calculate how deep you are in the directory structure, as you will need that to print blank spaces as a way to format the program's output. **preVisitDirectory** will get the current path as a parameter named **dir**. But it will also use the global path parameter (remember we start from **user.home**). Declare a variable called **depthInit** to store the how far you are in the directory structure when at path.

    ```
    String [] pathArray = path.toString().split("/");
    int depthInit = pathArray.length;
    ```

6. Repeat the operation but this time with the current directory, store the outcome in a variable called **depthCurrent**.

```
String [] fileArray = dir.toString().split("/");
int depthCurrent = fileArray.length;
```

7. Use a **for** loop to print a bunch of blank spaces in front of the current folder name.

```
for (int i = depthInit; i < depthCurrent; i++) {
    System.out.print("    ");
}
```

8. Finally, print out the name of the folder/file, and exit the method.

```
System.out.println(fileArray[fileArray.length - 1]);
return FileVisitResult.CONTINUE;
```

9. The second method to override within **SimpleFileVisitor** is **visitFileFailed**. This method is handling the exception that would be triggered when reading a path to which the user has no permission to enter, or similar. The full method looks like follows.

```
@Override
public FileVisitResult visitFileFailed(Path file, IOException exc) throws IOException
{
    System.out.println("visitFileFailed: " + file);
    return FileVisitResult.CONTINUE;
}
```

10. Try now how the program works. You will get to see the listing of the directories at your home folder in a similar fashion as the following one where each block of four blank spaces represents deepening one more level in the folder structure.

```
topeka
    snap
        gnome-calculator
        gnome-system-monitor
        libreoffice
    Downloads
    [...]
```

11. It is now a trivial exercise making the outcome be stored in a file instead of being simply printed out to the CLI. First you will need to declare a file name, in this case let's make one that will end up at the same folder where the Main class is to be found.

```
String fileName = "temp.txt";
Path pathFile = Paths.get(fileName);
```

12. Next you should check whether the logfile already exists in the folder, that will help deciding whether you create it or if you will simply append data to it instead.

```
if(!Files.exists(pathFile))  {
    try {
        // Create the file
        Files.createFile(pathFile);
        System.out.println("New file created at: " + pathFile);
    } catch (IOException ioe) {
        System.out.println("EXCEPTION when creating file: " + ioe.getMessage());
    }
}
```

13. You will have to modify the overridden **preVisitDirectory** to include the possibility of writing to the file you just created.

Activity01.java

```
27 public FileVisitResult preVisitDirectory(Path dir, BasicFileAttributes
     attrs) {
28
29     String toFile = "";
30
31     String [] pathArray = path.toString().split("/");
32     int depthInit = pathArray.length;
33     String [] fileArray = dir.toString().split("/");
34     int depthCurrent = fileArray.length;
35     for (int i = depthInit; i < depthCurrent; i++) {
36         toFile += "     ";
37     }
38     toFile += fileArray[fileArray.length - 1];
39
40     if(Files.exists(pathFile))
```

https://packt.live/35Ye4kR

14. Executing the code will now give as a result a file located in the same folder you are executing it from.

```
user@computer:~/[...]/Activity0801/out/production/Activity0801$ ls
'Main$1.class'   Main.class   temp.txt
```

Activity 2: Improving the EchoServer and EchoClient Programs

Solution

1. The expected results will require you to modify both the server and the client in a very similar way. On the client-side, you will have to do something like the following:

Client.java

```
1   import java.io.*;
2   import java.net.*;
3
4   public class Client {
5       public static void main(String[] args) throws IOException {
6           if (args.length != 2) {
7               System.err.println(
8                       "Usage: java EchoClient <host name> <port number>");
9               System.exit(1);
10          }
11
12          String hostName = args[0];
13          int portNumber = Integer.parseInt(args[1]);
14
```

https://packt.live/2MEFg0w

2. On the server, the modifications should look like the following:

Server.java

```
1   import java.net.*;
2   import java.io.*;
3
4   public class Server {
5       public static void main(String[] args) throws IOException {
6
7           if (args.length != 1) {
8               System.err.println("Usage: java EchoServer <port number>");
9               System.exit(1);
10          }
11
12          int portNumber = Integer.parseInt(args[0]);
13
14          try (
15                  ServerSocket serverSocket =
```

https://packt.live/2WbxAWv

The expected interaction between the server and the client should be as follows:

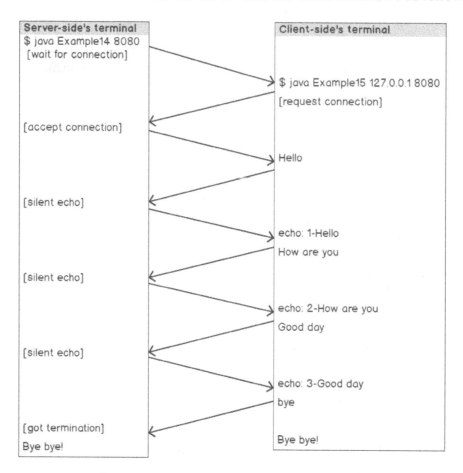

Figure 8:2: Interaction between server and client

Chapter 9: Working with HTTP

Activity 1: Using the jsoup Library to Download Files from the Web

Solution

The program is relatively short. The main task is to figure out the CSS query for the **select()** method call:

1. Create a class named **Activity1**.

2. In **main()**, start a **try-catch** block

   ```
   try {
   
   } catch (IOException e) {
       e.printStackTrace();
   }
   ```

3. Inside the **try** block, use the **Jsoup** library to download the contents of the remote Web page located at https://packt.live/2BqZbtq. This will result in the Web page contents stored in a **Document** object.

   ```
   String url = "http://hc.apache.org/";
       Document doc =
               Jsoup.connect(url).get();
   ```

4. Next, query the document for all elements of type **DIV** with a CSS class of **section**.

   ```
   Elements sections = doc.select("div.section");
   ```

5. You will need to iterate over each of these **DIV** elements.

   ```
   for (Element div : sections) {
       for (Element child : div.children()) {
       }
   }
   ```

6. Inside the inner for loop, look for **H3** headline tags.

```
String tag = child.tagName();
if (tag.equalsIgnoreCase("h3")) {
}
```

7. Finally, inside the **if** statement that detects if the tag is an H3 element, find all anchor (A) tags used for HTML links and print out the link text for each.

```
Elements links = child.getElementsByTag("a");
for (Element link : links) {
    System.out.println(link.text());
}
```

> **Note**
>
> The complete code for this activity can be found here: https://packt.live/33SEhPP

Chapter 11: Processes

Activity 1: Making a Parent Process to Launch a Child Process

Solution

1. The child should have an algorithm that looks like the following:

Child.java

```
9     public static void main(String[] args) throws java.io.IOException,
      InterruptedException {
10        int ch;
11        System.out.print ("Let's echo: ");
12        while ((ch = System.in.read ()) != '\n')
13            System.out.print ((char) ch);
14        BufferedWriter bw=new BufferedWriter(
15                new FileWriter(new File("mycal2022.txt")));
16            int cont = 0;
17            while(cont <= 50) {
18                System.out.println(cont++);
19                cont %= 50;
20                bw.write(cont + "\n");
```

https://packt.live/32I5Afu

Here, there is a call to **System.in.available()** to check whether there is any data in the output buffer from the child program.

2. On the other hand, the parent program should consider including something along the lines of:

Parent.java

```
18        try {
19            process.waitFor(5, TimeUnit.SECONDS);
20        } catch (InterruptedException ie) {
21            System.out.println("WARNING: interrupted exception fired");
22        }
23
24        System.out.println("trying to write");
25        OutputStream out = process.getOutputStream();
26        Writer writer = new OutputStreamWriter(out);
27        writer.write("This is how we roll!\n");
28        writer.flush();
29
30        File file = new File("data.log");
31        FileWriter fileWriter = new FileWriter(file);
32        BufferedWriter bufferedWriter = new BufferedWriter(fileWriter);
33
34        System.out.println("trying to read");
35        InputStream in = process.getInputStream();
36        Reader reader = new InputStreamReader(in);
37        BufferedReader bufferedReader = new BufferedReader(reader);
38        String line = bufferedReader.readLine();
39
40        // send to screen
41        System.out.println(line);
```

https://packt.live/2MEBlR9

Chapter 12: Regular Expressions

Activity 1: Regular Expressions to Check If the Entrance is Entered in the Desired Format

Solution

1. Visit https://packt.live/2MYzyFq.

2. To the already exisiting regular expression from Exercise 1, add the rule to allow an optional alphabet after the number:

   ```
   [a-zA-Z]{2,}\s{1}\d+[a-zA-Z]{1}
   ```

3. Check if the RE works for *Strandvagen 1a* and *Ringvagen 2b*.

Chapter 13: Functional Programming with Lambda Expressions

Activity 1: Modifying Immutable Lists

Solution

1. Write an application which modifies the ShoppingCart class found in Exercise 2 to allow for removing items from the cart.

```
public ShoppingCart removeItem(ShoppingItem item) {
    Map<String, Integer> newList = new HashMap<>(mShoppingList);
    int value = 0;
    if (newList.containsKey(item.name)) {
        value = newList.get(item.name);
    }
    if (value > 0) {
        newList.put(item.name, --value);
    }
    return new ShoppingCart(newList);
}
```

2. Add a new feature to the ShoppingCart class that allows users to add multiple items to the cart in a single invocation.

```
public ShoppingCart addItems(ShoppingItem... items) {
    Map<String, Integer> newList = new HashMap<>(mShoppingList);
    ShoppingCart newCart = null;
    for (ShoppingItem item : items) {
        newCart = addItem(item);
    }
}
```

3. Prove that the new features work as intended by modifying the code in the main application file to show how the features are used.

```
public class Activity1 {
    public static void main(String[] args) {
        ShoppingCart myFirstCart = new ShoppingCart(new HashMap<>());
        ShoppingCart mySecondCart = myFirstCart.addItem(new
            ShoppingItem("Chair", 150));
        ShoppingCart myThirdCart = mySecondCart.addItem(new
            ShoppingItem("Table", 350));
```

You can find the entire code for this activity at: https://packt.live/2q045er

Chapter 14: Recursion

Activity 1: Calculating the Fibonacci Sequence

Solution

1. Create a class named **Fibonacci**.

2. Create a static method called **fibonacci** to calculate the Fibonacci sequence for a given number. If the input number is greater than **1**, this method will call itself.

```
public static int fibonacci(int number) {
    if (number == 0) {
        return number;
    } else if (number == 1) {
        return 1;
    } else {
        return (fibonacci(number - 1) + fibonacci(number - 2));
    }
}
```

If the input number is **0** or **1**, this method returns the input number (**0** or **1**, respectively).

3. Create a **main()** method that calls the **fibonacci** method with inputs going from 0 to 16 (or to a value less than 17 as shown here).

```
public static void main(String[] args) {
    for (int i = 0; i < 17; i++) {
        System.out.println( fibonacci(i) );
    }
}
```

> **Note**
>
> The complete code for this activity can be found here: https://packt.live/32DtjNT.

Chapter 15: Processing Data with Streams

Activity 1: Applying Discount on the Items

Solution

Activity1.java

```
30          double sum = calculatePrice(fruitCart, vegetableCart, meatAndFishCart);
31          System.out.println(String.format("Sum: %.2f", sum));
32
33          Map<String, Double> discounts = Map.of("Cod", 0.2, "Salad", 0.5);
34
35          double sumDiscount = calculatePriceWithDiscounts(discounts, fruitCart, vegetableCart,
            meatAndFishCart);
36          System.out.println(String.format("Discount sum: %.2f", sumDiscount));
37      }
38
39      private static double calculatePrice(ShoppingCart... carts) {
40          return Stream.of(carts)
41                  .flatMap((cart) -> { return cart.mArticles.stream(); })
42                  .mapToDouble((item) -> { return item.price; })
43                  .sum();
44      }
```

https://packt.live/35Zm5Gj

Activity 2: Searching for Specifics

Solution

Activity2.java

```
61          private ShoppingArticle(String name, String category, double price, String unit) {
62              this.name = name;
63              this.category = category;
64              this.price = price;
65              this.unit = unit;
66          }
67
68          @Override
69          public String toString() {
70              return name + " (" + category + ")";
71          }
72      }
73
74      private static ShoppingArticle findCheapestFruit (List<ShoppingArticle> articles) {
75          return articles.stream()
76                  .filter((article) -> article.category.equals("Fruits"))
77                  .min(Comparator.comparingDouble(article -> article.price))
78                  .orElse(null);
79      }
80
81      private static ShoppingArticle findMostExpensiveVegetable (List<ShoppingArticle> articles) {
82          return articles.stream()
83                  .filter((article) -> article.category.equals("Vegetables"))
84                  .max(Comparator.comparingDouble(article -> article.price))
85                  .orElse(null);
86      }
```

https://packt.live/32EnOid

Chapter 16: Predicates and Other Functional Interfaces

Activity 1: Toggling the Sensor States

Solution

Activity1.java

```
52              for (Sensor sensor : sensors) {
53                  if (hasAlarmOrWarning.test(sensor)) {
54                      alarmOrWarning = true;
55                  }
56              }
57
58          if (alarmOrWarning) {
59              System.out.println("Alarm, or warning, was triggered!");
60
61
62              for (Sensor sensor : sensors) {
63                  System.out.println(sensor.batteryHealth() + ", " + sensor.triggered());
64              }
65          }
66      }
67
68 }
```

https://packt.live/33Vnc7X

Activity 2: Using a Recursive Function

Solution

Activity2.java

```
36      private static double loopedAverageHealth(Integer[] batteryHealths) {
37          double average = 0;
38          for (int i = 0; i < batteryHealths.length; i++) {
39              average += batteryHealths[i];
40          }
41          average = average / batteryHealths.length;
42          return average;
43      }
44
45      private static double streamedAverageHealth(Integer[] batteryHealths) {
46          return Stream.of(batteryHealths)
47                  .mapToDouble(Integer::intValue)
48                  .average()
49                  .orElse(0);
50      }
51
52      private static double recursiveAverageHealth(Integer[] batteryHealths, int index) {
53          double average = batteryHealths[index] / (double) batteryHealths.length;
54          if (index == 0) {
55              return average;
56          } else {
57              return average + recursiveAverageHealth(batteryHealths, index - 1);
58          }
59      }
60 }
```

https://packt.live/32EnJep

Activity 3: Using a Lambda Function

Solution

Activity3.java

```
37      private static double loopedAverageHealth(Integer[] batteryHealths) {
38          double average = 0;
39          for (int i = 0; i < batteryHealths.length; i++) {
40              average += batteryHealths[i];
41          }
42          average = average / batteryHealths.length;
43          return average;
44      }
45
46      private static double streamedAverageHealth(Integer[] batteryHealths) {
47          return Stream.of(batteryHealths)
48                  .mapToDouble(Integer::intValue)
49                  .average()
50                  .orElse(0);
51      }
52
53      private static double recursiveAverageHealth(Integer[] batteryHealths, int index) {
54          double average = batteryHealths[index] / (double) batteryHealths.length;
55          if (index == 0) {
56              return average;
57          } else {
58              return average + recursiveAverageHealth(batteryHealths, index - 1);
59          }
60      }
61 }
```

https://packt.live/2BxaoIK

Chapter 17: Reactive Programming with Java Flow

Activity 1: Let NumberProcessor Format Values as Integers

Solution

1. Change the processors published item type to Integer. Make the necessary changes in the implementation to match the new type:

`Activity1.java`

```
53                @Override
54                public void onComplete() {
55                    System.out.println("onComplete()");
56                }
57            });
58        }
59
60
61      private static String[] getStrings() {
62          String filePath = "res/numbers.txt";
63          try (Stream<String> words = Files.lines(Paths.get(filePath))) {
64              return words.flatMap((line) -> Arrays.stream(line.split("[\\s\\n]+")))
65                      .filter((word) -> word.length() > 0)
66                          .toArray(String[]::new);
67          } catch (IOException e) {
68              e.printStackTrace();
69          }
70          return null;
71      }
72 }
```

https://packt.live/32GPq6b

2. Change the subscriber for the processor, it should accept only Integer values in the **onNext** method:

```
@Override
        public void onSubscribe(Flow.Subscription subscription) {
            this.subscription = subscription;
            subscription.request(1);
        }
```

Chapter 18: Unit Testing

Activity 1: Counting the Words in the String

Solution

1. Create a class named `WordCount`.

2. Define a method named `countWords()` that takes as input a `String`. The method will count the words in the `String`.

```java
public int countWords(String text) {
    int count = 0;
    return count;
}
```

3. In `countWords()`, check if the input String is null. If not, trim any spaces at the beginning and end of the text. Then, split the `String` into words.

```java
if (text != null) {
    String trimmed = text.trim();
    if (trimmed.length() > 0) {
        String[] words = trimmed.split("\\s+");
        count = words.length;
    }
}
```

Note the use of a regular expression, **\s+**, that gets passed to the **split()** method. This will split the **String** into words. Also note that the leading backslash character needs to be escaped.

> **Note**
>
> The complete code for WordCount.java file can be found here: https://packt. live/32DtjNT.

Next, write a parameterized test as follows.

1. Create a class named **WordCountTest** in the **src/test** directory (not **src/main**).

2. Use the **ParameterizedTest** annotation and define a **CsvSource** with data for the test.

```
@ParameterizedTest
@CsvSource({
    "'A man, a plan, a canal. Panama',  7",
    "'Able was I ere I saw Elba',  7",
    ",  0",
    "'',  0",
    "'      ',  0",
    "' A cat in the hat with spaces  ', 7"
})
```

The test data takes in two values, a text string to check and then the word count. Note the placement of punctuation and spaces to see if the **WordCount** class works correctly.

3. Create the **test** method to use the input parameters and validate that the reported word count matches the expected word count.

```
public void testWordCounts(String text, int expected) {
    WordCount wordCount = new WordCount();
    int count = wordCount.countWords(text);
    Assertions.assertEquals(expected, count,
            "Expected " + expected + " for input[" + text + "]");
}
```

> **Note**
>
> The complete code for WordCountTest.java file can be found here: https://packt.live/2oafOq9.

Index

About

All major keywords used in this book are captured alphabetically in this section. Each one is accompanied by the page number of where they appear.

CPSIA information can be obtained
at www.ICGtesting.com
Printed in the USA
JSHW030227200920
7854JS00015B/153

9 781838 986698